PERFIDIOUS ALBION

The Untold Suffering Visited

Upon Humanity

Man Lee

TITLE : PERFIDIOUS ALBION

Copyright © First Edition 2025 by Man Lee.

All rights reserved. No part of this book may be used or reproduced in any manner whatsoever without written permission except in the case of brief quotations embodied in critical articles or reviews.

For information contact :
manlee2050@outlook.com

Book Cover : *Queen Elizabeth I by Nicholas Hilliard, circa 1575.* © National Portrait Gallery, London

ISBN: 978-1-7643910-0-9

Foreword

A Personal Journey from Colonial Malaya to Historical Reckoning

I grew up in 1960s Malaysia, in a world still saturated with the residue of British colonial rule. Though Malaya had achieved independence in 1957, and Malaysia was formed in 1963, the atmosphere in which I came of age remained profoundly shaped by over 150 years of British dominance. The colonial infrastructure was everywhere—not just in the physical landscape of government buildings, railway stations, and rubber plantations, but in the mental architecture of how society was organized, how we understood ourselves, and what we were taught to believe about our own history.

In school, we learned in English. Our textbooks came from Britain or were modeled on British curricula. We studied British history—the Tudors and Stuarts, the Industrial Revolution, the two World Wars—in far greater depth than we studied our own. The Malayan Emergency, which in 1960, was presented to us as a communist insurgency defeated by British military skill and wisdom, not as an anti-colonial struggle. The "New Villages" where half a million of our Chinese compatriots had been forcibly relocated were described, if mentioned at all, as protective measures rather than concentration camps. We learned nothing of the brutality that had characterized the Emergency, nothing of the torture and extrajudicial killings, nothing of the villages burned and the lives shattered.

The British were still everywhere in the 1960s and '70s. British companies dominated the economy—plantation agriculture, tin mining, banking, commerce. British expatriates held senior positions in government, education, and business, their presence a reminder that independence was more legal fiction than lived reality.

English was the language of power and prestige; those who spoke it fluently enjoyed advantages those who spoke only Malay, Chinese dialects, or Tamil could never access.

The assumption of British superiority was so naturalized that it rarely required articulation—it was simply understood that British ways were modern, efficient, and civilized, while local traditions were backward, inefficient, and in need of modernization. The colonial mentality persisted not only among the British who remained but among Malaysians who had internalized the colonizer's contempt for indigenous cultures and knowledge systems.

I remember the stark economic hierarchies that mapped imperfectly but unmistakably onto colonial categories. The wealthiest Malaysians were predominantly those whose families had collaborated with colonial rule or who had adopted British cultural norms. The poorest were often those from communities that had resisted most strongly or that colonial policies had most thoroughly marginalized. Rural Malays, estate workers of Indian descent, tin miners—these were the people whose labor had built colonial wealth but who had inherited only poverty from that history.

I remember the silences. Certain topics were not discussed, certain histories not acknowledged. The violence of colonial rule, the resistance movements, the reasons for ethnic tensions that colonialism had deliberately cultivated—these remained largely unexamined in public discourse. Malaysia, like many postcolonial nations, was attempting to build national unity, and confronting the divisions colonialism had created seemed dangerous to that project. So we inherited colonial ethnic categories—Malay, Chinese, Indian—and colonial tensions between them, but we were not taught how these divisions had been deliberately constructed and exploited by British

Foreword

administrators pursuing divide-and-rule strategies.

It was not until I left Malaysia and began studying history seriously that I started to understand how profoundly I had been shaped by colonial education and colonial frameworks of understanding. Reading scholarship on colonialism, encountering perspectives from colonized peoples rather than colonizers, I began to recognize the systematic nature of what had been done—not just in Malaysia but across the vast territories that Britain had conquered and exploited.

I learned that the famines I had vaguely heard about in India were not natural disasters but deliberately caused or catastrophically worsened by British policies. I learned that the "primitive" societies British colonizers described in Africa and the Pacific possessed sophisticated cultures, knowledge systems, and governance structures that colonialism systematically destroyed. I learned that the development Britain claimed to have brought—the railways, the plantations, the administrative systems—had been designed primarily to extract wealth rather than to serve colonized populations, and that they had been financed by those populations rather than by British benevolence.

Most painfully, I learned the truth about the Malayan Emergency that had ended when I was a toddler. Reading scholarly accounts—particularly by historians who had accessed documents Britain tried to suppress—I discovered the extent of British brutality: the systematic torture, the mass detention, the aerial bombardment of villages, the deliberate strategy of targeting civilian populations to separate them from guerrilla forces. The "New Villages" I had learned about as protective measures were revealed as concentration camps, built through forced removal and surrounded by barbed wire, designed to control populations whose loyalty Britain doubted.

Foreword

I realized that my education had been a form of continued colonization—that the mental frameworks I had inherited were designed to make colonial exploitation appear natural, British superiority appear self-evident, and resistance to colonial rule appear irrational or criminal. The silence about colonial violence, the emphasis on British achievements while minimizing British crimes, the presentation of independence as gift rather than hard-won victory—all of this served to perpetuate colonial hierarchies and assumptions even after formal colonial rule ended.

This book emerged from decades of reckoning with that inheritance. It is an attempt to document what we were not taught, to center the perspectives that were systematically marginalized, and to confront honestly the violence and exploitation that made the British Empire possible. It is written for those who, like me, grew up in former colonies absorbing colonial education and colonial assumptions, as well as for those in Britain who inherited a sanitized version of imperial history that celebrates achievements while erasing crimes.

The contrast between the world of my childhood and the world today is striking in some respects. Malaysia is now a confident middle-income nation with its own thriving culture, increasingly willing to examine its colonial past critically. The British expatriate community has shrunk to insignificance. The automatic prestige once attached to all things British has diminished considerably. Postcolonial scholarship has produced mountains of evidence documenting imperial crimes, making the comfortable myths of benevolent empire increasingly difficult to sustain.

Yet in other respects, the continuities are more striking than the changes. Britain continues to evade honest reckoning with imperial history, with politicians and public figures regularly celebrating empire while minimizing its violence. Imperial nostalgia remains politically potent, invoked to bolster Brexit nationalism and to justify Britain's continuing global military role. The wealth extracted from colonies during centuries of imperial rule remains concentrated in Britain and the West, while many former colonies struggle with poverty that has deep roots in colonial underdevelopment. The racial hierarchies colonialism established persist in modified but recognizable forms, shaping global inequalities and domestic politics in both former colonizers and colonized.

Most troublingly, the imperial habits of mind persist. Britain continues to assume the right to intervene militarily in other nations, as it did in Iraq, Afghanistan, and Libya, with catastrophic consequences each time. It continues to subordinate international law to perceived national interest, as with its refusal to return the Chagos Islands despite International Court of Justice rulings and UN votes demanding it do so. It continues to resist accountability for historical crimes, offering at most carefully worded expressions of "regret" while avoiding acknowledgment of systematic wrongdoing that might create legal or moral obligations.

I write this foreword from the perspective of someone who has lived between worlds—raised in postcolonial Malaysia still saturated with colonial residue, educated in Western universities where colonial history was taught from colonizers' perspectives, and now committed to recovering the histories that were suppressed. This perspective makes clear both how much has changed since the 1960s and how much fundamental reckoning remains undone.

The generation that experienced colonialism directly is now largely gone. My parents' generation remembered British rule firsthand; my generation inherited its immediate aftermath; today's young people in Malaysia know colonialism only as history. Yet the effects persist across generations. The economic structures colonialism established, the borders it drew, the ethnic tensions it cultivated, the languages it imposed, the self-

Foreword

conceptions it shaped—all continue influencing contemporary realities in ways that make colonial history anything but safely past.

This book is an attempt to document what colonialism actually was, stripped of the sanitizing myths that made it palatable to British audiences and that were exported to colonized populations through colonial education. It is based on extensive scholarship by historians, economists, and other researchers who have devoted careers to recovering suppressed evidence and challenging comfortable narratives. It centers the experiences and perspectives of colonized peoples rather than the self-justifications of colonizers.

The judgments offered will strike some readers as harsh or one-sided. They are harsh because the evidence demands harsh judgment—the scale of exploitation and violence was enormous. They may appear one-sided because the "other side"—the colonizers' perspective, the emphasis on railways and schools and British achievements—has dominated for generations. Correcting historical imbalance requires centering what has been marginalized.

I write this book also as an act of recovery—recovering the histories that my colonial education suppressed, recovering the voices that colonial archives silenced, recovering the dignity of peoples whom colonialism systematically dehumanized. The British Empire shaped my childhood world profoundly, but my childhood education taught me almost nothing truthful about how or why. This book attempts to provide the honest account that we who grew up in postcolonial societies should have received but rarely did.

To British readers, I offer this perspective from someone who experienced empire's residue firsthand: what you may have learned about the British Empire is likely fundamentally misleading. The benevolent narratives of development and civilization, the emphasis on infrastructure and institutions, the claims of gradual, voluntary decolonization—these are myths that served imperial purposes and that continue serving contemporary political purposes. The reality documented in this book is more disturbing but also more honest than the comfortable versions still taught in many British schools.

To readers from former colonies, I offer solidarity born of shared experience of inheriting colonial legacies we did not create but cannot escape. Our histories have been distorted, our ancestors' resistance has been erased or vilified, and our contemporary struggles often have deep roots in colonial policies we were not taught to recognize. Understanding this history is essential for understanding ourselves and our societies.

To all readers, I offer this book as contribution to the honest reckoning that remains desperately needed. Germany confronted Nazism, South Africa confronted apartheid, and many nations have begun confronting their histories of slavery and indigenous dispossession. Britain has yet to undertake comparable reckoning with empire, despite having created one of history's most extensive systems of exploitation and violence. Until that reckoning occurs, empire's long shadow will continue distorting British identity, policy, and international relationships while denying justice to empire's victims and their descendants.

I write this with no personal animosity toward Britain or British people. I studied in Britain, I have British friends and colleagues, and I recognize that contemporary Britons are not personally responsible for their ancestors' imperial crimes. But those crimes occurred, their effects persist, and honest acknowledgment is essential for justice and for genuine post-imperial relationships between Britain and former colonies.

Foreword

The world of my childhood—1960s Malaysia still soaked in colonial residue—is gone. But the imperial legacies that shaped that world persist in transformed forms. Until those legacies are honestly confronted, the work of decolonization remains incomplete. This book is offered as contribution to completing that work—by documenting what colonialism actually was, acknowledging what it did, and demanding the accountability that has been too long delayed.

The stories told in the following chapters are difficult and disturbing. They document systematic exploitation, mass death, cultural destruction, and persistent refusal to accept accountability. They challenge comfortable narratives about Britain's role in the world and demand recognition that empire was fundamentally criminal enterprise, however it has been subsequently mythologized. These are not easy truths, but they are necessary ones.

I hope that readers will engage with this book seriously and honestly, setting aside preconceptions and being willing to confront evidence that may disturb cherished beliefs. The victims of empire and their descendants deserve nothing less than honest acknowledgment of what was done to them. Britain deserves the opportunity to face its history honestly rather than hiding behind comforting fictions. And the world needs honest reckoning with colonialism's legacies if we are to build futures less haunted by imperial pasts.

This book is dedicated to all those who suffered under British imperial rule—the enslaved, the conquered, the dispossessed, the starved, the tortured, the culturally destroyed, and the systematically exploited. Their stories have been too long suppressed. It is time they were told.

Preface

This book exists because a comprehensive, accessible, and unflinchingly honest account of the British Empire's violence and exploitation has been needed for decades but rarely attempted. While academic scholarship has thoroughly documented specific atrocities, periods, and regions of British imperialism, few works synthesize this evidence into a comprehensive narrative accessible to general readers while maintaining rigorous standards of evidence and analysis. *Perfidious Albion* aims to fill this gap by documenting five centuries of systematic imperial violence—from Elizabethan slave trading through 21st-century interventions—in a single volume that neither minimizes crimes through euphemism nor sensationalizes them through polemic.

Why This Book Is Necessary

British imperialism killed tens of millions through famine, enslaved millions of Africans, committed genocide against indigenous peoples, destroyed cultures and languages, extracted trillions in wealth, and deliberately underdeveloped colonized economies while enriching Britain. Yet contemporary Britain persistently evades this history through selective education, imperial nostalgia in political discourse, and active resistance to accountability. Polls consistently show substantial British public opinion views the empire positively—a testament to successful historical mythologizing that this book challenges with comprehensive evidence.

The need for honest imperial history extends beyond Britain. For people in formerly colonized nations, British evasion adds insult to historical injury, preventing healing and reconciliation. For global understanding of contemporary inequality, recognizing that underdevelopment resulted from colonial exploitation

Preface

rather than pre-existing backwardness is essential. For addressing ongoing patterns of intervention and domination by Western powers, understanding imperial precedents matters urgently. The past is not past when its effects shape present realities and when perpetrators refuse to acknowledge what occurred.

What This Book Does

Perfidious Albion systematically documents British imperial violence across five centuries, seventeen chapters, and every inhabited continent. It examines the Atlantic slave trade's scale and brutality, the famines that killed over sixty million people through deliberate British policies, the genocides of Aboriginal Australians and other indigenous peoples, the systematic economic exploitation that enriched Britain while impoverishing colonies, the concentration camps pioneering mass detention and abuse, the cultural genocide destroying languages and identities, the covert operations overthrowing democratic governments, and the continuing evasion through evidence destruction and historical amnesia.

The book takes three methodological approaches that distinguish it from both traditional imperial histories and some recent critical works. First, it centers colonized peoples' experiences rather than British perspectives, treating imperial violence from victims' viewpoints rather than through colonizers' justifications. Second, it demonstrates systematic patterns rather than treating atrocities as isolated incidents—the famines, the genocides, the torture, the exploitation were not unfortunate excesses but deliberate policies implemented across the empire over centuries. Third, it connects historical crimes to contemporary effects, showing how colonial exploitation created present global inequalities, how colonial divisions fuel ongoing conflicts, and how imperial evasion prevents accountability.

Preface

The book's title, *Perfidious Albion*, invokes the phrase "perfidious Albion"—used for centuries to characterize British duplicity and untrustworthiness in international relations. The phrase aptly captures the gap between British rhetoric about civilization, law, democracy, and human rights versus British conduct involving systematic violence, exploitation, and refusal to accept legal or moral constraints. The subtitle, *The Untold Suffering Visited Upon Humanity*, emphasizes that this history focuses on victims rather than perpetrators, on suffering inflicted rather than glory achieved, and on truths systematically suppressed rather than myths comfortably maintained.

Structure and Organization

The seventeen chapters are organized to provide both chronological progression and thematic coherence. Chapters 1-2 examine the empire's foundations in Elizabethan slave trading and the triangular trade's development. Chapters 3-4 document the conquest of India and the famines that killed tens of millions. Chapters 5-8 examine imperial zenith through violence (crushing resistance), territorial expansion (the Scramble for Africa), economic warfare (the Opium Wars), and forgotten brutalities in the Caribbean and Pacific. Chapters 9-11 analyze strategies of division (divide and rule, suppressing independence movements, and partition violence). Chapters 12-14 examine structures of control and extraction (concentration camps, economic underdevelopment, and cultural genocide). Chapter 15 marks a turning point with the Suez Crisis revealing Britain's declining power. Chapters 16-17 document how imperialism continued after formal decolonization through the Anglo-American "special relationship" and examine empire's 21st-century legacies including ongoing evasion and resistance to accountability.

Each chapter includes an Author's Note providing scholarly context, acknowledging historiographical debates, explaining methodological choices, and guiding readers to key sources. These notes serve readers wanting deeper engagement with scholarship while remaining optional for those focused on the historical narrative. Detailed endnotes organized by chapter provide full citations for all factual claims, enabling verification and further research. The comprehensive bibliography lists 154 sources ranging from archival documents and government inquiries to academic monographs and investigative journalism.

Who Should Read This Book

Perfidious Albion is written for general readers seeking honest understanding of British imperial history, students requiring comprehensive overview of five centuries of imperialism, educators teaching colonial history and its legacies, activists working on reparations and historical justice, and anyone questioning comfortable narratives about British global influence. The book assumes no prior specialist knowledge, explaining contexts and defining terms while maintaining analytical rigor and comprehensive documentation. Readers already familiar with imperial history will find new connections across regions and periods, recognition of systematic patterns, and evidence of specific atrocities less commonly discussed.

The book will challenge readers who have accepted positive characterizations of British imperialism. It documents that railways served extraction not development, that British rule caused rather than alleviated famines, that economic "progress" measured by trade concealed systematic wealth extraction, that British law protected colonizers while denying colonized peoples' rights, and that claims about civilizing missions masked racist ideologies enabling violence. These arguments are not provocative revisionism but scholarly consensus supported by overwhelming evidence that traditional imperial histories ignored or minimized.

Preface

What Readers Should Expect

This book does not flinch from describing violence and suffering. The Middle Passage's horrors, famine victims' starvation, torture in detention camps, massacre victims' deaths, and cultural genocide's devastation are documented with specificity necessary for understanding scale and systematic nature of imperial violence. Yet the book avoids gratuitous detail or sensationalism, describing violence to inform rather than shock, and always connecting specific atrocities to broader patterns and policies.

The book maintains critical perspective throughout, challenging imperial justifications and exposing rhetorical strategies that masked exploitation as development, violence as pacification, and theft as legal appropriation. This critical stance reflects not political bias but honest engagement with evidence and centering of colonized peoples' experiences. The book does not claim that British imperialism was uniquely evil—other empires committed comparable atrocities—but focuses on British imperialism because that is its subject and because British society persistently evades honest reckoning with this history.

Readers will find the cumulative weight of evidence across seventeen chapters overwhelming—deliberately so. The point is not to catalog every imperial crime but to demonstrate through comprehensive documentation across regions, periods, and types of violence that exploitation and brutality were not aberrations but systematic features of imperial rule. The scale of suffering—tens of millions dead, hundreds of millions exploited, countless cultures destroyed—demands sustained attention rather than summary dismissal or comfortable minimization.

Continuing Relevance

This history matters urgently for contemporary politics

Preface

and ethics. The global inequality characterizing the present world results substantially from colonial exploitation and neo-colonial structures that replaced formal empire. Climate change's worst effects will be suffered by formerly colonized nations that contributed least to causing it, reflecting continuing injustice rooted in colonial-era industrialization financed by imperial extraction. Conflicts across Africa, Asia, and the Middle East trace substantially to colonial borders, divide-and-rule strategies, and arms Britain supplied to favored groups. Racism in contemporary Britain connects directly to imperial ideologies that characterized non-white peoples as inferior and requiring European domination.

Britain's persistent evasion of imperial history—through selective education, imperial nostalgia, resistance to reparations, and systematic evidence destruction revealed through Operation Legacy—demonstrates that confronting this past remains politically urgent work. Until Britain acknowledges systematic nature of imperial violence, accepts responsibility for ongoing effects, implements meaningful accountability including reparations, and fundamentally transforms relationships with former colonies, decolonization remains incomplete. The empire's shadow will continue darkening both Britain's present and the futures of billions experiencing imperialism's effects generations after formal independence.

A Note on Terminology

This book uses terminology centering colonized peoples' experiences rather than colonizers' justifications. It refers to "conquest" rather than "expansion," "extraction" rather than "trade," "detention camps" rather than "rehabilitation centers," "torture" rather than "enhanced interrogation," and "genocide" rather than "pacification." Where British sources use euphemistic language, the book notes this while employing more accurate terms. The book refers to colonized peoples and nations by

Preface

names they used for themselves where known, not only by colonial designations, though colonial names appear when necessary for clarity given historical sources' terminology.

Acknowledgment of Sources and Limitations

This book synthesizes extensive scholarship by historians across multiple continents and disciplines. The endnotes and bibliography acknowledge this intellectual debt. While the book strives for comprehensiveness, no single volume can document every aspect of five centuries of global imperialism. Some regions, periods, and topics receive more attention than others based on available evidence, historical significance, and thematic relevance. The book focuses primarily on British actions rather than providing comprehensive accounts of colonized peoples' societies, cultures, and resistance movements—not because these are less important but because the book's purpose is documenting British imperial crimes and their effects.

The interpretation offered—that British imperialism was systematic exploitation and violence, not civilizing mission—represents scholarly consensus supported by overwhelming evidence, though some historians dispute specific claims or emphasize different aspects. The Author's Notes accompanying each chapter acknowledge major scholarly debates and guide readers to works offering different perspectives. The book aims for honest engagement with evidence rather than neutral "balance" that would falsely equate perpetrators' self-justifications with victims' experiences or scholarly documentation.

The Moral Imperative

History is not merely academic exercise but moral and political endeavor with continuing relevance. The millions killed in famines, enslaved and transported, subjected to genocide, tortured in camps, whose cultures

Preface

were destroyed, whose lands were stolen, whose histories were erased—they deserve acknowledgment. They deserve truth. They deserve justice. And their descendants deserve futures not haunted by continuing shadow of unconfronted crimes.

This book contributes to the work of honest historical reckoning by providing comprehensive, accessible, and unflinching documentation of British imperial violence. It challenges comfortable mythologies, demands accountability, and insists that five centuries of systematic exploitation and violence cannot be evaded through selective memory, historical amnesia, or appeals to move past without acknowledging what occurred. The past must be confronted honestly before genuine post-imperial relationships, domestic racial justice, and global equity become possible.

The work of documenting imperial crimes, demanding accountability, supporting reparations, and building genuinely post-imperial world continues. *Perfidious Albion* aims to contribute to that work by ensuring that the suffering Britain inflicted across five centuries and every inhabited continent is remembered, acknowledged, and never again minimized or denied.

TABLE of CONTENTS

	Page
Chapter 1: The Seeds of Empire	1
Chapter 2: The Triangular Slave Trade	17
Chapter 3: The Conquest of India	39
Chapter 4: Famine by Design	65
Chapter 5: Crushing the Resistance	91
Chapter 6: The Scramble for Africa	115
Chapter 7: Opium, Gunboats and Humiliation of China	139
Chapter 8: The Caribbean, Australia and Pacific	169
Chapter 9: Divide and Rule	191
Chapter 10: Suppressing Freedom	217
Chapter 11: Partitions and the Bloody Aftermath	241
Chapter 12: Concentration Camps	263
Chapter 13: The Myth of Benevolent Development	287
Chapter 14: Cultural Genocide	315
Chapter 15: Suez and the End of Illusions	347
Chapter 16: The Anglo-American Empire	365
Chapter 17: The Long Shadow- Empire's Legacy	399
EPILOGUE	487
END NOTES	503
BIBLIOGRAPHY	561

CHAPTER ONE

The Seeds of Empire

Elizabethan Expansion and the Roots of Exploitation (1558-1603)

When Elizabeth I ascended to the English throne in 1558, England was a relatively minor European power, economically backward compared to Spain, Portugal, France, and the Italian city-states. By her death in 1603, the foundations had been laid for what would become the largest and most brutal empire in human history.˄5˄

The Elizabethan era saw the establishment of patterns that would persist for centuries: state-sponsored piracy rebranded as heroism, the treatment of non-European peoples as resources to be exploited, the use of extreme

Perfidious Albion

violence to establish trading advantages, and the deployment of legal fictions to justify theft and genocide. These were not unfortunate side effects of imperial ambition—they were its very essence.

The Privateer-Heroes: State-Sanctioned Piracy as National Policy

The mythology of Elizabethan England celebrates Francis Drake, Walter Raleigh, and John Hawkins as brave adventurers who built England's naval power. The reality is considerably darker. These men were pirates whose activities would be classified today as acts of terrorism, and they operated with the explicit approval and financial backing of the English Crown.^16^

John Hawkins pioneered England's participation in the Atlantic slave trade. In 1562, he sailed to West Africa, where he acquired approximately 300 enslaved Africans—the exact methods remain disputed, but later voyages clearly involved attacking Portuguese ships and raiding coastal villages.^7^ He transported these captives across the Atlantic in conditions of unimaginable horror, with many dying during the Middle Passage, then sold the survivors in Spanish Caribbean colonies, despite Spanish law forbidding foreign traders. When Spanish authorities objected to this illegal trade, Hawkins responded with threats of violence. Elizabeth I, far from condemning these act22ions, invested in his subsequent

Chapter 1: The Seeds of Empire

voyages and even loaned him the royal ship Jesus of Luanda for his 1564 expedition.^7^

The symbolism is worth dwelling on: the English queen's ship, bearing the name of Christianity's central figure, being used to transport human beings as cargo. This expedition saw Hawkins attack African towns to capture people for enslavement, with his chronicler John Sparke describing how they "burnt and spoilt" villages.^4^ The profits from these voyages of kidnapping and murder helped finance England's emerging naval power, and Hawkins was rewarded with a knighthood and a coat of arms featuring a bound African.^7^

Francis Drake took the model of state-sponsored criminality even further. His 1577-1580 circumnavigation of the globe, celebrated in English history books, was primarily a mission of plunder.^5,19^ Drake attacked Spanish settlements and ships along the Pacific coast of South America, seizing enormous quantities of silver and gold. The raid on the Spanish ship Nuestra Señora de la Concepción alone netted treasure worth approximately £126,000—equivalent to roughly half of Elizabeth's annual revenue.^5^ These weren't acts of war between equal powers; they were robberies carried out against civilian populations and merchant vessels.

The Spanish naturally viewed Drake as a pirate and a terrorist. When he raided Nombre de Dios in Panama in

1573, his men killed Spanish defenders and terrorized the town's inhabitants in their search for treasure.[1] When he attacked Spanish settlements on the Pacific coast, he burned churches, held priests and officials for ransom, and seized ships engaged in legitimate commerce.[5] Yet Elizabeth not only accepted the stolen goods—she personally took a substantial share—but knighted Drake aboard his ship Golden Hind in 1581.[18] The message was unmistakable: robbery and violence were not crimes when directed against non-Protestant peoples in the service of English enrichment.

Ireland: The First Laboratory of Colonial Brutality

While Drake and Hawkins were developing techniques of overseas exploitation, Elizabeth's government was perfecting methods of colonial control much closer to home. The Tudor conquest of Ireland, intensified dramatically during Elizabeth's reign, served as a template for later imperial ventures.[6,20] The Irish experience reveals the ideological foundations that would justify centuries of brutality: the dehumanization of the colonized, the use of overwhelming violence to destroy resistance, the theft of land justified by claims of superior civilization, and the deliberate destruction of indigenous culture.

The Elizabethan approach to Ireland was systematic and devastating. The "plantations" established in Munster

Chapter 1: The Seeds of Empire

(1580s) and Ulster (planned but not fully implemented until after Elizabeth's death) were exercises in ethnic cleansing and replacement.^6,9^ English and Scottish settlers were granted land confiscated from Irish owners, who were driven off, killed, or reduced to landless laborers on their ancestral territories. The plantations were justified by claims that the Irish were barbarous and uncivilized—a pattern of racist rationalization that would be repeated worldwide.^13^

The violence employed to establish English control was staggering. During the suppression of the Desmond Rebellions in Munster (1569-1573 and 1579-1583), English forces under Lord Deputy Arthur Grey and others deliberately targeted civilians and food supplies.^20^ Edmund Spenser, better known as a poet, served as Grey's secretary and later described the results with chilling detachment: "Out of every corner of the woods and glens they came creeping forth upon their hands, for their legs could not bear them. They looked like anatomies of death, they spoke like ghosts crying out of their graves."^2^ This was the result of a deliberate policy of starvation designed to break Irish resistance.

The campaign included what can only be described as acts of terror designed to instill fear. At the Siege of Smerwick in 1580, after a garrison of Italian and Spanish soldiers supporting Irish rebels had surrendered under promise of mercy, Grey ordered the execution of approximately 600 prisoners.[6,20] English forces also employed a systematic policy of killing all they encountered in rebel territories, making no distinction between combatants and civilians. Walter Raleigh, later celebrated as a founder of English colonization in America, participated in these massacres as a young commander.[6]

The English justified their brutality with claims that the Irish were barely human. English writers described the Irish as savage, treacherous, lazy, and priest-ridden—characteristics that would later be attributed to Africans, Asians, and indigenous peoples worldwide.[13] The supposed barbarism of the Irish was cited as justification for seizing their land and destroying their culture. This logic—that superior civilization gave the right to dispossess inferior peoples—became the foundation of British imperial ideology.[8]

Elizabeth and the Slave Trade: Royal Investment in Human Misery

Elizabeth's personal involvement in the slave trade deserves particular emphasis, as it demolishes any notion that the crown was merely an innocent beneficiary of her subjects' activities. The queen was a direct investor in slaving voyages and personally profited from the sale of human beings.[7]

Chapter 1: The Seeds of Empire

When John Hawkins planned his second slaving voyage in 1564, Elizabeth not only invested £1,000 of her own money. This was no passive investment; it was active participation in a venture whose business model was kidnapping, imprisonment, forced transportation in lethal conditions, and sale into lifetime bondage. The queen received her share of the profits, calculated in part on how many enslaved Africans survived the Middle Passage to be sold.˄7,14˄

The defense sometimes offered—that Elizabeth was merely operating within the commercial norms of her time—is historically illiterate. The slave trade was controversial even in the 16th century. Spanish authorities objected to English participation not just on mercantilist grounds but because they recognized the trade's horrors.˄5˄ Some English voices also expressed discomfort. Moreover, even if we accept that moral standards differ across eras, we cannot escape the fact that Elizabeth made a calculated decision that her own enrichment was more important than the lives, freedom, and dignity of thousands of African people.

The processes involved were horrific in ways that bear repeating. Enslaved people were held in suffocating conditions below deck, chained together in their own waste, with inadequate food and water.˄14˄ Disease spread rapidly. The death rate on Middle Passage voyages often exceeded 20 percent, sometimes reaching much higher.˄14˄ Those who died were thrown overboard. Those who resisted were tortured or killed as examples. And Elizabeth, invested in these ventures, received detailed reports of their progress and profited from their success.^7^

The Roanoke Disaster and the Genocidal Logic of Colonization

Elizabeth's attempts to establish English colonies in North America, while unsuccessful during her lifetime, revealed the assumptions that would guide later colonization. The Roanoke ventures of 1585 and 1587, organized by Walter Raleigh, demonstrated English willingness to use violence against indigenous peoples and the fundamentally extractive logic of colonization.^11^

The first Roanoke expedition, led by Ralph Lane, quickly deteriorated into conflict with local Algonquian peoples. When the English suspected a chief named Wingina of plotting against them, they launched a preemptive attack, killing Wingina and several others.^11^ This was not defensive action but aggressive intimidation designed to terrorize the indigenous population into submission. The expedition's scientific observer, Thomas Harriot, while genuinely interested in indigenous culture, also noted how disease devastated native communities after English contact—and he observed this not with horror but as a potential advantage, since it might facilitate English settlement.^3^

Chapter 1: The Seeds of Empire

The logic was already clear: indigenous peoples were obstacles to be removed, whether through violence, disease, or displacement.^15^ Their existing occupation of the land was irrelevant; English "discovery" and settlement created superior claims. This genocidal framework—and there is no softer word for a logic that accepts the elimination of indigenous peoples as natural and even desirable—would govern English and later British colonial expansion for centuries.

The East India Company: Corporate Plunder with State Backing

Elizabeth's granting of a royal charter to the East India Company on December 31, 1600, created an entity that would eventually bring unimaginable misery to hundreds of millions.^12^ While the Company's worst atrocities came later, its founding illuminates the fusion of state power and corporate avarice that characterized British imperialism.

The charter gave the Company monopoly rights over English trade with Asia, the power to acquire territory, administer justice, make war, and mint money.^12^ In other words, Elizabeth granted a private corporation the powers of a sovereign state, as long as it enriched England and returned profits to its shareholders—who included members of the royal family and aristocracy. This was a charter to exploit Asia with the full backing of

English state power.

The Company immediately began establishing trading posts through a combination of negotiation and intimidation. English ships, heavily armed, would arrive in Asian ports and demand trading rights.^5,12^ Local rulers, faced with the threat of naval bombardment, often had little choice but to acquiesce. The English sought not fair trade but monopoly control, aiming to eliminate competitors—whether Dutch, Portuguese, or indigenous Asian merchants—through whatever means necessary.

Even in this early period, the pattern was established: European demand for Asian goods (spices, textiles, indigo) would be met through systems that impoverished producers while enriching English merchants.^14^ The profits would return to England while the costs—social disruption, destroyed local industries, resource depletion—would be borne by Asian societies. Elizabeth created the legal and political framework that enabled this exploitation, and she did so knowingly and deliberately.

The Ideological Foundations: Race, Religion, and Rapacity

The Elizabethan era established the ideological justifications that would sustain centuries of British imperial atrocity.^8^ These interlocking ideas created a

Chapter 1: The Seeds of Empire

worldview in which exploitation and violence were not merely acceptable but righteous.

First was racial hierarchy. The English increasingly understood themselves as fundamentally superior to other peoples. Africans were described as savage and suited only for servitude. The Irish were denigrated as barbarous and untrustworthy. Indigenous Americans were dismissed as primitive.^8,13^ These weren't casual prejudices but systematic ideologies that justified dispossession and violence. The English claimed their superiority was rooted in civilization, Christianity, and commerce—but the practical effect was to place non-English peoples outside the moral community, rendering crimes against them invisible.

Second was religious justification. As a Protestant nation in conflict with Catholic Spain and France, England portrayed its expansion as a divine mission to spread true Christianity against Catholic corruption and pagan darkness.^8^ Drake and other privateers saw themselves as warriors for the faith, which conveniently absolved them from moral guilt when they slaughtered Spanish sailors or robbed Catholic churches. The fact that this religious mission was inseparable from the pursuit of gold and silver was rarely acknowledged.

Third was the transformation of greed into virtue. The Elizabethan age saw the emergence of an aggressive commercial ideology that celebrated wealth accumulation and portrayed trade—even when backed by violence—as a civilizing force.^5,14^ Merchants were celebrated as builders of national greatness. The theft of Spanish gold was reframed as weakening a tyrannical Catholic empire. The establishment of plantations on stolen Irish land was presented as bringing order and productivity to chaos and waste. Profit became patriotism.

These ideologies would be refined over subsequent centuries, but their essential elements were already present. They performed a crucial function: they allowed the English to commit terrible acts while maintaining their self-image as a civilized, Christian nation. This capacity for ideological self-deception would prove essential to the building and maintenance of empire.^8^

The Economic Foundations of Later Empire

The Elizabethan age also laid crucial economic foundations for later imperial expansion. The profits from piracy, the early slave trade, and the confiscation of Irish land flowed into England, where they were invested in new commercial ventures, including more aggressive overseas expansion.^5,14^ The wealth seized by Drake, Hawkins, and others helped finance England's naval development, creating the maritime power that would dominate global trade routes for three centuries.^16^

Moreover, Elizabethan England developed financial and

Chapter 1: The Seeds of Empire

legal innovations that facilitated imperial capitalism. The joint-stock company model, perfected with the East India Company, allowed the mobilization of capital on a new scale while distributing risks.^12^ Investors could profit from overseas exploitation without personal participation in violence or even geographical knowledge of where their money was working. This separation of profit from moral responsibility would be crucial to empire's expansion.

The enclosure of common lands (meaning the appropriation of 'waste' or common land) in England itself, a process accelerated during Elizabeth's reign, created a displaced rural population that would become both the labor force for early English industrialization and a source of colonists for overseas settlements.^17^ The dispossession of English peasants and the dispossession of Irish landowners were parallel processes, both justified by claims of economic efficiency and superior utilization of resources. The same logic would later justify the seizure of land in America, Africa, Asia, and Oceania.

Summary Conclusion: The Seeds Bear Poisoned Fruit

By Elizabeth's death in 1603, England had not yet built a true empire, but the foundations were unmistakable. The state had demonstrated its willingness to support piracy and slaving when profits beckoned. It had perfected techniques of colonial violence in Ireland. It

Perfidious Albion

had established corporate entities with sovereign powers to exploit Asia. It had developed ideologies that placed non-English peoples outside the bounds of moral consideration. It had created economic structures that channeled the profits of overseas exploitation into further expansion.

None of this was accidental or incidental. Elizabeth and her advisors made deliberate choices, knowing the human costs.^18^ When Drake returned with holds full of stolen Spanish silver, Elizabeth knew it represented not just metal but the extracted wealth of indigenous American mines worked by enslaved or forced labor. When Hawkins returned from Africa with profits from selling human beings, she knew exactly what crimes her investment had funded. When her commanders in Ireland reported success in suppressing rebellion, she knew this meant burned villages and starving populations.^2,6^

The mythology of Elizabethan England celebrates this era as a golden age of English culture and power. The historical reality is that this golden age was gilded with stolen wealth and built on foundations of violence that would support centuries of atrocity. The seeds planted during Elizabeth's reign—racial hierarchy, commercial ruthlessness, state-corporate fusion, and the transformation of greed into patriotic virtue—would grow into the vast apparatus of the British Empire,

Chapter 1: The Seeds of Empire

bringing death, exploitation, and destruction to hundreds of millions across the globe.

Understanding this origin story is essential to understanding how a small island nation came to inflict such suffering on such a monumental scale for so long. The evil was not in the DNA of the English people but in the structures, ideologies, and interests established during this formative period—structures that, once created, developed their own logic and momentum, carrying forward for centuries.

Author's Notes Chapter 1

This opening chapter establishes that British imperialism did not emerge suddenly but developed systematically during Elizabeth I's reign through the slave trade and Irish colonization. The chapter deliberately begins with Hawkins' slave voyages rather than earlier exploratory expeditions to emphasize that profit through human exploitation—not discovery or adventure—was the foundation of English imperial expansion.

On John Hawkins and the Slave Trade: Harry Kelsey's biography *Sir John Hawkins: Queen Elizabeth's Slave Trader* (2003) provides the most comprehensive modern account, drawing on Spanish, Portuguese, and English sources. Earlier treatments often minimized or romanticized Hawkins' slaving activities; Kelsey's work corrects this by centering the enslaved Africans' experiences. The naming of the slave ship *Jesus of Lübeck* represents one of history's most disturbing ironies—a vessel carrying human cargo named for a figure who preached human dignity and compassion.

On Irish Colonization: The connection between English strategies in Ireland and later imperial practices in the Americas and beyond is well-established in scholarship (particularly Nicholas Canny's work). Ireland served as a laboratory where English colonizers developed techniques—land confiscation, plantation systems, characterization of indigenous peoples as "savage," justifications based on "civilization"—that would be replicated globally. The deliberate brutality of the Irish campaigns was not aberrational excess but calculated policy designed to terrorize populations into submission.

Historiographical Context: Traditional British imperial history often portrayed Elizabethan expansion as glorious adventure, with figures like Drake and Raleigh celebrated as heroes. More recent scholarship (particularly since the 1990s) has centered colonized peoples' experiences and examined the violence and exploitation underlying expansion. This chapter follows the latter approach, treating the beginning of English imperialism as the beginning of a system of organized violence and extraction that would continue for centuries.

On Sources: Contemporary accounts from Hawkins himself and Richard Hakluyt's collections provide evidence of how English actors understood and justified their actions. These must be read critically, recognizing that they represent colonizers' perspectives designed to legitimate their conduct. Archaeological evidence, Spanish and Portuguese records, and African oral histories (though limited for this early period) provide alternative perspectives that challenge English self-justifications.

CHAPTER TWO

The Triangular Slave Trade

Britain's Foundation Built on Slavery (1600-1807)

The wealth of modern Britain was built on the bodies of enslaved Africans. This is not metaphor or exaggeration but documented historical fact. Between the early 17th century and the abolition of the British slave trade in 1807, British ships transported approximately 3.1 million Africans across the Atlantic, of whom at least 400,000 died during the Middle Passage.[1,2] These numbers represent only those who survived to be counted in ships' manifests; the true death toll—including those killed during capture in Africa, those who died in coastal holding facilities, and those who perished shortly after arrival in the

Americas—was vastly higher.[3] British merchants, ship owners, plantation owners, investors, and the British state itself profited from this industrialized system of kidnapping, torture, forced labor, and murder that operated for two centuries. The slave trade was not peripheral to British development but central to it, providing the capital that financed the Industrial Revolution and creating the commercial networks that sustained British global dominance.[4,5]

The Royal African Company: State-Organized Human Trafficking

The English slave trade began, as we saw in Chapter 1, with individual privateers like John Hawkins. But it was transformed into a systematic, industrialized operation with the creation of the Company of Royal Adventurers Trading to Africa in 1660, reconstituted as the Royal African Company (RAC) in 1672.[6] The RAC held a legal monopoly on English trade with West Africa, and its primary commodity was human beings.

The RAC was not a private enterprise operating independently of the state. It was chartered by the Crown, its investors included members of the royal family—King Charles II was a major shareholder—and it operated with the full backing of English naval and military power.[6,7] The company built and maintained a network of more than fifty fortified trading posts along

Chapter 2: The Triangular Slave Trade

the West African coast, from Senegal to Angola. These forts—with names like Cape Coast Castle, Elmina Castle, and Fort James—served as prisons where captured Africans were held, often for months, awaiting the arrival of ships.[8]

The conditions in these coastal dungeons were designed to break the spirit and resistance of the imprisoned. Captives were held in dark, airless chambers, packed so tightly that sitting or lying down was often impossible. They received minimal food and water. Disease spread rapidly in these conditions, and death rates in the coastal forts were horrific.[8,9] Those who resisted were tortured or killed as examples to others. Women and girls were routinely raped by the fort's personnel.[10] The forts' architecture reveals their purpose: the "Door of No Return" through which captives passed to the waiting ships became a symbol of the permanent destruction of their former lives.

Between 1672 and 1731, the RAC transported approximately 187,000 enslaved Africans across the Atlantic.[6] The company branded each captive with its initials—"DY" for Duke of York (the future King James II, the company's governor)—burning ownership into human flesh.[7] This practice reveals the fundamental premise of the trade: African people were property, commodities to be marked like cattle and sold like goods. The RAC's monopoly ended in 1698 when Parliament opened the slave trade to all English merchants, but this liberalization only intensified the horror.^11^ Previously restricted to a single company, the trade now attracted hundreds of merchants, ship owners, and investors. British participation in the slave trade exploded. By the mid-18th century, British ships were transporting more enslaved Africans than all other European nations combined, capturing approximately 40% of the entire Atlantic slave trade.^1,2^

The Mechanics of Capture: War, Kidnapping, and Collaboration

The popular myth suggests that European slavers simply purchased captives from African rulers who had already enslaved them, making Europeans merely participants in an existing African practice. This narrative, still repeated today to diffuse European responsibility, is fundamentally dishonest.^12^

European demand for enslaved labor transformed African warfare and politics. The presence of European traders on the coast, willing to exchange guns and manufactured goods for captives, created powerful incentives for warfare and raiding.^13^ African leaders who refused to participate in the slave trade found themselves at a military disadvantage against neighbors who acquired firearms through selling captives. This created a vicious cycle: communities needed to participate in slaving to obtain weapons to defend

Chapter 2: The Triangular Slave Trade

themselves against slavers.[13,14]

British and other European traders deliberately fostered this instability. They supplied weapons to rival groups, encouraged warfare, and created markets for captives that made peaceful alternatives economically unviable.[13] Ship captains would sometimes arm one group to raid another, effectively outsourcing the violence of capture while maintaining the fiction that they were merely passive purchasers.[14]

The methods of capture were brutal. Raiding parties, often equipped with British weapons, would attack villages at dawn, killing those who resisted and capturing those they could.[15] Kidnapping of individuals was common, particularly of children. People were seized while farming, traveling, or gathering resources, then marched to the coast in coffles—groups chained together by the neck—a journey that could take weeks or months and during which many died.[15,16]

The claim that this was simply African slavery that would have existed anyway ignores several crucial facts. First, while slavery existed in various forms in Africa, as in most pre-modern societies, the scale, brutality, and permanence of chattel slavery in the Americas was fundamentally different.[12] Second, European demand radically expanded and transformed African slavery, creating commercial incentives that had not previously existed.[13] Third, European traders were not passive purchasers but active agents who shaped, encouraged, and profited from the systems that produced captives. The moral responsibility lies squarely with those who created the demand and profited from it.[12,14]

The Middle Passage: Industrial-Scale Murder

The voyage across the Atlantic—the Middle Passage—was designed to transport the maximum number of people in the minimum space with the minimum cost.[17] Ships were specially designed for human cargo, with between-deck spaces often less than five feet high, forcing captives to crouch or lie flat. In these spaces, hundreds of people were chained in place, lying in rows, with as little as six square feet of space per person.[17,18]

The voyage typically lasted six to eight weeks, though bad weather could extend it much longer. During this time, captives were kept in nearly total darkness, in stifling heat, with inadequate ventilation. They lay in their own urine and excrement. Disease spread rapidly: dysentery, smallpox, measles, and other illnesses swept through the holds.[17,19] The mortality rate on British slave ships averaged 12-13% during the 18th century, though some voyages lost 30% or more of their human cargo.[2,17]

These deaths were not unfortunate accidents but the

Chapter 2: The Triangular Slave Trade

predictable result of deliberate decisions. Ship captains knew that tight packing increased mortality, but the profit calculation favored carrying more people even if more died.^17^ Insurance policies covered the loss of enslaved people who died during the voyage, removing any financial incentive for captains to improve conditions.^20^ The dead were thrown overboard, sometimes while still alive if they appeared unlikely to survive and their deaths would not be covered by insurance.^17^

Resistance was constant. Captives tried to starve themselves, requiring the invention of devices like the speculum oris—a metal instrument forced into the mouth to enable forced feeding.^21^ Suicide attempts were common; people threw themselves overboard when brought on deck, or found ways to strangle themselves below.^21^

Shipboard rebellions occurred on approximately 10% of slave voyages, though they were usually suppressed with overwhelming violence.^22^ The crew's responses to resistance were savage: torture, dismemberment, and execution were standard punishments designed to terrorize others into submission.^21,22^

Women and girls suffered additional horrors. Sexual violence was routine and systematic. Women were typically kept separately and had greater access to the deck, but this "privilege" meant increased vulnerability to rape by crew members.^10,23^ Many women arrived in the Americas pregnant from rapes during the voyage. The violence continued even after the voyage ended, as newly arrived women were often raped by plantation owners, overseers, or other enslaved men forced to "breed" more slaves.^10^

The Plantation Economy: Capitalism Built on Torture

The purpose of the slave trade was to supply labor for plantation agriculture in the Caribbean and Americas. British colonies—particularly Jamaica, Barbados, and other Caribbean islands—became vast forced labor camps producing sugar, tobacco, coffee, and cotton for European markets.^24,25^

Sugar plantations were the most profitable and the most deadly. Sugar cultivation and processing was backbreaking labor performed in tropical heat. The work day began before dawn and often continued past dark.^26^ Workers cleared land with machetes, planted and harvested cane, then processed it immediately—sugar cane begins to spoil within 24 hours of cutting. Processing required boiling the cane juice in huge copper vats, dangerous work that resulted in frequent burns and accidents.^26,27^

The mortality rate on sugar plantations was catastrophic. Recent estimates suggest that enslaved people on Caribbean sugar plantations had a life expectancy of only

Chapter 2: The Triangular Slave Trade

seven years after arrival.^25,26^ This was not an unfortunate byproduct but an accepted business model. It was often cheaper to work enslaved people to death and import new captives than to maintain conditions that would allow natural population reproduction.^25^ This calculation—that human beings could be treated as disposable equipment—reveals the fundamental inhumanity of the system.

The violence required to maintain this system was systematic and industrial in scale. Enslaved people who resisted, worked too slowly, attempted escape, or violated any of hundreds of arbitrary rules were subjected to torture.^28^ Whipping was so routine it was barely remarked upon in plantation records. Other punishments included being locked in stocks for days, forced to wear heavy iron collars with projecting spikes, mutilation (cutting off ears, nose, or genitals), branding, and execution by burning, hanging, or being broken on the wheel.^28,29^

The severity of punishment was designed not just to punish individual offenders but to terrorize the entire enslaved population into submission. After slave rebellions, British authorities engaged in orgies of retaliatory violence. Following the 1760 Tacky's Rebellion in Jamaica, approximately 60 rebels were executed, many by being burned alive or suspended in iron gibbets to die slowly of thirst and starvation.^30^ Their bodies were left on display as warnings. Such exhibitions of cruelty were standard practice across British slave colonies.^28,30^

The Economics of Slavery: Blood Money Built Britain

The profits from the slave trade and slave labor were staggering, and they flowed primarily to Britain. Conservative estimates suggest that British merchants and investors extracted £20 million in profits from the slave trade alone between 1750 and 1807, equivalent to billions in today's currency.^4^ The profits from slave-produced goods—sugar, tobacco, cotton—were vastly larger.^4,5^

These profits were not simply consumed but invested in ways that transformed Britain. Slave trade profits financed the construction of ports, particularly Liverpool and Bristol, which became major commercial centers.^31^ Merchants who made fortunes in the slave trade invested in banks, insurance companies, and industrial enterprises.^4,5^ Barclays Bank, Lloyds of London, and other major British financial institutions have their origins in slave trade capital.^32^ The Hibbert family fortune, built on Jamaican slavery, helped establish the Hibbert Trust, which funded educational institutions.^33^ Many British country estates, art collections, and aristocratic fortunes trace directly to slavery.^33,34^

The connection between slavery and the Industrial Revolution is particularly important. Slave-produced

Chapter 2: The Triangular Slave Trade

cotton from the Americas supplied Britain's textile mills, the leading sector of industrialization.^5^ The profits from colonial trade provided the capital for industrial investment.^4,5^ The commercial and financial infrastructure developed to manage the slave trade—international banking, insurance, commodity markets—became the foundation of modern capitalism.^4^ The slave economy created a vast market for British manufactured goods, particularly cheap textiles exported to Africa to purchase more captives.^5^ Britain's industrial supremacy was built on foundations of slave labor.

This is not mere historical accident or correlation. The slave economy was essential to British economic development. As historian Eric Williams demonstrated in his groundbreaking work Capitalism and Slavery, the wealth generated by slavery provided the capital accumulation necessary for industrialization.^4^ The notion that Britain's rise to global economic dominance was the result of superior culture, Protestant work ethic, or fortunate geography is mythology. It was built on the systematic exploitation of enslaved labor on an unprecedented scale.

Legal Fictions and Moral Contradictions

The legal framework supporting British slavery reveals the system's fundamental contradictions. In Britain itself, slavery was legally ambiguous. The famous

Perfidious Albion

Somerset case (1772) established that a slave brought to England could not be forcibly removed, which some interpreted as ending slavery on English soil.^35^ Yet this did not end British participation in the slave trade or slavery in British colonies. The British government, courts, and public claimed to value liberty while actively enforcing one of history's most oppressive systems.^35^

The law treated enslaved people simultaneously as property and as human beings responsible for their actions—whichever categorization was more convenient for slaveholders.^36^ Enslaved people could be bought, sold, mortgaged, and inherited like livestock. They could be branded, beaten, and killed with minimal legal consequences for the owner. Yet they could be prosecuted and punished for crimes, implying moral agency and responsibility that property does not possess.^36^

These contradictions occasionally produced cognitive dissonance among British observers. Some recognized the horror and injustice. But the vast majority of British people, particularly those who profited from the system, maintained their moral equilibrium through a combination of racism, willful ignorance, and economic rationalization.^37^

The development of scientific racism during this period was not coincidental. Theories of African inferiority

Chapter 2: The Triangular Slave Trade

were developed and promoted specifically to justify slavery.^38^ If Africans were inherently inferior, savage, childlike, or suited only for labor, then slavery could be presented as beneficial or at least not criminal. These racist ideologies, developed to justify economic exploitation, outlived slavery itself and continue to poison societies today.^38^

Resistance: The Struggle for Freedom

Despite the overwhelming violence deployed against them, enslaved people never accepted their bondage passively. Resistance took many forms, from individual acts of defiance to organized rebellions that shook the foundations of British colonial power.^39^

Day-to-day resistance was constant. Enslaved people worked slowly, damaged tools and equipment, feigned illness, and stole food and goods from their enslavers.^39^ These acts, while small, were dangerous—punishment for even minor resistance could be savage—but they represented refusals to fully cooperate in their own exploitation.

Escape was common despite the terrible risks. In Jamaica, escaped slaves established maroon communities in mountainous interior regions, where they successfully defended their freedom for generations.^40^ The British military launched repeated campaigns against these communities, but maroons' knowledge of terrain and guerrilla tactics made them difficult to defeat. The existence of maroon communities was both a practical challenge to slavery and a symbolic affront to the system.˄40˄

Large-scale rebellions were less common but more threatening to the system. The 1760 Tacky's Rebellion in Jamaica involved hundreds of enslaved people and briefly captured significant territory before being suppressed.˄30˄ The 1795-1796 Second Maroon War required thousands of British troops and extensive military operations to defeat.˄40˄ Most famous was the Haitian Revolution (1791-1804), which, while not directly British, terrified British slaveholders and demonstrated that enslaved people could successfully overthrow their oppressors.˄41˄

British responses to resistance reveal the system's fundamental dependency on violence. Every rebellion was met with overwhelming force and horrific retribution. Yet the constant resistance demonstrates that enslaved people never internalized their oppressors' ideology. They knew they were human beings unjustly imprisoned and forced to labor, and they fought for freedom however they could.˄39,41˄

The Abolitionist Movement: Too Little, Too Late
The movement to abolish the British slave trade

Chapter 2: The Triangular Slave Trade

emerged in the late 18th century, driven by Quakers, evangelical Christians, and Enlightenment thinkers who recognized slavery's moral horror.^42^ Figures like Granville Sharp, Thomas Clarkson, and William Wilberforce become celebrated in British historical memory as humanitarian heroes who brought about abolition.^42,43^

This narrative, while not entirely false, requires significant qualification. First, the abolitionist movement focused initially on ending the slave trade rather than slavery itself, accepting that existing enslaved people would remain enslaved.^42^ This was a morally compromised position that prioritized British sensitivity over enslaved people's freedom. Second, abolitionists often adopted racist and paternalist attitudes toward Africans, seeing them as objects of pity rather than as equals.^37,44^ Third, the campaign succeeded only when economic and political conditions made abolition palatable to British elites.^4,45^

The Slave Trade Act of 1807, which prohibited British ships from transporting enslaved people, was certainly a significant achievement.^43^ But Britain continued to allow slavery in its colonies until 1833, and even then, "abolition" came with massive compensation—£20 million, an enormous sum—paid to slave owners for their "loss of property."^46^ The enslaved people themselves received nothing. Moreover, they were required to serve "apprenticeships" to their former masters for years after nominal emancipation, meaning that actual freedom was delayed.˄46˄

British historical memory celebrates abolition as proof of British moral superiority and humanity. The reality is that Britain abolished slavery only after extracting centuries of wealth from enslaved labor, only after paying slaveholders handsomely for giving up their "property," and only after former slaves themselves rose up repeatedly to demand freedom. The credit belongs primarily to the enslaved people who resisted and rebelled, not to the British who finally, grudgingly, and incompletely dismantled a system they had built and profited from.˄39,41,46˄

The Legacy: Wealth Built on Bones

The Atlantic slave trade ended two centuries ago. Slavery in British colonies ended nearly two centuries ago. Yet the effects remain profoundly visible today. The wealth extracted from enslaved labor became the foundation of modern British prosperity.˄4,5˄ Meanwhile, the regions that supplied enslaved people—West and Central Africa—and the regions where they labored—the Caribbean and Americas—were left impoverished, depopulated, and traumatized.˄47˄

The demographic impact on Africa was catastrophic. An estimated 12-15 million Africans were transported across the Atlantic, with millions more dying during capture or

Chapter 2: The Triangular Slave Trade

before reaching the coast.^1,3^ This massive loss of primarily young, healthy people devastated African societies for generations.^47^ The economic distortions created by the slave trade—the focus on capturing people rather than productive activity—left African economies weakened precisely when European colonialism was intensifying.^47^

In the Caribbean and Americas, slave societies became societies built on racial hierarchy, with effects that persist today in economic inequality, political systems, and social relations.^48^ The racial ideologies developed to justify slavery outlived the institution itself, evolving into Jim Crow segregation, apartheid, and continuing racism.^38,48^

Britain has never adequately reckoned with this history. There has been no official apology, no reparations, no systematic education about slavery's centrality to British wealth.^49^ Instead, British historical memory emphasizes abolition, treating it as evidence of moral progress while minimizing the two centuries of industrialized atrocity that preceded it. The buildings constructed with slave wealth, the museums filled with slave-funded art, and the institutions built on slave capital continue to function without acknowledgment of their origins.^33,34^

Summary Conclusion: The Foundation of Empire
The British slave trade was not an unfortunate episode in

an otherwise admirable history of imperial expansion. It was fundamental to the creation of the British Empire and modern British wealth. For two centuries, British ships, British merchants, British investors, and the British state organized the largest forced migration in human history. They transported millions of people across the ocean in conditions designed to maximize profit while minimizing cost, accepting massive death rates as the price of business. They forced these people to labor under conditions of unimaginable brutality to produce commodities for British and European consumption. They used systematic violence—torture, mutilation, murder—to maintain control over populations whose labor they stole.

They did all this while developing elaborate ideologies to justify it: claims that Africans were inferior, that slavery was economically necessary, that it was even beneficial to those enslaved. These lies were never believed by the enslaved themselves, who resisted constantly and fought for freedom whenever possible. But they were believed, or at least professed, by the British people who benefited from the system, allowing them to maintain their self-image as civilized and Christian while building their prosperity on mass murder.

The wealth generated by this system did not disappear when slavery ended. It was invested, inherited, and compounded. It built institutions, industries, and infrastructure that continue to generate wealth today. The descendants of slave traders and slave owners

Chapter 2: The Triangular Slave Trade

inherited that wealth. The descendants of enslaved people inherited poverty, trauma, and continued discrimination. This is not ancient history but living legacy, and Britain's refusal to acknowledge it honestly is itself an ongoing injustice.

Understanding this history is essential to understanding everything that follows. The British Empire was built on slavery's foundation. The methods of control, the racial ideologies, the economic exploitation, and the casual brutality developed in the slave system were carried forward into Britain's subsequent imperial ventures. The mentality that could accept the horrors of the Middle Passage as acceptable business practice was the same mentality that would starve millions in colonial famines, massacre rebellious subjects, and extract the wealth of entire continents. Slavery was not an aberration in British imperial history—it was the template.

Author's Notes Chapter 2

This chapter examines Britain's dominance of the Atlantic slave trade and argues that slavery was not peripheral to British economic development but foundational. The approximately 3.1 million Africans transported on British ships represents the largest national participation in the trade, and the wealth generated fundamentally shaped British capitalism, industrialization, and global power.

On the Middle Passage: Marcus Rediker's *The Slave Ship: A Human History* (2007) provides harrowing detail about conditions aboard slave ships based on ship logs, crew testimonies, and survivor accounts. Stephanie Smallwood's

Saltwater Slavery (2007) examines the Middle Passage from enslaved Africans' perspectives, treating their commodification as fundamental violence rather than unfortunate necessity. The 10-20% mortality rate during the Atlantic crossing represents approximately 1.5-3 million deaths—a scale of suffering that defies adequate description.

On Economic Impact: Eric Williams' controversial thesis in *Capitalism and Slavery* (1944) argued that slavery profits directly financed Britain's industrial revolution. While subsequent scholarship has debated the precise mechanisms and magnitudes, Joseph Inikori's magisterial *Africans and the Industrial Revolution in England* (2002) demonstrates convincingly that slavery and the slave trade were central to British economic development through multiple pathways: direct profits, demand for manufactured goods, development of financial instruments and institutions, and creation of protected markets.

Historiographical Debates: Scholarly debate continues about slavery's precise contribution to British industrialization. Some economic historians (notably Stanley Engerman and David Eltis) argue that Williams overstated slavery's economic importance. Others (including Inikori and Catherine Hall) maintain that slavery was fundamental. This chapter follows the latter interpretation, arguing that attempting to calculate slavery's contribution through narrow economic metrics misses the systemic ways slavery shaped British economic, social, and political development.

On Resistance: The chapter emphasizes enslaved people's resistance—from shipboard revolts to everyday acts of defiance—to counter narratives presenting enslaved Africans as passive victims. Michael Craton's *Testing the Chains* (1982) documents the persistent, varied, and creative

Chapter 2: The Triangular Slave Trade

forms of resistance that characterized slavery across the Caribbean. This resistance ultimately contributed to slavery's abolition by making the system increasingly expensive and unstable.

Methodological Note: Reconstructing enslaved people's experiences from the historical record is challenging because most sources were produced by slavers, traders, and plantation owners. Slave narratives (like Olaudah Equiano's) provide invaluable first-person accounts, though their publication contexts shaped their content. Archaeological evidence, including slave quarters, burial sites, and material culture, increasingly supplements written records.

CHAPTER THREE

The Conquest of India

From Trading Post to Subjugation (1600-1857)

When the East India Company established its first trading post at Surat in 1608, the Mughal Empire was one of the world's wealthiest and most powerful states, controlling approximately a quarter of global GDP.[1] India's textile industry was the world's most advanced, its agricultural productivity sustained a population larger than Europe's, and its cultural and scientific achievements were extraordinary.[2] Two and a half centuries later, by the time of the 1857 Uprising, the Company had conquered virtually the entire subcontinent through warfare, treachery, and systematic violence.

India had been transformed from a prosperous center of global commerce into a colony designed to enrich Britain while impoverishing its own people.^3,4^ This conquest was not the inevitable triumph of superior civilization but the result of deliberate military aggression, economic manipulation, and the ruthless exploitation of internal divisions. It ranks among history's greatest thefts, with consequences that continue to devastate the subcontinent today.

The Company-State: Corporate Sovereignty as Imperial Weapon

The East India Company, chartered by Elizabeth I in 1600, was nominally a commercial enterprise seeking to trade with Asia. But from its inception, the Company possessed powers that no modern corporation could dream of: the authority to wage war, negotiate treaties, mint currency, administer justice, and govern territory.^5^ This fusion of corporate profit-seeking with sovereign power created an entity uniquely positioned to exploit and eventually conquer India.

The Company's early decades involved establishing trading posts through a combination of diplomacy and intimidation. Company representatives would approach local rulers requesting trading privileges, backed by the implicit threat of naval bombardment if cooperation was not forthcoming.^5,6^ The Company's ships carried far

Chapter 3: The Conquest of India

more cannon than legitimate merchant vessels required, advertising their dual function as instruments of commerce and coercion.

Initially, the Company traded British goods—primarily woolens and metals—for Indian textiles, spices, and other commodities. But British manufactures were inferior to Indian products and found limited markets in Asia.^7^ The Company increasingly paid for Indian goods with bullion, draining British silver reserves. This created a fundamental problem: how could the Company profit if it had to pay real money for Indian goods but couldn't sell British products in return?

The solution, developed over decades, was to stop operating as a legitimate trading company and instead use political and military power to extract wealth directly. The Company would conquer territory, impose taxes on the population, use that tax revenue to purchase Indian goods, then sell those goods in Britain and Europe for profit.^4,8^ In other words, the Company would force Indians to pay for their own exploitation. This model— using conquered peoples' resources to finance their continued subjugation—became the template for British imperialism worldwide.

The Battle of Plassey: Conquest Through Betrayal

The transformation of the Company from merchant to

sovereign began in earnest with the Battle of Plassey in 1757, one of history's most consequential acts of treachery.^9^ The battle itself was barely a battle—more an arranged surrender—but its consequences were catastrophic for India and enormously profitable for Britain.

Bengal in the mid-18th century was one of India's wealthiest regions, with a thriving textile industry, productive agriculture, and a population of approximately 30 million.^10^ The Nawab of Bengal, Siraj ud-Daulah, was the region's legitimate ruler. The East India Company, operating trading posts in Bengal, had been systematically abusing its privileges: smuggling to avoid taxes, fortifying its positions without permission, and generally acting as a state within a state.^9,11^

When Siraj ud-Daulah attempted to assert his authority by attacking the Company's unauthorized fortifications at Fort William in Calcutta (1756), the Company used this as pretext for regime change.^9^ Robert Clive, a Company military officer, assembled an army and made secret arrangements with Mir Jafar, one of Siraj's generals, to betray his ruler during battle. In exchange for his treachery, Mir Jafar was promised the throne and personal wealth.^9,11^

At Plassey on June 23, 1757, when battle was joined, Mir

Chapter 3: The Conquest of India

Jafar's forces stood aside or withdrew, leaving Siraj's much smaller actual fighting force to be defeated.^9^ Siraj was captured and murdered. Mir Jafar was installed as puppet Nawab, and the Company extracted enormous payments for its "services": immediate compensation of £2.5 million plus annual tribute.^11^ For comparison, the Company's total annual revenue at the time was approximately £1.5 million—Bengal's plunder more than doubled the Company's income in a single transaction.^8^

Robert Clive personally received £234,000 (equivalent to tens of millions today) as his share of the loot, making him instantly one of Britain's wealthiest men.^11^ He later testified to Parliament that he showed "restraint" in only taking this amount when he "could have taken more." This testimony, intended to defend himself against accusations of excessive greed, instead revealed the mentality of the conquest: India was a treasury to be looted, and the only question was how much each individual looter could carry away.^11^

The significance of Plassey extends far beyond the battle itself. It established the Company's military dominance in Bengal and demonstrated a method that would be repeated across India: exploit internal divisions, bribe local elites to betray their rulers, install puppets, then extract wealth while maintaining the fiction of native sovereignty.^9,12^ It marked the beginning of the

Company's transformation from merchant to conqueror.

The Great Bengal Famine: Ten Million Dead

The immediate consequence of the Company's conquest of Bengal was catastrophe. Between 1769 and 1773, a famine devastated Bengal, killing an estimated 10 million people—approximately one-third of the region's population.^13,14^ This was not a natural disaster but a direct result of Company policies.

Before Company rule, Bengal's agricultural system had been sophisticated and resilient, with stored grain reserves, irrigation systems, and mechanisms for distributing food during shortages.^15^ The Company destroyed this system. It dramatically increased the land tax burden—doubling or tripling rates in some areas—because it needed revenue to pay for continued military expansion and to remit profits to shareholders in Britain.^14,16^ These taxes had to be paid in cash, forcing farmers to sell crops immediately after harvest regardless of price, eliminating their ability to store grain for lean seasons.^14^

When drought struck in 1769, there were no reserves. Farmers, already impoverished by excessive taxation, had no cushion to survive a bad harvest.^13,14^ The Company, rather than reducing tax demands or

Chapter 3: The Conquest of India

providing relief, actually increased collection efforts because it needed revenue.^16^ Company officials enforced tax collection with violence, seizing property and even torturing villagers who could not pay.^14^ Meanwhile, Company merchants profited by hoarding grain to sell at inflated famine prices.^14^

The death toll was staggering. Contemporary accounts describe depopulated villages, roads lined with corpses, and desperate survivors eating grass, leaves, and even human flesh.^13^ Company officials documented the catastrophe in their reports, noting that tax revenue decreased because so many taxpayers had died—a bureaucratic observation that reveals the Company's fundamental indifference to human life.^14,16^

The Company's response was not to reform its policies but to adjust its expectations of revenue collection downward to account for the reduced population.^16^ The famine was treated as a natural disaster that reduced the productive capacity of the Company's asset (Bengal) rather than as a crime that demanded accountability. No Company officials were punished. The shareholders continued receiving dividends. Robert Clive, architect of the conquest, retired wealthy and was eventually buried with honors in Britain.^11^

Expansion Through Warfare: The Conquest Spreads

Following the conquest of Bengal, the Company spent

the next century systematically conquering the rest of India through a series of wars that killed millions and destroyed indigenous states.^17^ This expansion was driven by a combination of strategic paranoia—fear that rivals would threaten Company territory—and straightforward greed for more taxable land and loot.^12,17^

The Anglo-Mysore Wars (1767-1799) against Tipu Sultan's Kingdom of Mysore involved four separate conflicts over three decades.^18^ Tipu Sultan was one of India's most effective military leaders, employing modern tactics and weaponry, including rockets that would later inspire British military developments.^18^ He was also a substantial obstacle to Company expansion in South India. The Company eventually defeated Mysore through alliance with other Indian states, particularly the Maratha Confederacy and the Nizam of Hyderabad—a pattern of using some Indians to conquer others that the British would perfect.^18^

When Mysore's capital Seringapatam fell in 1799, Company forces engaged in an orgy of plunder and violence.^18,19^ Tipu Sultan was killed defending his capital. His treasury, accumulated over generations, was looted—with senior Company officers taking enormous personal shares. The palace was ransacked, with soldiers seizing everything of value. Civilians were killed or enslaved. Arthur Wellesley (later Duke of Wellington)

Chapter 3: The Conquest of India

participated in this campaign, beginning a military career that would culminate in defeating Napoleon—a trajectory that illustrates how British officers used India as a training ground and enrichment opportunity.^19^

The Anglo-Maratha Wars (1775-1818) were even longer and bloodier, involving multiple campaigns against the powerful Maratha Confederacy that controlled much of central and northern India.^20^ The Marathas were formidable opponents with large, well-organized armies and sophisticated administration. The Company defeated them not primarily through military superiority but through diplomatic manipulation, exploiting internal divisions within the Confederacy and allying with some Maratha factions against others.^20,21^

The Anglo-Sikh Wars (1845-1849) in Punjab involved some of the Company's hardest-fought campaigns.^22^ The Sikh Empire under Maharaja Ranjit Singh had been powerful and well-organized, with a modernized army trained by European officers. After Ranjit Singh's death, political instability weakened the empire, and the Company exploited this vulnerability to provoke war.^22^ Despite fierce Sikh resistance and heavy British casualties, the Company eventually conquered Punjab, completing its control over virtually all of India by 1849.^22^

Each of these conquests followed a similar pattern: the

Company would identify a wealthy independent state, manufacture a pretext for war (often through deliberate provocation), exploit internal divisions, deploy overwhelming violence, and then loot the defeated state's treasury while imposing permanent taxation on its population.^12,17^ The wealth seized in these conquests was staggering. The annexation of Awadh in 1856, for example, brought the Company control of a treasury containing approximately £3 million plus annual tax revenue of £1.3 million—this from a state that had been a British ally and had committed no offense except being wealthy and vulnerable.^23^

The Doctrine of Lapse: Legal Fiction as Theft

Not all conquests required warfare. Under Governor-General Lord Dalhousie (1848-1856), the Company adopted the "Doctrine of Lapse," a legal principle that allowed the Company to annex any princely state whose ruler died without a direct biological heir.^24^ This violated Indian traditions, which recognized adopted heirs as legitimate, and it was applied selectively—only to wealthy states the Company coveted.^24^

The doctrine was pure theft disguised as law. When a ruler died, Company officials would refuse to recognize his adopted heir, declare the state "lapsed" to British control, and seize its territory and treasury.^24^ This

Chapter 3: The Conquest of India

happened to Satara (1848), Jaitpur and Sambalpur (1849), Baghat (1850), Udaipur (1852), Jhansi (1853), and Nagpur (1854), among others.^24^ The annexation of these states was accomplished not through military conquest but through bureaucratic fiat—British officials simply declared them British property and sent troops to enforce the declaration if local populations objected.^24^

The economic motivations were transparent. These states had been paying tribute to the Company and maintaining their own administrations at their own expense. By annexing them directly, the Company could seize their accumulated wealth and impose higher taxes while eliminating the cost of maintaining puppet rulers.^24^ The annexed territories generated immediate windfalls—Nagpur's treasury alone contained £3 million—plus ongoing revenue.^23,24^

The Doctrine of Lapse created widespread insecurity among India's remaining princes, who realized that British protection was worthless and that their states would be annexed the moment British officials decided it was profitable.^24^ This contributed significantly to the alienation that would explode in the 1857 Uprising. More fundamentally, it revealed the Company's complete contempt for Indian law, custom, and sovereignty. Property rights, inheritance rules, and treaty obligations meant nothing when they conflicted with British avarice.^24^

Economic Extraction: The Deliberate Deindustrialization of India

Military conquest was only the beginning of British exploitation. Once territory was controlled, the Company and later the Crown implemented economic policies designed to extract wealth from India while destroying indigenous industries that competed with British manufactures.^3,4^

India in 1700 had the world's most advanced textile industry, producing cotton and silk fabrics of unmatched quality.^2,25^ Indian textiles were exported globally and were so superior to European products that British manufacturers demanded protection against Indian imports.^25^ The Company's solution was two-fold: destroy Indian industry while forcing India to import British textiles.^4,25^

The Company imposed tariffs and prohibitions on Indian textiles entering Britain, making them uncompetitive, while forcing India to accept British textiles duty-free or at minimal tariffs.^25,26^ This destroyed Indian export markets. Simultaneously, the Company manipulated its taxation and purchasing policies to impoverish Indian weavers. It forced artisans to sell only to Company agents at fixed, artificially low prices—essentially forced labor for below-market wages.^4^ Weavers who tried to sell to other buyers were punished. Some had their thumbs cut off to prevent them from weaving.^4,27^

Chapter 3: The Conquest of India

The result was the systematic deindustrialization of India. Towns that had been centers of textile production were abandoned. Weavers were reduced to poverty or driven to agricultural labor.^4,25^ By the mid-19th century, India had been transformed from the world's leading textile exporter to an importer of British textiles manufactured from Indian raw cotton.^25^ The economic logic was brutal: India would produce raw materials cheaply, export them to Britain where they would be manufactured into finished goods using British labor, then import those goods at high prices. India would be deindustrialized to eliminate competition while creating captive markets for British products.^4,26^

This was deliberate imperial policy, not market forces. Company and later Crown officials explicitly discussed the need to destroy Indian manufacturing to benefit British industry.^4,26^ Governor-General William Bentinck observed in 1834: "The misery hardly finds a parallel in the history of commerce. The bones of the cotton-weavers are bleaching the plains of India."^27^ This was not lament but observation—the destruction of Indian industry was policy, and its human costs were acceptable.

The Revenue System: Permanent Exploitation

The Company's land revenue system was designed to

Perfidious Albion

extract maximum wealth with minimum British investment or responsibility.^28^ Different systems were implemented in different regions, but all shared the goal of transferring as much agricultural surplus as possible from Indian producers to British coffers.^28,29^

The Permanent Settlement (1793) in Bengal created a class of zamindars—landlords who would collect taxes from peasant farmers and remit a fixed amount to the Company.^28^ The zamindars could keep any surplus they collected above the fixed demand, creating incentives for maximum extraction. The Company's demand was set deliberately high—approximately 90% of estimated agricultural productivity—leaving farmers with barely enough to survive.^28,29^

This system was catastrophic for farmers. Zamindars, seeking to maximize their profits, imposed crushing rents. Farmers who could not pay were evicted or had their property seized. The Company provided no relief during droughts or crop failures—the revenue demand remained constant regardless of harvest.^28,29^ Meanwhile, the Company accepted no responsibility for maintaining irrigation, roads, or other infrastructure. The zamindars, interested only in short-term profit extraction, had no incentive to make long-term investments.^28^

The Ryotwari system in Madras and Bombay presidencies nominally dealt directly with peasant

Chapter 3: The Conquest of India

cultivators, but with similar results.^29^ The revenue demand was set at approximately 50% of gross agricultural output—a rate vastly higher than had prevailed under previous Indian rulers.^29^ Farmers fell into debt, lost their land, and became dependent on moneylenders who charged usurious rates, creating cycles of poverty that persist today.^29,30^

The fundamental principle of British land revenue policy was extraction without investment. The Company and Crown took enormous wealth from Indian agriculture while providing nothing in return—no agricultural development, no famine relief, no infrastructure beyond what was necessary for military control and export of commodities.^4,28^ British officials openly acknowledged this. Charles Trevelyan, a senior official, described the British role as similar to "a sponge, drawing up all the good things from the banks of the Ganges, and squeezing them down on the banks of the Thames."^31^

Cultural Arrogance and the "Civilizing Mission"
British conquest was justified through an ideology of racial and cultural superiority that portrayed Indians as backward, barbaric, and in need of British governance to become civilized.^32^ This "civilizing mission" was propaganda designed to make theft and violence appear beneficent, but it was also genuinely believed by many British officials and shaped policy in destructive

ways.[32,33]

British officials dismissed Indian civilization as inferior despite overwhelming evidence to the contrary. India's mathematical achievements—including the concept of zero, the decimal system, advanced astronomy—were ignored or appropriated.[34] Its architectural wonders were acknowledged but attributed to foreign influences rather than indigenous genius.[33] Its philosophical and religious traditions were caricatured as superstition.[33]

This arrogance led to policies that destroyed India's educational system. Under previous Indian rulers, village schools had provided basic education, and centers of higher learning taught philosophy, science, and literature.[35] The Company largely ignored education, and when the Crown assumed control, British authorities created an education system designed to produce clerks and administrators who spoke English and absorbed British values rather than Indians educated in their own traditions.[35]

The explicit goal, articulated by Thomas Macaulay, was to create "a class of persons Indian in blood and colour, but English in taste, in opinions, in morals, and in intellect."[36] This policy of cultural imperialism aimed to alienate educated Indians from their own heritage and make them willing collaborators in British rule.[35,36]

Chapter 3: The Conquest of India

The British also intervened in Indian social and religious practices, sometimes in ways that seem progressive (banning sati, prohibiting female infanticide) but were implemented with cultural insensitivity and arrogance that alienated Indians.˄37˄

More often, British interventions were destructive: undermining traditional governance systems, dismissing Indian legal principles, and treating Indian customs with contempt. The fundamental premise was that nothing Indian was worth preserving unless it served British interests.˄32,33˄

Resistance and Suppression

Indians resisted British conquest from the beginning. Every major war involved fierce fighting by Indian armies. Between wars, there were constant smaller rebellions, riots, and acts of resistance.˄38˄ The British response was always overwhelming violence designed not just to defeat but to terrorize.˄38,39˄

The methods employed by Company forces were savage. Villages suspected of harboring rebels were burned. Captured resisters were executed, often after torture. Mass hangings and public executions were used to instill fear.˄39˄ Company military policy explicitly embraced terrorism—the deliberate targeting of civilians to break resistance.˄38,39˄

In the 1820s-30s, the Company waged a campaign of suppression against the Thuggee, portraying them as a cult of hereditary criminals who robbed and murdered travelers.^40^ While criminal gangs certainly existed, the British vastly exaggerated the threat and used anti-Thuggee operations as pretext for mass arrests, executions, and the extension of police-state surveillance systems.^40^ Thousands were hanged based on dubious evidence and coerced confessions. The campaign served British interests by justifying increased policing, eliminating potential sources of resistance, and providing propaganda about British civilization bringing order to savage India.^40^

These decades of piecemeal resistance were preludes to the greatest challenge to British rule: the Uprising of 1857, which demonstrated both the depths of Indian hatred for British rule and the extremes of violence Britain was willing to employ to maintain control.

The Uprising of 1857: When India Rose

In May 1857, sepoys (Indian soldiers in the Company's army) in Meerut mutinied, killed British officers and civilians, and marched to Delhi where they proclaimed the restoration of Mughal rule under the aged Emperor Bahadur Shah II.^41^ Within weeks, the uprising spread across northern and central India, involving not just

Chapter 3: The Conquest of India

soldiers but civilians, landlords, peasants, and princes.^41,42^

The immediate trigger was the introduction of new rifle cartridges rumored to be greased with cow and pig fat, offensive to both Hindu and Muslim soldiers.^41^ But the deeper causes were the accumulated grievances of a century of British exploitation: loss of sovereignty, economic devastation, cultural contempt, broken promises to soldiers, and the annexations under the Doctrine of Lapse.^41,42^

The uprising was not a unified independence movement with modern nationalist ideology—it was a diverse collection of groups with varying motivations, from soldiers seeking better treatment to princes wanting to restore their kingdoms to peasants seeking revenge for exploitation.^42^ But what united them was opposition to British rule and a desire to expel the foreign occupiers.^42^

The British portrayed the uprising as a "mutiny"—a breakdown in military discipline—rather than acknowledging it as widespread rejection of British rule.^43^ They also focused attention on atrocities committed against British civilians, particularly the killings at Cawnpore, while minimizing both the scale of Indian participation and the causes of Indian anger.^43^ The British response was genocidal in its fury. As British

Perfidious Albion

forces regained control, they engaged in systematic massacres. Villages were burned with their inhabitants inside. Prisoners were executed without trial—often by being blown from cannon, a method chosen for its spectacular brutality.^39,44^ At Delhi, when British forces retook the city, they engaged in days of indiscriminate slaughter, killing thousands of civilians regardless of whether they had participated in the uprising.^44^

British officers sent letters and reports describing these atrocities with satisfaction, even pride.^39,44^ General Neill boasted of his policy of forcing Muslim prisoners to lick blood from floors before execution, deliberately violating their religious beliefs before killing them.^39^ Colonel James Neill wrote: "I wish I had the power to place myself at the head of an Army of Extermination... I would take care that the streets of every place I entered should be running with blood."^44^ These were not rogue elements but official British military policy, documented in official communications.

The death toll of the uprising and its suppression is estimated at several hundred thousand, with some historians suggesting over a million when including famine and disease caused by the disruption.^42,44^ The British officially characterized their response as restoring order; in reality, it was collective punishment designed to terrorize India into permanent submission.~39,44~

The Crown Takes Control: Imperialism Formalized

The 1857 Uprising convinced British authorities that Company rule was unsustainable. In 1858, the British Crown assumed direct control of India, ending the Company's political authority while maintaining its trading operations.~45~ This transferred India from corporate to imperial sovereignty—a distinction without meaningful difference for Indians, who remained subjects of an exploitative foreign power.~45~

The Crown's assumption of control was accompanied by proclamations promising to respect Indian traditions and provide good governance.~45~ These promises were largely empty. The fundamental structure of exploitation—revenue extraction, economic subordination to British interests, political disenfranchisement—continued unchanged.~45~ If anything, Crown rule made exploitation more systematic and thorough, as the British government could deploy imperial resources more efficiently than the Company had.~46~

The British also implemented policies designed to prevent future uprisings. The Indian army was reorganized to ensure British units outnumbered Indian ones, and Indian soldiers were deliberately recruited from groups the British considered "martial races" and unlikely to unite across ethnic and religious lines.~47~ This policy of divide and rule would characterize British policy for the next ninety years.~47~

Summary Conclusion: Conquest as Catastrophe

By 1857, Britain had conquered India through a systematic campaign of warfare, treachery, and economic manipulation lasting two and a half centuries. This was not the spread of civilization but the destruction of one of the world's great civilizations for profit. India, which had accounted for approximately 23% of global GDP in 1700, would account for less than 4% by 1950, while Britain's share increased dramatically.~1,3~ This was not natural economic evolution but deliberate exploitation—wealth was systematically extracted from India to Britain through unfair trade, land revenue, and direct plunder.~3,4~

The human costs were staggering: millions dead in famines caused or exacerbated by British policies, millions more killed in wars of conquest and suppression, countless lives destroyed by economic policies that impoverished farmers and destroyed industries.~3,13,14,42~ India's political sovereignty was eliminated, its economic systems destroyed, and its cultural traditions were denigrated and suppressed.~4,32~

British historical memory portrays the conquest of India as Britain bringing civilization, rule of law, and

Chapter 3: The Conquest of India

modernity to a backward region. The reality is that Britain brought exploitation, violence, and systematic theft on a scale rarely matched in human history. The wealth extracted from India helped finance British industrialization, enriched British elites, and created the power that allowed Britain to dominate globally.˄4,5˄ Meanwhile, India was reduced from prosperity to poverty, from industrial leadership to colonial dependency, from sovereign civilization to subject population.˄3,4˄

The conquest of India was not complete by 1857—that would require another ninety years and would be the subject of later chapters. But by the mid-19th century, the pattern was firmly established: British rule meant Indian impoverishment, British profit meant Indian loss, and British civilization meant the destruction of Indian civilization. Every aspect of subsequent British rule in India would follow from these foundations laid between 1600 and 1857.

Author's Notes Chapter 3

This chapter traces how the East India Company transformed from a trading corporation into a territorial power ruling most of the Indian subcontinent. The Company's history demonstrates that imperialism was not incidental to capitalism but that corporate profit-seeking led directly to conquest, exploitation, and mass violence when commercial goals could be achieved through force.

On the East India Company: William Dalrymple's *The Anarchy* (2019) provides the most recent comprehensive account, emphasizing the Company's extraordinary violence and the active resistance it faced. The Company operated as private corporation with its own army—larger than Britain's national army by the early 19th century—demonstrating that imperialism was not merely state policy but also corporate strategy. The Company's directors and shareholders in London profited directly from Indian conquest and exploitation.

On the Battle of Plassey (1757): This battle, though militarily minor, marked a crucial turning point enabling Company territorial expansion in Bengal. Robert Clive's victory through bribery and betrayal (rather than military superiority) established a pattern: the Company exploited internal divisions, bribed local officials, and manufactured conflicts to justify intervention. The subsequent looting of Bengal's treasury—Clive personally took £234,000 (equivalent to tens of millions today)—exemplifies the Company's extractive character.

On Economic Exploitation: The "drain of wealth" from India to Britain has been quantified by economic historians including Utsa Patnaik, who estimates approximately $45 trillion (in today's values) was extracted from India during British rule through various mechanisms: artificially low prices for Indian exports, high prices for British imports, "Home Charges" requiring India to pay for British administration, and direct taxation financing British military operations. This systematic extraction impoverished India while enriching Britain.

On the 1857 Uprising: British sources called this the "Mutiny," characterizing it as illegitimate rebellion by disloyal troops. Indian historians more accurately term it the "First War of Independence"—a widespread uprising against Company rule involving not just soldiers but civilians across northern India. The uprising's brutal

Chapter 3: The Conquest of India

suppression, including mass executions and collective punishments, demonstrated the violence required to maintain British control. The Crown's assumption of direct rule from the Company (1858) represented administrative reorganization, not fundamental change in exploitative character.

Historiographical Note: Traditional British imperial history portrayed the Company as bringing order, development, and civilization to chaotic India. Post-colonial scholarship has thoroughly debunked these claims, documenting instead the Company's role in creating poverty, destroying Indian industries, and causing famines. Indian historians including Romesh Dutt, R.C. Dutt, and more recently Shashi Tharoor have documented the systematic economic exploitation underlying British rule.

CHAPTER FOUR

Famine by Design

Economic Policies and Mass Death (1770-1943)

Famine is commonly understood as a natural disaster—the result of drought, crop failure, or other environmental catastrophes beyond human control. This understanding is fundamentally wrong when applied to famines under British rule.

The great famines that killed tens of millions across the British Empire were not natural disasters but the predictable, and often deliberate, consequences of British economic policies.^1^ From the Great Famine in Ireland (1845-1852) that killed over one million people, to the repeated Indian famines that claimed tens of millions of lives, to the less-documented but equally devastating famines in Africa, British authorities prioritized profit extraction and ideological commitments over human life.[1,2] In many cases, food was exported from famine-stricken regions while people starved, markets were allowed to operate "freely" while the poor couldn't afford to eat, and relief efforts were deliberately minimized to avoid "encouraging dependency."[3,4] These were not failures of governance but the logical outcomes of a system designed to extract maximum wealth with minimum responsibility. The famines of the British Empire were acts of policy, and they rank among history's greatest crimes.

The Irish Great Famine: Ideology as Murder Weapon

The Great Famine that devastated Ireland between 1845 and 1852 killed at least one million people—approximately 12% of Ireland's population—and forced another million to emigrate.[5] The immediate cause was potato blight (Phytophthora infestans), a fungal disease that destroyed the potato crop on which the Irish poor depended.[5] But the potato blight affected other European countries without causing comparable catastrophe.[6] What made Ireland's experience uniquely deadly was British policy.

Ireland in 1845 was part of the United Kingdom, governed directly from Westminster. The Irish population of approximately 8.5 million was largely

Chapter 4: Famine by Design

Catholic, poor, and systematically disadvantaged by laws that favored Protestant landlords—many of them absentee English owners.^7^ The land system, a legacy of centuries of conquest and confiscation, concentrated ownership in few hands while the mass of Irish people were tenant farmers working tiny plots.^7^ Subdivision of land had created increasingly small holdings, and by the 1840s, much of the rural population survived almost entirely on potatoes, which could produce sufficient calories from small plots.^5,7^

When the blight struck in autumn 1845, destroying much of the potato crop, the consequences were immediately catastrophic. Without potatoes, millions had no food.^5^ The blight returned in 1846, 1848, and 1849, making the crisis prolonged and devastating.^5^ But crucially, Ireland continued to produce substantial quantities of other foods—wheat, oats, barley, beef, pork, butter—throughout the famine years.^8^ These foods were not consumed by starving Irish people but were exported to Britain, where they fetched higher prices.^8^

The British government's response was shaped by laissez-faire economic ideology and a racist contempt for the Irish. Prime Minister Lord John Russell and his ministers believed that government interference in markets was economically harmful and morally corrupting.^9^ They feared that providing relief would create "dependency" and undermine Irish "character."^9^

Perfidious Albion

Charles Trevelyan, the senior Treasury official responsible for famine relief, wrote that the famine was "a direct stroke of an all-wise and all-merciful Providence" that would teach the Irish proper economic behavior.^10^ This wasn't merely callous indifference but active ideological commitment to letting people die rather than violating free-market principles.

The British government did implement some relief measures, but these were deliberately inadequate and often counterproductive.^11^ Public works schemes employed people at below-subsistence wages to build roads and other infrastructure—work that was deliberately pointless, so the destitute wouldn't benefit from anything useful.^11^ Soup kitchens were established but then shut down because officials feared they were too effective and would create dependency.^11^ The Poor Law Extension Act of 1847 made Irish property owners responsible for relief, bankrupting many small landlords while large landowners evaded responsibility.^12^ Throughout, the principle remained: minimal aid, maximum "self-reliance," and above all, no interference with food exports or market operations.^9,12^

The result was mass death from starvation and disease. Contemporary accounts describe skeletal figures, abandoned villages, roads lined with corpses, and desperate attempts to eat grass, seaweed, or anything

Chapter 4: Famine by Design

remotely edible.^13^ Entire families died in their cottages. Children's bodies were found with green stains around their mouths from eating nettles and grass.^13^ Diseases associated with malnutrition—typhus, relapsing fever, dysentery—killed hundreds of thousands.^5,13^ Meanwhile, food continued to leave Ireland. During the worst famine year of 1847, Ireland exported approximately 4,000 vessels of food to Britain—enough to feed millions.^8^ Armed guards protected food shipments from starving people who sometimes tried to seize them.^8^ British officials justified this by arguing that interfering with exports would damage trade and violate property rights. The property rights of Irish and British landowners to profit from their produce were more important than the right of Irish people to live.^8,9^

British public opinion was divided, but significant segments accepted the government's framing that the Irish were themselves responsible for their suffering through overpopulation, laziness, and dependence on a single crop.^14^ British newspapers published cartoons depicting the Irish as ape-like and savage, racially inferior beings who couldn't manage their own affairs.^14^ This racism made the mass death easier to tolerate—these weren't quite fellow citizens dying but racially inferior others whose suffering was somehow their own fault.^14^

The long-term consequences were catastrophic. Ireland's population, which had been growing rapidly before the famine, fell from 8.5 million in 1845 to 6.5 million in 1851 and continued declining for decades.^15^ Entire regions were depopulated. The social fabric was shredded. The famine convinced many Irish that British rule was inherently murderous, fueling independence movements that would eventually succeed.^15^ And it established a pattern: British officials would allow populations to starve rather than compromise their economic ideology or profit margins.^1,9^

The Indian Famines: Repeated Atrocity

While Ireland suffered one great famine, India endured repeated famines under British rule that collectively killed tens of millions. Major famines struck in 1770, 1783-1784, 1791-1792, 1837-1838, 1860-1861, 1865-1867, 1868-1870, 1873-1874, 1876-1878, 1896-1897, 1899-1900, and 1943-1944.^16^ These were not isolated incidents but a pattern of recurring catastrophe directly linked to British economic policies.^1,16^

We have already discussed the Bengal Famine of 1770 in Chapter 3, which killed approximately 10 million people shortly after the East India Company's conquest.^17^ That famine established the template: excessive taxation, elimination of traditional grain reserves, prioritization of revenue extraction over human welfare, and complete

Chapter 4: Famine by Design

indifference to mass death.[17] Subsequent famines followed the same pattern with depressing consistency. The Great Famine of 1876-1878 killed between 5.5 and 10 million people across southern and western India.[1,18] The immediate trigger was drought associated with a strong El Niño event, but the death toll was determined by British policy.[1,18] The Viceroy, Lord Lytton, was hosting an elaborate Imperial Assemblage in Delhi to proclaim Queen Victoria Empress of India—a spectacle of grotesque opulence costing millions—while millions of Indians starved.[18,19]

During this famine, India exported record quantities of wheat.[1,18] In 1877, at the height of the death toll, India exported 6.4 million hundredweight of wheat to Britain.[18] The logic was identical to Ireland: market principles must not be violated, exports must continue, and government intervention would create "moral hazard."[1,18] Lytton explicitly rejected proposals to ban grain exports or regulate prices, arguing that this would interfere with trade.[18] He reduced relief spending, closed relief camps, and implemented policies designed to minimize the number of people receiving aid.[18,20]

Relief, when provided, was deliberately punitive. The Temple-Famine Code, which governed relief efforts, specified that aid should be less than the wages of the poorest independent laborer, to avoid creating incentives for "malingering."[20] Relief camps required

Perfidious Albion

exhausting labor in exchange for minimal food—often less than the caloric intake provided in Nazi concentration camps.[1,20] The death rate in relief camps sometimes exceeded 90%.[20] People were literally worked to death for handfuls of grain.

British officials documented the horror with bureaucratic detachment. Reports noted the death toll, the emaciation of victims, the social breakdown.[18] But they expressed no shame, accepted no responsibility, and implemented no meaningful reforms. The famine was treated as an unfortunate natural event, not a policy-created catastrophe.[18] Some officials even argued that famine was beneficial, reducing population pressure and eliminating the weak.[1,21] This Social Darwinist logic—that mass death was natural selection improving the population—was explicitly stated in official documents.[21]

The famine of 1896-1897 killed an estimated 5 million people, and that of 1899-1900 killed another 1-3 million.[16,22] Again, these occurred not because India had insufficient food but because British policies ensured food went where it was profitable rather than where it was needed.[22] Again, exports continued, markets remained "free," and relief was minimal and punitive.[22] The pattern was so consistent that it defies interpretation as anything but intentional policy: British authorities knew their policies caused mass death, and

Chapter 4: Famine by Design

they continued those policies anyway.^1,16^

The economic impact of these famines extended far beyond the immediate death toll. Survivors were weakened, productivity declined, social systems fractured, and debt burdens increased as desperate people borrowed at usurious rates to survive.^23^ Each famine transferred wealth upward—from poor peasants to moneylenders, landlords, and grain merchants—while leaving rural populations more vulnerable to the next crisis.^23^ The famines were not just failures to prevent death but mechanisms of economic exploitation that benefited colonial authorities and their allies.^1,23^

The Bengal Famine of 1943: Churchill's Atrocity

The Bengal Famine of 1943-1944, which killed approximately 3 million people, deserves particular attention because it occurred during World War II, was extensively documented, and involved direct decisions by Winston Churchill, celebrated as a hero in British historical memory.^24,25^

Bengal in 1943 was Britain's most important colony during the war, supplying resources and soldiers for the fight against Japan.^24^ The famine was triggered by a combination of factors: cyclone and flood damage to crops, wartime inflation, panic buying, and disruption of rice imports from Burma (occupied by Japan).^24,25^ But these factors created shortage, not famine. The

Perfidious Albion

famine resulted from policy decisions that prioritized military and economic considerations over Bengali lives.[24,25]

The British government, focused on the war effort, requisitioned grain and boats from Bengal for military use.[24] This removed food from circulation and destroyed transportation networks that normally distributed grain within Bengal.[24] Simultaneously, the government refused to divert shipping to bring grain imports to Bengal, arguing that ships were needed for military purposes.[26] This was demonstrably false—shipping was available, but the British government chose not to use it to save Bengali lives.[26]

Most damningly, the British government actively prevented other countries from sending aid. When Canada and the United States offered to send grain, Churchill's government refused, claiming it would interfere with wartime shipping priorities.[26] Australia was prevented from sending wheat.[26] The British government preferred to let Bengalis die rather than accept foreign assistance that might embarrass them or establish precedents for future obligations.[26]

Churchill personally expressed racist contempt for Indians and indifference to their suffering. When told of the famine, he asked why Gandhi hadn't died yet if the famine was so bad.[27] He wrote that he "hated Indians"

Chapter 4: Famine by Design

and considered them "a beastly people with a beastly religion."[27] He argued that Indians were responsible for the famine through "breeding like rabbits."[27] These weren't private prejudices but views that shaped policy decisions affecting millions of lives.

Churchill's Secretary of State for India, Leopold Amery, recorded in his diary that arguing with Churchill about India was like "hitting a sponge" because of his racial hatred.[27] When the Viceroy of India, Field Marshal Wavell, pleaded for food imports and emergency aid, Churchill consistently refused or delayed.[28] Wavell's diary records his frustration with London's indifference and obstruction.[28]

The death toll—approximately 3 million people—was comparable to the Holocaust in Eastern Europe occurring simultaneously.[24,25] Bodies lined the streets of Calcutta. Rural Bengal was devastated, with entire villages depopulated.[25] Survivors resorted to eating grass, leaves, and bark. Women and children were sold into prostitution or servitude in desperate attempts to survive.[25] Disease killed hundreds of thousands.[25]

British authorities in India were divided. Some officials, recognizing the catastrophe, tried to organize relief despite obstruction from London.[28] Others maintained the traditional indifference, arguing that market mechanisms should be allowed to work and that relief would create dependency.^20,28^ But all were constrained by London's refusal to provide adequate resources or prioritize Bengali lives.^28^

The Bengal Famine was investigated after the war by the Famine Inquiry Commission, whose report documented the policy failures while largely exonerating British officials.^29^ Churchill was never held accountable. He went on to be celebrated as Britain's wartime savior, while his role in enabling a famine that killed 3 million people was minimized or ignored in British historical memory.^30^ This selective memory is itself a crime— the deliberate erasure of mass death to preserve the reputation of those responsible.^30^

African Famines: The Forgotten Catastrophes

While Irish and Indian famines receive some historical attention, the famines that devastated British African colonies are less documented and remembered, despite killing millions.^31^ This historical erasure reflects the continuing devaluation of African lives and suffering.^31^

The concentration camp system implemented during the Second Boer War (1899-1902) in South Africa created famine conditions that killed approximately 48,000 people, most of them women and children.^32^ British forces, pursuing a scorched-earth policy, burned Boer

Chapter 4: Famine by Design

farms and forcibly relocated civilians to concentration camps.^32^ Conditions in these camps were deliberately harsh: inadequate food, no sanitation, overcrowding, and minimal medical care.^32,33^ The mortality rate, especially among children, was staggering—reaching 50% in some camps.^33^

Significantly, the British also established separate camps for Black Africans, which received even less attention and worse conditions.^34^ Approximately 20,000 Black Africans died in these camps, but their deaths were barely recorded and have been largely forgotten.^34^ The racial hierarchy was explicit: even in suffering, Black Africans were considered less important than white Boers, who themselves were considered less important than British lives.^34^

East Africa experienced repeated famines under British rule. The "Great Hunger" of 1918-1919 in Kenya killed an estimated 100,000-300,000 people.^35^ This followed the conscription of hundreds of thousands of Kenyans as porters and laborers for British military operations during World War I.^35^ The forced removal of working-age men from agriculture, combined with colonial requisitions of food and livestock for military purposes, devastated food production.^35^ British authorities provided minimal relief, and the famine's death toll went largely unrecorded and unacknowledged.^35^

The Kenyan famine of 1942-1943, coinciding with the Bengal Famine, killed tens of thousands more.^36^ Again, British military requisitions combined with drought to create crisis, and again, British authorities prioritized wartime needs over African lives.^36^ Food was exported from Kenya to support British military operations while Kenyans starved.^36^

Nigeria experienced significant famines during British colonial rule, particularly in 1927-1928 and during World War II.^37^ Colonial policies that prioritized cash crop exports over food security, combined with inadequate infrastructure and relief systems, made Nigerian populations vulnerable to crop failures.^37^ British authorities' responses were minimal, guided by the same laissez-faire ideology and racial indifference that characterized famine policy elsewhere.^37^

The pattern across British Africa was consistent: colonial economic policies prioritized extraction and export, traditional food security systems were destroyed, and when famine struck, British authorities provided minimal relief while maintaining that market mechanisms and "African resilience" would solve the problem.^31,38^ The death tolls were rarely accurately recorded—African lives were not considered important enough to count carefully.^31,38^

The Economics of Famine: Profit From Death

Chapter 4: Famine by Design

British famine policy was not simply negligent but economically rational within the perverse logic of colonial exploitation.[1,39] Famines, while killing millions, served several economic and political functions that benefited British interests.

First, famines facilitated land consolidation. When smallholders died or were forced to sell their land to survive, that land was acquired by larger landowners, moneylenders, or colonial authorities.[23,39] In Ireland, the famine accelerated the transformation from a landscape of small tenant farms to one of larger estates.[40] In India, famines increased indebtedness and land loss, transferring control from peasant cultivators to moneylenders and landlords allied with British interests.[23,39]

Second, famines maintained downward pressure on wages. A population desperate for survival would work for minimal pay, benefiting employers.[1,39] British officials explicitly noted that famine relief should not provide enough to live on independently, as this would reduce the labor supply.[20,39]

Third, famines justified increased colonial control. Each crisis was used as evidence that indigenous populations couldn't govern themselves and needed British administration.[41] The fact that British policies caused the famines was ignored while the supposed incompetence of colonial subjects was emphasized.[41]

Fourth, grain merchants and traders profited enormously from famines. Prices skyrocketed, and those who controlled grain stocks made fortunes.^1,23^ British merchants and allied Indian merchants were well-positioned to profit, and they did.^23^ The free-market ideology that British authorities claimed to follow actually meant freedom for merchants to charge whatever the market would bear while millions starved.^1,23^

Fifth, famines never threatened British officials or elites. Colonial administrators, military officers, merchants, and landlords always had access to food.^1,42^ The suffering was imposed on the colonized poor—people whose deaths were economically and politically convenient.^1^ This class dimension was inseparable from the racial dimension: it was always brown and black people who starved while white administrators dined comfortably.^1,42^

Ideology and Indifference: The Mentality of Mass Murder

Understanding how British officials could watch millions die requires examining the ideologies that made this possible.^43^ These weren't monsters who enjoyed suffering but people who believed they were acting correctly within their worldview.^43^ That worldview

Chapter 4: Famine by Design

was structured by three interlocking beliefs: laissez-faire economic ideology, racism, and Social Darwinism.˄1,43˄ The laissez-faire ideology held that government intervention in markets was harmful, creating "dependency" and "moral hazard."˄9,44˄ Relief efforts, according to this view, would discourage self-reliance and damage character.˄9,44˄ It was better to let people die than to interfere with market mechanisms or violate property rights.˄9,44˄ This ideology was selectively applied—the British government readily intervened in markets when it served British interests—but was invoked as absolute principle when relief for the starving was proposed.˄3,44˄

Racism made the death of non-British, non-white people easier to accept. The Irish were portrayed as racially inferior, lazy, and over-breeding—responsible for their own suffering.˄14,43˄ Indians were similarly depicted as irrational, fatalistic, and prone to excess reproduction.˄21,43˄ Africans were seen as barely human, their lives of minimal value.˄43˄ This racism operated both at the level of explicit statements (like Churchill's comments about Indians) and implicit assumptions that made British lives valuable and colonial subjects' lives expendable.˄27,43˄

Social Darwinism provided pseudo-scientific justification. British officials argued that famine was nature's way of eliminating the unfit and controlling overpopulation.~21,45~ This logic appeared in official documents, with administrators arguing that preventing all deaths would be counterproductive because it would preserve weak individuals and encourage population growth.~21,45~ Mass death was reframed as natural selection, an impersonal natural process rather than policy-caused catastrophe.~45~

These ideologies formed a coherent worldview that absolved British officials of responsibility. They weren't causing death—they were simply refusing to interfere with natural economic and biological processes.~43,44~ The fact that these processes operated within political and economic structures they controlled, and that their policies directly caused millions of deaths, was intellectually elided.~43,44~ This capacity for self-deception—the ability to rationalize mass death as something other than murder—was essential to maintaining colonial rule.~43~

The Alternative That Wasn't Taken

Famines under British rule were not inevitable. Alternative policies were available and were often proposed by observers at the time.~46~ The British government chose not to implement them.
During the Irish Famine, many proposed banning food exports, providing free relief, or implementing public works at living wages.~8,11~ These proposals were

Chapter 4: Famine by Design

rejected as too expensive or ideologically unacceptable.~9,11~ Yet Britain was simultaneously spending enormous sums on military operations elsewhere—the first Afghan War cost £15 million, far more than comprehensive famine relief would have required.~47~ The resources existed; the political will did not.~47~

During Indian famines, indigenous leaders and some British officials proposed creating grain reserves, regulating prices, banning exports during crises, and providing adequate relief.~46~ The Famine Commission reports that followed each disaster recommended reforms.~46~ Yet subsequent famines continued to follow the same pattern, demonstrating that British authorities learned nothing or, more accurately, that preventing famine was never the priority.~1,16,46~
Traditional Indian governance systems had maintained grain reserves and implemented relief during famines.~48~ The Mughal Empire, despite its flaws, had never experienced famines on the scale of those under British rule.~48~ British policies destroyed these systems without replacing them with anything adequate, because maintaining food security for Indians was not considered important.~48~

Other colonial powers, while also exploitative, sometimes implemented more effective famine relief. The Dutch in Java, despite running a brutal colonial system, maintained rice reserves and provided relief during shortages.^49^ The death toll from famines in Dutch colonies was lower than in comparable British territories.^49^ This demonstrates that even within colonial systems, British policy was distinctively lethal.^49^

The fundamental issue was priority. British authorities prioritized profit extraction, ideological purity, and the convenience of administrators over human life.^1,3^ Preventing famine would have required reducing exploitation, maintaining reserves, regulating markets, and accepting financial costs.^46^ These were considered unacceptable.^1,3^ Millions of deaths were more acceptable than any reduction in colonial profit or compromise of free-market ideology.^1,3^

Accountability That Never Came

No British official was ever held criminally accountable for policies that killed tens of millions.^50^ Charles Trevelyan, whose policies exacerbated the Irish Famine, was later knighted for his service.^10^ Lord Lytton, whose policies during the 1876-1878 Indian Famine killed millions while he hosted lavish imperial ceremonies, faced no consequences.^18,19^ Winston Churchill, whose decisions contributed directly to the Bengal Famine's death toll, is celebrated as Britain's greatest wartime leader.^30^

Chapter 4: Famine by Design

This absence of accountability extends beyond individuals to institutions. The British government never officially apologized for famine policies, never paid reparations, never even acknowledged that its policies caused these deaths.^50^ British historical memory celebrates imperial achievements while minimizing or ignoring the famines.^50^ School curricula teach about industrialization and the empire's "positive" contributions while devoting minimal attention to the deaths of tens of millions.^50^

This historical erasure is ongoing violence. By refusing to acknowledge the scale and causes of famine deaths, British society evades moral reckoning and maintains myths of imperial benevolence.^50^ The dead remain uncounted, unnamed, and unmourned in British memory.^50^ Their deaths are treated as unfortunate background events rather than policy-driven catastrophes, as if millions of people dying was simply bad weather rather than the result of deliberate choices made by people with names and titles who could have chosen differently.^50^

Summary Conclusion: The Banality of Atrocity

The famines that killed tens of millions under British rule were not natural disasters but policy outcomes.

Perfidious Albion

British economic theories, racial ideologies, and administrative priorities systematically prioritized profit and ideological purity over human life across multiple continents and over nearly two centuries.^1,3^ The death toll—conservatively estimated at 30-60 million people across Ireland, India, and Africa—rivals the great deliberate atrocities of the twentieth century.^1,16^

Yet these deaths retain an undeserved ambiguity in historical memory. They are classified as famines—natural events—rather than as crimes, despite the overwhelming evidence that British policies caused them and that alternative policies were available.^1,50^ The officials responsible are remembered, when they are remembered at all, as administrators facing difficult circumstances rather than as architects of mass death.^50^

This reflects the enduring power of the ideologies that enabled the famines in the first place. We still tend to separate economic policy from moral responsibility, to treat market mechanisms as natural forces rather than human choices, and to value some lives more than others.^43,51^ The famines under British rule demonstrate where these tendencies lead when unconstrained by accountability: to the industrialized production of mass death while maintaining the illusion of innocence.^43,51^

Chapter 4: Famine by Design

The famines were not failures of the British Empire but expressions of its essential nature: a system designed to extract maximum wealth from colonized peoples with minimum responsibility for their welfare, justified by ideologies of racial superiority and economic theory, and maintained through violence and the threat of violence.^1,3^ The millions who starved while food was exported, while officials dined comfortably, while ideologues insisted that aid would damage character— they died not despite British rule but because of it.^1,3^ Their deaths were the price Britain decided was acceptable for profit, and their erasure from memory is the price Britain continues to pay to avoid confronting what the empire actually was.^50^

Author's Notes Chapter 4

This chapter examines major famines under British rule— the 1770 Bengal Famine, the 1845-52 Irish Famine, late Victorian Indian famines (1876-1902), and the 1943 Bengal Famine—arguing that these were not natural disasters but resulted from deliberate policies prioritizing British economic interests and ideological commitments over colonized peoples' lives. The combined death toll across these famines likely exceeds 60 million people.

On Categorizing These Famines Together: While separated by geography and time, these famines share crucial commonalities: they occurred under British rule; they resulted substantially from British policies rather than unavoidable natural causes; they involved food exports from famine-stricken regions; British officials refused adequate relief based on ideological objections or indifference; and racism shaped British responses. Examining them together reveals systematic patterns rather than isolated tragedies.

On Mike Davis' Work: *Late Victorian Holocausts* (2001) revolutionized understanding of 19th-century famines by demonstrating that they were created substantially by market integration under imperial rule, not by climate alone. Davis shows that El Niño droughts affected global regions similarly, but famines occurred primarily in colonized areas where market mechanisms and colonial policies prevented local populations from accessing food. His work has faced some criticism regarding specific details but the fundamental thesis—that colonialism created conditions enabling famines—has been broadly accepted.

On the Irish Famine: The debate over whether the Irish Famine constitutes genocide continues. Cormac Ó Gráda argues that while British policies were catastrophically inadequate, genocide requires intent to destroy a group that wasn't clearly present. Christine Kinealy and others argue that British policies were so systematically harmful— continuing food exports, inadequate relief, evictions during famine—that they constituted genocide in effect if not explicit intent. This chapter takes the latter position, arguing that indifference to mass death when remedy was possible constitutes a form of genocide.

On Churchill and Bengal (1943): Madhusree Mukerjee's *Churchill's Secret War* (2010) documents Churchill's direct role in the Bengal Famine through his refusal to divert shipping for relief, his racist statements about Indians, and his priority on maintaining stockpiles in Europe and the Mediterranean. Some Churchill defenders argue that wartime shipping constraints made relief impossible; Mukerjee and others demonstrate that ships were available but Churchill refused to allocate them, and that Australian

Chapter 4: Famine by Design

wheat offers were rejected. Amartya Sen's work on "entitlement" shows that the famine resulted from distribution failures and policy choices rather than absolute food shortage.

Methodological Challenges: Calculating famine death tolls is difficult because official records are incomplete and British authorities often undercounted deaths. Numbers cited represent scholarly estimates based on demographic data, burial records, and population census comparisons. The actual tolls may be higher. Even conservative estimates reveal mass death on a scale that should be central to understanding British imperialism.

On "Famine Codes": After the 1876-78 famine killed millions, British India developed "Famine Codes" establishing relief procedures. Yet famines continued, suggesting that the problem was not absence of knowledge about how to prevent famine but lack of political will to prioritize Indian lives over British economic and political interests. The 1943 Bengal Famine occurred despite a century of supposed learning about famine prevention.

CHAPTER FIVE

Crushing Resistance

Violence and the Maintenance of Empire (1757-1920)

The British Empire was not maintained through consent but through violence. Wherever Britain established control, resistance emerged, and wherever resistance emerged, Britain responded with systematic brutality designed not merely to defeat opponents but to terrorize entire populations into submission.^1^ From the Indian Uprising of 1857, to the Morant Bay Rebellion in Jamaica, to the suppression of the Mau Mau in Kenya, British forces employed tactics that would be recognized today as war crimes and crimes against humanity: mass executions, torture, collective punishment, destruction of villages, and deliberate targeting of civilians.[1,2] These were not isolated incidents or the actions of rogue commanders but established policy, approved at the highest levels of government and documented in official records.[2,3] The violence was both instrumental—meant to crush specific resistance movements—and expressive, demonstrating to colonized peoples that opposition to British rule would be met with overwhelming force.[1,4] Understanding this violence is essential to understanding the empire: it was not an unfortunate side effect of otherwise benign rule but the foundation on which colonial control rested.[1,4]

The 1857 Indian Uprising: Genocidal Reprisals

We have already discussed the 1857 Uprising in Chapter 3, but the British response to that uprising deserves detailed examination as it established patterns of counter-insurgency violence that would be repeated throughout the empire.[5] When the uprising began in May 1857, it spread rapidly across northern and central India, involving sepoys (Indian soldiers), landlords dispossessed by the Doctrine of Lapse, peasants suffering under British exploitation, and various other groups united by opposition to British rule.[5,6]

The British response, once they regained military advantage, was consciously genocidal in intent and effect.[7] British commanders explicitly called for extermination. Brigadier-General Neill wrote: "I wish I

Chapter 5: Crushing Resistance

had the power to place myself at the head of an Army of Extermination... I would take care that the streets of every place I entered should be running with blood."~7~ These were not private sentiments but statements appearing in official correspondence and approved by superior officers.~7~

The methods employed were designed for maximum brutality and public impact. Prisoners were blown from cannons—strapped to the muzzle and literally disintegrated when the gun was fired.~8~ This was chosen specifically because it was horrifying and because it violated Hindu and Muslim religious beliefs about body integrity, adding spiritual terror to physical annihilation.~8~ British officers wrote about these executions with satisfaction, describing them as appropriate punishment and effective deterrence.~8~

Mass hangings were conducted across recaptured territories. At Delhi, when British forces retook the city in September 1857, they engaged in days of indiscriminate slaughter.~9~ Thousands of civilians were killed regardless of whether they had participated in the uprising. British soldiers looted homes, raped women, and murdered randomly.~9~ Colonel Hodson, who captured the aged Mughal Emperor Bahadur Shah II, personally shot the Emperor's sons and grandson in cold blood after they had surrendered.~9~ Their bodies were displayed publicly at a major Delhi gate as a warning.~9~

Perfidious Albion

The policy of collective punishment meant that entire villages suspected of harboring rebels were destroyed. British forces would surround a village, kill all male inhabitants, burn houses, destroy crops, and poison wells.^10^ Women and children were often killed as well, though official reports sometimes euphemized this by claiming they were accidentally caught in crossfire.^10^ Contemporary British accounts describe this violence proudly, as necessary severity to restore order.^7,10^

Religious and cultural sites were deliberately targeted. Mosques were desecrated, Hindu temples destroyed, and holy sites converted to barracks or latrines as acts of humiliation.^11^ The famous Red Fort in Delhi was partially demolished, and many of its treasures looted.^11^ This was cultural warfare designed to break Indian spirit and demonstrate British dominance.^11^

The violence continued long after military victory was assured. Summary executions, torture to extract information or confessions, and arbitrary imprisonment characterized British rule in the uprising's aftermath.^12^ Estimates of the death toll range from several hundred thousand to over a million when including deaths from famine and disease caused by the disruption.^6,12^ No British official faced any accountability for ordering or conducting this violence. Many were promoted and honored.^12^

Chapter 5 Crushing Resistance

The uprising and its suppression marked a turning point. It demonstrated to Indians that British rule rested on overwhelming violence and would not be dislodged easily.^5^ It demonstrated to British officials that maintaining control required constant readiness to employ extreme brutality.^5^ And it established the template: when resistance emerged, crush it with maximum force and accept no limits on violence.^2,5^

Morant Bay Rebellion: Terror in Jamaica

In October 1865, a small uprising occurred in Morant Bay, Jamaica, triggered by oppressive conditions facing freed slaves in the decades after emancipation.^13^ Approximately 400 people, primarily Black Jamaicans, marched on the courthouse protesting poverty, lack of land access, and the corrupt judicial system.^13^ Violence broke out, and 18 people, mostly white officials and planters, were killed.^13^ The uprising was swiftly contained—it never involved more than a few hundred participants and posed no serious military threat to British control.^14^

The British response was staggeringly disproportionate. Governor Edward Eyre declared martial law and unleashed a campaign of state terror.^15^ Over the following weeks, approximately 439 people were executed, often after drumhead courts-martial that lasted minutes and provided no real defense.^15,16^ Many were hanged from makeshift gallows, their bodies left on display. Others were shot by firing squads. Some were flogged to death—receiving hundreds of lashes until they expired.^16^

More than 600 people, including pregnant women, were flogged with rawhide whips that stripped flesh from bone.^16^ Flogging was conducted publicly to terrorize communities. Over 1,000 homes, mostly belonging to poor Black farmers, were burned.^16^ Crops were destroyed, and livestock killed. The violence was deliberately indiscriminate—many victims had no connection to the uprising but were punished because they were Black and poor and therefore suspected of disloyalty.^14,16^

One victim requires particular mention: George William Gordon, a wealthy mixed-race politician and landowner who had criticized Governor Eyre's administration.^17^ Gordon was not at Morant Bay during the uprising and had no involvement in the violence, but he was arrested, subjected to a sham trial, and executed by hanging.^17^ His judicial murder was clearly intended to eliminate a political opponent who had championed poor Black Jamaicans' rights.^17^

The Morant Bay suppression sparked controversy in Britain. Some public figures, including John Stuart Mill and Charles Darwin, condemned the violence as excessive and illegal.^18^ Others, including Thomas

Chapter 5: Crushing Resistance

Carlyle and Charles Dickens, defended Eyre, arguing that harsh measures were necessary to maintain white rule over supposedly inferior Black populations.^18^ The debate revealed deep divisions in British society about empire, race, and violence.^18^

Eyre was eventually recalled and faced prosecution in Britain for Gordon's murder, but the prosecution failed.^19^ Eyre never faced meaningful consequences and was lionized by many as a hero who had saved Jamaica from "savagery."^19^ A defense fund raised substantial sums for his legal costs, with contributions from prominent Britons including Alfred Tennyson and John Ruskin.^18,19^ The message was clear: extreme violence against colonized peoples, even when technically illegal, would be tolerated and even celebrated by significant portions of British society.^19^
The Morant Bay suppression demonstrated several patterns that would recur throughout imperial violence. First, colonial authorities consistently interpreted any resistance, however minor, as existential threat requiring maximum force.^14^ Second, violence was racialized—the severity of punishment reflected assumptions about racial hierarchy and the supposed need to keep Black populations terrorized.^14,20^ Third, the violence served economic interests—many of those killed or dispossessed were small farmers whose land was subsequently acquired by large estates.^21^ Fourth, even when violence was controversial in Britain, perpetrators

rarely faced serious accountability.[19]

The Amritsar Massacre: Peacetime Atrocity

On April 13, 1919, in the Punjabi city of Amritsar, British Brigadier-General Reginald Dyer ordered his troops to open fire on an unarmed crowd gathered in an enclosed garden called Jallianwala Bagh.[22] The crowd, estimated at 10,000-20,000 people, included men, women, and children attending a peaceful gathering during the Sikh festival of Baisakhi.[22,23] Some were there to protest recent repressive laws; others were simply socializing or attending the festival.[23]

Dyer had recently banned all public gatherings, though it's unclear how widely this order was known.[22] Rather than dispersing the crowd with warnings or non-lethal means, Dyer positioned his troops to block the main exit, then ordered them to fire into the densest parts of the crowd.[22,24] The soldiers fired for approximately ten minutes, only stopping when they had exhausted their ammunition—1,650 rounds.[24]

The official death toll was 379, with over 1,200 wounded.[22] These figures are certainly undercounts, as many injured people fled or were carried away by families who feared British reprisals if they sought medical help.[25] The real death toll was likely 500-1,000 or more.[25] People were killed attempting to

Chapter 5: Crushing Resistance

escape by climbing walls or jumping into a well—the well later yielded over 100 bodies.[22,26]

Dyer made no attempt to provide medical care for the wounded or remove the dead. He marched his troops away, leaving the dying to suffer through the night.[27] The next day he imposed a curfew, preventing relatives from retrieving bodies or helping survivors.[27] This deliberate cruelty reflected Dyer's stated intention not just to disperse a gathering but to inflict maximum terror.[27]

In the days following the massacre, Dyer implemented collective punishment across Amritsar. He ordered public floggings, forced Indians to crawl on their bellies down a street where a British woman had been attacked, and conducted arbitrary arrests.[28] These humiliations were designed to establish British dominance and demonstrate what resistance would cost.[28]

When investigated, Dyer was unapologetic. He testified that he had fired to create "a sufficient moral effect" and that his purpose was "to produce a moral and widespread effect... not only on those who were present, but more especially throughout the Punjab."[29] In other words, terrorism—the deliberate targeting of civilians to inspire fear in a broader population.[29] He stated he would have used machine guns and armored cars if he could have gotten them into the garden.[29]

British reaction in India and Britain was divided. The Hunter Commission investigation condemned Dyer's actions as excessive, and he was forced to resign.^30^ However, he faced no criminal prosecution. In Britain, conservative opinion rallied to his defense. The House of Lords passed a motion approving his conduct.^31^ The right-wing Morning Post newspaper raised £26,000 (equivalent to millions today) for Dyer as a reward, with thousands of Britons contributing.^31^ Rudyard Kipling called him "the man who saved India."^31^

This response demonstrated that significant portions of British society endorsed terrorizing colonized populations. The violence at Amritsar was not an aberration but an expression of colonial logic: when Indians challenged British authority, even peacefully, they must be taught through bloodshed that resistance would not be tolerated.^32^ The fact that Dyer was celebrated rather than imprisoned revealed the empire's essential nature.^32^

The Amritsar Massacre had profound political consequences. It convinced many Indians that British rule could never be reformed, only ended.^33^ Gandhi, who had previously sought accommodation, moved toward demanding complete independence.^33^ The massacre became a symbol of British brutality and accelerated the independence movement.^33^

Chapter 5: Crushing Resistance

The Boer War: Scorched Earth and Concentration Camps

The Second Boer War (1899-1902) in South Africa saw British forces implement a scorched earth policy combined with concentration camps that killed tens of thousands of civilians.^34^ The war began as a conventional conflict between British forces and Boer republics, but when Boer forces shifted to guerrilla tactics, Britain responded with a strategy designed to eliminate civilian support for resistance.^34,35^

British forces under Lord Kitchener systematically destroyed Boer farms—burning houses, slaughtering livestock, destroying crops, and poisoning wells.^35^ The goal was to deny Boer commandos supplies and shelter while making the cost of resistance unbearable.^35^ Entire regions were depopulated as British columns swept through, destroying everything they encountered.^36^

The displaced civilians—primarily women, children, and elderly—were forcibly relocated to concentration camps.^37^ The British established approximately 45 camps for white Boers and 60 camps for Black Africans.^37^ The term "concentration camp" was coined in this context—the first systematic use of such facilities to control civilian populations.^37^

Conditions in the camps were deliberately harsh. Overcrowding was severe, with families crammed into tents providing minimal shelter.[38] Rations were intentionally inadequate, especially for families of men still fighting—a policy of collective punishment designed to pressure Boers to surrender.[38] Sanitation was minimal or non-existent, leading to rapid spread of disease.[38] Medical care was grossly insufficient.[38]

The death toll was catastrophic. Approximately 28,000 Boer civilians died in the camps, roughly 22,000 of them children.[39] The mortality rate reached extraordinary levels—up to 50% in some camps.[39] Measles, typhoid, dysentery, and pneumonia killed thousands.[39] These deaths were not unfortunate accidents but the predictable result of deliberate policies.[39]

The camps for Black Africans were even worse and received less attention both at the time and subsequently.[40] Approximately 20,000 Black Africans died in these segregated camps, but the death toll was poorly documented because British authorities considered Black lives less important.[40] Conditions in the Black camps were worse than in the Boer camps—less food, less medical care, more brutal treatment.[40]

British authorities were fully aware of the mortality rates. Emily Hobhouse, a British welfare campaigner, visited the camps and documented the conditions in a report that shocked British public opinion.[41] She described children dying from malnutrition,

Chapter 5: Crushing Resistance

preventable diseases killing hundreds, and deliberate policies of starvation being used as weapons.^41^ Her testimony to the British government included detailed evidence of the death rates and their causes.^41^

The government response was to defend the camps while making minimal improvements. Lord Kitchener argued the camps were necessary for military success and that improving conditions would be too expensive.^42^ Some improvements were eventually implemented—primarily in the Boer camps after public pressure—and death rates declined, but thousands had already died.^42^

The concentration camp system in South Africa established several precedents that would be repeated in later colonial conflicts. First, it normalized the idea of interning entire civilian populations to suppress resistance.^43^ Second, it demonstrated that Britain would accept mass civilian death if it served military objectives.^43^ Third, it showed that even when atrocities became public, political will to stop them was limited.^43^ Fourth, it revealed the racial hierarchy of suffering—Black African deaths were barely counted while Boer deaths eventually provoked reforms.^40,43^

The Boer War concentration camps would directly inspire later systems of civilian internment, including those used by the British in Kenya during the Mau Mau uprising and, tragically, the Nazi camps that would emerge decades later.^44^ The British had pioneered industrial-scale civilian detention and demonstrated its effectiveness as a counter-insurgency tool.^44^

Suppressing the Irish: Centuries of Violence

British violence in Ireland was so extensive and prolonged that it could fill volumes alone, but several episodes particularly illustrate the patterns of imperial brutality.^45^ We have already discussed the Elizabethan conquest in Chapter 1 and the Great Famine in Chapter 4, but the period from 1916-1921 saw a renewed cycle of violence that demonstrated Britain's unchanged willingness to terrorize Irish populations.^45,46^

The Easter Rising of 1916, a rebellion in Dublin seeking Irish independence, was quickly suppressed by British forces using artillery that destroyed much of central Dublin.^47^ The military suppression itself killed approximately 450 people, many of them civilians caught in crossfire or killed by indiscriminate British shelling.^47^ But the post-rebellion reprisals were more significant.^48^

British authorities executed 16 leaders of the rising, including several signatories of the Irish Declaration of Independence.^48^ The executions were conducted over ten days, prolonging the terror.^48^ One leader, James

Chapter 5: Crushing Resistance

Connolly, was so badly wounded he couldn't stand for execution and was tied to a chair to be shot.^48^ These executions transformed the leaders into martyrs and turned Irish public opinion decisively against British rule.^49^

During the Irish War of Independence (1919-1921), British forces and paramilitary groups (the Black and Tans and Auxiliaries) implemented a campaign of state terror.^50^ They conducted reprisal attacks on Irish towns, burning buildings and killing civilians.^50^ In November 1920, Black and Tans burned much of Cork city center, destroying businesses and homes.^51^ In Balbriggan, they burned the town and killed two civilians in revenge for an IRA attack.^51^

The policy of "official reprisals" was explicitly approved at high levels of British government. Prime Minister Lloyd George and other officials discussed and endorsed reprisal attacks, even as they publicly denied responsibility.^52^ British forces would attack villages suspected of harboring IRA members, destroy property, and sometimes kill civilians, all while claiming these were spontaneous actions by uncontrollable troops rather than official policy.^52^

Torture was routinely used by British forces to extract information. Suspects were beaten, deprived of sleep, and subjected to mock executions.^53^ Some were thrown from moving vehicles, while others were shot "while attempting to escape"—the standard cover story for extrajudicial execution.^53^ These practices, documented in Irish testimony and some British sources, were denied by British authorities but were systematic rather than exceptional.^53^

The violence in Ireland during this period killed approximately 2,000 people, with British forces and their proxies responsible for the majority of civilian deaths.^54^ The campaign failed to suppress Irish resistance and instead strengthened support for independence.^54^ When Britain eventually negotiated Irish independence (initially as the Irish Free State in 1922), it was because the violence had become politically unsustainable, not because British authorities had developed moral objections to terrorizing Irish civilians.^54^

Colonial Policing: Routine Violence

Beyond spectacular massacres and major suppressions, the British Empire was maintained through routine, everyday violence.^55^ Colonial police forces, often commanded by British officers and staffed by local recruits, employed violence as standard practice.^55,56^

In India, the police used lathi charges—baton charges that often resulted in serious injuries or death—to

Chapter 5: Crushing Resistance

disperse protests.^56^ Suspects were routinely beaten during interrogation. Prisoners in colonial jails faced brutal conditions and harsh punishments including flogging.^56^ Political prisoners, including those guilty only of advocating independence, were imprisoned under repressive laws that allowed indefinite detention without trial.^57^

In Africa, colonial police forces employed violence with even less restraint. In Kenya, routine practices included beating suspects, public floggings as punishment for minor infractions, and forced labor enforced through violence.^58^ Chiefs and headmen who collected taxes or enforced colonial orders were backed by police violence.^58^ The entire system of colonial administration rested on the credible threat that resistance would be met with physical harm.^58^

The flogging of colonial subjects was widespread and systematic.^59^ British colonial regulations specified maximum numbers of lashes (often 24 or 36) but these limits were frequently ignored.^59^ Flogging was conducted publicly to terrorize communities and was applied for infractions ranging from tax evasion to "disrespect" to British officials.^59^ The practice was opposed by some humanitarian campaigners in Britain but continued well into the 20th century.^59^

Collective punishment was routine. If taxes weren't paid, entire villages might be punished. If a British official was attacked and the perpetrator not identified, nearby communities would suffer reprisals.^60^ This policy, explicitly authorized in colonial regulations, meant that colonized populations lived under constant threat of violence for offenses they didn't commit.^60^

This routine violence was essential to maintaining colonial control with minimal British personnel. A handful of British officials could govern millions because the colonized knew that resistance meant violence from police, from local collaborators, or eventually from military forces.^55,61^ The empire was not a consensual political arrangement but a protection racket enforced through violence and the threat of violence.^61^

The Ideology of Violence: How Brutality Was Justified

British officials and soldiers who implemented this violence required ideological justification to maintain their self-image as civilized people.^62^ Several interlocking beliefs made extreme violence psychologically acceptable.^62,63^

First was racism. British ideology portrayed colonized peoples—Irish, Indians, Africans, and others—as racially inferior, savage, and violent.^63^ This justified treating them with violence, as supposedly they only understood force.^63^ The idea that "natives" were like children who needed firm discipline appeared repeatedly in British discourse.^63^ This paternalistic racism framed violence

Chapter 5: Crushing Resistance

as beneficial correction rather than criminal brutality.^63^

Second was the doctrine of collective responsibility. British authorities held that entire communities were responsible for individual acts of resistance.^64^ This justified collective punishment—if one person from a village attacked British forces, the entire village could be destroyed.^64^ This violated basic principles of justice but was accepted as necessary for imperial control.^64^

Third was the idea of exemplary violence. British commanders explicitly argued that spectacular brutality was necessary to deter future resistance.^65^ Blowing rebels from cannons, public hangings, and displayed corpses were defended as creating "moral effect"—terrorizing populations into submission.^65^ This was not seen as terrorism but as efficient governance.^65^

Fourth was the civilization mission. Even as they committed atrocities, British officials maintained they were bringing civilization, law, and order to barbarous peoples.^66^ The contradiction between claiming to represent civilization while massacring unarmed civilians was resolved through the belief that temporary violence was necessary to establish permanent order.^66^ The civilizing mission became justification for any level of brutality.^66^

Finally, there was legal impunity. British soldiers and officials rarely faced prosecution for violence against colonized peoples.^67^ When prosecutions occurred, they usually failed or resulted in minimal punishment.^67^ This impunity sent a clear message: colonized lives had little value, and violence against them was not really criminal.^67^

These ideological justifications were sincerely believed by many British perpetrators and supporters. They genuinely saw themselves as maintaining necessary order against savage resistance, not committing crimes against humanity.^62^ This capacity for self-deception—the ability to commit atrocities while maintaining moral self-regard—was essential to the empire's functioning.^62^

Summary Conclusion: Violence as System

The violence described in this chapter was not aberrational but systematic. From 1757 to well into the 20th century, Britain maintained its empire through the consistent application of extreme force against resistance movements.^1,2^ The methods were refined over time but remained essentially unchanged: mass executions, torture, collective punishment, destruction of property, and deliberate targeting of civilians to create terror.^1,2^ The scale was staggering. Hundreds of thousands, possibly millions, were killed in these suppressions—the exact number will never be known because many victims

Chapter 5: Crushing Resistance

were never counted.˄68˄ Millions more were injured, displaced, or traumatized. The psychological impact of living under constant threat of violence shaped generations of colonized peoples.˄68˄

British authorities learned lessons from each suppression and applied them to subsequent conflicts. Techniques developed in Ireland were used in India and Africa. The concentration camps pioneered in South Africa were refined and reused in Kenya.˄44˄ The legal frameworks authorizing collective punishment and detention without trial were standardized across colonies.˄2˄ Violence became systematized, bureaucratized, and normalized.˄2,4˄

Yet this violence ultimately failed in its strategic objective. Rather than securing permanent British control, it generated hatred and resistance that eventually made empire unsustainable.˄69˄ The 1857 Uprising, though crushed, convinced British authorities that holding India would require constant military readiness.˄5˄ The Irish violence created martyrs and strengthened independence movements.˄49˄ The Amritsar Massacre accelerated Indian nationalism.˄33˄ Even when violence achieved tactical success, it undermined strategic sustainability.˄69˄

The violence also contradicted every claim Britain made about its empire. Britain claimed to bring civilization, yet massacred civilians. It claimed to bring law, yet

Perfidious Albion

employed collective punishment that violated basic legal principles. It claimed to bring progress, yet responded to resistance with medieval brutality.^70^ The gap between imperial rhetoric and imperial reality was nowhere more apparent than in the violence required to maintain control.^70^

This chapter has documented only a fraction of imperial violence—the episodes that were significant enough, or controversial enough, to be extensively recorded.^68^ Countless smaller acts of violence, routine beatings, individual killings, and everyday coercion are lost to history but were no less real to those who experienced them.^68^ The British Empire was built on violence, maintained through violence, and left a legacy of violence that continues to shape post-colonial societies today.^68,70^

Author's Notes Chapter 5

This chapter examines British counterinsurgency and suppression of resistance movements, focusing on the 1857 Indian Uprising, various African wars of resistance, and the 1919 Amritsar Massacre. The chapter argues that systematic violence and terror were not aberrations but essential tools for maintaining imperial control against populations that consistently resisted subjugation.

On the 1857 Uprising: The scale and ferocity of the British response—summary executions, mass hangings, village burnings, collective punishments—reveals the violence required to maintain imperial control. William Dalrymple's

Chapter 5: Crushing Resistance

The Last Mughal (2006) documents that British forces killed tens of thousands of civilians in recapturing Delhi alone. The violence was both punitive (revenge for British deaths) and terroristic (designed to prevent future resistance through fear).

On Amritsar (1919): General Dyer's massacre of peaceful protesters remains among the most documented and infamous atrocities of British rule. Nigel Collett's *The Butcher of Amritsar* (2005) demonstrates that the massacre was premeditated—Dyer deliberately trapped protesters in an enclosed space (Jallianwala Bagh) with one exit, then ordered troops to fire into the densest crowds to maximize casualties. The "crawling order" requiring Indians to crawl on hands and knees down a street where an Englishwoman had been assaulted reveals the racial humiliation underlying imperial control.

On Colonial Counterinsurgency Doctrine: C.E. Callwell's *Small Wars* (1896) codified British counterinsurgency tactics used across the empire, explicitly advocating collective punishment, village destruction, and use of overwhelming force to terrorize populations. Modern counterinsurgency doctrine claims to have learned from colonial "excesses," but David French's *The British Way in Counter-Insurgency* (2011) shows that systematic abuse characterized British counterinsurgency into the 1960s.

Historiographical Context: Traditional military history often portrayed colonial wars as adventures or defensive operations protecting British interests. Recent scholarship treats them as wars of conquest and imperial maintenance requiring systematic violence against populations resisting foreign domination. The language matters: "pacification" obscures conquest; "rebels" delegitimizes resistance; "savages" dehumanizes opponents. This chapter uses language recognizing colonized peoples' legitimate resistance to invasion and exploitation.

On Public Knowledge and Support: Detailed reports of British atrocities often appeared in British newspapers and parliamentary debates, yet rarely provoked fundamental policy changes. After Amritsar, substantial British public opinion supported Dyer, raising funds for him and celebrating him as a hero. This demonstrates that imperial violence was not hidden from British public but was often actively supported, revealing deep-seated racism and imperialism in British society.

CHAPTER SIX

The Scramble for Africa

Colonialism at Its Zenith (1880-1914)

Between 1880 and 1914, European powers partitioned Africa with breathtaking speed and brutality, seizing control of virtually the entire continent in a period later termed the "Scramble for Africa."[1] Britain was the dominant player in this scramble, acquiring vast territories through a combination of treaty manipulation, military conquest, and corporate plunder.[1,2] By 1914, Britain controlled approximately 30% of Africa's population and territory, including Egypt, Sudan, Kenya, Uganda, Northern and Southern Rhodesia, Nyasaland, South Africa, Nigeria, Gold Coast, Sierra Leone, and Gambia.[2] This expansion was driven by economic greed—the desire for raw materials, markets, and investment opportunities—strategic competition with other European powers, and racist ideologies that portrayed African colonization as a civilizing mission.[3,4] The human cost was staggering: millions died in wars of conquest, from diseases introduced or spread by colonial disruption, from forced labor regimes, and from famines caused by economic exploitation.[5] The Scramble for Africa represented imperialism at its most rapacious, justified by racism at its most virulent, and executed with violence at its most systematic.[1,5]

The Berlin Conference: Carving Up a Continent

The Scramble for Africa is often dated from the Berlin Conference of 1884-1885, where European powers met to establish rules for African colonization.[6] No African representatives were invited to this conference that would determine their continent's fate.[6] The Europeans treated Africa as terra nullius—empty land—ignoring the complex societies, states, and civilizations that had existed for millennia.[6,7]

Britain arrived at Berlin as a major player, already controlling strategic positions in Africa and determined to expand.[8] The conference established principles that would govern the Scramble: European powers must demonstrate "effective occupation" of territories they claimed, meaning they needed physical presence and

Chapter 6: The Scramble for Africa

administration, not just treaties with African rulers.^6^ This principle encouraged rapid military conquest, as powers raced to establish control before rivals could.^6^ The conference also established rules about Congo, navigation rights, and spheres of influence, but its deeper significance was ideological.^6^ It formalized the European consensus that Africa was available for taking, that African sovereignty was irrelevant, and that European powers had the right to divide the continent among themselves.^6,7^ The racist assumptions undergirding this consensus were explicit: Africans were portrayed as savage, backward, and incapable of self-governance.^9^ European colonization was presented as beneficial, bringing civilization, Christianity, and commerce to darkness.^9^

Britain's strategy at Berlin and subsequently was to secure maximum territory with minimum European competition.^8^ British diplomats negotiated spheres of influence with other powers, agreeing which regions each could colonize.^8^ This cynical horse-trading divided ethnic groups, split kingdoms, and created arbitrary borders that ignored African political and social realities—borders that persist today and continue to generate conflict.^10^

Cecil Rhodes: The Colossus of Greed

No figure better embodies the Scramble for Africa than Cecil Rhodes, the British businessman and politician who sought to paint the map of Africa red (the color used for British territories).^11^ Rhodes made his fortune in South African diamond and gold mining, building De Beers into a monopoly that controlled the global diamond trade.^11^ He used this wealth to finance territorial expansion, founding the British South Africa Company, which conquered and administered vast territories that would become Rhodesia (now Zimbabwe and Zambia).^11,12^

Rhodes's vision was grandiose and racist. He dreamed of a continuous belt of British territory from Cape Town to Cairo, an "All-Red Route" that would make Britain dominant in Africa.^13^ He saw Africans as obstacles to be removed or exploited. His famous statement captured his ideology: "I contend that we are the finest race in the world and that the more of the world we inhabit the better it is for the human race."^14^ This wasn't casual prejudice but the ideological foundation for systematic conquest and exploitation.^14^

The British South Africa Company, chartered in 1889, was given governmental powers over territories it conquered—the same fusion of corporate and sovereign power that had characterized the East India Company.^12^ The Company organized military expeditions to seize African land, suppress resistance, and establish extractive economic systems.^12^ Africans who resisted were killed; those who survived were forced

Chapter 6: The Scramble for Africa

into labor.^12^

The conquest of Matabeleland and Mashonaland (1890s) demonstrated Rhodes's methods.^15^ The British South Africa Company invaded these territories, defeated the Ndebele and Shona kingdoms through superior firepower, and seized their land.^15^ When the Ndebele and Shona rebelled in 1896-1897 against British occupation and abuse, the Company forces suppressed the rebellions with extreme violence.^15,16^ Villages were burned, cattle were seized, and rebels were executed.^16^ Estimates suggest 20,000-50,000 Africans died in these conflicts and subsequent famines.^16^

Rhodes implemented systems of racial segregation and labor exploitation that would later be formalized as apartheid.^17^ The 1894 Glen Grey Act in Cape Colony, which Rhodes championed, restricted African land ownership and was designed to force Africans into wage labor for white employers.^17^ Rhodes explicitly stated his goal was to make Africans "go out to work" by denying them alternatives.^17^ This was social engineering designed to create a permanent underclass of African laborers serving white economic interests.^17^

Rhodes died in 1902, but his legacy endured. Rhodesia was named after him, and his British South Africa Company continued exploiting the region until 1923.^18^ His scholarships, still awarded today, were funded by wealth extracted from African labor and land.^19^ He is remembered in Britain as a great empire-builder, while in Africa he is recognized as an architect of racist exploitation.^19^

Egypt and Sudan: Strategic Conquest

British control of Egypt demonstrates how economic interests, strategic considerations, and military power combined in the Scramble.^20^ Egypt was nominally independent, ruled by a Khedive under Ottoman suzerainty, but became increasingly indebted to European creditors in the 1870s.^20,21^ When the Egyptian government defaulted on loans, Britain and France imposed joint financial control, triggering Egyptian nationalist resistance.^21^

In 1882, a nationalist movement led by Colonel Urabi Pasha challenged foreign control.^22^ Britain responded by bombarding Alexandria and invading Egypt with military force.^22^ The Battle of Tel el-Kebir saw British forces defeat the Egyptian army, and Britain established military occupation that would last until 1956.^22,23^ This invasion was justified as protecting European financial interests and the Suez Canal, the strategic waterway linking Europe to India.^23^

British rule in Egypt was formalized as a "veiled protectorate"—Britain claimed Egypt remained

Chapter 6: The Scramble for Africa

independent while in practice controlling its government.^24^ This fiction allowed Britain to exploit Egypt economically while avoiding formal annexation that might provoke other powers.^24^ British officials governed through Egyptian institutions, implementing policies that prioritized cotton production for export to British textile mills.^25^ Egyptian agriculture was reoriented to serve British industry, making Egypt dependent on food imports while exporting cash crops.^25^

British expansion into Sudan followed from Egyptian control. Sudan had been nominally under Egyptian rule, but the Mahdist Uprising (1881-1899) established an independent Islamic state.^26^ Britain, claiming to act on behalf of Egypt, launched a campaign to reconquer Sudan.^26^ The campaign was led by General Kitchener and culminated in the Battle of Omdurman (1898), one of the most one-sided massacres in military history.^27^ At Omdurman, British and Egyptian forces armed with modern rifles and Maxim machine guns faced Sudanese forces armed primarily with spears and outdated firearms.^27^ The result was slaughter. Approximately 10,000-12,000 Sudanese were killed while British forces suffered fewer than 50 deaths.^27,28^ The young Winston Churchill, who participated, described it as "the most signal triumph ever gained by the arms of science over barbarians."^29^ This framing—technological superiority as proof of civilizational superiority justifying conquest—was typical of imperial ideology.^29^

The aftermath of Omdurman revealed British brutality. Kitchener ordered the Mahdi's tomb destroyed and the Mahdi's body desecrated—his skull was reportedly kept as a trophy before public outcry forced its burial.^30^ Wounded Sudanese soldiers were killed rather than treated.^30^ The city was looted. Prisoners were massacred.^30^ These war crimes were documented but never prosecuted.^30^

British rule in Sudan, established as an Anglo-Egyptian condominium, was extractive and authoritarian.^31^ Sudanese were denied political rights, their resources were exploited for British benefit, and their resistance was met with violence.^31^ The legacy includes the arbitrary division between northern and southern Sudan that contributed to decades of civil war.^32^

The Boer War: White on White Violence

The Second Boer War (1899-1902) in South Africa was primarily a conflict between British imperial forces and Dutch-descended Boer republics, but it demonstrated British willingness to employ total war tactics even against white Europeans when economic and strategic interests were at stake.^33^ The war was triggered by the discovery of gold in the Transvaal, which made the Boer

Chapter 6: The Scramble for Africa

republics wealthy and strategically important.^34^ Britain, seeking to dominate southern Africa, provoked conflict with demands for political rights for British settlers that the Boers refused.^34^

When war began, Britain expected quick victory, but Boer guerrilla tactics proved effective against conventional British forces.^35^ Britain responded with a scorched earth policy and concentration camps, discussed in Chapter 5.^36^ What bears emphasis here is that these tactics—considered acceptable against Africans—were controversial when applied to white Boers, revealing the racial hierarchy of imperial violence.^37^

The war killed approximately 75,000 people: 22,000 British soldiers (mostly from disease), 7,000 Boer soldiers, 28,000 Boer civilians (mostly women and children in concentration camps), and an estimated 20,000 Black Africans who died in separate, worse camps or were killed as "collateral damage."^38^ The Black African death toll is least certain because British authorities didn't consider Black lives worth counting carefully.^38,39^

British victory in 1902 led to the Union of South Africa (1910), which granted substantial autonomy to white settlers while excluding the Black majority from political power.^40^ Britain essentially handed power to white

Perfidious Albion

settlers who would establish the apartheid system.˄40˄ British policy prioritized maintaining white dominance and ensuring continued access to South African gold and diamonds.˄41˄ The interests and rights of the Black African majority—who comprised over 75% of the population—were ignored.˄41˄

Kenya: Settler Colonialism and Dispossession

British conquest of Kenya (initially the East Africa Protectorate) combined strategic interests—controlling the headwaters of the Nile and the route to Uganda—with settler colonialism that dispossessed indigenous peoples of their land.˄42˄ The process began in the 1890s with the construction of the Uganda Railway, built by Indian indentured laborers at tremendous human cost.˄43˄ Over 2,500 Indian workers died during construction from disease, accidents, and attacks by wildlife.˄43˄

Once the railway was complete, Britain encouraged white settler immigration to make the territory "pay for itself."˄44˄ The problem was that the most fertile land—the Kenya Highlands—was already occupied by the Kikuyu, Maasai, and other peoples.˄45˄ The British solution was simply to seize it, declaring the Highlands "Crown Land" available for white settlers.˄45˄ This was justified by claiming Africans didn't properly "use" the land and therefore had no real ownership rights.˄45˄

Chapter 6: The Scramble for Africa

The dispossession was systematic. The Maasai were forcibly relocated twice (1904 and 1911) through fraudulent treaties and military pressure, losing their best grazing lands.^46^ The Kikuyu were pushed onto "reserves"—marginal land insufficient for their population.^47^ By 1915, about 5.5 million acres of the most fertile land had been transferred to approximately 1,000 white settlers, while millions of Africans were confined to reserves.^47,48^

White settlers in Kenya established a system of racial domination that made South African apartheid look moderate by comparison.^49^ Africans were required to carry identification passes (kipande), were subject to forced labor, and faced the constant threat of violence for any perceived disrespect to whites.^49^ The colonial legal system enforced a rigid racial hierarchy with different laws for Europeans, Asians, and Africans.^50^

Labor exploitation was particularly brutal. Africans were forced to work on white-owned plantations and farms through hut and poll taxes that could only be paid with cash, obtainable only through wage labor.^51^ Workers were subjected to corporal punishment, including flogging, which continued into the 1920s despite humanitarian protests.^52^ Wages were kept deliberately low—often below subsistence—forcing entire families to work.^51,52^

The process of dispossession and exploitation generated resistance, which was met with systematic violence.~53~ When Africans protested land seizures or refused forced labor, British colonial forces responded with punitive expeditions that burned villages, destroyed crops, and killed resisters.~53~ This pattern of violence was routine throughout the colonial period and would culminate in the Mau Mau Uprising of the 1950s, discussed in later chapters.~54~

West Africa: Commercial Exploitation

British expansion in West Africa followed a different pattern than in East or Southern Africa.~55~ The climate and disease environment made large-scale white settlement impractical—West Africa was called "the white man's grave" because of high European mortality from tropical diseases.~55~ Instead, British colonization focused on commercial exploitation through African labor.~55,56~

Nigeria became Britain's most populous African colony, created by amalgamating disparate territories and peoples with distinct cultures, languages, and political systems.~57~ The conquest involved defeating established states including the Sokoto Caliphate, the largest and most powerful Islamic state in West Africa.~58~ British forces, using superior weaponry, defeated Sokoto armies and occupied the territory in 1903.~58~

Chapter 6: The Scramble for Africa

British rule in Nigeria was implemented through "indirect rule"—governing through existing traditional authorities who were co-opted or coerced into serving British interests.˄59˄ This system was cost-effective but preserved and ossified ethnic divisions while giving traditional rulers incentives to exploit their subjects for British benefit.˄59˄ The arbitrary amalgamation of northern and southern Nigeria into one colony created an unstable entity whose ethnic and religious divisions persist today.˄60˄

The Gold Coast (now Ghana) was colonized for its gold, cocoa, and strategic position.˄61˄ The Asante Empire, powerful and sophisticated, resisted British encroachment, leading to multiple Anglo-Asante Wars throughout the 19th century.˄61,62˄ The final conquest came in 1900-1901 when British forces captured Kumasi and exiled Asante leadership.˄62˄ The conquest was brutal: villages were burned, resisters were executed, and the Asante kingdom was dismantled.˄62˄

British economic policy in West Africa prioritized extracting raw materials—palm oil, cocoa, rubber, minerals—for export while importing British manufactured goods.˄63˄ This trade pattern deliberately prevented African industrialization.˄63˄ Africans were forced to produce cash crops for export instead of food for consumption, making them vulnerable to famines when global commodity prices fell or harvests failed.˄64˄

The colonial taxation system was designed to force Africans into the cash economy on unfavorable terms.^65^ Hut taxes, poll taxes, and other levies required cash payment, forcing people to sell their labor or crops.^65^ Those who couldn't pay faced punishment including imprisonment, forced labor, or confiscation of property.^65^ This was economic coercion systemized as governance.^65^

The Mythology of the Civilizing Mission

British colonization of Africa was justified through an ideology that portrayed conquest as beneficent—the "civilizing mission" or "white man's burden."^66^ According to this ideology, Africans were backward, savage, and childlike, requiring European tutelage to become civilized.^67^ Europeans had a duty (the "burden") to bring Christianity, commerce, and civilization to Africa, even if Africans resisted for their own good.^67^

This mythology was thoroughly racist, portraying Africans as inherently inferior and incapable of self-governance.^68^ It was also fundamentally dishonest, concealing economic exploitation and violence behind claims of benevolence.^68^ The reality was that British colonization enriched Britain while impoverishing Africa, destroyed African political systems while claiming to bring good governance, and imposed

Chapter 6: The Scramble for Africa

Christianity while suppressing African religions and cultures.˄68,69˄

The "3 Cs"—Christianity, Commerce, and Civilization—were invoked as justifications, but each was hypocritical.˄70˄ Christianity was spread through missions that often served as advance agents for colonial conquest, teaching Africans to accept European authority.˄70˄ Commerce meant extracting African resources for European benefit while preventing African economic development.˄63˄ Civilization meant imposing European cultural norms while treating African cultures as worthless.˄69˄

The civilizing mission ideology served multiple functions. It justified colonization to European publics who might otherwise question the morality of conquest.˄71˄ It provided psychological comfort to colonizers, allowing them to see themselves as benefactors rather than thieves.˄71˄ And it established a framework for continued exploitation—since Africans were supposedly inferior, they needed indefinite European rule.˄71˄

Contemporary African responses demolished these claims. Educated Africans pointed out the contradiction between European claims of civilization and European violence.˄72˄ They noted that Africa had civilizations before Europe arrived, that African political systems often provided better governance than colonial administrations, and that the supposed benefits of colonization—education, infrastructure, medicine—were minimal and primarily served colonial interests.^72,73^

Economic Extraction: The Purpose Behind Conquest

The Scramble for Africa was fundamentally about economics—securing raw materials, creating captive markets, and generating profits for European investors.^74^ British colonies in Africa were integrated into a global economic system designed to benefit Britain while subordinating African interests.^74,75^

Raw materials extraction was paramount. Britain imported African gold, diamonds, copper, tin, palm oil, rubber, cocoa, coffee, cotton, and numerous other commodities.^76^ These resources were extracted using African labor paid minimal wages, then exported to Britain where they were processed into manufactured goods.^76^ Some manufactured goods were then sold back to African colonies at high prices, completing a cycle of exploitation.^76^

The terms of trade were systematically rigged against Africa. Colonial governments imposed trade policies favoring British goods while restricting African economic development.^77^ Tariffs protected British manufacturers from competition while forcing Africans

Chapter 6: The Scramble for Africa

to export raw materials cheaply.˄77˄ African colonies were forbidden from industrializing—they were to remain sources of raw materials and markets for British products.˄77˄

Investment patterns reflected these priorities. British capital flowed into African mining, plantation agriculture, and transportation infrastructure connecting resource areas to ports.˄78˄ Little investment went to African education, health, or economic development.˄78˄ Railways were built not to serve African needs but to transport minerals and crops to coastal ports for export.˄78˄ When independence came, African nations inherited economies designed for extraction, not self-sustaining development.˄79˄

Labor systems were coercive. Africans were forced into wage labor through taxation, land dispossession, and sometimes direct compulsion.˄80˄ Wages were kept artificially low through racial wage scales that paid Africans a fraction of what Europeans received for similar work.˄80˄ Working conditions were often brutal, especially in mines where death and injury rates were extremely high.˄80,81˄

The profits from this system flowed to Britain. Shareholders in companies like De Beers, British South Africa Company, United Africa Company, and numerous mining concerns became wealthy from

Perfidious Albion

African labor and resources.^82^ British government revenues increased from colonial taxes and customs duties.^82^ The British economy benefited from cheap raw materials that fueled industry.^82^ Meanwhile, African societies were impoverished, their resources extracted, their labor exploited, and their development prevented.^79,82^

Resistance and Its Suppression

Africans resisted colonization from the beginning, and British forces suppressed resistance with systematic violence.^83^ Every major British colony in Africa was established through military conquest that killed thousands or tens of thousands.^83^

The conquest of the Sokoto Caliphate involved multiple campaigns and thousands of deaths.^58^ The Asante Wars killed thousands and destroyed Asante political structures.^62^ The conquest of Sudan saw mass slaughter at Omdurman.^27^ The suppression of the Ndebele and Shona rebellions in Rhodesia killed tens of thousands.^16^ The Maji Maji Rebellion in German East Africa (neighboring British territories) killed 75,000-300,000, providing a cautionary example that Britain observed and sometimes assisted in suppressing.^84^

British counter-insurgency tactics were consistent: overwhelming firepower, collective punishment,

Chapter 6: The Scramble for Africa

destruction of economic resources, and exemplary violence designed to terrorize.^85^ Villages suspected of harboring resisters were burned. Crops and livestock were destroyed to starve populations into submission. Leaders were captured and executed publicly. Entire regions were subjected to martial law with summary justice.^85^

The technological advantage was overwhelming. African forces armed with spears, old muskets, or captured rifles faced British forces with modern breech-loading rifles, machine guns, and artillery.^86^ The results were one-sided massacres described by British participants as battles.^86^ At Omdurman, at the Rongai massacre in Kenya, at numerous smaller engagements, Africans died in hundreds or thousands while British casualties numbered in dozens.^27,87^

Yet resistance persisted. Despite overwhelming odds, Africans continued fighting for their freedom, their land, and their dignity.^83^ Some resistance was military, others was cultural or economic—refusing to pay taxes, maintaining traditional practices, or withdrawing labor.^88^ This resistance demonstrates that Africans never accepted colonial rule as legitimate, contradicting the claim that colonization was accepted or welcomed.^88^

Summary Conclusion: The Zenith of Empire, The Depth of Crime

The Scramble for Africa represented British imperialism at its most extensive and most brutal. In three decades, Britain seized control of millions of square miles and tens of millions of people, destroying indigenous political systems, appropriating resources, and imposing racial hierarchies that denied Africans basic human rights.[1,89]

The human cost was catastrophic and can never be fully calculated. Conservative estimates suggest hundreds of thousands died in wars of conquest, but the total death toll—including deaths from disease, famine, and forced labor—was certainly in the millions.[5,90] Entire societies were disrupted or destroyed. Ethnic groups were divided by arbitrary borders. Political systems that had governed effectively for centuries were dismantled. Economies were reoriented from meeting local needs to serving European interests.[90]

The economic extraction was staggering. Billions of pounds worth of resources flowed from Africa to Britain.[91] African labor built the infrastructure of colonial exploitation—the mines, railways, plantations—while receiving minimal compensation.[91] The wealth Britain gained from African colonization helped finance industrialization, enriched investors, and created economic dominance that persisted long after formal colonization ended.[91]

British historical memory treats the Scramble for Africa as an adventure, celebrating explorers and empire-

Chapter 6: The Scramble for Africa

builders while minimizing the violence and exploitation.^92^ Cecil Rhodes, who orchestrated racist dispossession and violence, has universities, scholarships, and formerly a country named after him.^19^ Kitchener, who presided over the Omdurman massacre, is remembered as a military hero.^93^ The actual costs imposed on Africans are forgotten or denied.^92^

The Scramble for Africa was not civilization meeting barbarism but one of history's greatest thefts, executed with systematic violence and justified by racist ideology.^1,94^ Understanding this is essential to understanding both British imperial history and contemporary Africa, where the borders, economic structures, and political problems created during the Scramble continue to shape lives.^94^ The crimes of the Scramble were never acknowledged, the wealth was never returned, and the damage endures.^94^

Author's Notes Chapter 6

This chapter examines the late 19th-century partition of Africa among European powers, with Britain seizing vast territories across the continent. The "Scramble" exemplifies imperialism's rapaciousness—the division of an entire continent among European powers with no concern for African peoples' rights, interests, or existing political systems.

On the Berlin Conference (1884-85): The conference

established ground rules for European colonization of Africa, treating African territories as ownerless lands available for European appropriation. No African representatives participated in discussions dividing their continent. The conference's provisions—requiring "effective occupation" to claim territory—accelerated European military conquest, making the 1880s-1910s a period of intense colonial violence across Africa.

On Thomas Pakenham's *The Scramble for Africa* (1991): This remains the most comprehensive narrative history of the partition, based on extensive archival research in European sources. However, Pakenham's work focuses heavily on European actors and rivalries, treating African peoples largely as objects rather than subjects with agency. More recent African-centered histories, including work by scholars such as A.G. Hopkins and Toyin Falola, foreground African experiences, resistance, and the devastating consequences of partition.

On Comparing Imperial Atrocities: This chapter references the Congo Free State under King Leopold II of Belgium to provide comparative context—Leopold's regime killed an estimated 10 million Congolese through forced labor, violence, and starvation. While Britain did not perpetrate atrocities on quite this scale in any single territory, British colonial rule collectively killed millions across Africa through wars of conquest, punitive expeditions, forced labor, and created famine conditions. The comparison is not to excuse British conduct but to situate it within the systematic violence characterizing European colonialism in Africa.

On "Effective Occupation": Berlin Conference provisions requiring occupying powers to maintain effective control led directly to increased military operations and violence. "Effective occupation" meant suppressing resistance,

Chapter 6: The Scramble for Africa

establishing administrative control, and extracting resources—all requiring force against populations opposing foreign domination. The diplomatic language obscured the violence involved.

On Economic Motivations: The Scramble was driven by multiple factors including strategic rivalry among European powers, missionary activity, and genuine belief in European racial and civilizational superiority. But fundamentally, as J.A. Hobson argued in *Imperialism: A Study* (1902), economic interests drove expansion—desire for raw materials, markets for manufactured goods, and investment opportunities. The resources Britain extracted from African colonies (minerals, agricultural products, labor) enriched British corporations and financed British development while impoverishing colonized territories.

CHAPTER SEVEN

Opium, Gunboats, and the Humiliation of China (1839-1860)

F ew episodes in imperial history expose Britain's moral bankruptcy more completely than its wars against China to force opium addiction upon the Chinese people. When the Qing government, confronting a public health catastrophe of staggering proportions, attempted to suppress the drug trade devastating its population, Britain responded with military force—deploying the world's most powerful navy to compel China to accept narco-colonialism at gunpoint. The Opium Wars represent imperialism in its purest, most indefensible form: wars fought explicitly to protect drug trafficking, justified through racist contempt for Chinese civilization, and prosecuted through overwhelming military violence against a society whose only crime was attempting to protect its people from addiction and social destruction.

The wars' consequences extended far beyond immediate military defeats. They shattered China's self-conception as the Middle Kingdom, the civilizational center of the world, reducing it to semi-colonial status where foreign powers dictated terms, occupied territory, and operated beyond Chinese law. The "Century of Humiliation" that followed—from the First Opium War in 1839 through the Communist Revolution in 1949—saw China dismembered by foreign powers, its government subordinated to foreign interests, its people subjected to racist violence and exploitation, and its ancient civilization treated with contempt by European nations whose own claims to civilization were exposed as fraudulent by their conduct in China.

Britain's responsibility for initiating and perpetuating this catastrophe was central and undeniable. British merchants trafficked the opium, British officials protected the trade, British politicians justified it through parliamentary debates revealing stunning moral depravity, and British military forces prosecuted wars whose explicit purpose was forcing China to accept drug addiction as the price of dealing with the West. The opium trade and the wars fought to protect it represent among the most cynical and destructive episodes in

Chapter 7: Humiliation of China

imperial history—a calculated program of narco-colonialism that destroyed millions of lives, humiliated one of humanity's greatest civilizations, and established patterns of Western domination over China that poisoned relationships for generations.

The Opium Trade: Deliberate Narco-Colonialism

The opium trade was not incidental to British imperialism in Asia but central to its economic structure and strategic objectives. After Britain's East India Company conquered Bengal in the mid-18th century, it established monopoly control over opium production. Company officials recognized that opium cultivation offered enormous profit potential and, crucially, provided the means to solve Britain's "China problem"—the massive trade deficit resulting from British demand for Chinese tea, silk, and porcelain.^1^

China in the late 18th and early 19th centuries was the world's largest economy, accounting for approximately one-third of global GDP. Chinese products—particularly tea, which had become essential to British culture and economy—were in enormous demand in Britain. Yet China had little interest in British manufactured goods. Chinese officials, viewing their civilization as superior and self-sufficient, permitted limited trade only through the port of Canton (Guangzhou) and demanded payment in silver. The resulting trade imbalance drained British silver reserves, creating economic pressure that

British merchants and officials were determined to reverse.^2^

Opium provided the solution. Despite Chinese government prohibitions on opium importation and consumption dating from 1729, British merchants discovered that demand existed and could be cultivated. The East India Company, operating through nominally independent merchant houses to maintain deniability, began systematically shipping opium from Bengal to China. What began as relatively modest trade in the 1780s—approximately 4,000 chests annually—exploded over subsequent decades as British merchants deliberately cultivated addiction. By 1838, on the eve of the First Opium War, approximately 40,000 chests containing roughly 2,400 tons of opium were being smuggled into China annually.^3^

The trade was consciously designed to create and exploit addiction. British merchants understood that opium was powerfully addictive and that initial users would become dependent customers requiring regular supplies. They deliberately marketed opium to maximize addiction rates, offering free samples, establishing opium dens, and creating distribution networks reaching deep into Chinese society. Company correspondence reveals explicit awareness that the trade depended on addiction and deliberate strategy to maximize the number of Chinese addicts.^4^

Chapter 7: Humiliation of China

The human consequences were catastrophic. By the 1830s, conservative estimates suggest between 2 and 10 million Chinese were addicted to opium, with actual figures likely higher given underreporting and the trade's illegal nature. Addiction devastated families as wage earners spent income on opium rather than food, housing, or children's welfare. It destroyed productivity as workers became incapable of sustained labor. It corrupted government as officials were bribed to permit smuggling. And it drained China's silver reserves as the trade deficit reversed, with silver now flowing out of China to pay for imported opium.^5^

The social destruction was immense. Chinese sources from the period describe communities devastated by opium addiction. One memorial to the Emperor from 1836 reported: "Of the rich who smoke opium, nine out of ten are reduced to poverty; of the poor who smoke it, nine out of ten are reduced to stealing and robbery."^6^ Families were torn apart, children abandoned, theft and prostitution increased as addicts desperately sought means to purchase opium. The drug corrupted Chinese officialdom as coastal officials responsible for preventing smuggling were systematically bribed, creating networks of corruption that undermined government authority.^7^

British officials and merchants were fully aware of the destruction they were causing. Missionaries, diplomats, and travelers sent regular reports describing opium's devastating effects on Chinese society. Yet rather than acknowledging moral responsibility, British merchants and officials justified the trade through arguments revealing the racism and moral bankruptcy underlying imperialism. They claimed that Chinese were racially predisposed to addiction and would obtain opium from other sources if Britain ceased supplying it. They argued that opium use was a personal choice and that Chinese who became addicted bore sole responsibility. They insisted that trade restrictions were unacceptable interference with British commercial rights. And they maintained that Chinese government prohibitions were illegitimate constraints on free trade that civilized nations had the right to ignore.^8^

The free trade argument was particularly cynical. Britain defended opium trafficking as legitimate commerce while simultaneously maintaining strict prohibitions on opium sales in Britain itself. The hypocrisy was explicit: opium was too dangerous for British consumption but acceptable to force upon Chinese. When Chinese officials pointed out this contradiction, British representatives dismissed their arguments with contempt. Lord Palmerston, as Foreign Secretary, exemplified this attitude, arguing that China had no right to restrict British trade and that British military force was justified to compel Chinese acceptance of opium imports.^9^

The trade also had strategic dimensions beyond

Chapter 7: Humiliation of China

immediate profit. British officials recognized that opium weakened China militarily and politically. A population debilitated by mass addiction, a government corrupted by smuggling networks, and an economy drained of silver reserves made China vulnerable to Western pressure and unable to resist British demands. The opium trade was not merely profitable commerce but deliberate policy to subordinate China to British interests through narco-colonialism—the systematic use of drug trafficking to weaken and control another society.^10^

Commissioner Lin and the Crisis of 1839

By the late 1830s, the Qing government faced a crisis. Opium addiction was destroying Chinese society, corrupting government, and draining the economy. The Daoguang Emperor, recognizing the catastrophic nature of the situation, appointed Lin Zexu as Imperial Commissioner with extraordinary powers to suppress the opium trade. Lin was a distinguished official known for integrity, competence, and determination—precisely the qualities needed to confront the British-dominated smuggling networks.^11^

Lin arrived in Canton in March 1839 and immediately took decisive action. He demanded that foreign merchants surrender all opium in their possession and sign bonds pledging to cease opium trafficking on penalty of death. When British merchants, encouraged by the British Superintendent of Trade Charles Elliot, refused, Lin imposed a blockade, confining foreign merchants to their Canton factories (trading compounds) and cutting off food and water supplies until they complied. Elliot, recognizing that resistance was futile, ordered British merchants to surrender their opium stocks—approximately 20,000 chests worth millions of pounds—promising British government compensation for their losses.^12^

Lin supervised the destruction of the surrendered opium in elaborate public ceremonies designed to demonstrate Qing authority. Over several weeks in June 1839, workers dissolved the opium in lime and salt water and flushed it into the sea. Lin composed a prayer to the Sea Spirit apologizing for polluting the ocean and asking protection for sea creatures. The destruction was both practical measure eliminating contraband and symbolic demonstration that the Qing government would no longer tolerate foreign drug trafficking.^13^

Lin then sent a famous letter to Queen Victoria, appealing to her sense of morality and reciprocity: "We have heard that in your honorable nation, too, the people are not permitted to smoke opium... Suppose there were people from another country who carried opium for sale to England and seduced your people into buying and smoking it; certainly your honorable ruler would deeply hate it and be bitterly aroused."^14^ The letter never reached Victoria—British officials intercepted it—but its

Chapter 7: Humiliation of China

logic was irrefutable. Lin was asking Britain to apply to China the same standards it applied to itself: if opium was too dangerous for British subjects, why was it acceptable to force upon Chinese?

The British response ignored Lin's moral arguments entirely and focused instead on claims that British rights had been violated. British merchants demanded compensation for destroyed opium. Charles Elliot reported to London that British dignity had been insulted by Lin's "coercive" measures. And British officials, led by Foreign Secretary Palmerston, determined that military force was necessary to compel China to accept British terms including compensation for destroyed opium, access to multiple ports beyond Canton, and legal guarantees protecting British trade including opium.^15^

The cynicism was breathtaking. China was defending its population against drug trafficking and Britain was claiming victim status because its drug profits had been interrupted. British officials explicitly acknowledged that they were preparing to wage war to protect opium trafficking. Palmerston wrote to the Prime Minister in 1840: "The Chinese must be made to understand that we will not tolerate their insolent behaviour and that if they continue their obstructions to our trade, we will use force."^16^ The "obstructions" in question were Chinese efforts to prevent mass addiction of their population.

Parliamentary debates in 1840 revealed the moral depravity underlying British policy. William Gladstone, then a young MP, delivered a devastating critique: "A war more unjust in its origin, a war more calculated to cover this country with permanent disgrace, I do not know... the British flag is hoisted to protect an infamous contraband traffic."^17^ Yet Gladstone's position was minority. The majority of Parliament, driven by commercial interests and racist contempt for China, supported military action. The vote to authorize war passed 271 to 262—a narrow margin that reflected moral unease but insufficient to prevent catastrophe.^18^

The First Opium War: Military Aggression and Imposed Humiliation

The First Opium War (1839-1842) demonstrated the devastating effectiveness of industrial military technology deployed against a society that had not experienced European-style warfare. British forces, consisting of modern warships, steam-powered gunboats, and well-armed infantry, faced Chinese forces equipped with outdated weapons and naval vessels designed for coastal defense rather than engagement with European battleships.^19^

The military campaign was systematic and brutal. British forces blockaded Chinese ports, bombarded coastal cities, seized strategic positions, and moved up the Yangtze River threatening to cut off the Grand Canal—

Chapter 7: Humiliation of China

China's crucial internal transportation artery supplying Beijing with southern grain. Each engagement demonstrated British technological superiority and Chinese military inadequacy against European industrial warfare. Chinese coastal fortifications, designed to repel pirates, proved useless against British naval artillery. Chinese war junks were destroyed by steamships that could maneuver regardless of wind. Chinese infantry armed with matchlocks faced British troops with modern rifles and artillery.^20^

The British conduct of the war involved systematic atrocities. Naval bombardments of civilian areas killed thousands. The sack of cities involved looting, rape, and murder of civilians. British forces showed contempt for Chinese military resistance and civilian suffering alike. Contemporary British accounts describe the violence with disturbing casualness, treating Chinese deaths as insignificant and Chinese attempts at defense as futile resistance to inevitable British superiority.^21^

The war's outcome was never in doubt. By 1842, British forces controlled key coastal positions and threatened to advance on Beijing. The Qing government, recognizing military helplessness, sued for peace. The resulting Treaty of Nanjing (Nanking), signed in August 1842, imposed terms that fundamentally altered China's relationship with the outside world and established patterns of foreign domination that would persist for over a century.^22^

The treaty's terms were deliberately humiliating and economically exploitative:

Territorial cession: China ceded Hong Kong Island to Britain in perpetuity, establishing a British colony on Chinese territory that would endure until 1997.

Indemnity: China was forced to pay 21 million silver dollars to Britain—including 6 million as compensation for destroyed opium, explicitly requiring China to pay for its own attempts to prevent drug trafficking.

Treaty ports: China was forced to open five ports (Canton, Amoy, Foochow, Ningpo, and Shanghai) to British trade, residence, and consular representation.

Tariff limitations: China lost the right to set its own tariffs, with rates fixed at levels favorable to British commerce.

Most-favored-nation clause: Any privileges China granted to other nations would automatically extend to Britain.

Extraterritoriality: British subjects in China would be subject only to British law administered by British consuls, removing them from Chinese legal jurisdiction regardless of crimes committed on Chinese soil.˄23˄

Each provision was calculated to subordinate China to British interests. The indemnity drained Chinese

Chapter 7: Humiliation of China

finances. The treaty ports opened China to foreign penetration. Tariff limitations prevented China from protecting domestic industries. Most-favored-nation status ensured Britain automatically received any concessions China was forced to grant other powers. And extraterritoriality established that foreigners operated above Chinese law, creating legal immunity for foreign merchants, missionaries, and criminals.^24^

Crucially, the Treaty of Nanjing did not explicitly address opium, but British officials ensured that opium trafficking continued and expanded. The opened treaty ports became centers for opium distribution. British merchants, now operating legally from treaty ports, increased smuggling operations. And the Qing government, militarily defeated and financially drained, lacked capacity to enforce its opium prohibitions effectively.^25^

The Arrow War: Doubling Down on Humiliation

The Second Opium War (1856-1860), also known as the Arrow War, demonstrated that the First Opium War's humiliations were merely the beginning of China's subordination. When China attempted to assert minimal sovereignty and resist further foreign encroachments, Britain—joined by France—launched an even more destructive war that deepened China's semi-colonial status and demonstrated Western powers' determination to dominate China regardless of cost to Chinese

Perfidious Albion

society.[26]

The war's pretext was transparently cynical. In October 1856, Chinese authorities in Canton boarded the Arrow, a Chinese-owned vessel flying the British flag, and arrested several Chinese crew members suspected of piracy. The British consul claimed this violated British sovereignty. Yet the Arrow's registration had actually expired, its claim to British protection was legally dubious, and the arrested men were Chinese subjects. Nevertheless, British officials seized upon the incident as justification for military action they had been seeking to expand British privileges in China.[27]

France joined Britain after a French missionary was killed in Guangxi province, using this as pretext to support British demands. The combined Anglo-French force attacked Canton in late 1857, capturing the city and installing a puppet administration. They then moved north, attacking the Taku Forts guarding access to Beijing and advancing on the capital itself.[28]

The Qing government, hoping to negotiate settlement, sent representatives to meet Anglo-French forces. When negotiations stalled and Chinese forces attempted to defend the approaches to Beijing, Anglo-French forces responded with systematic violence. In October 1860, in an act of cultural destruction that shocked even contemporary observers, British and French forces looted and burned the Yuanmingyuan—the Old

Chapter 7: Humiliation of China

Summer Palace—one of China's greatest architectural and cultural treasures.^29^

The destruction of the Summer Palace represented cultural genocide enacted to inflict maximum humiliation. The palace complex, developed over 150 years, contained priceless art, rare books, historical artifacts, and architectural wonders representing the pinnacle of Chinese craftsmanship and aesthetic achievement. Anglo-French soldiers spent days looting everything portable—gold, jade, silk, porcelain, paintings, calligraphy, rare books, scientific instruments. What could not be stolen was destroyed. Soldiers smashed porcelain, shredded silk, burned books, and vandalized buildings. Then, on orders from British commander Lord Elgin, the entire complex was burned.^30^

The justification offered—retaliation for Chinese mistreatment of British prisoners—was pretextual. The actual purpose was terroristic: to demonstrate that Western powers would destroy China's most cherished cultural treasures if China resisted Western demands. Victor Hugo, the French writer, condemned the destruction: "One day two bandits entered the Summer Palace. One plundered, the other burned... Before history, one of the bandits will be called France; the other will be called England."^31^

The Treaty of Tianjin (1858) and Convention of Beijing

(1860), imposed at gunpoint after the Summer Palace's destruction, expanded Western privileges beyond even the Treaty of Nanjing's humiliating terms:

Additional treaty ports: Ten more ports opened to foreign trade and residence, extending foreign penetration deep into interior.

Foreign travel rights: Foreigners gained right to travel in China's interior, previously restricted.

Foreign legations in Beijing: Western powers established permanent diplomatic presence in the capital.

Christian missionary rights: Missionaries gained right to own property and proselytize throughout China, protected by extraterritoriality.

Opium legalization: Opium trade was formally legalized, eliminating any pretense that China could protect its population from drug trafficking.

Additional indemnities: China was forced to pay another 16 million taels to Britain and France as "compensation" for the costs of the war Britain and France had initiated.

Territorial cessions: China ceded Kowloon Peninsula to Britain, expanding the Hong Kong colony, and ceded coastal and border territories to Russia (which had

Chapter 7: Humiliation of China

mediated the settlement and extracted its own territorial gains as payment).˄32˄

The opium legalization clause was particularly cynical. Having fought two wars ostensibly over trade issues, Britain now forced China to legalize the drug trade that had precipitated the conflicts. Chinese opium imports continued growing, reaching over 6,500 tons annually by the 1880s. Domestic Chinese opium production also expanded as the government, unable to prevent importation, attempted to promote domestic cultivation to reduce silver drain. The result was catastrophic expansion of addiction. By century's end, estimates suggest 10-20% of Chinese adult males were addicted to opium, with rates even higher in coastal provinces.˄33˄

Impact on Chinese Society and Psychology

The Opium Wars and unequal treaties' impact on Chinese society extended far beyond territorial losses and economic exploitation. They shattered China's self-conception and initiated a crisis of confidence that would take a century to resolve. For millennia, China had understood itself as the Middle Kingdom—the center of civilization, superior to barbarian peoples at its periphery. The Confucian worldview presumed Chinese cultural superiority, with foreign peoples expected to acknowledge this through tributary relationships that reinforced Chinese centrality.˄34˄

Perfidious Albion

The Opium Wars demolished these assumptions through traumatic military defeats that exposed Chinese military weakness, technological backwardness, and inability to resist Western demands. The unequal treaties forced China to accept subordinate status in diplomatic relationships based on European international law rather than Chinese tributary system. The establishment of foreign enclaves operating under foreign law within Chinese territory created spaces where Chinese sovereignty did not operate. And the forced legalization of opium demonstrated that China could not protect its population from foreign exploitation even when that exploitation involved mass drug addiction.^35^

The psychological impact was profound and persists in Chinese consciousness today. The period from 1839 to 1949 is known in Chinese as the "Century of Humiliation" (百年国耻)—a term that captures the collective trauma of a civilization that understood itself as supreme being reduced to semi-colonial status, carved into spheres of influence by foreign powers, and subjected to racist contempt by Europeans who treated Chinese as inferior. The humiliation was not merely political or economic but existential—a challenge to China's fundamental understanding of itself and its place in the world.^36^

Chinese intellectuals struggled desperately to understand how China, with its ancient civilization and vast resources, had been so easily defeated by technologically superior but culturally younger

Chapter 7: Humiliation of China

European powers. This produced decades of painful self-examination and debates about whether China should adopt Western technology while preserving Chinese cultural essence (the "self-strengthening" approach), or whether deeper transformation was necessary requiring Western political and social institutions.^37^

The social destruction from opium addiction compounded the psychological trauma. As millions of Chinese became addicted, families disintegrated, productivity collapsed, and communities were devastated. Contemporary Chinese accounts describe the horror of mass addiction: government officials, soldiers, merchants, and laborers all falling victim to the drug that British merchants continued importing despite witnessing the destruction it caused. The combination of military humiliation and social destruction from British-trafficked opium created deep anger toward Western imperialism that shaped Chinese nationalism and anti-foreign sentiment for generations.^38^

The Treaty Port system created physical spaces where Chinese subordination was visible and enforced daily. In Shanghai and other treaty ports, foreigners established separate settlements governed by foreign law where Chinese could enter only as servants or laborers. Parks famously posted signs reading "No Dogs or Chinese Allowed"—a racist humiliation that became symbolic of the broader indignity of semi-colonial status. Chinese witnessed foreigners living in luxury extracted from

Chinese labor and trade while Chinese themselves were excluded from spaces in their own country.^39^

The extraterritoriality provisions created legal immunity that foreigners routinely abused. Foreign criminals knew they faced only consular courts typically staffed by their own nationals who regularly rendered lenient judgments or dismissed charges entirely. Chinese victims of foreign crimes had no legal recourse. This created atmosphere where foreigners operated with impunity, committing assaults, property crimes, and murders knowing Chinese authorities could not prosecute them and foreign consuls would not.^40^

The missionary presence, while less overtly violent than military or commercial imperialism, contributed to cultural humiliation. Missionaries, protected by extraterritoriality and backed by foreign military power, condemned Chinese religion and culture as heathen superstition requiring replacement with Christianity. They established churches, schools, and orphanages that provided services but demanded cultural submission. Missionary activities produced intense local resentment that periodically exploded into violence, which foreign powers then used as pretext for further intervention and extraction of new concessions.^41^

The Broader "Century of Humiliation"

The Opium Wars initiated what would become

Chapter 7: Humiliation of China

systematic dismemberment of China by multiple foreign powers. Following Britain's example, other Western nations and Japan extracted their own concessions through military pressure. France seized concessions in southern China. Germany occupied Qingdao. Russia expanded into Manchuria and extracted railway and mining rights. Japan, having modernized rapidly after its own forced opening by the West, defeated China in the 1894-1895 Sino-Japanese War, seizing Taiwan, Korea, and additional concessions. By 1900, China had been carved into spheres of influence with each foreign power dominating particular regions while maintaining the fiction of Chinese sovereignty.^42^

The Boxer Uprising of 1900—a violent anti-foreign movement that besieged foreign legations in Beijing—represented desperate attempt to expel foreign influence. The Eight-Nation Alliance (Britain, France, Germany, Russia, USA, Japan, Italy, Austria-Hungary) responded with military expedition that captured Beijing, engaged in widespread looting and atrocities, and imposed the Boxer Protocol requiring China to pay 450 million taels in indemnities over 39 years—an astronomical sum calculated to equal the foreign powers' costs plus punitive damages, ensuring Chinese economic subjugation for decades.^43^

The dynasty that had ruled China for nearly three centuries collapsed in 1911, unable to defend China against foreign predation or implement reforms sufficient to modernize while preserving imperial system. The Republic that followed remained weak, divided by warlordism, and subject to continuing foreign intervention. Japan's invasion in 1937 and the subsequent eight-year war killed tens of millions. Only with the Communist victory in 1949 did China finally expel foreign domination, close the treaty ports, abolish the unequal treaties, and reassert sovereignty—ending the Century of Humiliation that the Opium Wars had initiated.^44^

Britain's Moral Responsibility and Historical Legacy

Britain's responsibility for initiating and perpetuating China's Century of Humiliation is undeniable. British merchants trafficked the opium, British officials protected the trade, British politicians justified it through parliamentary debates revealing stunning moral depravity, and British military forces prosecuted wars explicitly to force opium upon the Chinese people. The unequal treaties Britain imposed established the template other powers followed. The Treaty Port system Britain created became the mechanism for foreign exploitation. And the precedent Britain set—that Western military power could override Chinese sovereignty whenever Chinese policies conflicted with Western commercial interests—encouraged the broader imperial assault on China.^45^

Chapter 7: Humiliation of China

Yet Britain has never acknowledged this responsibility honestly or offered meaningful accountability. The opium trafficking is typically presented, when discussed at all, as unfortunate commercial excess rather than deliberate narco-colonialism. The wars are often characterized as resulting from Chinese "inflexibility" or "misunderstanding" of international law rather than British military aggression to protect drug trafficking. The Summer Palace's destruction is sometimes acknowledged as regrettable excess but not as deliberate cultural terrorism. And the broader pattern of British responsibility for initiating China's subordination is obscured through narratives emphasizing China's own weaknesses rather than British violence and exploitation.^46^

The comparison with Britain's contemporary horror at drug trafficking is instructive. Modern Britain spends billions combating drug trade, imprisons traffickers, and cooperates internationally to suppress narcotics. Government officials routinely characterize drug trafficking as among the most serious crimes, destroying lives and communities. Yet these same moral principles were inverted when Britain trafficked opium to China: the drug dealers were protected by the state, their victims were blamed for weakness, and military force was deployed to ensure the drug trade continued.^47^

The human cost of British narco-colonialism was staggering. Millions of Chinese lives were destroyed by

Perfidious Albion

addiction. Families disintegrated as wage earners spent income on opium rather than supporting children. Communities were devastated as productive workers became incapable of labor. The Chinese economy was drained as silver flowed out to pay for imported poison. And Chinese society was weakened, corrupted, and humiliated—made vulnerable to the broader imperial assault that would follow British precedent.˄48˄

The legacy persists in contemporary China-West relations. The Century of Humiliation remains central to Chinese historical consciousness and shapes how China understands Western power and intentions. When Western nations criticize Chinese policies, Chinese officials routinely reference the historical humiliation and resist what they characterize as renewed attempts at Western domination. The determination to prevent any return to semi-colonial status drives Chinese assertions of sovereignty, resistance to Western pressure, and insistence on non-interference in internal affairs. Understanding contemporary China's behavior requires acknowledging the trauma of the Century of Humiliation—trauma for which Britain bears primary responsibility.˄49˄

Summary Conclusion

The Opium Wars represent British imperialism in its purest, most indefensible form. They were wars fought explicitly to protect drug trafficking, wars that killed tens

Chapter 7: Humiliation of China

of thousands in combat and millions more through the addiction Britain forced upon China, wars whose purpose was subordinating one of humanity's greatest civilizations to British commercial interests regardless of human cost. The justifications offered—free trade, diplomatic rights, Chinese "obstinacy"—were transparent pretexts for naked aggression and exploitation.

Commissioner Lin's question to Queen Victoria remains unanswered and unanswerable: if opium was too dangerous for British subjects, why was it acceptable to force upon Chinese? The British response—military violence, imposed humiliation, and forced legalization of the drug trade—revealed the moral bankruptcy at imperialism's heart. British officials knowingly trafficked poison, deliberately cultivated mass addiction, protected smuggling networks through military force, and then imposed treaties requiring China to legalize the trade destroying millions of lives.

The Century of Humiliation that followed—the systematic subordination of China to foreign domination, the carving of Chinese territory into spheres of influence, the legal immunity that allowed foreigners to commit crimes with impunity, the racist exclusions and daily humiliations, and the destruction of Chinese lives and property through wars, rebellions, and continuing opium addiction—traces directly to British aggression of 1839-1860. Other powers followed Britain's

Perfidious Albion

precedent, extracted their own concessions, and contributed to China's dismemberment. But Britain initiated the pattern, established the mechanisms, and demonstrated that military force could override Chinese sovereignty whenever Chinese policies conflicted with Western interests.

The trauma persists in Chinese historical consciousness and shapes contemporary China-West relations. The determination to prevent any return to semi-colonial status, the resistance to Western pressure, the assertions of sovereignty, the celebration of national strength—all reflect memory of the Century of Humiliation and determination to ensure it never recurs. Understanding contemporary China requires acknowledging this historical trauma—trauma for which Britain bears primary responsibility through its decision to wage war to force opium addiction upon the Chinese people.

Britain has never honestly confronted this history, never acknowledged the full extent of harm inflicted, never offered meaningful apology or accountability. The opium trafficking is minimized as unfortunate commercial excess. The wars are characterized as resulting from Chinese inflexibility rather than British aggression. The unequal treaties are presented as typical 19th-century diplomacy rather than imposed subordination. And British responsibility for initiating China's Century of Humiliation is obscured through narratives emphasizing Chinese weakness rather than

Chapter 7: Humiliation of China

British violence.

Yet the evidence is overwhelming and the judgment inescapable. Britain waged wars to force drug addiction upon millions of Chinese, destroyed one of humanity's greatest civilizations' confidence and autonomy, and initiated a century of humiliation whose effects persist today. The Opium Wars represent among the most cynical, destructive, and morally indefensible episodes in imperial history—a program of deliberate narco-colonialism that British officials understood was destroying Chinese society yet prosecuted with military violence because drug profits and commercial access mattered more than millions of Chinese lives.

Author's Notes Chapter 7

This chapter examines the two Opium Wars through which Britain forced China to accept British opium imports, demonstrating imperialism at its most naked—deploying military force to compel a nation to permit drug trafficking that was enriching British merchants while addicting millions of Chinese.

On the Moral Dimension: The Opium Wars represent imperialism stripped of any pretense to civilization or benevolence. Britain used military force to protect drug trafficking that British officials acknowledged was morally indefensible and harmful to Chinese society. William Gladstone, speaking in Parliament, called the First Opium War "a war more unjust in its origin, a war more calculated in its progress to cover this country with permanent disgrace." Yet the war continued, revealing that economic interests trumped moral concerns.

On Sources: Julia Lovell's *The Opium War* (2011) provides an accessible narrative based on Chinese and British sources, emphasizing Chinese perspectives often marginalized in English-language accounts. Stephen Platt's *Imperial Twilight* (2018) offers detailed examination of the period leading to the First Opium War, showing how the conflict developed gradually through escalating tensions over trade and sovereignty. Both works benefit from recent Chinese scholarship that has been increasingly accessible to Western historians.

On the East India Company's Opium Monopoly: The Company controlled opium production in British India, running what was essentially a state-sponsored drug cartel. Opium represented the Company's most profitable export to China, making up the majority of the value of British exports. The revenue was so important to Company finances that when China attempted to suppress the trade, Britain went to war to protect it. This reveals the fundamentally criminal nature of imperialism—deploying state violence to protect illegal drug trafficking.

On the "Century of Humiliation": Chinese historians characterize the period from the First Opium War (1839) through the founding of the People's Republic (1949) as the "Century of Humiliation"—110 years during which foreign powers imposed unequal treaties, seized Chinese territory, and exploited China's weakness. The Opium Wars initiated this period and remain powerfully symbolic in Chinese historical memory. Understanding this history is essential for comprehending contemporary Chinese nationalism and foreign policy positions.

On the Destruction of the Summer Palace (1860): During the Second Opium War, British and French forces looted and burned the Yuanming Yuan (Summer Palace)—one of China's greatest architectural and artistic treasures. The

Chapter 7: Humiliation of China

destruction was ordered by Lord Elgin (son of the man who removed the "Elgin Marbles" from Greece) in retaliation for Chinese treatment of prisoners. The deliberate cultural destruction exemplifies imperialism's contempt for non-European civilizations. Artifacts looted from the Summer Palace remain in British and French museums, with Chinese demands for their return ongoing.

On Contemporary Relevance: The Opium Wars' legacy shapes China-Britain relations today. Chinese officials frequently reference these wars when discussing Western imperialism, sovereignty issues, and the need for China to be strong enough to resist foreign domination. Britain's role in forcing opium on China represents perhaps the clearest example of imperial economic exploitation through violence, making it particularly powerful symbolically.

CHAPTER EIGHT

The Caribbean, Australia and Pacific
Forgotten Brutalities (1600-1900)

British imperial history focuses disproportionately on India and Africa, treating the Caribbean, Australia and Pacific as peripheral theaters despite centuries of exploitation and violence in these regions.^1^ The Caribbean islands were sites of some of slavery's worst horrors, where enslaved Africans were worked to death on sugar plantations generating enormous British wealth.^2^ After slavery's abolition, the exploitation continued through indentured labor, economic subordination, and political domination.^3^ In the Pacific, British colonization brought genocide to Australia's Aboriginal peoples, dispossession to New Zealand's Māori, and exploitation to countless Pacific islands.~4,5~ These regions' historical marginalization in British memory reflects a hierarchy of imperial concerns where crimes against Black and indigenous peoples receive less attention than those against populations Britain deemed more significant.~6~ Yet the human cost was staggering, the wealth extracted was enormous, and the legacies persist today—as evidenced by recent demands from Jamaica and Barbados for reparations for slavery and colonial exploitation.~7,8~ This chapter examines Britain's forgotten brutalities in the Caribbean and Pacific, connecting historical crimes to contemporary calls for justice.~7,8~

The Caribbean: Sugar, Slavery, and Super-Exploitation

The Caribbean was Britain's most profitable colonial region for much of the 18th and early 19th centuries, generating wealth that exceeded that from North America or India.~9~ This wealth came from sugar, produced by enslaved Africans laboring under conditions so brutal that the death rate exceeded the birth rate, requiring constant imports of new captives to maintain the workforce.~10~ We have discussed the Atlantic slave trade in Chapter 2, but the Caribbean plantation system deserves specific attention for its extremity.~10~

Sugar cultivation was labor-intensive and dangerous. Enslaved workers cleared land with machetes, planted

Chapter 8: The Caribbean and Pacific

and tended cane in tropical heat, harvested the sharp-edged stalks by hand, then processed them immediately—sugar cane begins fermenting within hours of cutting.[11] Processing involved boiling cane juice in huge copper vats, work that caused frequent burns and accidents.[11] The work day during harvest season could extend to 18 hours.[11] Enslaved people were driven to exhaustion and beyond, whipped when they slowed, and provided minimal food and shelter.[11,12]

The mortality rate on Caribbean sugar plantations was catastrophic. Enslaved people on sugar estates had a life expectancy of only 7-9 years after arrival.[10] This wasn't an unfortunate side effect but an accepted business model: it was cheaper to work people to death and import replacements than to maintain conditions allowing natural population growth.[10] British plantation owners calculated the cost of a new enslaved person versus the cost of better food, housing, and working conditions, and chose death.[10]

Jamaica was Britain's most profitable sugar colony and the site of particular brutality.[13] By 1774, Jamaica had approximately 200,000 enslaved people and only 18,000 whites—a ratio of more than 10:1 that required constant terror to maintain control.[13] The legal system granted slaveholders near-absolute power over enslaved people, including the right to inflict any punishment short of death without legal consequence.[14] Even murders of enslaved people rarely resulted in prosecution, as the testimony of Black witnesses wasn't accepted in court.^14^

Punishments were designed to terrorize. Whipping was routine—the lash cutting flesh from backs until bone showed.^15^ The treadmill, a device forcing prisoners to climb continuously or be crushed, was invented in Jamaica for punishing enslaved people.^15^ Enslaved people were hanged, burned alive, or broken on the wheel for offenses like attempted escape or striking an overseer.^15^ During slave rebellions, British authorities engaged in orgies of retaliatory violence, as we saw with the Morant Bay Rebellion discussed in Chapter 5.^16^

Barbados, Britain's first major sugar colony, established patterns that would be repeated elsewhere.^17^ The island was transformed from a diverse agricultural economy into a sugar monoculture, with forests cleared, food production eliminated, and virtually all land devoted to cane.^17^ This made Barbados dependent on food imports, creating vulnerability during wars or trade disruptions.^17^ The entire society was restructured around sugar production, with a small white elite controlling enslaved Black majority through systematic violence.^17,18^

The wealth generated by Caribbean slavery was enormous. By the late 18th century, British West Indies colonies were producing approximately £4 million

Chapter 8: The Caribbean and Pacific

worth of sugar and other products annually—more valuable than all British North American colonies combined.^9^ This wealth flowed to Britain, enriching plantation owners, merchants, shippers, insurers, and investors.^9^ Caribbean slavery profits helped finance the Industrial Revolution, built country estates, and created family fortunes that persist today.^19^

Post-Emancipation Exploitation: Apprenticeship and Indentured Labor

When Britain abolished slavery in 1833, Caribbean slaveholders received £20 million in compensation—approximately 40% of the British government's annual expenditure.^20^ The enslaved people themselves received nothing.^20^ Moreover, they were required to serve "apprenticeships" to their former masters for up to six years—continued forced labor disguised as a transition period.^21^ The apprenticeship system was marked by continued violence, with former slaveholders retaining the power to punish their "apprentices" through flogging and imprisonment.^21^

Full emancipation came in 1838, but economic freedom proved elusive.^22^ Former slaveholders still controlled land and capital, while formerly enslaved people had neither.^22^ Planters deliberately kept wages low and used various coercive measures—vagrancy laws, tenancy requirements, manipulation of provision grounds—to force people to continue working on plantations.^22,23^

Perfidious Albion

When Black workers demanded fair wages or left plantations to establish independent farms, planters turned to imported labor.^23^

British authorities organized massive importation of indentured laborers from India—approximately 500,000 to the Caribbean between 1838 and 1917.^24^ These workers, predominantly from impoverished regions of India, were recruited under contracts committing them to five or more years of labor.^24^ While technically not enslaved, they faced conditions little better than slavery: confined to estates, punished harshly for contract violations, paid minimal wages, and subjected to violence and sexual abuse.^24,25^

The indenture system allowed Caribbean planters to maintain exploitative labor arrangements after slavery's abolition.^25^ It also created ethnic divisions—between formerly enslaved Africans and indentured Indians—that planters exploited and that persist in some Caribbean societies today.^26^ British authorities facilitated this system, providing ships, recruiting agents, and legal frameworks that favored planters over workers.^24,25^

Colonial Administration: Crushing Self-Governance

Throughout the 19th and early 20th centuries, British authorities systematically crushed Caribbean movements toward self-governance and economic

Chapter 8: The Caribbean and Pacific

independence.˄27˄ After the Morant Bay Rebellion in 1865, Britain dissolved Jamaica's elected assembly and imposed direct Crown Colony rule, eliminating even limited local self-government.˄28˄ This pattern was repeated across the Caribbean—whenever colonized peoples demanded political rights or economic justice, Britain responded by reducing their autonomy and increasing direct imperial control.˄28˄

British economic policies kept Caribbean colonies dependent and underdeveloped.˄29˄ Islands were forced to specialize in single export crops—sugar, bananas, cotton—making them vulnerable to price fluctuations.˄29˄ Tariffs favored British manufactured goods while hindering Caribbean industrialization.˄29˄ Investment went to extraction and export infrastructure, not to development benefiting local populations.˄30˄ Education systems were minimal, preparing a small elite to serve colonial administration while denying the masses access to education.˄30˄

The result was systematic underdevelopment. Despite centuries of wealth extraction, Caribbean colonies remained poor, with inadequate infrastructure, limited economic opportunity, and social systems still bearing slavery's imprint.˄31˄ When independence finally came in the 1960s-1980s, Caribbean nations inherited economies designed for exploitation, social divisions rooted in slavery and indenture, and minimal resources for development.˄31˄

Reparations Claims: The Bill Comes Due

In recent years, Caribbean nations have formally demanded reparations from European powers, particularly Britain, for slavery and colonialism.^7^ The Caribbean Community (CARICOM), a regional organization of 15 Caribbean nations, established a Reparations Commission in 2013 to pursue these claims.^7^ Jamaica and Barbados have been particularly vocal in demanding accountability.^7,8^

The case for reparations rests on several arguments.^32^ First, slavery was a crime against humanity that enriched Britain while devastating African and Caribbean populations.^32^ The wealth extracted has never been returned or compensated.^32^ Second, post-emancipation compensation went to slaveholders, not enslaved people—a fundamental injustice that should be rectified.^32^ Third, the underdevelopment Caribbean nations experience today directly results from centuries of extractive colonialism that deliberately prevented economic development.^33^

CARICOM's reparations claim includes ten specific demands: formal apology, repatriation programs (facilitating return to Africa for those who wish), indigenous peoples' development program, cultural institutions, public health crisis programs, illiteracy eradication, African knowledge program, psychological rehabilitation, technology transfer, and debt

Chapter 8: The Caribbean and Pacific

cancellation.^7^ These demands acknowledge that simple monetary payment cannot address centuries of harm, but comprehensive programs might begin to repair the damage.^7^

Britain's response has been dismissive. British governments have refused to apologize, rejected reparations claims, and argued that slavery, while morally wrong, was legal at the time and therefore cannot be subject to retroactive justice claims.^34^ Prime Minister David Cameron, visiting Jamaica in 2015, refused to apologize or discuss reparations, instead offering to build a prison.^35^ This response was widely criticized as insulting—Britain would help imprison Jamaicans but not address the historical crimes that contributed to Jamaica's current challenges.^35^

Barbados has taken the strongest stance, with Prime Minister Mia Mottley explicitly linking Britain's historical extraction of wealth to current Barbadian economic challenges.^8^ In 2020, Barbados announced plans to remove Queen Elizabeth II as head of state and become a republic, a move framed partly as addressing colonial legacies.^36^ The transition to republic status in 2021 was celebrated as a step toward decolonization, though economic relationships remain largely unchanged.^36^

The reparations debate reveals Britain's continuing refusal to acknowledge the full scope of its imperial

Perfidious Albion

crimes or accept responsibility for their ongoing consequences.˄37˄ The wealth extracted from Caribbean slavery remains in British institutions, banks, and families.˄19˄ The underdevelopment caused by colonial policies persists in Caribbean economies.˄33˄ Yet Britain acts as though history is past, with no contemporary obligations arising from centuries of exploitation.˄37˄

Australia: Genocide by Design and Neglect

British colonization of Australia, beginning in 1788, brought catastrophe to Aboriginal peoples who had inhabited the continent for at least 65,000 years.˄38˄ The British claimed Australia as terra nullius—empty land—ignoring the presence of hundreds of distinct Aboriginal nations with complex societies, laws, and cultures.˄39˄ This legal fiction justified seizing the entire continent without treaties or compensation.˄39˄

The impact was genocidal. Australia's Aboriginal population, estimated at 750,000-1.5 million in 1788, fell to approximately 93,000 by 1900—a decline of at least 90%.˄40˄ This demographic catastrophe resulted from multiple causes, all flowing from British colonization: disease, direct violence, dispossession from land, destruction of food sources, and deliberate policies of cultural genocide.˄40,41˄

European diseases—smallpox, influenza, measles,

Chapter 8: The Caribbean and Pacific

tuberculosis—devastated Aboriginal populations who had no immunity.[42] Some epidemics may have been deliberately introduced. In 1789, a smallpox epidemic killed approximately 50% of the Aboriginal population around Sydney Cove within months of British arrival.[43] While debate continues about whether this was deliberate biological warfare, documentary evidence exists of colonists discussing using smallpox against Aboriginal people, and some historians argue the timing and spread pattern suggest deliberate introduction.[43,44]

Direct violence was systematic and widespread. British colonists and colonial authorities conducted what they euphemistically called "dispersals"—military or settler attacks on Aboriginal camps that killed men, women, and children.[45] These massacres occurred across the continent for over a century.[45] Historian Lyndall Ryan's Colonial Frontier Massacres project has documented over 400 massacres of Aboriginal people, with the actual number certainly much higher.[46]

Some massacres are particularly well-documented. The Myall Creek Massacre (1838) saw white settlers kill 28 Aboriginal people, including children, then burn the bodies.[47] Unusually, some perpetrators were prosecuted and hanged, but this was exceptional—most massacres resulted in no accountability.[47] The Coniston Massacre (1928) killed at least 31 Aboriginal people, possibly over 100, in "reprisal" for the death of a white dingo hunter.^48^ Police and civilians conducted the killings, which were initially defended by authorities before public outcry forced an inquiry that whitewashed the events.^48^

Queensland had particularly horrific policies. Native Police units—Aboriginal men recruited to track and kill other Aboriginal people—were used extensively from the 1840s-1900s to "disperse" Aboriginal populations from land wanted by settlers.^49^ These units committed countless massacres, with officers' reports sometimes boasting of large numbers killed.^49^ The actual death toll will never be known because many killings were never recorded.^49^

Poisoning was another method of extermination. Settlers laced food with strychnine or arsenic, leaving poisoned flour or meat for Aboriginal people, then collecting and disposing of bodies.^50^ Documented cases exist across multiple regions, though the full scale is unknown because perpetrators rarely faced consequences and had little incentive to document their crimes.^50^

Dispossession from land was itself genocidal. Aboriginal peoples' cultures, economies, and spiritual lives were intimately connected to specific territories.^51^ Forced removal from land meant loss of food sources, sacred sites, and cultural identity.^51^ British colonists seized the best land for farming and grazing, pushing

Chapter 8: The Caribbean and Pacific

Aboriginal people onto marginal land that couldn't sustain traditional lifestyles.^51^ Waterholes were controlled by settlers, game was hunted out or displaced by cattle and sheep, and traditional burning practices that had managed the landscape for millennia were prohibited.^51,52^

Starvation was systematic. Once dispossessed from land, Aboriginal people faced hunger.^52^ Some colonial authorities provided minimal rations—as a "humanitarian" gesture—but these were often inadequate and came with requirements to live on reserves under white supervision.^52^ Others simply allowed starvation to occur, viewing it as inevitable and perhaps desirable elimination of inconvenient populations.^52^

Cultural Genocide: Stolen Generations and Forced Assimilation

Beyond physical genocide, British Australia implemented cultural genocide designed to eliminate Aboriginal identity and culture.^53^ Children were systematically removed from their families—the "Stolen Generations"—in policies continuing into the 1970s.^54^ An estimated 100,000 Aboriginal children were forcibly taken from their parents and placed in missions, orphanages, or white foster homes.^54^

The stated purpose was assimilation—to "breed out"

Aboriginality by raising children as whites and preventing transmission of Aboriginal culture.^55^ Mixed-race children were particularly targeted, with authorities believing they could be successfully assimilated.^55^ Children were forbidden to speak their languages, practice their cultures, or maintain contact with families.^55^ Many were subjected to abuse, forced labor, and cultural indoctrination teaching them to be ashamed of their heritage.^56^

The trauma was intergenerational. Stolen children grew up disconnected from families, communities, languages, and cultures.^56^ As adults, many struggled with identity, mental health, and parenting—having never experienced normal family relationships.^56^ Their children and grandchildren continue to suffer the effects.^57^ Communities were devastated by the loss of children, who were the future and the transmission of culture.^57^

Missions and reserves where Aboriginal people were confined imposed totalitarian control.^58^ Superintendents regulated every aspect of life: work, movement, marriage, childrearing, religious practice, and cultural expression.^58^ Aboriginal people needed permission to leave reserves, to marry, to spend money.^58^ Traditional practices including ceremonies, languages, and body painting were often prohibited.^58^ The goal was destroying Aboriginal culture and identity.^58^

Chapter 8: The Caribbean and Pacific

Australian authorities justified these policies through racist ideology portraying Aboriginal people as dying race whose extinction was inevitable.^59^ This "doomed race" theory conveniently absolved colonizers of responsibility—Aboriginal people were supposedly naturally inferior and would disappear regardless of colonial actions.^59^ The fact that Aboriginal deaths resulted from deliberate policies was ignored or rationalized as speeding an inevitable process.^59^

Tasmania: Genocide Completed

The most extreme case was Tasmania (Van Diemen's Land), where British colonization led to the near-complete extermination of the indigenous population.^60^ Tasmania's Aboriginal people, isolated from mainland Australia for over 10,000 years, had developed distinct cultures and languages.^60^ When British colonists arrived in 1803, they pursued aggressive expansion, seizing Aboriginal land and responding violently to any resistance.^60^

The "Black War" (1824-1831) saw colonial authorities attempt to eliminate Tasmania's Aboriginal people through a combination of military operations, settler violence, and bounty hunting.^61^ Martial law was declared, giving settlers and soldiers license to kill Aboriginal people on sight.^61^ Bounties were offered for capturing Aboriginal people—£5 for adults, £2 for children.^61^ The infamous "Black Line" (1830) saw over 2,000 armed colonists form a human chain across

Tasmania attempting to drive all remaining Aboriginal people into a peninsula where they could be captured or killed.^62^

The operation largely failed in its immediate objective, but the systematic violence had devastating effect.^62^ By 1835, only approximately 200 Tasmanian Aboriginal people remained.^63^ George Augustus Robinson, a "conciliator," convinced most survivors to relocate to Flinders Island, promising safety and provisions.^63^ The conditions were catastrophic: inadequate food, disease, and despair killed most within a few years.^63^ By 1847, only 47 remained.^63^

The last full-blooded Tasmanian Aboriginal person, Truganini, died in 1876.^64^ Her death was widely portrayed as the extinction of an entire people—though this ignored the mixed-race descendants who survived and today identify as Tasmanian Aboriginal people.^64^ The near-total destruction of Tasmania's Aboriginal population within 70 years of colonization represents one of the most complete genocides in recorded history.^64^

New Zealand: A Different Pattern, Familiar Outcomes

British colonization of New Zealand (Aotearoa) followed a somewhat different pattern due to the Treaty of Waitangi (1840), which theoretically protected Māori land rights and sovereignty.^65^ However, the treaty's

Chapter 8: The Caribbean and Pacific

English and Māori versions contained significant differences, and British authorities consistently violated even the English version's terms.[66]

Land was systematically seized from Māori through fraudulent purchases, confiscations following conflicts, and legal mechanisms designed to facilitate transfer to European settlers.[67] By 1900, Māori had lost approximately 95% of their land.[67] The New Zealand Wars (1845-1872) saw British military forces and colonial militia defeat Māori resistance, though Māori warriors fought with extraordinary skill and tenacity.[68] Following British victories, massive land confiscations punished entire tribes, including those who hadn't participated in fighting.[68]

The demographic impact was severe. Māori population fell from approximately 100,000-200,000 at first contact to fewer than 43,000 by 1900—a decline of at least 75%.[69] Disease, warfare, land loss, and disruption of traditional food sources all contributed.[69] As in Australia, British colonizers saw this decline as evidence of a dying race, rationalizing their role in causing it.[69]

Unlike Australia, where Aboriginal people were denied citizenship and relegated to reserves, New Zealand eventually granted Māori nominal equality while maintaining structural discrimination.[70] The treaty remained legally recognized, providing a framework for later redress that has no parallel in Australia.[70]

Beginning in the 1970s, the Waitangi Tribunal began hearing claims of treaty breaches and recommending settlements.~71~ While these settlements have returned some land and provided compensation, they represent only a fraction of what was taken, and fundamental inequalities persist.~72~

Pacific Islands: Exploitation and Blackbirding

British influence extended across the Pacific through both formal colonies and informal dominance.~73~ Fiji became a Crown colony in 1874, with British authorities importing Indian indentured laborers to work sugar plantations after Fijian chiefs resisted providing labor.~74~ This created ethnic divisions that dominate Fijian politics today.~74~

"Blackbirding"—the kidnapping or coercion of Pacific islanders for labor on Australian or Fijian plantations—operated with British complicity from the 1860s-1900s.~75~ While technically illegal after 1872, enforcement was minimal, and an estimated 60,000 islanders were recruited, many under false pretenses or by force.~75~ Conditions on plantations were brutal, mortality rates were high, and many never returned home.~75~

British and Australian authorities classified this as "labor recruiting," but contemporary observers recognized it as slavery under another name.~76~ Ships would arrive at

Chapter 8: The Caribbean and Pacific

Pacific islands, and through a combination of deception, alcohol, violence, and outright kidnapping, would collect laborers who were then transported to plantations and held in conditions of forced labor.^76^ Death rates on some voyages reached 30%, and plantation conditions killed many more.^76^

Summary Conclusion: Remembering the Forgotten

The Caribbean and Pacific regions experienced some of British imperialism's worst brutalities, yet these crimes remain marginalized in British historical memory.^1,6^ Caribbean slavery's super-exploitation generated enormous wealth while killing millions.^2,10^ Australian colonization brought genocide to Aboriginal peoples through violence, disease, dispossession, and cultural destruction.^40,41^ Pacific peoples faced exploitation, kidnapping, and land theft.^73,75^

These aren't distant historical events but living legacies. Caribbean nations struggle with underdevelopment directly resulting from centuries of extractive colonialism and are demanding reparations Britain refuses to pay.^7,33^ Aboriginal Australians experience poverty, health disparities, and continued marginalization resulting from genocide and dispossession—with only minimal efforts at reconciliation.^77^ Pacific island nations face existential threats from climate change caused largely by industrial development in nations that colonized them.^78^

Britain's refusal to acknowledge these legacies, to apologize, to provide reparations, or even to teach this history honestly represents ongoing injustice.^34,37^ The wealth extracted from Caribbean slavery remains in British institutions.^19^ The land stolen from Aboriginal peoples remains in settler hands.^51^ The artifacts looted from Pacific cultures sit in British museums.^79^ These are not resolved historical events but continuing colonial relationships that demand accountability.^80^

The recent reparations movements in the Caribbean and ongoing reconciliation efforts in Australia and New Zealand represent attempts to force historical accountability.^7,71^ They insist that history matters, that crimes have consequences, and that justice delayed is not justice denied.^80^ Britain's response will determine whether it can move beyond empire's legacies or whether it will continue benefiting from historical crimes while refusing to acknowledge them.^80^

Author's Notes Chapter 8

This chapter examines British imperialism in the Caribbean (focusing on slavery and its aftermath) and the Pacific (focusing on indigenous genocide in Australia and New Zealand). These regions are often marginalized in British imperial history despite experiencing some of colonialism's most devastating impacts.

On Caribbean Slavery: The Caribbean was the epicenter of British slavery, with sugar plantations in Jamaica, Barbados,

Chapter 8: The Caribbean and Pacific

and other islands generating enormous wealth for British planters and merchants while inflicting systematic violence on enslaved Africans. Hilary Beckles' *Natural Rebels* (1989) documents the specific experiences of enslaved women, who faced both the violence endemic to slavery and sexual exploitation by slaveholders. Trevor Burnard's examination of Thomas Thistlewood's diaries (*Mastery, Tyranny, and Desire*, 2004) provides disturbing detail about daily violence on Jamaican plantations.

On Post-Emancipation Exploitation: The 1833 Abolition Act freed slaves but compensated owners rather than the enslaved, and established "apprenticeship" systems requiring freed slaves to continue working for former owners for years. Even after full freedom, Caribbean societies remained structured around plantation economies controlled by white elites, with freed slaves denied access to land and forced to work for wages insufficient for survival. Thomas Holt's *The Problem of Freedom* (1992) demonstrates that emancipation did not end exploitation but transformed it.

On Aboriginal Genocide: The destruction of Aboriginal peoples in Australia represents one of history's clearest cases of genocide—the deliberate destruction of populations through killing, dispossession, and cultural annihilation. Benjamin Madley's research on Tasmania documents near-complete extermination of the indigenous population through what he terms "genocide." Henry Reynolds' *An Indelible Stain?* (2001) examines whether Australian colonization constitutes genocide under international law, concluding that it meets the legal definition.

On the Stolen Generations: The forcible removal of Aboriginal children from their families, continuing into the 1970s, represented systematic cultural genocide. The 1997

Bringing Them Home report documented that between one-in-three and one-in-ten indigenous children were forcibly removed, experiencing abuse, neglect, and deliberate cultural erasure in government and missionary institutions. The trauma continues affecting Aboriginal communities today.

On Māori and the Treaty of Waitangi: British colonization of New Zealand differed from Australia in that Britain signed a treaty (1840) with Māori chiefs ostensibly recognizing Māori sovereignty and property rights. Yet British authorities systematically violated the treaty, seizing Māori land and waging wars against Māori who resisted. Claudia Orange's work on the treaty documents the fundamental disconnect between what Māori understood they were agreeing to and how British authorities interpreted and implemented the treaty.

On Forgotten Brutalities: The chapter's title refers to how Caribbean and Pacific violence are often marginalized in British historical memory despite their scale. British imperialism killed more people in these regions than in any single military conflict Britain fought in the 20th century, yet these deaths receive far less attention in British education and public discourse. This selective memory allows imperial nostalgia to persist unchallenged by evidence of imperialism's devastating violence.

CHAPTER NINE

Divide & Rule

Engineering Ethnic Conflict (1880-1960)

Divide and rule was not an accidental byproduct of British imperial administration but a deliberate strategy employed systematically across the empire.[1] British authorities consciously created, manipulated, or exacerbated ethnic, religious, and communal divisions to facilitate colonial control and prevent unified resistance.[1,2] The logic was straightforward: populations divided against each other were easier to govern and less likely to unite against British rule.[2] This policy was implemented through census classifications that hardened fluid identities into fixed categories, through legal systems that treated different groups unequally, through favoritism that elevated some communities over others, and through deliberate manipulation of historical grievances.˄3,4˄ The human cost was catastrophic: millions died in communal violence during British rule and in the conflicts that followed independence.˄5˄ The political cost persists today: the borders, ethnic divisions, and communal conflicts that plague post-colonial states from India to Kenya to Burma (modern day Myanmar) to Palestine can be traced directly to British divide-and-rule policies.˄6˄ This chapter examines how Britain deliberately engineered ethnic conflict across multiple continents, creating problems that continue to kill people decades after the empire's formal end.˄6˄

India: Partition's Deadly Legacy

British divide-and-rule policy in India was implemented systematically over centuries and culminated in the 1947 Partition that killed between one and two million people and displaced 15 million.˄7,8˄ The communal violence of Partition—Hindus, Muslims, and Sikhs killing each other in horrific massacres—is often portrayed as ancient hatred finally exploding, but this narrative is false.˄9˄ While religious differences existed, large-scale communal violence was largely a product of British policies that deliberately fostered Hindu-Muslim

Chapter 9: Divide & Rule

antagonism.^9,10^

The British census, first systematically implemented in the 1870s, played a crucial role in hardening religious identities.^11^ Census categories required Indians to identify primarily by religion, transforming complex, overlapping identities into fixed, mutually exclusive categories.^11^ The census counted "Hindus," "Muslims," "Sikhs," etc., as distinct populations, implying they were separate peoples with different interests rather than overlapping communities sharing geography, language, and culture.^11,12^

British authorities used census data to allocate government positions, educational opportunities, and political representation proportionally, creating zero-sum competition between religious communities.^13^ If Muslims received more positions in one province, Hindus in that province perceived it as discrimination. If Hindus dominated in another, Muslims felt marginalized.^13^ This framework transformed every administrative decision into a communal issue, fostering perpetual grievance and competition.^13^

British legal and administrative systems treated religious communities differently. Personal law—governing marriage, divorce, inheritance, and family matters—was organized along religious lines, with different courts and rules for Hindus, Muslims, and others.^14^ This made religion the primary legal identity and prevented the

Perfidious Albion

development of a common citizenship.^14^ It also allowed colonial authorities to play communities against each other by favoring one group's legal claims over another's.^14^

The introduction of separate electorates—where Muslims voted for Muslim representatives, Hindus for Hindu representatives—explicitly organized politics along communal lines.^15^ First implemented in 1909 and expanded in 1919, separate electorates meant politicians represented religious communities rather than geographic constituencies or ideological positions.^15^ This institutionalized communalism, making it impossible for political movements to transcend religious divisions.^15,16^

British officials explicitly articulated divide-and-rule strategy in internal correspondence. Secretary of State for India John Morley wrote in 1906 that British rule depended on "the division of religious feelings" and that supporting Muslim political organization would provide "a counterpoise to Hindu predominance."^17^ Governor-General Lord Minto noted that encouraging Muslim separate identity would create "a natural source of division... which we are bound in honesty to encourage."^17^ These weren't inadvertent consequences but deliberate policies.^17^

The creation and support of the Muslim League as a counterweight to the Indian National Congress was

Chapter 9: Divide & Rule

calculated strategy.^18^ British authorities encouraged Muslim political organization, provided official recognition and support, and portrayed the League as representing Muslim interests against Hindu-dominated Congress.^18^ This wasn't because British officials cared about Muslim rights—they consistently denied Muslim demands that didn't serve imperial interests—but because fostering Hindu-Muslim division weakened the independence movement.^18,19^

When independence became inevitable, Britain's rush to withdraw ensured the worst possible outcome. Lord Mountbatten, the last Viceroy, accelerated the independence timeline from June 1948 to August 1947, giving only months to implement Partition—the division of India into Hindu-majority India and Muslim-majority Pakistan.^20^ The boundary commission, chaired by lawyer Cyril Radcliffe who had never visited India, was given five weeks to draw borders dividing Bengal and Punjab.^21^

The resulting borders were arbitrary and catastrophic. Communities that had coexisted for centuries found themselves on opposite sides of new international borders.^22^ Radcliffe's lines divided Punjab—home to intermixed Hindu, Muslim, and Sikh populations—with little regard for settlement patterns, water resources, or economic integration.^21,22^ The eastern boundary in Bengal similarly ignored ground realities.^22^

Perfidious Albion

The Partition violence that followed killed between one and two million people in some of history's most brutal communal massacres.^7,8^ Entire train loads of refugees were slaughtered. Villages were burned with inhabitants inside. Women were raped, mutilated, and killed. The trauma was unprecedented in scale and intimacy—neighbors killing neighbors, communities that had lived peacefully for generations suddenly engaged in genocidal violence.^23^

British forces, still present during Partition, did little to prevent the violence. Some historians argue they could have stopped much of the killing had preventing it been a priority.^24^ But British authorities were focused on orderly withdrawal, not on protecting the populations they had ruled for two centuries.^24^ The speed of British departure ensured chaos, and the divide-and-rule policies had ensured populations were primed for violence.^24^

The legacy persists. India and Pakistan have fought four wars, possess nuclear weapons, and maintain hostile relations driven partly by Partition trauma.^25^ Kashmir remains disputed, claimed by both nations, with ongoing violence that has killed tens of thousands.^26^ The communal divisions British policies created continue to shape South Asian politics, with periodic outbreaks of Hindu-Muslim violence and political movements exploiting religious division.^27^

Chapter 9: Divide & Rule

Kenya: Kikuyu, Luo, and Manufactured Tribalism

British colonization of Kenya systematically created ethnic divisions where previously more fluid identities had existed.^28^ Pre-colonial Kenya was home to diverse peoples with overlapping identities based on clan, age-set, geography, and language, but these were not the fixed "tribal" categories that British administrators imposed.^28,29^

The British colonial state required legible categories for administration, so they created "tribes."^30^ Census takers, anthropologists, and administrators identified distinct groups—Kikuyu, Luo, Luhya, Kamba, etc.—and codified them as natural, unchanging ethnic groups.^30^ This process transformed fluid identities into rigid categories with supposed distinct characteristics, territories, and political interests.^30,31^

British authorities then allocated resources, land, and political representation based on these tribal categories.^32^ Different ethnic groups were assigned to different areas, creating geographic segregation. Access to education, government positions, and economic opportunities was often distributed along ethnic lines.^32^ This created zero-sum competition between groups for colonial favor and resources.^32^

The system of indirect rule, where British authorities governed through appointed chiefs and headmen, was

Perfidious Albion

organized tribally.^33^ Each "tribe" had chiefs who governed "their people" under British supervision.^33^ These chiefs were often selected not for traditional legitimacy but for willingness to collaborate with colonial authorities.^33^ The system gave chiefs incentives to emphasize ethnic boundaries and loyalty to strengthen their own positions.^33,34^

Land policy was explicitly organized along ethnic lines. The "White Highlands"—prime agricultural land—was reserved for European settlers.^35^ Africans were confined to "tribal reserves," each designated for a specific ethnic group.^35^ The Kikuyu, whose traditional territories included much of the prime land seized for white settlement, were pushed into overcrowded reserves, creating grievances that would fuel the Mau Mau uprising.^36^

During the Mau Mau rebellion (1952-1960), British authorities deliberately exploited ethnic divisions.^37^ They portrayed Mau Mau as a specifically Kikuyu phenomenon—"Kikuyu savagery"—rather than as nationalist resistance to colonial rule.^37^ They recruited loyalist Kikuyu and members of other ethnic groups to fight against Mau Mau, creating intra-Kikuyu violence and inter-ethnic tensions.^37,38^ The goal was preventing united African resistance.^38^

British authorities employed collective punishment against Kikuyu communities, implementing a pass

Chapter 9: Divide & Rule

system, forced villagization, and detention camps that imprisoned over 150,000 Kikuyu.^39^ Simultaneously, they recruited heavily from Luo, Kamba, and other groups for security forces, creating ethnic resentment and associating certain groups with colonial collaboration.^39^

At independence in 1963, Kenya inherited these manufactured ethnic divisions. Political parties organized along ethnic lines, with different groups competing for power and resources.^40^ The first post-independence government, led by Jomo Kenyatta (Kikuyu), favored Kikuyu communities in land distribution and government positions, generating resentment from other groups.^40^ Ethnic tensions, largely absent in pre-colonial Kenya, became central to Kenyan politics.^41^

Post-independence Kenya has experienced periodic ethnic violence, particularly around elections. The 2007-2008 post-election violence killed over 1,100 people and displaced 600,000, largely along ethnic lines.^42^ While post-independence politicians have exploited these divisions, the divisions themselves were created and institutionalized by British colonial rule.^42^

Palestine: Creating Permanent Conflict

British rule in Palestine (1917-1948) created one of the world's most intractable conflicts through policies that deliberately fostered Jewish-Arab antagonism while British authorities positioned themselves as necessary arbiters.^43^ The Balfour Declaration (1917), promising British support for "a Jewish homeland in Palestine" while supposedly protecting Arab rights, was contradictory and designed to be.^44^ It committed Britain to mutually incompatible goals, ensuring perpetual conflict requiring British presence to manage.^44^

British authorities implemented separate legal systems for Jews and Arabs, maintained separate education systems, and governed through different administrative structures.^45^ Jews developed parallel state institutions—the Jewish Agency, Haganah militia, and extensive self-governing bodies—that were tolerated or encouraged by British authorities.^45^ Arabs were governed through traditional notable families and religious authorities that British officials appointed and manipulated.^45,46^

British immigration policy allowed large-scale Jewish migration to Palestine despite Arab opposition, radically changing the demographic balance.^47^ In 1917, Jews comprised about 10% of Palestine's population; by 1947, they were about 33%.^47^ This demographic transformation was achieved through British policy facilitating Jewish immigration while Arab political demands were ignored.^47^

Chapter 9: Divide & Rule

British authorities armed and trained Jewish security forces while suppressing Arab armed resistance.˄48˄ The Haganah, officially illegal, was tolerated and sometimes cooperated with British forces.˄48˄ Arab armed groups were crushed with extreme violence during the Arab Revolt (1936-1939), when British forces killed approximately 5,000 Arabs and implemented collective punishment including house demolitions, detentions, and executions.˄49˄

When Jewish groups turned to violence against British rule (1945-1947), Britain suddenly discovered that maintaining control was untenable and rapidly withdrew.˄50˄ The withdrawal was designed to ensure conflict. Britain refused to implement any coherent transition plan, instead handing the problem to the United Nations, which proposed partition.˄50˄ The partition plan allocated 55% of Palestine to a Jewish state despite Jews owning only 7% of the land and comprising 33% of the population.˄51˄

The 1948 war that followed British withdrawal killed thousands and created approximately 750,000 Palestinian refugees through expulsion and flight—the Nakba (catastrophe) that remains central to Palestinian identity.˄52˄ The conflict continues today, having killed tens of thousands and displaced millions. While many parties bear responsibility for its continuation, the conflict's origins lie in British policies deliberately designed to foster Jewish-Arab antagonism while Britain positioned itself as indispensable mediator.^53^

Cyprus: Greeks, Turks, and Imperial Manipulation
British rule in Cyprus (1878-1960) transformed an island where Greek and Turkish Cypriots had largely coexisted into one divided by ethnic conflict.^54^ British authorities implemented policies that emphasized ethnic difference, created separate institutions, and fostered antagonism that erupted in violence and eventual partition.^54,55^

The British census classified Cypriots by religion/ethnicity—Greek Orthodox and Muslim Turkish—rather than by language, geography, or other identities.^56^ This created the framework for ethnic politics. British authorities governed through separate communal institutions, with different schools, different legal systems for personal law, and different political representation for Greeks and Turks.^56,57^

British policy deliberately fostered Turkish Cypriot fear of Greek Cypriot domination to prevent unified anti-colonial resistance.^58^ When Greek Cypriots began demanding enosis (union with Greece), British authorities encouraged Turkish Cypriot opposition, providing support and recognition to Turkish political organizations and portraying Turkish Cypriots as needing British protection.^58^

During the EOKA insurgency (1955-1959), Greek Cypriot

Chapter 9: Divide & Rule

guerrillas fought for independence and union with Greece.^59^ British forces suppressed the insurgency with extreme violence—torture, collective punishment, detention camps, and executions.^59^ Simultaneously, British authorities recruited Turkish Cypriots for security forces and encouraged formation of Turkish Cypriot paramilitary groups.^60^ This created inter-communal violence, with Greeks and Turks killing each other while both fought against or alongside British forces.^60^

British withdrawal in 1960 left Cyprus independent but deeply divided. The constitution imposed by Britain (negotiated with Greece and Turkey) included provisions guaranteeing Turkish Cypriot veto power and separate communal institutions.^61^ This framework ensured political deadlock and continued ethnic tension.^61^

Intercommunal violence erupted in 1963-1964, with UN peacekeepers deployed.^62^ The 1974 Turkish invasion, triggered by a Greek-backed coup, resulted in Cyprus's partition into Greek and Turkish zones that persists today.^63^ While Turkey's invasion was the immediate cause of partition, the ethnic divisions and antagonism that made invasion thinkable were products of British colonial policy.^63^

Burma (Myanmar): Bamar, Karen, and Colonial

Fragmentation

British colonization of Burma (1824-1948) deliberately fragmented what had been a relatively integrated kingdom into antagonistic ethnic groups.^64^ The Konbaung Dynasty that Britain defeated ruled a multi-ethnic polity where various peoples—Bamar, Karen, Kachin, Shan, and others—were integrated into common administrative and cultural systems.^64,65^

British authorities divided Burma into "Ministerial Burma" (Bamar heartland) directly administered by colonial officials, and "Frontier Areas" (Karen, Kachin, Chin, Shan territories) governed under separate systems.^66^ This geographic and administrative separation created distinct political identities and interests where previously there had been variation within unity.^66^

British recruitment policies explicitly favored ethnic minorities for military and police forces while excluding Bamar.^67^ Karen, Kachin, and Chin peoples were recruited extensively, creating military forces predominantly composed of ethnic minorities commanded by British officers.^67^ This served multiple purposes: it prevented Bamar-dominated military forces that might resist colonial rule, and it created ethnic resentment as Bamar experienced policing and military control by ethnic minority forces.^67,68^

Chapter 9: Divide & Rule

Christian missionaries, operating with British support, concentrated efforts on ethnic minority populations, particularly Karen.^69^ Significant numbers of Karen converted to Christianity, creating religious divisions that overlapped with ethnic ones.^69^ British authorities favored Christian Karen for education and government positions, creating both privilege and resentment.^69,70^

Economic policy reinforced divisions. Bamar areas were integrated into export agriculture (rice), while frontier areas remained relatively isolated.^71^ Indian immigration, encouraged by British authorities, led to Indians dominating urban commerce and money-lending, generating anti-Indian sentiment while British authorities remained above the fray.^71^

During World War II, these divisions became violent. The British recruited heavily from Karen and other minorities to fight the Japanese, while the Burma Independence Army (predominantly Bamar) initially collaborated with the Japanese.^72^ This created civil war conditions, with Karen and Bamar forces fighting each other while Japanese and British forces competed for control.^72^ The Burma Independence Army switched sides in 1945, but the damage was done—Karen and other minorities viewed Bamar as collaborators, while Bamar resented minority cooperation with colonial forces.^72,73^

British withdrawal in 1948 was rapid and chaotic, leaving unresolved the constitutional status of ethnic minority regions.^74^ Karen leaders had requested guarantees of autonomy or a separate state, but Britain granted independence without resolving these issues.^74^ Civil war began almost immediately, with Karen, Kachin, and other groups fighting for autonomy against the Bamar-dominated central government.^75^

These conflicts continue today. Burma/Myanmar has experienced continuous civil war since independence, with ethnic minority groups fighting for autonomy or independence.^76^ The military regime that has dominated Myanmar politics since 1962 has committed extensive human rights violations against ethnic minorities, including genocide against the Rohingya.^77^ While the military regime bears direct responsibility, the ethnic divisions it exploits were created and institutionalized by British colonial policy.^76,77^

British Malaya: Chinese, Malays, and Indians

British colonization of Malaya created ethnic divisions through immigration policy and administrative practices that organized society along rigid racial lines.^78^ Pre-colonial Malaya was ethnically diverse but not organized into the fixed racial categories that British rule imposed.^78^

British authorities imported massive numbers of

Chapter 9: Divide & Rule

Chinese and Indian laborers to work rubber plantations and tin mines.^79^ By independence, Malaya's population was approximately 50% Malay, 37% Chinese, and 12% Indian—dramatic demographic transformation from the predominantly Malay population of the early 19th century.^80^ This immigration was deliberately encouraged to provide cheap labor while preventing any single ethnic group from achieving overwhelming demographic dominance.^79,80^

British administrative policy organized society explicitly along racial lines.^81^ Different ethnic groups were subject to different laws, had different legal statuses, and were governed through separate institutions.^81^ Malays were considered indigenous and given certain privileges (reserved land, preference for government positions), but were also stereotyped as lazy and backward.^82^ Chinese were seen as industrious but politically dangerous. Indians were imported labor with minimal rights.^82^

Economic roles were racialized. Malays were predominantly rural agriculturalists. Chinese dominated urban commerce, tin mining, and some rubber plantations. Indians worked rubber estates and provided administrative labor.^83^ This economic segregation created mutual dependence but also resentment, with each group perceiving the others as competition or exploitation.^83^

Education systems were segregated by ethnicity. British authorities maintained separate schools for Malays (teaching in Malay), Chinese (teaching in Mandarin or dialects), and English-medium schools (primarily for elites and Europeans).[84] This prevented development of common identity or shared language, ensuring each ethnic group maintained separate cultural identity.[84]

During the Malayan Emergency (1948-1960), British authorities fought a communist insurgency that was predominantly Chinese.[85] The British response included mass detention of Chinese in "New Villages"—concentration camps that imprisoned approximately 500,000 people.[86] These operations, while directed at communist insurgents, affected entire Chinese communities and generated ethnic resentment.[86]

British authorities portrayed the conflict as racial—Chinese communists versus Malay loyalty—rather than as class-based insurgency.[87] They armed and trained Malay security forces, created Malay-dominated Home Guard units, and presented the conflict as defending Malays against Chinese.[87] This racialization of political conflict ensured ethnic tensions would persist.[87]

At independence in 1957 (fully 1963 with formation of Malaysia), the new nation inherited these ethnic divisions. The constitution included provisions protecting Malay "special rights" while guaranteeing Chinese and Indian citizenship.[88] This framework

Chapter 9: Divide & Rule

institutionalized ethnic politics, with political parties organized along racial lines and politics centered on ethnic competition for resources and power.^88^

The result was periodic ethnic violence, most dramatically in the May 13, 1969 riots that killed hundreds (officially 196, likely more) in Kuala Lumpur.^89^ The government responded with affirmative action policies favoring Malays (Bumiputera policies) and restrictions on political discussion of ethnic issues.^90^ While ostensibly addressing Malay grievances, these policies institutionalized ethnic preferences and ensured continued ethnic politics.^90^

Malaysia remains divided along ethnic lines today, with political parties, economic policies, and social relations organized around the racial categories British colonialism created.^91^ Periodic ethnic tensions and political crises revolve around these divisions.^91^

The Middle East: Borders Drawn in Sand

British and French division of the Ottoman Empire after World War I created states with borders deliberately designed to maximize ethnic and religious division.^92^ The Sykes-Picot Agreement (1916) divided the region into spheres of influence without regard for existing political entities, ethnic distributions, or sectarian boundaries.^92,93^

Perfidious Albion

British-created Iraq combined three Ottoman provinces—Mosul (predominantly Kurdish), Baghdad (Sunni Arab), and Basra (Shia Arab)—into an artificial state with no historical precedent.[94] The borders ensured no ethnic or sectarian group would dominate, requiring British presence to arbitrate among factions.[94] British authorities installed a Sunni Arab minority government over a Shia Arab majority and restive Kurdish population, guaranteeing instability.[94,95]

In Jordan (Transjordan), Britain created a kingdom from territory that had no historical unity, installing the Hashemite monarchy as reward for Arab Revolt participation.[96] The artificial state was designed to be dependent on British support against more powerful neighbors.[96]

Throughout the Middle East, British authorities employed divide-and-rule by favoring certain sects or ethnicities over others.[97] In Iraq, they favored Sunni Arabs for government and military positions despite Shia Arab majority.[97] They manipulated Kurdish aspirations for autonomy while preventing actual Kurdish independence.[98] They played Christian minorities against Muslim majorities and vice versa.[98]

The legacy is clear: Iraq has experienced decades of ethnic and sectarian conflict, including genocide against Kurds, civil war between Sunni and Shia, and state

Chapter 9: Divide & Rule

collapse.^99^ Syria's civil war, while recent in outbreak, is partly rooted in the sectarian divisions British and French policies created.^100^ The entire region remains plagued by conflicts along ethnic, sectarian, and national lines drawn by colonial powers.^100^

Summary Conclusion: The Death Toll of Division

Divide-and-rule was not a mistake but a strategy, not an unintended consequence but deliberate policy.^1,2^ British authorities consciously created, manipulated, and exacerbated ethnic, religious, and communal divisions across the empire because divided populations were easier to control.^2^ Internal correspondence, policy documents, and published memoirs demonstrate that British officials understood what they were doing and did it anyway.^101^

The human cost is incalculable. Partition of India killed one to two million people and displaced 15 million.^7,8^ Ethnic conflicts in Kenya, Uganda, Nigeria, and other African states have killed hundreds of thousands.^102^ The Israel-Palestine conflict has killed tens of thousands and displaced millions.^52^ Burma's civil wars have killed and displaced hundreds of thousands.^76^ Malaysia's ethnic riots killed hundreds.^89^ Cyprus remains divided.^63^ Iraq experienced genocidal ethnic cleansing.^99^

These conflicts didn't emerge from ancient hatreds but

from colonial policies that deliberately fostered division.[103] While post-colonial leaders bear responsibility for exploiting these divisions, the divisions themselves were British creations.[103] The census categories, separate institutions, differentiated legal systems, ethnic favoritism, and zero-sum resource competition were colonial policies designed to prevent unified resistance.[3,4,103]

Britain has never acknowledged this. No apologies have been offered. No reparations paid. No serious effort made to help resolve the conflicts British policies created.[104] Instead, British historical memory treats these divisions as natural features of the colonized societies rather than as British constructions.[104] The narrative claims Britain brought order to chaotic, divided societies, inverting reality—Britain created division in societies that had managed diversity for centuries.[104]

The divide-and-rule legacy persists because the institutions, borders, and ethnic categories created by British colonialism remain.[105] Post-colonial states inherited administrative systems organized along ethnic lines, borders that divided ethnic groups or combined antagonistic ones, and constitutions that institutionalized ethnic politics.[105] Changing these structures would require acknowledging their origins, but that acknowledgment would implicate Britain in

Chapter 9: Divide & Rule

ongoing conflicts.˄105˄

Understanding divide-and-rule is essential to understanding contemporary conflicts in South Asia, Africa, the Middle East, and Southeast Asia.˄106˄ These conflicts weren't inevitable products of ethnic or religious differences but deliberate constructions of colonial policy.˄106˄ They could have been prevented. They could be resolved. But doing so requires acknowledging their origins in British imperial strategy—an acknowledgment Britain has consistently refused to make.˄104,106˄

Author's Notes Chapter 9

This chapter examines how British colonial authorities deliberately created, exacerbated, or exploited ethnic and communal divisions to maintain control, with particular focus on India/Pakistan partition, British Guiana's racial politics, and various African contexts. The legacy of these British-engineered divisions continues producing violence and instability in former colonies.

On "Divide and Rule": This was explicit British colonial strategy, not incidental outcome. Mahmood Mamdani's *Citizen and Subject* (1996) documents how British colonial authorities in Africa created rigid ethnic categories, elevated some groups over others, and institutionalized divisions through law and administration. The strategy aimed to prevent unified anti-colonial resistance by fostering competition and conflict among colonized groups. While divisions often pre-existed colonialism, British rule hardened, politicized, and weaponized them.

On Partition Violence (1947): The partition of India and Pakistan killed approximately one million people and displaced 15 million in one of history's largest forced migrations. Yasmin Khan's *The Great Partition* (2007) and Urvashi Butalia's *The Other Side of Silence* (2000) document the horrific violence—massacres, sexual violence, forced conversions—that accompanied partition. British authorities share responsibility: the partition plan was hastily implemented with inadequate security provisions, borders were drawn carelessly dividing communities, and British forces withdrew precipitously rather than maintaining order during the transition.

On British Guiana: Stephen Rabe's *U.S. Intervention in British Guiana* (2005) documents how British and American intelligence services deliberately inflamed racial tensions between Afro-Guyanese and Indo-Guyanese populations to prevent Cheddi Jagan's multi-racial party from governing. The racial violence that resulted (killing hundreds in the early 1960s) was not spontaneous communal conflict but manufactured crisis serving British and American strategic interests.

On Kenya: British authorities in Kenya exploited and hardened divisions between ethnic groups, and between "loyal" Africans and Mau Mau "terrorists," to divide opposition to colonial rule. Caroline Elkins' *Imperial Reckoning* (2005) documents how British authorities forced hundreds of thousands into detention camps, extracted "confessions" through torture, and created networks of informants that sowed lasting distrust within Kenyan communities.

Historiographical Note: Earlier scholarship sometimes portrayed communal conflicts as arising from ancient ethnic hatreds that colonialism unsuccessfully tried to mediate. More recent scholarship—particularly post-

Chapter 9: Divide & Rule

colonial studies and work by historians from formerly colonized regions—demonstrates that many supposedly ancient hatreds were actually recently constructed or intensified through colonial policies. This doesn't deny that pre-colonial conflicts existed, but recognizes that colonialism fundamentally transformed their nature and intensity for colonial authorities' benefit.

On Continuing Effects: The divisions British colonialism created or intensified continue producing violence: India-Pakistan conflict, Hutu-Tutsi tensions in Rwanda (influenced by Belgian colonial policies similar to British), ethnic politics in Kenya and other African nations, and racial divisions in Guyana and Trinidad. Understanding colonialism's role in creating these divisions is essential for addressing their ongoing effects.

CHAPTER TEN

Suppressing Freedom

The Long War Against Independence Movements (1919-1963)

Throughout the 20th century, as colonized peoples demanded freedom, Britain responded with systematic violence designed to crush independence movements and delay decolonization as long as possible.˄1˄ From Ireland's War of Independence to India's struggle for freedom, from Malaya's Emergency to Kenya's Mau Mau uprising to Cyprus's EOKA insurgency, Britain employed remarkably consistent tactics: mass detention without trial, torture, collective punishment, emergency powers suspending civil liberties, censorship, and targeted killings.^2,3^ These counter-insurgency campaigns killed hundreds of thousands, displaced millions, and established precedents for state violence that influenced military and intelligence operations worldwide.^4^ Britain portrayed these conflicts as bringing order to chaos, civilization to savagery, and security against terrorism.^5^ The reality was that Britain was fighting against peoples demanding the same freedoms Britain claimed to represent, using methods that violated the very principles of law and humanity Britain professed to uphold.^5^ This chapter examines Britain's long war against freedom, documenting the violence employed to delay the inevitable collapse of empire and the human cost of Britain's refusal to relinquish control.^1,6^

Ireland: The Black and Tans and State Terror

Ireland's War of Independence (1919-1921) saw Britain deploy paramilitary forces—the Black and Tans and Auxiliaries—who conducted a campaign of state terrorism that shocked even some British observers.^7^ These forces, recruited from World War I veterans and given minimal training, were deployed to suppress the Irish Republican Army's guerrilla campaign for independence.^7,8^ They operated with effective impunity, conducting reprisal attacks, burning towns, killing civilians, and employing torture.^8^

Chapter 10: Suppressing Freedom

The Black and Tans (named for their mixed police and military uniforms) and Auxiliaries numbered approximately 10,000 men, supplementing the Royal Irish Constabulary.^9^ Unlike regular police or military forces, they operated under loosened rules of engagement and faced minimal accountability for violence against civilians.^9^ British authorities officially denied these forces conducted reprisals while privately authorizing and encouraging such actions.^10^

The pattern was consistent: after IRA attacks on British forces, the Black and Tans would retaliate against nearby towns or villages.^11^ On November 21, 1920—"Bloody Sunday"—the IRA killed 14 British intelligence officers in Dublin.^12^ That afternoon, Black and Tans fired into a crowd at a Gaelic football match in Croke Park, killing 14 civilians including a player.^12^ The same night, three IRA prisoners were killed "while attempting to escape."^12^ A week later, 18 Auxiliaries were killed in an IRA ambush at Kilmichael.^13^ In response, Auxiliaries burned much of Cork city center, destroying businesses and homes in a carefully orchestrated act of collective punishment.^14^

Similar attacks occurred across Ireland. In Balbriggan, Black and Tans burned the town and killed two civilians after an RIC officer was killed.^15^ In Thurles, they burned the town hall and businesses.^15^ In Trim, they destroyed much of the town center.^15^ These weren't isolated incidents by rogue elements but systematic policy—punishing communities for IRA actions to deter support for independence.^15,16^

Torture was routine. Suspects were beaten during interrogation, denied sleep, subjected to mock executions, and sometimes killed.^17^ Some were thrown from moving vehicles. Others were shot "while attempting to escape"—the standard cover story for extrajudicial execution.^17^ British forces operated under the tacit understanding that violence against Irish civilians and suspected IRA members would not be prosecuted.^17^

The death toll reached approximately 2,000: about 750 IRA members, 550 British forces (including police), and over 700 civilians.^18^ Thousands more were imprisoned, often without trial, in detention camps where conditions were harsh and abuse common.^19^ The conflict ended not because Britain defeated the IRA but because the violence became politically unsustainable in Britain, where public opinion was divided about the methods employed.^20^

The Anglo-Irish Treaty (1921) granted Ireland dominion status (full independence would come in 1937-1949), but partitioned the island, keeping six northern counties under British control.^21^ This partition, imposed against the wishes of the Irish majority, created Northern Ireland—a Protestant-majority statelet within which a large Catholic minority was systematically discriminated

Chapter 10: Suppressing Freedom

against.^21^ The partition and its legacy of sectarian division led to decades of continued violence, including "The Troubles" (1968-1998) that killed over 3,500 people.^22^

India: From Amritsar to Quit India

We have discussed the 1919 Amritsar Massacre in Chapter 5, but India's independence struggle involved decades of British suppression beyond that single atrocity.^23^ British authorities employed a sophisticated apparatus of repression combining emergency laws, mass detention, censorship, and selective violence to delay independence as long as possible.^24^

The Rowlatt Acts (1919) allowed detention without trial, arrest without warrant, and trials without juries for those suspected of sedition.^25^ These laws were imposed despite unanimous opposition from Indian legislators in the Imperial Legislative Council—a stark demonstration that Indian opinion was irrelevant to British policy.^25^ The Acts remained in force throughout the independence struggle, providing legal cover for mass repression.^25^

Gandhi's non-violent civil disobedience campaigns were met with mass arrests and brutal police violence.^26^ The Salt March (1930), where Gandhi led thousands to the sea to make salt in defiance of British monopoly, resulted in over 60,000 arrests.^27^ At Dharasana, police attacked non-violent protesters with steel-tipped lathis (batons), fracturing skulls and breaking bones while protesters refused to resist.^28^ American journalist Webb Miller's eyewitness account shocked the world, but British authorities continued the violence.^28^

The Quit India Movement (1942), launched during World War II when Britain was fighting fascism, demanded immediate independence.^29^ Britain's response was overwhelming repression. The entire leadership of the Indian National Congress was arrested and imprisoned without trial.^30^ Police and military forces fired on demonstrations, killing approximately 1,000 protesters.^30^ Collective fines were imposed on villages, and entire communities were punished through confiscation of property and mass detentions.^30^

British authorities employed agents provocateurs and intelligence operations to infiltrate and undermine independence movements.^31^ Censorship was pervasive—newspapers were shut down, political literature was banned, and discussing independence could result in imprisonment.^32^ The British portrayed independence activists as criminals or terrorists, not as people demanding freedom.^32^

Throughout this period, Britain maintained that India wasn't ready for self-governance, that different

Chapter 10: Suppressing Freedom

communities would fight if British rule ended, and that British presence was necessary for stability.^33^ These were self-serving rationalizations: Britain was profitable for Britain, regardless of Indian suffering. When World War II devastated Britain's finances and made holding India militarily and economically untenable, Britain suddenly discovered that India was ready for independence.^34^

Malaya: The Emergency and New Villages

The Malayan Emergency (1948-1960) saw Britain fight a communist insurgency led primarily by ethnic Chinese guerrillas.^35^ Britain's response included one of the 20th century's largest forced population relocations, detention without trial of tens of thousands, extensive use of torture, and military operations that killed thousands.^36^

The "Emergency" label was itself propaganda—insurance policies didn't cover losses during wars but did during "emergencies."^37^ This was a war, but calling it an emergency served British economic interests.^37^ The conflict began when communist insurgents (the Malayan National Liberation Army) began attacking plantations, mines, and British forces, seeking to end colonial rule.^35^

Britain's response centered on "population control."^38^ British authorities believed the insurgents depended on support from Chinese rural communities, so they implemented forced relocation on a massive scale.[38] Approximately 500,000 people—mostly ethnic Chinese squatter farmers—were forcibly moved to "New Villages," concentration camps surrounded by barbed wire and guard towers.[39]

Life in the New Villages was regimented and controlled.[40] Residents needed passes to leave, faced curfews, and were subjected to constant surveillance and searches.[40] Food supplies were rationed to prevent excess that might be given to insurgents.[40] While some villages eventually developed into functioning communities, the initial years involved forced removal from land, inadequate housing, disrupted livelihoods, and military control over daily life.[40,41]

Detention without trial was used extensively. The Emergency Regulations allowed indefinite detention of anyone suspected of supporting communists.[42] Approximately 34,000 people were detained during the Emergency, many held for years without charge or trial.[42] Detention camps were harsh, with torture reported and conditions designed to break detainees' resistance.[42,43]

British and Commonwealth forces (including Malay, Gurkha, and British units) conducted extensive military operations in jungles where the insurgents operated.[44] These "search and destroy" missions killed

Chapter 10: Suppressing Freedom

approximately 7,000 insurgents and an unknown number of civilians caught in crossfire.ˆ44ˆ British forces sometimes engaged in summary executions, with soldiers shooting suspects and later claiming they were armed insurgents.ˆ45ˆ

Torture was systematic. Interrogators used beatings, sleep deprivation, stress positions, waterboarding, and psychological torture to extract information.ˆ46ˆ Some victims died. While officially prohibited, torture was so widespread that it was clearly policy rather than aberration.ˆ46ˆ The methods developed in Malaya would be exported to other colonial conflicts including Kenya and Northern Ireland.ˆ46,47ˆ

The Emergency ended in 1960 with communist defeat, but at tremendous human cost.ˆ48ˆ Approximately 11,000 people died: 6,710 insurgents, 2,478 civilians, 1,865 security forces.ˆ48ˆ These official figures likely undercount civilian deaths. Half a million people were forcibly relocated. Tens of thousands were detained. The "success" came through overwhelming force and population control that violated basic human rights.ˆ48ˆ

Kenya: Mau Mau and the Gulags

The Mau Mau uprising in Kenya (1952-1960) provoked Britain's most extreme counter-insurgency operation, involving detention camps that held over 150,000 people, systematic torture, extrajudicial killings, and collective punishment that devastated Kikuyu communities.[49] The official death toll was approximately 11,000 Mau Mau killed; the actual total was certainly much higher, possibly 20,000-50,000.[50]

Mau Mau emerged from Kikuyu grievances about land dispossession, economic exploitation, and political disenfranchisement under British rule.[51] The movement sought to expel European settlers and regain control of land seized during colonization.[51] British authorities portrayed Mau Mau as savage atavism—Kikuyu reverting to primitive barbarism—rather than as political resistance to colonial oppression.[52]

Britain declared a State of Emergency in October 1952, granting authorities sweeping powers.[53] Mass arrests began immediately. "Operation Jock Scott" rounded up suspected leaders; within months, thousands of Kikuyu were detained.[53] The detention system eventually held over 150,000 people—approximately 10% of the entire Kikuyu population.[49]

The detention camp system, which historian Caroline Elkins called "Britain's gulag," operated with three categories: those with minor suspicions against them, those requiring "rehabilitation," and those deemed hardcore requiring more extreme measures.[49] The goal was breaking resistance through a combination of forced labor, political indoctrination, and violence.[49]

Chapter 10: Suppressing Freedom

Torture was not incidental but central to the system.˄54˄ Techniques included severe beatings, sexual violence, forced labor to the point of collapse, starvation rations, stress positions, waterboarding, and psychological torture.˄54˄ Camp guards used violence as punishment, interrogation, and deterrent.˄54˄ Some detainees were castrated, burned with cigarettes, or subjected to electric shocks.˄54,55˄

The "dilution technique" involved separating Kikuyu from their communities and resettling them with other ethnic groups to break Kikuyu solidarity.˄56˄ Entire villages were demolished, and residents were forced into concentration villages surrounded by ditches, barbed wire, and guard posts.˄56˄ Movement required passes. Collective punishment meant that if Mau Mau activity occurred near a village, all residents faced punishment.˄56˄

British forces conducted military operations including aerial bombardment of suspected Mau Mau areas in forests and mountains.˄57˄ Ground forces conducted "pseudo-gangs"—British soldiers disguised as Mau Mau, sometimes with captured Mau Mau forced to cooperate, who infiltrated rebel groups and conducted assassinations.˄58˄ Summary execution was common; soldiers shot suspects and later claimed they were armed Mau Mau fighters.˄58,59˄

The conflict's racial character was stark. European

Perfidious Albion

settlers formed militias and conducted their own operations with official sanction.^60^ Kikuyu loyalists—those who opposed Mau Mau or were coerced into collaboration—were armed and used against their own communities.^60^ This created civil war within Kikuyu society, with casualties on all sides.^60^

Official statistics claimed 32 European settlers killed, 1,819 "loyalist" Africans killed, and 11,503 Mau Mau killed.^50^ These figures are certainly false. They ignore civilians killed in military operations, those who died from maltreatment in camps, and those who died from displacement and starvation.^50^ Realistic estimates suggest 20,000-50,000 deaths, overwhelmingly Kikuyu.^50^

The systematic destruction and concealment of documents when Kenya approached independence revealed consciousness of criminality.^61^ British authorities burned files documenting torture, killings, and camp operations.^61^ Surviving documents, discovered decades later, proved the systematic nature of abuse and that it was known and approved at high levels of British government.^61^

In 2013, Britain paid compensation to 5,228 Kenyans tortured during the Emergency—an admission, finally, that crimes had occurred.^62^ But most victims received nothing. Most perpetrators were never held accountable. The compensation was carefully framed to avoid

Chapter 10: Suppressing Freedom

admitting full responsibility or setting precedents for other colonial crimes.^62^

Cyprus: EOKA and the Dirty War

The Cyprus Emergency (1955-1959) saw Britain fight EOKA (Ethniki Organosis Kyprion Agoniston), a Greek Cypriot guerrilla organization seeking independence and union with Greece (enosis).^63^ British counter-insurgency operations included detention camps, torture, collective punishment, and targeted killings that created lasting bitterness and contributed to Cyprus's eventual partition.^63,64^

Cyprus was strategically valuable to Britain—a base for Middle East operations after withdrawal from Egypt.^65^ When Greek Cypriots demanded self-determination, Britain refused, claiming Cyprus could never be independent.^65^ EOKA began a campaign of bombings and assassinations targeting British forces and installations.^66^

Britain's response replicated tactics from Malaya and would soon be used in Kenya.^67^ Emergency regulations allowed detention without trial, curfews, censorship, and collective punishment.^67^ Approximately 3,000 suspected EOKA members or supporters were detained, many held in camps for years.^68^

Torture was systematic and documented. Detainees were beaten, subjected to waterboarding, forced into stress positions, and psychologically tortured.~69~ The European Commission of Human Rights investigated and found Britain guilty of torture and inhuman treatment.~70~ This was one of the first international legal findings against Britain for human rights violations, though Britain faced no real consequences.~70~

British forces conducted targeted killings of suspected EOKA members.~71~ While officially engaging armed guerrillas, evidence suggests many "killed in action" were actually executed after capture or assassination targets.~71~ Bodies would be displayed publicly as deterrents.~71~

Collective punishment was routine. Villages suspected of harboring EOKA faced mass detentions, property destruction, and curfews that prevented farming and normal life.~72~ The goal was making support for EOKA so costly that communities would withdraw cooperation.~72~

British intelligence operations included infiltration, informants recruited through coercion, and psychological operations.~73~ The dirty war included allegations of false-flag operations—violence attributed to EOKA that was actually British provocation designed to discredit the independence movement.~73~

Chapter 10: Suppressing Freedom

The conflict killed approximately 600 people: 100+ British forces, 200+ EOKA fighters, 300+ civilians (Greek and Turkish Cypriots).^74^ These deaths, the torture, and the fostering of Greek-Turkish antagonism poisoned Cyprus's politics.^74^ When independence came in 1960, Britain retained sovereign base areas and ensured the constitution created deadlock between Greek and Turkish Cypriots.^75^ The 1974 Turkish invasion and continuing partition are partly legacies of British policy during the Emergency.^75^

The Machinery of Repression: Common Tactics

Across these conflicts, British counter-insurgency employed remarkably consistent tactics that reveal systematic rather than improvised repression.^76^

Emergency Powers: Britain consistently declared "emergencies" or "states of emergency" granting authorities sweeping powers including detention without trial, suspension of habeas corpus, censorship, and collective punishment.^77^ These powers, justified as temporary measures for security, often lasted years or decades and became normalized.^77^

Mass Detention: Britain detained hundreds of thousands across these conflicts: Ireland's internment camps, India's mass arrests during Quit India, Malaya's 34,000 detainees, Kenya's 150,000+ in camps, Cyprus's 3,000.^78^ Detention without trial allowed authorities to imprison people indefinitely based on suspicion rather than evidence, violating fundamental legal principles Britain claimed to uphold.^78^

Torture: Systematic torture occurred in Ireland, Malaya, Kenya, and Cyprus (and in other conflicts not detailed here).^79^ Techniques were remarkably similar—beatings, stress positions, sleep deprivation, waterboarding, psychological torture—suggesting knowledge transfer between operations.^79^ The Compton Report (1971) investigating Northern Ireland claimed these were "interrogation in depth," not torture, establishing official terminology that euphemized abuse.^80^

Collective Punishment: Punishing entire communities for actions of resistance fighters violated international law but was standard British practice.^81^ Villages were fined, property was destroyed, populations were forcibly relocated, and restrictions were imposed on communities suspected of supporting insurgents.^81^

Information Control: Censorship prevented colonized peoples from knowing the extent of repression or organizing resistance.^82^ British authorities controlled newspapers, prohibited political literature, and imprisoned journalists and editors who criticized colonial rule.^82^ Meanwhile, British media often accepted official narratives portraying insurgents as terrorists and British forces as maintaining order.^82^

Chapter 10: Suppressing Freedom

Psychological Operations: Britain conducted sophisticated propaganda portraying independence movements as criminal, savage, or communist rather than as political resistance.^83^ Mau Mau was portrayed as atavistic cult, EOKA as terrorist organization, Malayan communists as foreign-influenced troublemakers— never as people seeking freedom from colonial rule.^83^

Divide and Rule: British counter-insurgency exploited ethnic, religious, and political divisions, recruiting local forces to fight their own people.^84^ Loyalist Kikuyu fought Mau Mau, Malays fought Chinese communists, Turkish Cypriots were armed against Greek Cypriots, Indians fought for Britain against other Indians.^84^ This created civil wars and lasting divisions beyond the immediate conflicts.^84^

The Personnel: Connecting the Dots

Key figures moved between these conflicts, transferring tactics and training others.^85^ General Sir Gerald Templer, celebrated as architect of Malayan Emergency "success," had served in Palestine and would advise on later operations.^86^ Brigadier Frank Kitson developed counter-insurgency doctrine in Kenya and Malaya, then applied it in Cyprus and Northern Ireland.^87^ Sir Arthur Young served in Malaya, then became Commissioner of Police in Cyprus.^88^

This wasn't coincidence but institutional knowledge

transfer. The Colonial Office, military staff colleges, and intelligence services maintained continuity of personnel and methods.^85,89^ What worked in one colony was adapted for another. Lessons learned suppressing freedom in India informed tactics in Malaya. Malayan methods were refined in Kenya. Kenyan operations influenced Cyprus. And eventually, these colonial methods came "home" to Northern Ireland.^89^

The Costs: Bodies and Burdens

The human cost of suppressing independence was staggering. Conservative estimates suggest:

- Ireland: 2,000+ dead, thousands detained
- India: Thousands killed over decades of resistance, hundreds of thousands imprisoned
- Malaya: 11,000+ dead, 500,000 forcibly relocated, 34,000 detained
- Kenya: 20,000-50,000 dead (realistic estimate), 150,000+ detained, entire communities destroyed
- Cyprus: 600+ dead, 3,000 detained, systematic torture

These figures represent documented deaths and detentions; the true totals—including those who died from conflict's indirect effects—are certainly higher.^90^

Chapter 10: Suppressing Freedom

The psychological costs are incalculable. Torture survivors carry lifelong trauma. Communities were fractured by collaboration and resistance. Families were destroyed. The violence and division these conflicts created persist in post-independence politics.^90^

The economic costs fell primarily on colonized populations. British military operations destroyed infrastructure, disrupted economies, and impoverished communities. The cost of suppressing independence was paid by those seeking freedom, not by the colonizers fighting to maintain control.^91^

Why Britain Lost: The Inevitable Collapse

Despite overwhelming force, Britain eventually lost all these conflicts. Independence came to Ireland (1921/1937), India (1947), Malaya (1957), Kenya (1963), and Cyprus (1960).^92^ Britain delayed freedom but couldn't prevent it permanently.

Several factors made colonial rule unsustainable. First, colonized peoples were determined to be free and willing to endure tremendous suffering to achieve it.^93^ Repression could suppress movements temporarily but couldn't eliminate the desire for independence.^93^

Second, the costs of maintaining empire escalated. Military operations were expensive. International criticism was damaging. Domestic British opinion was divided—many Britons questioned whether maintaining colonies was worth the violence required.ˆ94ˆ

Third, World War II fundamentally changed the global system. The war devastated Britain's economy and military capacity.ˆ95ˆ The United States and Soviet Union—both opposed to traditional European colonialism (for different reasons)—became superpowers.ˆ95ˆ The UN Charter's principles of self-determination created international norms that made colonialism increasingly illegitimate.ˆ95ˆ

Fourth, the violence required to suppress independence contradicted British claims about democracy and human rights.ˆ96ˆ Britain couldn't simultaneously claim to represent Western civilization while torturing detainees and massacring civilians.ˆ96ˆ The contradiction became untenable, especially when documented by journalists and human rights observers.ˆ96ˆ

Summary Conclusion: The Last Gasps of Empire

The suppression of independence movements from 1919-1963 represents Britain fighting against the inevitable collapse of empire. The violence employed—detention without trial, torture, collective punishment, and mass killing—revealed that empire could only be maintained through force, not consent.ˆ1ˆ Every tactic Britain deployed contradicted the values Britain claimed to represent.ˆ97ˆ

Chapter 10: Suppressing Freedom

The ultimate futility is clear: despite decades of violence, despite hundreds of thousands killed and millions detained, Britain lost its empire anyway.˄92˄ The colonies became independent. The people Britain tortured, imprisoned, and tried to break became citizens of free nations. The movements Britain called terrorism became founding narratives of independent states.˄98˄

Britain has never fully acknowledged this history. The torture, the camps, the killings remain marginalized in British historical memory.˄99˄ When forced to acknowledge specific crimes—like compensating Kenyan torture victims—Britain frames them as isolated incidents rather than systematic policy.˄99˄ The documents destroyed, the cover-ups maintained, and the refusal to conduct comprehensive truth and reconciliation processes all demonstrate continuing denial.˄99˄

For the colonized peoples who fought for freedom, this history is central to national identity. Ireland commemorates its independence struggle. India celebrates freedom fighters Britain called terrorists. Kenya honors Mau Mau. These aren't distant history but living memory shaping how these nations see themselves and their relationship with Britain.˄100˄

Understanding Britain's long war against independence is essential to understanding both how empire ended and why its legacies persist. The violence Britain employed created lasting trauma and division. The borders drawn during hasty withdrawals created ongoing conflicts. The refusal to acknowledge crimes prevents genuine reconciliation.^100^ Britain's suppression of freedom movements was ultimately futile, but its effects continue to shape post-colonial realities today.^100^

Author's Notes Chapter 10

This chapter examines British counterinsurgency operations against independence movements from the post-WWI period through decolonization, focusing on Palestine, Malaya, Kenya, Cyprus, and Aden. The chapter argues that Britain consistently deployed systematic violence—detention without trial, torture, collective punishment, and extrajudicial killing—to suppress legitimate demands for self-determination.

On the Pattern Across Theaters: Despite different contexts, British counterinsurgency operations shared common features: mass detention in camps, systematic torture during interrogation, collective punishments targeting civilians, censorship and propaganda, and minimal accountability for abuses. John Newsinger's *British Counterinsurgency* (2002) and David French's *The British Way in Counter-Insurgency* (2011) document these patterns across multiple conflicts, showing they represented deliberate policy rather than isolated misconduct.

On Kenya (Mau Mau Emergency): This remains the best-documented case of systematic British abuses during counterinsurgency. David Anderson's *Histories of the Hanged* (2005) focuses on judicial killings, documenting that British authorities hanged over 1,000 Kenyans—more than any other British colony during decolonization. Caroline Elkins'

Chapter 10: Suppressing Freedom

Imperial Reckoning (2005) documents the detention camp system where over 150,000 Kenyans were held, many tortured. The 2011 discovery of concealed archives (discussed further in Chapter 17) provided documentary evidence of British officials' knowledge and approval of systematic torture.

On Malaya: The Malayan Emergency (1948-60) is often portrayed in British accounts as "successful" counterinsurgency demonstrating that British tactics could defeat communist insurgency. Yet this success came through systematic detention of hundreds of thousands, widespread torture, forced resettlement of rural populations into "New Villages" (concentration camps by another name), and extensive use of collective punishment. The insurgency's military defeat did not make these tactics ethically acceptable or legally justified.

On Cyprus: British operations against EOKA independence fighters involved extensive torture, with techniques including beatings, near-drowning, electric shocks, and mock executions. When complaints surfaced, British authorities denied the practices, blamed "bad apples," and resisted accountability. The pattern mirrors British responses to torture allegations in other conflicts—deny, minimize, avoid prosecution.

On the Rhetoric of "Terrorism": British authorities consistently characterized independence movements as "terrorist" organizations engaged in illegitimate violence, contrasting them with British "security forces" maintaining order. This rhetorical strategy delegitimized colonized peoples' demands for self-determination and justified British violence as defensive. Yet from colonized peoples' perspectives, they were fighting for freedom from foreign domination—a legitimate goal under international law (particularly after the UN Declaration on Decolonization,

1960).

Methodological Note: Much of our knowledge about British counterinsurgency abuses comes from former victims' testimonies, investigative journalism, and recently declassified archives. British official histories typically minimize abuses, characterizing them as isolated incidents. The systematic pattern evident across multiple conflicts over decades suggests that abuse was policy rather than aberration, even when officially denied.

CHAPTER ELEVEN

Partitions and Their Bloody Aftermath

Dividing and Departing (1921-1948)

When Britain could no longer maintain control over territories, it frequently responded by dividing them—creating new borders that separated previously integrated populations, often along religious or ethnic lines.^1^ These partitions were presented as solutions to intractable communal conflicts, but the conflicts themselves were often British creations, and the partitions were designed primarily to serve British strategic interests rather than the welfare of affected populations.[1,2] The three major British partitions—Ireland (1921), Palestine (1947), and India (1947)—share disturbing similarities: borders drawn hastily by people with minimal local knowledge, populations given little say in decisions affecting their futures, inadequate preparation for the human consequences, and British authorities withdrawing rapidly while violence exploded.[3] The death toll from these partitions numbers in the millions, with India's Partition alone killing 1-2 million people and displacing 15 million.[4] The conflicts created by partition persist today: Northern Ireland experienced decades of violence, Israel-Palestine remains unresolved after 75 years, and India-Pakistan have fought multiple wars and maintain hostile nuclear-armed confrontation.[5] This chapter examines Britain's partitions as deliberate policy choices that prioritized imperial interests over human life, creating lasting divisions and conflicts that continue to kill people generations later.[6]

Ireland: The Manufactured Statelet

The partition of Ireland in 1921 created Northern Ireland, a political entity that had never existed and that most Irish people opposed.[7] The partition was not a recognition of natural divisions but a strategic decision to retain British control over part of Ireland while conceding the rest to independence.[8] The border

Chapter 11: Partitions Aftermath

drawn was designed to maximize territory under British control while maintaining a Protestant majority that would support continued union with Britain.^8,9^

The Government of Ireland Act 1920, passed by Westminster without Irish consent, divided Ireland into two Home Rule territories: Northern Ireland (six counties) and Southern Ireland (26 counties).^10^ The southern parliament was never established—Irish nationalists rejected partition and established an independent Irish state instead.^11^ But Northern Ireland was imposed and maintained despite majority Irish opposition to partition.^11^

The border's design reveals its political rather than natural character. The six counties included in Northern Ireland (Antrim, Armagh, Down, Fermanagh, Londonderry, Tyrone) were selected to maximize territory while maintaining a Protestant majority of approximately 65%.^12^ If the historic province of Ulster (nine counties) had been taken, Protestants would have been only 55% and Protestant dominance would have been insecure.^12^ If fewer counties were included, less territory would remain under British control.^12^ The six-county compromise prioritized British strategic interests over the preferences of people living there.^9,12^

The border itself was arbitrary and destructive. It divided counties, split communities, separated farmers from

Perfidious Albion

their fields, and created an international frontier where none had existed.^13^ Towns were divided—Pettigo was split between Donegal and Fermanagh. Railway lines were cut. Economic networks were severed.^13^ The border created immediate practical problems and long-term economic distortions.^13^

More fundamentally, partition created a Catholic minority of approximately 35% within Northern Ireland who opposed the state's existence and were systematically discriminated against.^14^ The Northern Ireland government, dominated by Protestant unionists, implemented policies ensuring Protestant political and economic dominance: gerrymandering electoral boundaries, discriminatory housing allocation, exclusion of Catholics from government employment, and tolerance of discrimination in private employment.^14,15^

The result was a state with a built-in structural conflict between a Protestant majority determined to maintain union with Britain and a Catholic minority demanding equality or reunification with Ireland.^16^ This wasn't ancient hatred but the predictable consequence of creating a state where a large minority fundamentally rejected its legitimacy.^16^

Violence marked partition from the beginning. Between 1920 and 1922, approximately 500 people were killed in sectarian violence in Northern Ireland, with Catholics

Chapter 11: Partition's Aftermath

suffering disproportionately.^17^ Pogroms in Belfast forced thousands of Catholics from their homes and jobs.^17^ The government established the Ulster Special Constabulary—an almost entirely Protestant paramilitary police force—that engaged in attacks on Catholic communities.^18^

The Northern Ireland government ruled through emergency powers that allowed detention without trial, arrest without warrant, and severe restrictions on civil liberties.^19^ These "temporary" emergency powers, introduced in 1922, remained in force until 1972—a fifty-year "emergency."^19^ They were used almost exclusively against the Catholic minority, creating a permanent state of siege.^19^

Partition's failure became undeniable in the late 1960s when Catholic civil rights marches demanding equal treatment were met with police violence and Protestant mob attacks.^20^ This sparked "The Troubles"—three decades of violence (1968-1998) that killed over 3,500 people, injured tens of thousands, and devastated communities.^21^ While many forces contributed to the Troubles, the conflict's roots lie in partition: the creation of a state that a large minority opposed and within which systematic discrimination was structural.^21,22^

The Good Friday Agreement (1998) brought an official end to the Troubles, but Northern Ireland remains divided.^23^ Separate Catholic and Protestant neighborhoods, divided schools, peace walls separating communities, and political parties organized along sectarian lines all testify to partition's enduring legacy.^23^ Brexit's impact on the Irish border (2020-present) demonstrates that partition remains a source of instability and conflict a century after its imposition.^24^

Palestine: The Impossible Mandate

The partition of Palestine represents perhaps Britain's most cynical imperial act—creating a deliberately unsustainable situation that guaranteed perpetual conflict.^25^ The British Mandate for Palestine (1920-1948) was based on contradictory promises: the Balfour Declaration promising support for a Jewish homeland, and commitments to Arab populations not to prejudice their rights.^26^ These promises were mutually incompatible, and British authorities knew it.^26,27^

Britain facilitated large-scale Jewish immigration to Palestine despite Arab opposition.^28^ The Jewish population increased from approximately 10% of Palestine's population in 1917 to 33% by 1947.^28^ This dramatic demographic change was achieved through British policy allowing Jewish immigration while suppressing Arab political demands.^28^ The inevitable result was increasing conflict between Jewish settlers seeking to establish majority control and Arabs resisting dispossession.^29^

Chapter 11: Partitions Aftermath

The Arab Revolt (1936-1939) saw Palestinians rise against British rule and Jewish immigration.^30^ British suppression was brutal: approximately 5,000 Arabs were killed, thousands detained without trial, homes demolished, collective fines imposed, and entire villages punished for resistance activities.^31^ Emergency regulations suspended civil liberties and allowed summary justice.^31^ British forces armed and trained Jewish defense forces while crushing Arab resistance.^32^

By the mid-1940s, when Jewish militant groups turned violence against British targets (the King David Hotel bombing killed 91 in 1946), Britain decided Palestine was no longer worth the cost.^33^ The decision to withdraw was made rapidly, with minimal preparation for consequences.^33^ Britain handed the problem to the United Nations, which proposed partition—dividing Palestine into Jewish and Arab states.^34^

The UN Partition Plan (1947) allocated 55% of Palestine to a Jewish state despite Jews owning only 7% of the land and comprising 33% of the population.^35^ The proposed borders were geographically incoherent—the Jewish state would consist of three separate territories connected by narrow corridors.^35^ The plan was fundamentally unworkable and unjust, allocating more land to the minority population.^35^

Perfidious Albion

Arabs rejected the plan as rewarding immigration by dispossessing indigenous populations.^36^ Fighting began immediately. As British forces withdrew in 1948, violence escalated into full-scale war between Jewish and Arab forces.^37^ The war resulted in the establishment of Israel and the Nakba (catastrophe) for Palestinians.^37^

Approximately 750,000 Palestinians—over half the Arab population—became refugees through expulsion or flight during 1947-1949.^38^ Zionist forces destroyed approximately 400 Palestinian villages to prevent refugees from returning.^39^ Massacres at Deir Yassin and elsewhere terrorized Palestinians into fleeing.^40^ The ethnic cleansing was systematic and deliberate, creating facts on the ground that made partition's borders irrelevant.^40^

The partition created Israel but no Palestinian state. Egypt occupied Gaza, Jordan occupied the West Bank, and Palestinian refugees scattered across the Middle East in camps where many remain today.^41^ The borders created by the 1948 war (the "Green Line") were never intended to be permanent but became de facto frontiers for two decades.^41^

The 1967 Six-Day War saw Israel occupy the West Bank, Gaza, Golan Heights, and Sinai, creating new realities.^42^ Israel's subsequent settlement expansion in occupied territories and refusal to allow Palestinian statehood means that partition's original vision—two

Chapter 11: Partitions Aftermath

states—has never been realized.^42^ Instead, there is one state (Israel) and occupied territories where Palestinians lack sovereignty or equal rights.^42^

The conflict continues today. The death toll since 1948 exceeds 100,000, with Palestinians suffering disproportionately.^43^ Millions of Palestinians remain stateless refugees or live under occupation.^44^ Periodic wars and ongoing violence make this one of the world's most intractable conflicts.^44^

Britain's role was to create conditions for this catastrophe: facilitating demographic transformation through immigration policy, suppressing Arab resistance while arming Jewish forces, making contradictory promises, then rapidly withdrawing while violence exploded.^45^ British authorities prioritized strategic interests (maintaining Middle East influence, securing oil access, managing relationships with both Zionist and Arab leaders) over Palestinian welfare or long-term stability.^45^ The partition was not a solution but the creation of a permanent problem.^45^

India/Pakistan: The Greatest Catastrophe

The partition of India in 1947 was the largest and deadliest of Britain's partitions, killing 1-2 million people and displacing 15 million in some of history's worst communal violence.^4,46^ The division of British India into Hindu-majority India and Muslim-majority

Pakistan was presented as the inevitable solution to irreconcilable Hindu-Muslim differences, but those differences were largely British creations through divide-and-rule policies examined in Chapter 9.^47^

The decision to partition was made quickly and implemented hastily. Lord Mountbatten, appointed Viceroy in March 1947, was instructed to oversee British withdrawal by June 1948.^48^ He accelerated the timeline to August 1947—giving barely five months from announcement to implementation.^48^ This rush ensured chaos.^48^

The boundary commission, chaired by Cyril Radcliffe, had five weeks to draw borders dividing Bengal and Punjab—provinces with populations of 88 million and 30 million respectively.^49^ Radcliffe had never visited India before his appointment and worked with outdated maps and census data.^49^ He was given an impossible task: drawing lines through provinces where religious communities were intermixed, with no clear geographic or demographic basis for separation.^49,50^

The borders announced on August 17, 1947—two days after independence—were arbitrary and catastrophic.^51^ In Punjab, the line divided the province roughly in half, with some districts going to Pakistan and others to India based primarily on religious majority.^51^ But Punjab was home to Sikhs, Muslims, and Hindus living in intermixed communities.^51^ No border could

Chapter 11: Partitions Aftermath

separate them cleanly.~51~

The Bengal partition was equally arbitrary. Eastern Bengal (with Muslim majority) became East Pakistan, despite being separated from West Pakistan by 1,000 miles of Indian territory.~52~ This geographic absurdity—a nation in two parts separated by a thousand miles—was unstable from inception and would lead to Bangladesh's independence in 1971.~52~

The borders created immediate crises. The Radcliffe Line divided the Punjab's irrigation system, with headworks in India controlling water for fields in Pakistan.~53~ Railway lines were cut. Cities were divided from their agricultural hinterlands. Economic networks were severed.~53~ These practical problems compounded the human catastrophe.~53~

The violence began before partition and exploded after the borders were announced. In Punjab, trains carrying refugees were stopped and all passengers massacred—entire trains arriving at stations filled with corpses.~54~ Villages were attacked, with residents killed or expelled based on religion.~54~ Women were abducted, raped, and killed in horrific numbers—estimates suggest 75,000-100,000 women were abducted during Partition.~55~

The migration was the largest in human history up to that time. Approximately 15 million people moved—

Hindus and Sikhs fleeing Pakistan for India, Muslims fleeing India for Pakistan.^56^ The refugee columns, sometimes stretching for miles, were attacked by mobs. Families were separated. Children were lost. The elderly and weak died on the roads.^56^

The death toll is uncertain—official estimates suggested 200,000-500,000, but most historians now believe 1-2 million is more accurate.^4,57^ In Punjab alone, possibly one million died.^57^ The violence was intimate and horrific: neighbors killing neighbors, communities that had coexisted for generations suddenly engaged in genocidal killing.^58^

British forces, still present during partition, did little to prevent the violence. Some historians argue they could have stopped much of the killing had preventing it been a priority.^59^ But British authorities focused on orderly withdrawal, protecting British personnel, and managing the transfer of power.^59^ Indian and Pakistani leaders were overwhelmed by events neither had anticipated.^59^

The legacy is profound and lasting. India and Pakistan have fought four wars (1947-48, 1965, 1971, 1999) and numerous smaller conflicts.^60^ Both possess nuclear weapons, making future war potentially catastrophic.^60^ Kashmir remains disputed, with ongoing violence that has killed tens of thousands.^61^ The trauma of Partition shapes both nations' politics and

Chapter 11: Partitions Aftermath

identities.~61~

Partition created Pakistan as an explicitly Islamic state, setting precedent for religious rather than secular nationalism in South Asia.~62~ India, while officially secular, has experienced periodic Hindu-Muslim violence and Hindu nationalist movements that exploit partition's legacy.~63~ The division created in 1947 continues to poison South Asian politics.~63~

Bangladesh's creation in 1971 demonstrated partition's failure even on its own terms. East Pakistan, separated from West Pakistan by geography, language, and culture, was exploited economically and politically by West Pakistan.~64~ When East Pakistan demanded autonomy, West Pakistan responded with military crackdown and genocide.~64~ An estimated 300,000-3,000,000 people were killed (with most credible estimates around 300,000-500,000), and 10 million refugees fled to India.~65~ India's military intervention led to Pakistan's defeat and Bangladesh's independence.~65~ The original partition created conditions for this subsequent catastrophe.~65~

The Pattern: Partition as British Strategy

The three major partitions share disturbing commonalities that reveal partition as British imperial strategy rather than unavoidable solution to local conflicts.~66~

Perfidious Albion

Created Divisions: In each case, British policies had created or exacerbated the divisions used to justify partition. Irish sectarianism was fostered by British support for Protestant ascendancy.^67^ Palestinian-Jewish conflict resulted from British facilitation of Zionist immigration.^68^ Hindu-Muslim divisions were deliberately fostered through divide-and-rule policies.^69^

Minimal Consultation: None of the affected populations were meaningfully consulted. Ireland's partition was imposed by Westminster.^10^ Palestine's partition was proposed by the UN with British influence but without Palestinian consent.^34^ India's partition was decided by British authorities with Congress and Muslim League leaders but not through popular referendum.^70^

Arbitrary Borders: Borders were drawn quickly by people with minimal local knowledge. Ireland's border was designed politically, not geographically.^9^ Palestine's UN partition borders were geographically incoherent.^35^ India's Radcliffe Line was drawn in five weeks by a man who had never visited.^49^

Strategic British Interests: Each partition served British strategic goals. Irish partition retained Northern Ireland's strategic location and industrial capacity.^71^ Palestinian partition was supposed to secure British influence with both Zionist and Arab populations.^45^ Indian partition weakened the subcontinent through

Chapter 11: Partitions Aftermath

division, preventing a united India that might challenge British interests.˄72˄

Inadequate Preparation: British authorities made minimal preparation for partition's human consequences. Insufficient security forces were deployed, refugee relief was inadequate, and communal violence prevention was not prioritized.˄73˄ In each case, British authorities withdrew rapidly while violence exploded.˄73˄

Lasting Conflict: Each partition created ongoing conflicts. Northern Ireland experienced the Troubles.˄21˄ Israel-Palestine remains unresolved after 75 years.˄44˄ India-Pakistan have fought repeated wars and maintain hostile nuclear confrontation.˄60˄ The conflicts persist because partition addressed symptoms (communal tensions) rather than causes (British divide-and-rule policies).˄74˄

The Human Cost: Millions Dead, Millions Displaced

The combined death toll from these partitions exceeds two million people:

- Ireland: Approximately 500 killed in initial partition violence (1920-22), over 3,500 in the Troubles (1968-98)˄17,21˄

- Palestine/Israel: Over 100,000 killed in conflicts since 1948~43~
- India/Pakistan: 1-2 million killed in Partition violence, hundreds of thousands in subsequent wars, ongoing Kashmir conflict~4,60~

The displacement toll exceeds 20 million:

- Ireland: Thousands displaced in initial partition, ongoing segregation in Northern Ireland~75~
- Palestine/Israel: 750,000 Palestinians in 1948 Nakba, millions of descendants remain refugees~38~
- India/Pakistan: 15 million displaced in Partition, 10 million in 1971 Bangladesh crisis~56,65~

These numbers represent documented deaths and displacements; the true totals including indirect deaths from disease, starvation, and conflict-related deprivation are certainly higher.~76~ Each number represents an individual life destroyed, a family shattered, a community devastated.~76~

The psychological trauma is generational. Partition survivors carry lifelong wounds. Their children and grandchildren inherit trauma and division.~77~ Communal identities hardened by partition persist across generations.~77~ The conflicts created by partition shape how hundreds of millions of people understand themselves and their relationship to others.~77~

Chapter 11: Partitions Aftermath

Could Partitions Have Been Avoided?

The question whether these partitions were necessary or could have been avoided is critical. British authorities presented partitions as reluctant responses to intractable local conflicts, but the evidence suggests alternatives existed.~78~

In Ireland, some form of Home Rule or dominion status for all Ireland was feasible. Ulster unionists opposed this, but they were themselves a minority (approximately 25% of Ireland's total population).~79~ Protecting minority rights within a united Ireland was possible—many constitutional arrangements exist for this.~79~ Partition was chosen not because it was the only option but because it served British strategic interests in retaining part of Ireland.~80~

In Palestine, honoring the mandate's commitment to protect Arab rights would have meant limiting Jewish immigration to levels the existing population could accommodate, or implementing genuine power-sharing arrangements.~81~ The choice to facilitate mass immigration without Arab consent created the conflict that partition supposedly solved.~81~ A unitary binational state or genuinely equal federal arrangement were alternatives never seriously pursued.~81~

In India, the question is more complex because Congress and Muslim League leaders eventually accepted partition.˄82˄ But their acceptance came after decades of British divide-and-rule policies that created the communal tensions making partition seem necessary.˄69˄ Had British authorities governed India as a unified polity rather than deliberately fostering communal division, partition might have been avoidable.˄69˄ Alternative arrangements including federalism or power-sharing were proposed but rejected.˄83˄

In each case, partition was not the only option but a choice—a choice that prioritized British interests and accepted massive human suffering as the price of protecting those interests.˄84˄

Summary Conclusion: The Legacy of Division

Britain's partitions were deliberate policies that created lasting conflicts killing millions and displacing tens of millions. They were presented as solutions to conflicts Britain had often created, implemented hastily with minimal regard for human consequences, and designed primarily to serve British strategic interests.˄1,85˄

The conflicts created by partition persist today. Northern Ireland remains divided, with Brexit threatening renewed instability.˄24˄ Israel-Palestine continues as one of the world's most intractable conflicts.˄44˄ India-Pakistan maintain hostile nuclear-armed confrontation.˄60˄ These aren't ancient hatreds

Chapter 11: Partitions Aftermath

but modern conflicts rooted in British imperial policy.^86^

Britain has never meaningfully acknowledged responsibility for partition's consequences. No apologies have been offered for the deaths caused. No reparations paid for the displacement. No serious effort made to help resolve the conflicts created.^87^ Instead, British historical memory treats partitions as unfortunate necessities, obscuring British agency in creating the problems partition supposedly solved.^87^

Understanding these partitions as British policy choices rather than inevitable solutions to local hatreds is essential to understanding contemporary conflicts. The borders drawn hastily in 1921-1947 continue to shape geopolitics, cause violence, and structure how hundreds of millions of people understand their identities and relationships to others.^88^ Partition was not a solution but a problem-creation mechanism—dividing and departing while leaving populations to suffer the consequences.^88^

Author's Notes Chapter 11

This chapter examines partitions as colonial strategy—dividing formerly unified territories along ethnic, religious, or political lines to serve imperial interests or facilitate withdrawal. The focus is primarily on India/Pakistan partition (1947) as the largest and most violent, with additional attention to other partitions including Ireland

(1921) and Palestine (1948).

On Partition Violence (1947): The scale of partition violence—approximately one million dead, 15 million displaced—makes this one of the 20th century's worst humanitarian disasters. Yasmin Khan's *The Great Partition* (2007) provides the most comprehensive recent account, emphasizing that the violence was not spontaneous religious hatred but emerged from the partition process itself—the hasty imposition of borders, inadequate security, and political mobilization around religious identity. Gyanendra Pandey's *Remembering Partition* (2001) examines how partition violence is remembered differently by different communities, with trauma transmitted across generations.

On British Responsibility: Debate continues about British culpability for partition violence. Some historians argue that religious tensions made violence inevitable regardless of how partition was conducted. Others (including Khan) argue that British decisions substantially worsened violence: announcing withdrawal only months before departing (creating urgency and panic), drawing borders carelessly without adequate consultation, providing insufficient security during the transition, and failing to prepare for predictable refugee movements. Lord Mountbatten, the last Viceroy, prioritized rapid British withdrawal over preventing violence.

On Sexual Violence: Partition involved horrific sexual violence against women—rape, abduction, forced conversion, and murder. Urvashi Butalia's *The Other Side of Silence* (2000) documents that both Muslim and Hindu/Sikh communities perpetrated sexual violence as a weapon against the other community, viewing women's bodies as territory to be conquered. Approximately 75,000-100,000 women were abducted during partition. Many were later "recovered" through agreements between India and Pakistan, but recovery often traumatized women further as families rejected them as "polluted."

On Other Partitions: While India/Pakistan receives most attention, Britain engineered multiple partitions: Ireland (1921), Palestine (1947, through UN but heavily influenced by British positions), and Cyprus (de facto partition after independence). Each created lasting conflicts and human suffering. The pattern suggests partition was colonial strategy—dividing and withdrawing while leaving populations to deal with violent consequences—rather than unfortunate necessity.

On Counterfactuals: Scholars debate whether partition could have been avoided or conducted less violently. Some argue that Hindu-Muslim tensions made partition inevitable. Others argue that united India remained possible until late in the independence process, and that British authorities and Indian politicians made choices accelerating division. While counterfactual history is speculative, it's clear that the partition as actually conducted—hastily, with inadequate preparation, with carelessly drawn borders—maximized suffering.

On Continuing Effects: India-Pakistan tensions rooted in partition have produced multiple wars, ongoing conflict over Kashmir, and continuing mutual suspicion affecting hundreds of millions of people. Understanding partition's origins in colonial policy is essential for addressing its continuing legacy. Both nations' nuclear arsenals make resolving partition's legacy urgently important for global peace.

CHAPTER TWELVE

Concentration Camps: Britain's Forgotten Gulags (1900-1960)

The term "concentration camp" carries profound historical weight, yet Britain's role in pioneering and perfecting this instrument of imperial control remains largely absent from popular memory. While the horrors of Nazi camps rightly dominate twentieth-century consciousness, Britain operated extensive camp systems across multiple continents for six decades, incarcerating hundreds of thousands of civilians without trial, subjecting them to forced labor, starvation, disease, and systematic brutality. These were not aberrations born of wartime panic or rogue commanders exceeding their authority. They were calculated instruments of colonial policy, sanctioned at the highest levels of government, designed to break resistance movements by targeting entire populations.

From the veldt of South Africa to the highlands of Kenya, from the jungles of Malaya to the detention centers of Cyprus, Britain constructed an archipelago of camps that prefigured totalitarian systems of the mid-twentieth century. The architects of these policies—celebrated military commanders, decorated colonial administrators, and elected British politicians—implemented strategies of collective punishment, forced resettlement, and social engineering on a massive scale with full knowledge that their actions would result in thousands of deaths.

This chapter examines four major British camp systems spanning 1900 to 1960, revealing a consistent pattern of official violence, deliberate neglect, and subsequent historical amnesia. It demonstrates that concentration camps were not a temporary expedient of the Boer War but became a standard tool of imperial control, refined and redeployed whenever colonial subjects dared to challenge British rule.

The Boer War: Inventing the Concentration Camp (1900-1902)

Chapter 12: Concentration Camps

Britain's systematic use of concentration camps began during the Second Boer War in South Africa, where military commanders confronted an unexpectedly resilient guerrilla insurgency by Afrikaner commandos. Unable to defeat mobile Boer forces through conventional military engagement, the British high command, under Lord Kitchener, implemented a scorched-earth strategy of unprecedented scope. Between 1900 and 1902, British forces systematically destroyed Boer farms, burned crops, slaughtered livestock, poisoned wells, and forcibly removed the entire civilian population—predominantly women, children, and elderly men—to what the military euphemistically termed "refugee camps."[1]

The camps were anything but refuges. Kitchener's strategy explicitly targeted the civilian support base sustaining Boer guerrillas. By removing this population to enclosed camps, British authorities aimed to deprive the guerrillas of sustenance while demonstrating the futility of continued resistance. Emily Hobhouse, the Cornish activist who became the camps' most prominent critic, understood the military logic immediately: the civilian population was being held hostage to force Boer surrender.[2]

The concentration camp system expanded with shocking rapidity. By late 1901, approximately 116,000 Afrikaners and 120,000 Black Africans were imprisoned in separate camp systems.[3] The racial segregation was deliberate: white Boers and Black Africans were confined in distinct facilities with the Black camps receiving even less attention and fewer resources than those holding whites.

Conditions in the camps defied basic standards of human decency. Overcrowding was endemic, with families of six or more crammed into twelve-by-ten-foot bell tents offering no protection from South Africa's climate extremes. Sanitation was catastrophic. Open latrines, contaminated water supplies, and inadequate sewage systems created ideal conditions for epidemic disease. Rations were deliberately kept minimal, reduced further as punishment for families whose menfolk continued fighting. The official ration scale provided just 1,363 calories daily—well below subsistence level—and was frequently cut to half or quarter rations for "undesirables."[4]

The mortality statistics reveal the camps' lethal character. Between June 1901 and February 1902, the death rate in the white camps reached 344 per 1,000 per annum—more than six times the rate in British cities.[5] Children suffered disproportionately, with infant and child mortality exceeding 600 per 1,000 per annum in some camps.[6] Of the estimated 28,000 Boer deaths in the camps, approximately 22,000 were children under sixteen.[7] The Black camps experienced even higher absolute mortality, with official figures recording at least 14,000 deaths, though the true toll likely exceeded

Chapter 12: Concentration Camps

20,000.^8^

Emily Hobhouse's visit to the camps in early 1901 exposed these conditions to British public opinion. Her report described scenes of almost unimaginable suffering: children dying of starvation and preventable diseases, mothers too weak from malnutrition to nurse their infants, families sleeping on bare earth without blankets in freezing temperatures. "I call this camp system," she wrote, "a wholesale cruelty... To keep these Camps going is murder to the children."^9^

The British government's response combined defensive denial with grudging reform. Kitchener initially dismissed Hobhouse as a "hysterical woman" and attempted to bar her return to South Africa.^10^ The government appointed the Fawcett Commission to investigate, which confirmed many of Hobhouse's findings while attributing deaths primarily to Boer ignorance rather than British policy.^11^ Improvements were eventually implemented, and death rates declined in the final months of the war, but this belated action came after the bulk of mortality had already occurred.

The camps achieved their strategic objective. By mid-1902, with their farms destroyed, their families imprisoned, and their support networks shattered, Boer commandos accepted peace terms. Yet the historical legacy has been remarkably constrained. In Britain, the camps are frequently presented as a regrettable mistake rather than a deliberate strategy of civilian targeting. The term "concentration camp" itself, coined during this conflict, has been retrospectively sanitized, with many British historians emphasizing that these facilities bore little resemblance to later Nazi death camps—a comparison that obscures rather than illuminates the camps' actual character as instruments of collective punishment.^12^

More significantly, the Boer War camps established precedents and techniques that would be refined and redeployed throughout the twentieth century. The strategic logic of targeting civilian populations to undermine insurgencies, the use of barbed wire and guards to concentrate dispersed rural populations, the manipulation of food rations as control instruments, and the bureaucratic systems for mass internment—all these elements would reappear in subsequent British colonial emergencies.

Kenya: The Gulag in the Kikuyu Highlands (1952-1960)

Half a century after the Boer War, Britain constructed a vastly more extensive camp system in Kenya during the Mau Mau Emergency. Between 1952 and 1960, colonial authorities detained approximately 1.5 million Kikuyu people—nearly the entire Kikuyu population—in a system of detention camps, "villages," and restricted areas that bore striking resemblances to Stalin's Gulag.^13^ This was mass internment on a scale

Chapter 12: Concentration Camps

unprecedented in British colonial history, implemented to crush the Kenya Land and Freedom Army (derisively termed "Mau Mau" by the British) and to restructure Kikuyu society according to colonial preferences.

The Mau Mau uprising emerged from decades of accumulated grievances: massive land alienation that transferred the most fertile Kikuyu territory to white settlers, exploitative labor practices, racial discrimination, and political repression that denied Africans meaningful participation in governance.^14^ When armed resistance began in 1952, the colonial government declared a State of Emergency and unleashed a counterinsurgency campaign of extraordinary brutality centered on a detention camp system serving multiple functions: punishment, intimidation, forced labor, and what authorities termed "rehabilitation"—a euphemism for systematic efforts to break prisoners psychologically and ideologically.

Governor Sir Evelyn Baring and his military commander, General Sir George Erskine, oversaw a camp network that encompassed multiple categories of detention. At the apex were "special detention camps"—including the notorious facilities at Manyani, Mackinnon Road, and Hola—which held suspected Mau Mau fighters and hardcore resisters. Below these were "works camps" where detainees performed forced labor. The "Pipeline" system categorized detainees into white (cooperative), grey (wavering), and black (resistant) groups, with treatment severity escalating according to classification.^15^

The vast majority of detained Kikuyu experienced the "villagization" program, which forcibly relocated approximately one million people into fortified settlements surrounded by barbed wire and watchtowers.^16^ Entire populations were uprooted from traditional farmsteads and confined in these villages, ostensibly to separate them from Mau Mau guerrillas but actually to facilitate surveillance, control movement, and provide labor for colonial projects.

Conditions throughout the camp system were deliberately harsh. Overcrowding, malnutrition, disease, inadequate shelter, and brutal discipline were endemic. Official rations provided approximately 1,400 calories daily—barely above starvation level for men engaged in heavy forced labor.^17^ The death toll remains contested, obscured by incomplete records, deliberate destruction of documents, and systematic underreporting. Official British figures acknowledged just 11,000 Mau Mau deaths during the entire Emergency, a number historian David Anderson characterized as "a fraction of the true total."^18^ More recent scholarship suggests that deaths in the camps and during counterinsurgency operations likely exceeded 50,000 and may have reached 100,000 or more.^19^

Systematic torture and abuse pervaded the detention

Chapter 12: Concentration Camps

system. Guards, operating with near-total impunity, employed horrific techniques to extract confessions and break prisoners' will. Testimonies documented prisoners being subjected to beatings, electric shocks, sexual assault, and castration.[20] Women detainees experienced particular forms of gendered violence. In 1954 at Kamiti detention camp, guards subjected approximately 100 women to systematic torture, including sexual assault with bottles.[21]

The most infamous incident occurred at Hola camp in March 1959, when guards beat eleven detainees to death during a forced labor detail.[22] The prisoners had refused to work, adhering to their classification as political detainees not required to perform manual labor. Camp Commandant G.M. Sullivan ordered guards to use "compelling force," which quickly escalated to frenzied clubbing. The dead were initially reported as victims of contaminated water, but post-mortem examinations revealed the truth: skulls fractured, ribs broken, internal organs ruptured.[23]

The Hola massacre finally penetrated British public consciousness. Enoch Powell delivered a devastating speech in Parliament, declaring that Britain could not maintain different standards in Africa than at home.[24] Yet Powell's condemnation obscured a crucial reality: Hola was not an aberration but the logical culmination of a detention system designed to inflict suffering. The camps operated according to official policy approved at the highest levels.^25^

After Hola, international pressure prompted Britain to wind down the detention system. Kenya gained independence in 1963, but the British government systematically destroyed evidence of camp abuses, burning or spiriting away thousands of documents.^26^ When Kenyan survivors brought legal action in British courts in 2009, government lawyers initially denied the existence of extensive documentation, only for historians to discover a secret archive of 8,800 files concealed in a Foreign Office facility.^27^ In 2013, the British government agreed to compensate 5,228 survivors while carefully avoiding admissions that might establish broader legal liability.^28^

Malaya: New Villages and the Technology of Population Control (1948-1960)

Britain's response to communist insurgency in Malaya represented concentration camp logic adapted to jungle warfare and dressed in more palatable language of "resettlement" and "protected villages." Between 1950 and 1954, British authorities forcibly relocated approximately 500,000 ethnic Chinese rural dwellers—roughly one-tenth of Malaya's entire population—into 480 fortified settlements known as "New Villages."^29^ This massive social engineering project, conceived and directed by General Sir Harold Briggs, aimed to sever the Malayan Communist Party's guerrilla army from its

Chapter 12: Concentration Camps

civilian support base by physically separating potential sympathizers from insurgents operating in the jungle.

The Chinese "squatter" population became the primary target of resettlement. These communities practiced small-scale agriculture on the jungle fringes, living in dispersed settlements beyond effective government control. Some provided support to communist guerrillas. British planners concluded that the entire population must be relocated, regardless of individual sympathies or involvement.

Families received minimal notice—sometimes only days—to abandon their homes, farms, and possessions. Security forces burned evacuated settlements, destroyed crops, and killed livestock.^30^ Relocated families were transported to designated New Village sites where they found minimal infrastructure: cleared land, rudimentary fencing, and little else. Residents were required to construct their own housing, often while living in temporary shelters or exposed to the elements.

The New Villages were concentration camps by another name, though British authorities vehemently rejected this terminology. Each village was surrounded by barbed wire perimeter fencing, watchtowers, and floodlit approaches. Residents required passes to exit and faced strict curfews. Police and military personnel conducted frequent searches and interrogations.^31^ Food supplies were tightly controlled through rationing systems that tracked rice purchases to prevent surpluses being smuggled to insurgents.

Conditions in many New Villages were initially appalling. A 1951 report by Major General Boucher described New Villages as having "no drainage, no water supply, and most of them no dispensary," with residents living in "really deplorable" conditions.^32^ Disease flourished: malaria, typhoid, dysentery, and tuberculosis ravaged communities weakened by malnutrition and stress. Economic devastation accompanied physical relocation. Farmers lost their land and livelihoods, receiving minimal or no compensation.

The colonial administration gradually improved conditions, recognizing that permanent squalor would breed resentment. By 1952, authorities were investing in infrastructure: piped water, electricity, schools, clinics.^33^ This development was strategic, not humanitarian. British planners understood that winning "hearts and minds" required demonstrating that cooperation with the government offered advantages over supporting insurgents.

General Sir Gerald Templer, who became High Commissioner in 1952, intensified both repressive and developmental aspects. He expanded collective punishment measures, including imposing food restrictions and extended curfews on villages suspected of aiding guerrillas. In the Tanjong Malim area, Templer

Chapter 12: Concentration Camps

reduced rations to starvation levels, closed schools, and restricted movement after guerrillas ambushed a bus.^34^ Yet Templer simultaneously accelerated New Village development, creating carrot-and-stick approach that defined later Emergency years.

The resettlement program achieved its military objective. By physically separating rural Chinese populations from communist guerrillas and implementing comprehensive surveillance, British forces severely degraded insurgent logistics. Guerrilla numbers declined from approximately 8,000 in 1951 to fewer than 2,000 by 1957.^35^ The Emergency officially ended in 1960, with Britain declaring victory.

British authorities promoted Malaya as a counterinsurgency success story, a template for defeating communist insurgencies. Yet this triumphalist narrative obscures the human costs. Approximately half a million people were forcibly relocated, their communities destroyed, their lives disrupted. Thousands died from disease, malnutrition, and violence.^36^ The "minimum force" doctrine permitted scorched-earth tactics, aerial bombardment, and shoot-on-sight orders.^37^ The success derived partly from the insurgents representing an ethnic minority and lacking external sanctuary—advantages impossible to replicate in other conflicts.^38^

Cyprus: The Last of Britain's Camp Systems (1955-1959)

Britain's final major deployment of concentration camps occurred in Cyprus during the Greek Cypriot struggle for independence. Confronting the EOKA (National Organization of Cypriot Fighters) insurgency led by Colonel George Grivas, British authorities detained approximately 12,000 Greek Cypriots without trial.^39^ Though smaller in scale than Kenya or Malaya, the Cyprus detention network demonstrated that mass internment remained Britain's default response to colonial resistance even in the late 1950s, after exposure of abuses in Kenya and growing international criticism.

Cyprus, a strategically vital Mediterranean base, became increasingly restive after World War II as Greek Cypriots, who constituted 80% of the island's population, demanded enosis (union with Greece). When EOKA launched its armed campaign in April 1955, Governor Sir Robert Armitage declared a State of Emergency and implemented draconian security measures.^40^

The detention system expanded rapidly as British forces conducted mass arrest sweeps through villages suspected of harboring EOKA sympathizers. Detainees included suspected guerrillas, political activists, students, clergy, and anyone whose behavior attracted suspicion. No judicial process was required: colonial authorities could detain anyone indefinitely under Emergency regulations modeled on those employed in Malaya and Kenya.^41^

Chapter 12: Concentration Camps

The main detention facility at Pyla Kokkinotrimithia held up to 1,000 detainees in a tented camp surrounded by barbed wire and guard towers.^42^ Conditions were harsh though generally not reaching the levels of deliberate brutality documented in Kenya. International Committee of the Red Cross inspections documented inadequate sanitation, limited medical care, and insufficient protection from climate extremes.^43^

British authorities employed detention for both punishment and interrogation. Suspected EOKA members faced intense pressure to provide information. Interrogation techniques included physical abuse, sleep deprivation, forced standing, and psychological torture, though systematic torture was less institutionalized than in Kenya.^44^ The European Commission of Human Rights later found that British forces in Cyprus had employed torture and inhuman treatment.^45^

Collective punishment accompanied mass detention. British forces imposed curfews, conducted cordon-and-search operations, destroyed suspected safe houses, and deported community leaders deemed insufficiently cooperative. In January 1956, following EOKA attacks, authorities imposed collective fines on villages totaling £30,000 and conducted mass arrests.^46^

Governor Sir John Harding, who replaced Armitage in late 1955, intensified the counterinsurgency campaign while simultaneously pursuing political negotiations. He expanded detention capacity, increased troop deployments to 25,000, and authorized aggressive measures against suspected EOKA supporters.˄47˄ The detention policy generated significant international criticism, with Greece bringing Cyprus to the United Nations.˄48˄

Within Cyprus, detention radicalized rather than pacified. Families of detainees became staunch EOKA supporters. Young men released from detention often joined the insurgency, their commitment hardened by imprisonment. The camps functioned as recruiting grounds where detained activists organized and maintained morale.˄49˄

Britain eventually conceded independence through negotiation rather than military victory. The 1959 Zurich-London agreements established the Republic of Cyprus, with Britain retaining two Sovereign Base Areas. Cyprus gained independence in 1960, and Britain closed its detention camps.˄50˄

The Cyprus experience demonstrated both the continuing appeal of detention as counterinsurgency policy and its ultimate futility against determined nationalist movements. Yet even under constraints of international scrutiny and declining public tolerance for colonial violence, Britain resorted to mass detention, collective punishment, and coercive interrogation—the familiar toolkit of imperial control.

Chapter 12: Concentration Camps

Patterns, Precedents, and Historical Amnesia

Britain's concentration camp systems from 1900 to 1960 share consistent characteristics revealing them as expressions of systematic policy rather than isolated aberrations. Each system emerged in response to anti-colonial resistance that could not be suppressed through conventional military force alone. Each targeted entire populations rather than just active insurgents, implementing collective punishment on massive scales. Each operated in legal twilight zones where normal protections did not apply. Each inflicted severe suffering through overcrowding, malnutrition, disease, forced labor, and physical abuse.

The evolution from South Africa through Kenya, Malaya, and Cyprus shows both continuity and adaptation. The crude brutality of Boer War camps gave way to more sophisticated systems incorporating "rehabilitation," political education, and development alongside repression. The language shifted from frank acknowledgment of punishment to euphemistic terminology: "protected villages," "rehabilitation camps," "emergency detention." Yet the essential character remained: coercive institutions designed to break resistance through suffering and intimidation.

The camps established precedents influencing colonial practice globally. The Boer War camps provided a template for civilian internment that informed German

Perfidious Albion

practices in Southwest Africa, Spanish camps in Cuba, and American "concentration zones" in the Philippines.^51^ The Malayan New Villages inspired American "strategic hamlet" programs in Vietnam.^52^ The Kenya detention system's interrogation and psychological manipulation techniques prefigured methods employed by security services worldwide.

The death tolls from British camps remain disputed, but conservative estimates suggest at least 50,000 deaths across the four systems examined here—28,000 in South Africa, 15,000-50,000 in Kenya, several thousand in Malaya, and hundreds in Cyprus. More expansive estimates push the total substantially higher. These figures exclude those who died during forced relocations, from indirect effects of malnutrition and trauma, or in military operations associated with the camp systems.

Perhaps most striking is the comprehensive historical amnesia surrounding these camps in British collective memory. While educated Britons generally know of Nazi concentration camps and Soviet gulags, awareness of British camps remains minimal. School curricula rarely address them; popular histories marginalize or ignore them. When British camps are mentioned, they are typically presented as exceptional responses to exceptional circumstances, disconnected from broader patterns of colonial governance.

Chapter 12: Concentration Camps

This amnesia is not accidental. The British government's systematic destruction of potentially incriminating documents—the files burned before Kenyan independence, the "migrated archives" concealed from historians and courts—represents official policy aimed at preventing accountability.˄53˄ The careful legal language used in recent settlements with camp survivors—expressing "regret" while avoiding "apology"—demonstrates continuing reluctance to confront this history honestly.

The camps reveal limitations of the "good empire, bad empire" narrative that distinguishes supposedly enlightened British imperialism from more brutal continental variants. The same empire that prided itself on parliamentary democracy, rule of law, and humanitarian values operated concentration camps across multiple continents for six decades. This contradiction reflects the fundamental nature of colonial rule: however benevolent its self-presentation, imperialism ultimately rested on violence deployed as necessary to maintain control over populations that did not consent to their subjugation.

Summary Conclusion

Britain's concentration camps from 1900 to 1960 constitute a central aspect of twentieth-century imperial history. They were not regrettable exceptions to generally humane colonial governance but integral instruments of imperial control, deployed systematically when colonized peoples resisted British rule. The scale is staggering: more than two million people confined in camp systems across four continents, tens of thousands dead, countless lives destroyed.

Yet this history remains largely unknown in Britain, absent from national memory and public consciousness. This amnesia serves contemporary political purposes, allowing continued celebration of empire's supposed benefits while evading serious reckoning with its systematic violence. Understanding Britain's concentration camps illuminates broader truths about colonial rule: imperialism was fundamentally about power—establishing it, maintaining it, and ruthlessly suppressing challenges to it.

As debates about empire's legacy continue in contemporary Britain, honest acknowledgment of concentration camps and the systematic violence they represented is essential. This history cannot be dismissed as the work of a few bad actors or explained away as unavoidable wartime necessity. It must be recognized as deliberate policy, implemented by celebrated figures, supported by parliamentary majorities, and defended by large sections of British public opinion. Only such recognition can prompt the deeper reckoning with imperial history that Britain has yet to undertake, confronting the uncomfortable truth that the violence employed in the colonies was not an aberration from but

Chapter 12: Concentration Camps

an expression of empire's essential character.

Author's Notes Chapter 12

This chapter examines British use of concentration camps from the Boer War through the Kenya Emergency, arguing that Britain pioneered concentration camps as counterinsurgency tools and that systematic abuse characterized British camp systems across multiple conflicts. The chapter title deliberately uses "gulags" to emphasize camps' role as instruments of political repression and mass detention without trial, drawing parallels to Soviet camps without claiming exact equivalence.

On the Boer War Camps (1900-1902): Thomas Pakenham's *The Boer War* (1979) remains the standard account. Emily Hobhouse's contemporary reports documented catastrophic conditions—overcrowding, inadequate food, poor sanitation, minimal medical care—that killed approximately 28,000 Boer civilians (mostly women and children) and 14,000 black Africans. Hobhouse's work forced British government to improve conditions, but only after the death toll became politically embarrassing. S.B. Spies' *Methods of Barbarism?* (1977) documents that camp mortality resulted from deliberate underfunding and official indifference rather than logistical impossibility.

On "Concentration Camps" as British Innovation: Britain did not invent the concept of concentrating populations—Spanish forces used similar tactics in Cuba in the 1890s, and earlier examples exist. But Britain's Boer War camps were among the first large-scale implementations and directly influenced later developments. Nazi concentration camps drew on multiple precedents including British camps, though Nazi camps' industrialized killing represents distinct and more extreme evil. The comparison is not to claim equivalence but to acknowledge British camps' place in the history of this form of mass detention and abuse.

On Kenya Detention Camps: Caroline Elkins' *Imperial Reckoning* (2005) documents that Britain detained over 150,000 Kenyans in camps characterized by forced labor, systematic torture, sexual violence, and killings. The camps were explicitly designed to "rehabilitate" detainees through coerced renunciation of Mau Mau oaths and pledges of loyalty to British rule—political indoctrination through violence and deprivation. Camp guards and interrogators received training in torture techniques, demonstrating systematic rather than rogue abuse.

Historiographical Controversy: Elkins' work initially faced criticism from some historians who questioned her death toll estimates and characterization of camps as comparable to Soviet gulags. Yet subsequent archival discoveries—particularly the 2011 revelation of concealed Foreign Office documents (discussed in Chapter 17)—confirmed Elkins' core arguments about systematic torture and abuse. David Anderson's *Histories of the Hanged* (2005), using different methodology, reached similar conclusions about systematic British violence. The 2013 legal settlement with Kenyan torture survivors represented British government acknowledgment that systematic abuse occurred.

On the "Pipeline" System: British authorities in Kenya developed a "pipeline" system moving detainees through camps of increasing harshness based on their perceived cooperation. Detainees who refused to cooperate faced escalating abuse, starvation rations, and torture designed to break their resistance. This systematic approach—bureaucratized torture with formal procedures and recordkeeping—reveals the rationalized, organized nature of British camp violence rather than chaos or isolated

Chapter 12: Concentration Camps

misconduct.

On Black Africans in Boer War Camps: The deaths of approximately 14,000 black Africans in Boer War camps receive less attention than Boer deaths, exemplifying how non-white suffering is marginalized in historical accounts. Black South Africans were detained on flimsier grounds than Boers (often merely for being in "wrong" areas), received worse rations and care, and died at higher rates. Their deaths and suffering are rarely centered in popular accounts of the Boer War.

On Legal Status: Concentration camps detained people without trial based on collective suspicion rather than individual evidence of wrongdoing. This violated fundamental legal principles including habeas corpus and presumption of innocence. British authorities justified detention through emergency powers and characterizations of security threats, establishing precedents for suspending civil liberties during counterinsurgency operations that influenced detention policies in later conflicts.

On Forgotten History: These camps are largely absent from British public historical memory despite killing tens of thousands and traumatizing hundreds of thousands more. British education rarely covers the Boer War camps comprehensively or the Kenya camps at all. This amnesia allows British politicians and public to invoke British values and respect for law without confronting systematic British violations of those principles across decades of colonial conflicts.

CHAPTER THIRTEEN

The Myth of Benevolent Development: Economic Extraction and Underdevelopment (1700-1960)

Few narratives about the British Empire have proven as resilient or as politically useful as the claim that colonial rule, whatever its flaws, brought modern development to backward territories. Railways threading through jungles, irrigation systems transforming arid plains, hospitals treating tropical diseases, schools teaching literacy—these images populate defenses of empire, offered as evidence that

British rule, on balance, benefited its subjects. Even critics of imperial excesses often concede this point, acknowledging exploitation and violence while crediting Britain with infrastructure and institutions that supposedly laid foundations for postcolonial progress.

This chapter dismantles the myth of benevolent development by examining what the British Empire actually built, for whom, and at what cost. It demonstrates that colonial infrastructure served primarily extractive purposes, facilitating the removal of wealth from colonized territories to Britain. Educational and medical systems remained deliberately limited, designed to produce compliant intermediaries rather than educated citizens. Where development occurred, colonized populations typically paid for it through taxation, forced labor, and land appropriation, receiving minimal benefits while bearing all costs. Most devastatingly, British economic policies systematically underdeveloped colonial economies, destroying indigenous industries, distorting economic structures toward export dependence, and draining capital that might have financed genuine development.

The development myth serves crucial ideological functions in contemporary Britain, allowing comfortable narratives about empire's legacy while obscuring exploitation's reality. It transforms theft into gift-giving, representing infrastructure built to extract resources as benevolence toward primitive peoples. This

Chapter 13: Benevolent Development?

chapter challenges such comforting fictions, revealing colonial development as a system designed to enrich Britain while impoverishing its colonies—a pattern whose effects persist in contemporary global economic structures that continue extracting wealth from the formerly colonized world.

Railways: Arteries of Extraction

Railways constitute the centerpiece of development mythology, routinely cited as Britain's great gift to its colonies. India's vast rail network, spanning 41,000 miles by 1947, appears as irrefutable evidence of British benevolence.^1^ Yet examining who built these railways, who paid for them, and whom they served reveals a very different story.

Indian railways were not built by British taxpayers' largesse but financed almost entirely through Indian revenues and Indian debt. The colonial government guaranteed British investors extraordinary returns—typically 5% annually—on railway capital, regardless of profitability.^2^ When lines proved unprofitable, as many did, the Indian treasury covered the shortfall. British investors enjoyed risk-free returns while Indians bore all financial risk. Between 1849 and 1947, India paid approximately £500 million in guaranteed interest to British railway investors, representing a massive transfer of wealth from one of the world's poorest populations to British shareholders.^3^

Perfidious Albion

The construction contracts themselves constituted systematic looting. British law required that railway materials—rails, engines, carriages, bridges—be manufactured in Britain and shipped to India, even when Indian manufacturers could have supplied them more cheaply.^4^ This "Home Charges" system guaranteed profits for British steel makers, engine manufacturers, and shipping companies while preventing development of Indian heavy industry. When Indian entrepreneurs proposed manufacturing railway equipment domestically, colonial authorities rejected their proposals, insisting on British supplies to protect metropolitan industries.^5^

Railway routes reflected extractive rather than developmental logic. Lines connected resource-rich interiors to ports, facilitating export of raw materials to Britain. The network radiated from Bombay, Calcutta, and Madras—the great port cities—into cotton-growing districts, coal fields, and agricultural regions producing exportable commodities.^6^ Railways moved Indian cotton to Bombay for shipment to Lancashire mills, carried wheat from Punjab to export terminals during famines, and transported coal from Bihar to fuel British industry. They were built to extract, not to develop.

The human cost of railway construction was staggering. Hundreds of thousands of Indian laborers, working under brutal conditions for minimal wages, built the railways. Contemporary accounts describe workers

Chapter 13: Benevolent Development?

dying from exhaustion, disease, and industrial accidents at rates that would have provoked scandals in Britain.^7^ No comprehensive mortality records exist, but fragmentary evidence suggests tens of thousands died during construction. They were not building their own railways; they were building extraction infrastructure with their labor and lives.

Moreover, railways actively harmed certain sectors of Indian economy. India possessed extensive indigenous transportation networks—river navigation, coastal shipping, and bullock cart systems—that provided employment to millions. Railways destroyed these networks, putting boatmen, carters, and associated trades out of business without providing alternative livelihoods.^8^ The efficiency gains went to British exporters; the economic losses fell on Indian workers.

The famine railways—the supposed humanitarian justification for the network—proved largely ineffective or counterproductive. During the famines of 1876-1878 and 1896-1902, railways efficiently transported grain out of famine-stricken districts to ports for export rather than bringing relief supplies inward.^9^ British officials prioritized commercial exports over famine relief, using railways to deepen rather than alleviate starvation.

Similar patterns characterized railways across the empire. East African railways, particularly the Uganda Railway built 1896-1901, served to facilitate British access

Perfidious Albion

to the interior and extraction of resources.^10^ The Rhodesian railway system, built by Cecil Rhodes's British South Africa Company, existed solely to extract minerals from the interior and transport them to ports for export.^11^ After independence, these extractive railway systems imposed enormous burdens on successor states. The networks required constant maintenance but generated insufficient revenue because they served external markets rather than internal development needs.

Irrigation: Engineering Dependency

Irrigation systems represent another supposed triumph of British engineering benevolence, particularly in India and Egypt. Yet examining these projects' purposes and effects reveals development rhetoric masking commercial agriculture designed for British benefit.

Indian irrigation works aimed to expand production of export crops—particularly cotton, wheat, and indigo—to supply British markets and industries. The canal colonies in Punjab deliberately created new agricultural zones producing wheat for export and cotton for Lancashire mills.^12^ British engineers designed the systems, British administrators allocated water rights, and the colonial government directed production toward export crops rather than food security for local populations.

The financing model paralleled railways: Indians paid

Chapter 13: Benevolent Development?

through taxation and debt for infrastructure serving British commercial interests. Between 1867 and 1938, irrigation works cost approximately £60 million, paid largely by Indian revenues while generating profits primarily for British traders and manufacturers who bought the expanded output.^13^ Indian cultivators who actually used the water paid fees for access while bearing all risks of crop failure, price fluctuations, and debt.

Irrigation systems also created new forms of dependency and vulnerability. Perennial irrigation in Punjab and Sind encouraged intensive cash crop cultivation, reducing diversified subsistence farming that had provided food security.^14^ When international prices for cotton or wheat collapsed, cultivators faced disaster, unable to fall back on diverse food production. Canal colonies became zones of chronic indebtedness, with peasants mortgaging land to pay for seeds, tools, and water fees, eventually losing their holdings to moneylenders and large landlords.^15^

The engineering itself often proved problematic. Inadequate drainage led to waterlogging and salinization, rendering previously fertile land uncultivable. By the 1920s, hundreds of thousands of acres in Punjab suffered from salinity caused by perennial irrigation, destroying the productive capacity that justified the projects.^16^

Egypt's irrigation transformation under British control

Perfidious Albion

exemplifies colonial development's contradictions most clearly. When Britain occupied Egypt in 1882, one justification was modernizing the country's irrigation to benefit Egyptian fellahin (peasants). In reality, the system served British cotton interests almost exclusively. Perennial irrigation expanded cotton cultivation dramatically—Egypt became a major cotton exporter, supplying Lancashire—but at enormous cost to food production and peasant welfare.^17^ Land previously growing wheat and food crops shifted to cotton. Egypt, which had been self-sufficient in grain, became a food importer. When World War I disrupted imports, Egypt experienced severe food shortages despite its agricultural abundance, because that abundance consisted of cotton rather than food.^18^

The irrigation infrastructure also concentrated land ownership. Large landowners who could afford investments in cotton cultivation benefited enormously.^19^ Small peasants, lacking capital and access, often lost their land through debt. British rule accelerated Egypt's transformation from a society of small peasant proprietors to one dominated by large landlords and landless laborers—a shift irrigation projects facilitated rather than prevented.

Education: Training Subordinates, Not Citizens

The British education system in the colonies represents perhaps the most pernicious form of

Chapter 13: Benevolent Development?

underdevelopment, deliberately designed to produce a narrow class of intermediaries capable of serving colonial administration while denying education to the vast majority.

Educational expenditure in British colonies remained extraordinarily low throughout the imperial period. In India, education spending never exceeded 1.5% of government revenues and typically hovered around 1%.[20] For comparison, contemporary Britain spent approximately 15% of government revenues on education.[21] This massive disparity reflected deliberate policy: colonial subjects required minimal education to serve imperial purposes.

The 1835 Macaulay Minute, which established education policy for British India, stated the objective with remarkable candor: "We must at present do our best to form a class who may be interpreters between us and the millions whom we govern; a class of persons, Indian in blood and colour, but English in taste, in opinions, in morals, and in intellect."[22] The goal was creating intermediaries, not educating a population.

This educational philosophy shaped systems across the empire. Colonial schools taught in English, deliberately suppressing indigenous languages. The curriculum centered on British history, literature, and values, systematically denigrating local cultures, histories, and knowledge systems.[23] Students learned about British kings and parliamentary democracy while remaining ignorant of their own societies' histories and political traditions.

The racial and class hierarchies embedded in colonial education were explicit. European children attended well-funded schools with qualified teachers and modern facilities. Elite indigenous children might attend similar institutions, though typically segregated. The vast majority attended poorly funded, understaffed schools offering minimal instruction, if they attended school at all.˄24˄

Literacy rates reveal the system's failure by any development metric. In India, after nearly 200 years of British rule, literacy stood at approximately 12% in 1947—one of the lowest rates in the world.˄25˄ For women, the rate was under 9%.˄26˄ In sub-Saharan African colonies, literacy rarely exceeded 10% at independence.˄27˄ These abysmal figures reflected not unfortunate oversight but deliberate underfunding and restricted access.

The subjects taught reflected imperial priorities rather than developmental needs. Colonial schools emphasized rote learning, classical languages, and British history, while providing minimal instruction in practical skills, sciences, or technical subjects that might have supported economic development.˄28˄ The system produced clerks and administrators but few engineers, scientists, or skilled technicians.

Chapter 13: Benevolent Development?

Higher education remained even more restricted. Universities in British colonies were few, poorly funded, and designed to mimic British institutions rather than address local needs.^29^ Most colonies had no universities at all until late in the colonial period, forcing those seeking higher education to study in Britain—an option available only to tiny wealthy elite.

The educational legacy proved devastating after independence. Post-colonial states inherited systems designed to produce colonial subordinates, not educated citizens. Literacy rates were abysmal, technical skills lacking, and indigenous knowledge systems suppressed or destroyed. Building functional educational systems required enormous investments that cash-strapped newly independent states struggled to afford.

Medicine: Selective Salvation

British medical services in the colonies constitute another area where mythology diverges sharply from reality. Yet examining what medical infrastructure existed, whom it served, and what Britain chose not to address reveals a system designed to protect British interests rather than colonized populations' health.

Medical spending in colonies remained negligible throughout most of the imperial period. In India, health expenditure comprised less than 1% of government revenues until the 1930s.^30^ Even at independence,

India had one doctor per 6,000 people—compared to one per 700 in Britain—and hospital beds were concentrated in major cities, leaving rural areas where 90% of the population lived with virtually no access to modern medicine.[31]

The medical services that existed served primarily Europeans and imperial priorities. Colonial hospitals in major cities provided Western medicine to European residents, colonial officials, and urban elites who could pay fees. The Indian Medical Service functioned primarily as a corps of military doctors serving the British Indian Army, with civilian medicine a distant secondary concern.[32]

Public health measures targeted diseases threatening British military effectiveness and economic interests rather than those causing the most suffering among colonized populations. Malaria control efforts concentrated on areas with British military cantonments or European plantations. Sanitation improvements focused on European residential quarters while Indian neighborhoods received minimal attention.[33]

Indigenous medical systems were systematically suppressed or marginalized. India possessed sophisticated Ayurvedic and Unani medical traditions, practiced by trained physicians serving communities for centuries. British authorities dismissed these systems as primitive superstition, refusing to fund indigenous

Chapter 13: Benevolent Development?

medical training and denying traditional practitioners official recognition.^34^ This suppression destroyed knowledge systems and reduced healthcare access.

The most damning evidence of medical neglect lies in health outcomes. Life expectancy in India actually declined during British rule, falling from approximately 25-27 years in the early 19th century to 22-23 years by 1921.^35^ Infant mortality remained catastrophically high, with over 200 deaths per 1,000 live births.^36^ The 1918 influenza pandemic killed an estimated 12-18 million Indians—approximately 5% of the entire population—in part because decades of British rule had left India with virtually no public health infrastructure capable of responding to such crises.^37^

Maternal mortality remained shockingly high throughout British rule. Indian women faced death rates from pregnancy and childbirth approximately 50 times higher than British women.^38^ This reflected not inevitable technological limitations but deliberate choices: Britain chose not to invest in maternal health services, train midwives, or provide obstetric care for Indian women.

In Africa, colonial medical policy focused almost exclusively on diseases threatening European health or economic productivity. Sleeping sickness control aimed to protect European settlers and maintain African labor supplies rather than to serve African health.^39^

Meanwhile, diseases affecting Africans but not threatening European interests received minimal resources.

After independence, the health infrastructure legacy proved catastrophic. Post-colonial states inherited systems designed to serve tiny urban elites and protect departed Europeans, utterly inadequate for providing healthcare to entire populations.

Economic Development: Systematic Underdevelopment

Beyond specific infrastructure sectors, British colonial economic policies systematically underdeveloped colonized economies, destroying indigenous industries, distorting economic structures toward export dependency, and draining capital that might have financed genuine development. This was not unfortunate side effect of otherwise beneficial rule but central objective: Britain's prosperity depended on keeping colonies economically subordinate.

The destruction of Indian textile industries exemplifies this process. India possessed the world's most advanced textile sector before British conquest, producing high-quality cotton and silk fabrics exported globally.^40^ British policy deliberately destroyed this industry through multiple mechanisms. High tariffs on Indian textiles entering Britain protected Lancashire

Chapter 13: Benevolent Development?

manufacturers while India's colonial administration imposed minimal or no tariffs on British textiles entering India.^41^ By 1820s, this asymmetric trade regime had reversed patterns: India transformed from textile exporter to importer of British cloth.

The destruction was not market competition but state-enforced underdevelopment. When Indian manufacturers attempted to modernize with mechanized production, colonial policies prevented machinery imports, denied credit, and maintained tariff structures favoring British imports.^42^ By late 19th century, India's once-thriving textile cities had been reduced to poverty while Lancashire boomed. Millions of Indian weavers, spinners, and associated workers lost their livelihoods without alternative employment.

This pattern repeated across industries. Indian shipbuilding was deliberately destroyed through policies favoring British shipping.^43^ Indian steel production was suppressed until late 19th century when Jamshedji Tata finally secured permission to establish an integrated steel plant over intense British opposition.^44^ In each case, colonial policy protected British industry by preventing Indian competition.

African economies experienced even more severe underdevelopment. Pre-colonial African societies possessed diverse economic systems—agriculture, pastoralism, metal working, textile production, long-distance trade networks. Colonial rule destroyed or distorted these economies, forcing them into narrow roles as raw material suppliers.~45~ Land alienation transferred the most fertile territory to white settlers or plantations producing export crops. Labor coercion—through taxation, land loss, or direct force—compelled Africans to work in mines and plantations for minimal wages.

The "hut tax" implemented across British Africa exemplified this coercion. The tax, payable only in cash, forced Africans into wage labor in the colonial economy to earn money for tax payments.~46~ This destroyed subsistence economies and created labor reserves for European enterprises.

Capital extraction drained wealth from colonies to Britain throughout the imperial period. The mechanisms were multiple: repatriation of profits from European-owned enterprises, payment for British manufactured imports, "Home Charges" for colonial administration and military costs, interest on railway and irrigation debt, pensions for British officials, and enforced sterling currency reserves.~47~ Economic historian Utsa Patnaik estimates that Britain extracted approximately $45 trillion (in current value) from India alone between 1765 and 1938.~48~ This represented wealth that could have financed Indian development but instead enriched Britain.

Chapter 13: Benevolent Development?

Trade patterns reflected colonial underdevelopment. Colonies exported raw materials at prices determined in London markets. They imported British manufactured goods at prices inflated by British manufacturers' monopoly power.^49^ This terms-of-trade disadvantage systematically transferred wealth from colonies to Britain. Moreover, colonial administrations prohibited or restricted trade between colonies, forcing them to route commerce through Britain even when direct trade would have been more efficient.^50^

Infrastructure investment patterns maximized extraction while minimizing development. British capital invested in colonies went overwhelmingly to extractive sectors—mines, plantations, export transport—rather than industries serving local needs.^51^ Where manufacturing developed, it consisted of simple processing of export commodities rather than industrial production serving domestic markets.

Agricultural policies forced production toward exports while undermining food security. Colonial administrations encouraged or coerced cultivation of cotton, jute, indigo, tea, coffee, rubber, and other export crops at the expense of food production.^52^ This made colonies vulnerable to famine during harvest failures, as land previously growing food now produced commercially valuable crops while food had to be imported.

Perfidious Albion

The economic legacy of colonial underdevelopment proved nearly insurmountable after independence. Post-colonial states inherited economies distorted toward raw material export, lacking industrial capacity, dominated by foreign capital, and depleted of investment resources. Diversifying these economies, building industries, achieving food security, and reducing external dependency required decades of effort and enormous investments.

Development Comparisons: The Divergent Paths

Comparing development trajectories illuminates colonial rule's effects. Britain entered the 20th century as the world's leading industrial power, with advanced infrastructure, widespread literacy, and rising living standards. Its colonies remained desperately poor, overwhelmingly agricultural, largely illiterate, and experiencing stagnant or declining living standards.~53~ These divergent trajectories were not coincidental but causally related: British prosperity depended on colonial poverty, and colonial poverty resulted from British policies.

India provides the starkest comparison. India's share of global GDP declined from approximately 23% in 1700 to under 4% by 1950, while Britain's share rose from 3% to approximately 9% before declining as other European powers industrialized.~54~ Indian per capita income declined or stagnated under British rule while British per

Chapter 13: Benevolent Development?

capita income rose dramatically.^55^ When Britain's Industrial Revolution lifted British living standards, Indians experienced deindustrialization and impoverishment.

Literacy comparisons are equally revealing. Britain achieved near-universal literacy by early 20th century through state investment in education. India, under the same government, remained 88% illiterate at independence.^56^ This gap reflected not different inherent capacities but political choices.

Life expectancy diverged dramatically. British life expectancy rose from approximately 40 years in 1820 to 67 years by 1945.^57^ Indian life expectancy stagnated at 22-27 years throughout British rule, actually declining in late 19th and early 20th centuries.^58^ Medical knowledge and public health measures that extended British lives were deliberately not applied in India at scale.

Comparisons with societies that avoided or escaped colonial rule further illuminate British rule's effects. Japan, which maintained independence and pursued autonomous development, industrialized rapidly in late 19th century, achieving literacy, living standards, and industrial capacity comparable to European nations by mid-20th century.^59^ These comparisons suggest that colonial rule, far from accelerating development, actively retarded it.

Summary Conclusion: From Colonial to Neocolonial Extraction

The myth of benevolent development constitutes one of imperialism's most persistent and pernicious legacies. It inverts reality, transforming systematic exploitation into supposed benevolence, representing infrastructure built for extraction as gifts to primitive peoples. This chapter has demonstrated that British colonial development served imperial interests, not colonized populations. Railways facilitated resource extraction; irrigation expanded export agriculture; education produced subordinate intermediaries; medicine protected British health while neglecting colonized populations; economic policies systematically destroyed indigenous industries and drained capital.

The infrastructure Britain left behind appears substantial when viewed in isolation. But examining what was not built, what was destroyed, what was prevented, and whom infrastructure actually served reveals development rhetoric as ideological camouflage for exploitation. India's railway mileage appears impressive until compared with what India might have built with capital extracted over two centuries. Irrigation works seem benevolent until recognizing they expanded cotton for Lancashire while reducing food security.

The human costs are nearly incalculable but undeniable. Millions died in famines that need not have occurred.

Chapter 13: Benevolent Development?

Hundreds of millions lived in poverty while wealth they produced enriched Britain. Generations grew up illiterate because Britain chose not to invest in education. Indigenous knowledge systems and industries were destroyed, representing irretrievable cultural and economic losses.

After independence, successor states inherited economies deliberately structured for subordination, requiring decades of effort to partially overcome colonial underdevelopment's effects. Many former colonies remain poor not despite colonial rule but largely because of it. The developmental gap between former colonizers and colonized represents not inherent differences but historical exploitation's legacy.

Yet the patterns of extraction and underdevelopment did not end with formal decolonization. The mechanisms evolved but the fundamental relationship persisted, transformed into what scholars term "neocolonialism"—the continuation of economic domination through ostensibly independent relationships. International financial institutions established in the post-war period—the International Monetary Fund and World Bank—inherited and institutionalized colonial patterns of extraction and subordination.

The debt crisis of the 1980s and subsequent structural adjustment programs imposed by the IMF and World

Bank replicated colonial economic policies with striking fidelity. Developing nations were required to: prioritize export production over food security; open markets to foreign imports while Western markets remained protected; privatize state assets (often sold to foreign corporations at bargain prices); cut social spending on health and education; and maintain debt service payments regardless of social costs.^60^ These policies produced results remarkably similar to colonial rule: wealth extraction from poor to rich nations, destruction of local industries unable to compete with subsidized Western imports, and perpetuation of economic structures serving Western interests rather than local development.

The contemporary global economic system maintains colonial-era hierarchies through different mechanisms. Former colonies remain primary exporters of raw materials and agricultural commodities, importing manufactured goods and technology at disadvantageous terms of trade. Capital continues flowing from poor to rich nations through debt service, profit repatriation, and illicit financial flows that dwarf development aid.^61^ The estimated $1 trillion in annual illicit financial outflows from developing nations represents a wealth drain comparable in proportion to colonial extraction.^62^

Western banks and financial institutions play roles analogous to colonial trading companies, extracting

Chapter 13: Benevolent Development?

wealth through debt service and investment returns while bearing minimal risk. When debt crises occur, the costs are socialized through IMF/World Bank bailouts that protect Western financial institutions while imposing austerity on populations who had no role in creating the debts. The pattern—privatized profits, socialized losses, continued subordination—mirrors colonial political economy.

Moreover, intellectual property regimes established through World Trade Organization agreements and bilateral trade deals recreate colonial monopolies in new forms. Patents on seeds, medicines, and technologies transfer wealth from poor to rich nations while preventing the technological development that might enable genuine economic independence.˄63˄ Pharmaceutical companies charge prices for essential medicines that guarantee millions of preventable deaths in poor nations, justified through the same logic that defended colonial exploitation: property rights and market mechanisms that, coincidentally, systematically advantage the already powerful.

The myth of benevolent development persists in contemporary form through narratives about globalization, foreign aid, and development assistance. Western nations and institutions present themselves as helping poor nations develop, just as colonial powers claimed to be civilizing backward peoples. Yet the net flows of wealth remain from poor to rich, just as under formal colonialism. For every dollar of aid provided, multiple dollars flow back through debt service, profit repatriation, and trade imbalances structured by rules that rich nations write.ˆ64ˆ

Confronting this history honestly requires abandoning comfortable mythologies about empire bringing development to backward peoples. It demands recognizing that British prosperity was built substantially on colonial exploitation, and that contemporary global inequality reflects, in significant measure, this extractive relationship's long-term effects and its continuation through transformed mechanisms. The development Britain claims to have brought its colonies was largely mirage—infrastructure serving extraction dressed in humanitarian rhetoric. The actual legacy was systematic underdevelopment whose effects persist generations after independence, continuing to shape global inequality through economic structures that maintain colonial patterns of extraction and subordination.

Until these realities are acknowledged—both the historical extraction and its contemporary continuations—the work of genuine decolonization remains incomplete. Economic justice requires not merely recognizing past exploitation but dismantling the systems that perpetuate it, systems that operate through debt, trade rules, and financial mechanisms rather than through direct colonial administration but that produce

Chapter 13: Benevolent Development?

remarkably similar results: the enrichment of the West and the continued impoverishment of the formerly colonized world.

Author's Notes Chapter 13

This chapter challenges the persistent myth that British imperialism brought development to colonized territories, arguing instead that systematic economic exploitation impoverished colonies while enriching Britain. The chapter draws on dependency theory and world-systems analysis to demonstrate that underdevelopment was not unfortunate side effect but direct result of colonial economic structures designed to benefit Britain at colonies' expense.

On the "Development" Myth: British imperial apologists claim that colonialism brought infrastructure (railways, ports), institutions (legal systems, administration), and economic progress to supposedly backward territories. This narrative persists in contemporary British discourse despite overwhelming historical evidence contradicting it. The chapter systematically debunks these claims by demonstrating that infrastructure served extraction rather than local development, that institutions protected British interests rather than colonized peoples' rights, and that economic "progress" measured by trade volumes obscures wealth extraction impoverishing local populations.

On Wealth Extraction Estimates: Utsa Patnaik's estimate that Britain extracted approximately $45 trillion (in today's values) from India between 1765-1938 represents the most comprehensive recent quantification. This figure includes direct revenue extraction, trade surpluses through artificially manipulated prices, and "Home Charges" requiring India to pay for British administration and military operations. While some economists question specific methodological choices, the fundamental reality of massive wealth transfer from India to Britain is well-established. Similar patterns characterized British rule across Africa, the Caribbean, and elsewhere.

On Deindustrialization: India possessed substantial manufacturing capacity—particularly textiles—before British conquest. British policies deliberately destroyed Indian industry through tariffs protecting British manufacturers, import of British factory-made goods, and extraction of raw materials to British factories. India's share of global manufacturing output declined from approximately 25% in 1750 to under 2% by 1900. This was not "natural" economic development but deliberate policy benefiting British industry at Indian expense.

On Railway Mythology: British-built railways in India and elsewhere are frequently cited as colonial benevolence. Yet as economic historians demonstrate, railways primarily served extraction—moving raw materials from interior regions to ports for export to Britain. Railway construction enriched British companies through guaranteed returns paid by Indian taxes, used British-imported materials and equipment (rather than supporting local manufacturing), and was designed for British strategic and commercial benefit rather than Indian development needs. Railways facilitated British control and exploitation more than Indian economic advancement.

On Walter Rodney and African Underdevelopment: *How Europe Underdeveloped Africa* (1972) remains a foundational text arguing that African poverty results from European colonialism rather than pre-existing backwardness. Rodney demonstrates that colonialism deliberately prevented African industrialization, extracted resources without compensation, and structured African economies around European needs. While Rodney's work has been criticized

Chapter 13: Benevolent Development?

on some specifics, his fundamental thesis that colonialism caused underdevelopment has been broadly validated by subsequent scholarship.

On Contemporary Relevance: Colonial economic exploitation's effects persist through multiple mechanisms: colonial-era debts that some countries continue repaying, economic structures oriented toward primary commodity export rather than diversified development, destroyed industries that were never rebuilt, and psychological legacies of dependency. Understanding this history is essential for addressing contemporary global inequality, which reflects not market outcomes but centuries of colonial wealth extraction and deliberately prevented development.

Historiographical Note: Traditional development economics often treated colonized regions' poverty as pre-existing condition that development aid should address. Dependency theorists and world-systems analysts demonstrated instead that poverty resulted from colonial exploitation and continuing neo-colonial economic relationships. While dependency theory faced criticisms regarding specifics, its core insight—that underdevelopment and development are connected processes with underdevelopment resulting from exploitation—fundamentally changed understanding of global inequality.

CHAPTER FOURTEEN

Cultural Genocide and the Colonized Mind: The Erasure of Languages, Histories, and Identities (1800-1960)

When the British Empire seized territories, it conquered not merely land and peoples but entire universes of meaning. Languages spoken for millennia were suppressed or allowed to die. Historical traditions stretching back centuries were dismissed as myth and superstition. Indigenous knowledge systems—astronomy, mathematics, medicine, agriculture, philosophy—were systematically

Perfidious Albion

devalued and replaced with European frameworks. Religious practices were banned or ridiculed. Art forms disappeared. Entire ways of understanding the world, transmitting knowledge, and constituting identity were attacked, eroded, or obliterated.

Yet perhaps the most devastating achievement of British cultural imperialism was not the direct destruction it inflicted but the psychological colonization it accomplished—the creation of colonized elites who internalized the colonizer's values so thoroughly that they became empire's most effective advocates, continuing to champion British superiority long after formal colonial rule ended. From Singapore's Lee Kuan Yew praising British governance as the model for his authoritarian modernization, to Hong Kong lawyers defending British legal traditions with greater fervor than the British themselves, to Indian and Pakistani elites perpetuating "colonial club" culture decades after independence, to African and Caribbean leaders educated at British institutions who returned home as evangelists for British culture—these represent colonialism's deepest victory: convincing the colonized themselves that their subjugation was beneficial and that their colonizers' culture was superior to their own.

This chapter examines both dimensions of British cultural imperialism: the systematic destruction of colonized cultures through suppression of languages, rewriting of histories, and attack on indigenous

Chapter 14: Cultural Genocide

traditions; and the creation of what Frantz Fanon termed the "colonized mentality"—the internalization of colonial hierarchies that produces elites who identify more with their colonizers than with their own people.^1^ Understanding this dual process—external destruction and internal colonization—is essential for grasping how empire's cultural effects persist generations after political independence.

Linguistic Imperialism and the Creation of Anglophone Elites

Language constitutes the foundation of culture, encoding not merely communication tools but entire worldviews and knowledge systems. The British Empire presided over the death or severe endangerment of hundreds of languages across its territories, through policies that deliberately marginalized indigenous languages while imposing English as the language of power, prestige, and advancement. More insidiously, these policies created Anglophone elites who internalized linguistic hierarchies so thoroughly that they perpetuated English dominance long after political independence, often with greater rigidity than the colonizers themselves had imposed.

India, with its extraordinary linguistic diversity, experienced the most comprehensive linguistic imperialism. At the time of British conquest, the subcontinent supported hundreds of languages and

Perfidious Albion

thousands of dialects, each embedded in complex literary, religious, and cultural traditions.^2^ The 1835 Macaulay Minute, which established education policy, declared English "preeminent" and indigenous languages inadequate for modern knowledge: "I have never found one amongst them [Orientalists] who could deny that a single shelf of a good European library was worth the whole native literature of India and Arabia."^3^ This dismissal of millennia of intellectual achievement was calculated strategy: making English the exclusive language of administration, higher education, and social advancement forced those seeking power to abandon their linguistic heritage.

The consequences were profound and enduring. English became the language of elite aspiration, with middle and upper-class families increasingly adopting it at home and sending children to English-medium schools.^4^ Indigenous languages, denied institutional support and associated with backwardness, lost prestige and speakers. Even major languages suffered degradation, as their vocabularies failed to develop technical and scientific terminology because such knowledge was transmitted exclusively in English.

Yet the most insidious effect was the creation of an Anglophone elite that genuinely believed in English superiority and actively worked to maintain English dominance after independence. Indians educated in English-medium schools often developed contempt for

Chapter 14: Cultural Genocide

their own linguistic heritage, speaking English at home, consuming British literature and culture, and viewing indigenous languages as provincial and limiting.^5^ After independence, this Anglophone elite dominated Indian politics, education, and culture, perpetuating English's privileged status through multiple mechanisms. They argued that English provided access to global knowledge and united India's diverse linguistic communities—justifications that, while containing elements of truth, also served to preserve their own class advantages.^6^

The reproduction of linguistic hierarchies across generations reveals colonialism's success in creating self-perpetuating elite identification with colonizers' language. The children of India's Anglophone elite attend English-medium schools where they are socialized into linguistic and cultural norms that distance them from majority populations. They consume primarily English-language media, think in English, and express complex ideas more easily in English than in their nominal "mother tongue." This creates a fundamental divide within Indian society, with English fluency marking class boundaries more sharply than almost any other characteristic.^7^

Africa experienced even more catastrophic linguistic destruction, and African elites' perpetuation of colonial language policies has been even more consequential. The continent's extraordinary linguistic diversity—over 2,000 languages—represented millennia of human cultural evolution.[8] British colonial policy treated this diversity as primitive chaos requiring rationalization through imposed linguistic uniformity. English became the language of education and administration, with African children forbidden to speak their mother tongues in schools, facing corporal punishment for violations. The famous Kenyan writer Ngũgĩ wa Thiong'o recalls being caned for speaking Gikuyu at school: "One of the most humiliating experiences was to be caught speaking Gikuyu in the vicinity of the school. The culprit was given corporal punishment."[9]

Yet again, the most profound effect was psychological colonization of African elites who then perpetuated colonial language policies after independence. Most Anglophone African countries retained English as sole official language after independence despite it being spoken fluently by tiny minorities—typically less than 10% of populations.[10] The justifications offered were pragmatic, yet these obscured how English-language policies preserved advantages of English-educated elites while disadvantaging majority populations.

Ngũgĩ wa Thiong'o's decision in 1977 to abandon English and write exclusively in Gikuyu represented direct challenge to this linguistic colonialism. His book *Decolonising the Mind: The Politics of Language in African Literature* (1986) articulated how African writers' use of European languages perpetuated mental colonization: "The effect of a cultural bomb is to annihilate a people's

Chapter 14: Cultural Genocide

belief in their names, in their languages, in their environment, in their heritage of struggle."^11^ Yet Ngũgĩ's position remained controversial even among African intellectuals, many of whom argued that European languages allowed African writers to reach global audiences. This debate revealed colonized elites' ambivalence: recognizing linguistic colonialism's damage while depending on colonial languages for their professional identities.

The Caribbean experienced linguistic colonization with different dynamics given its settler-colonial character and the prevalence of creole languages. Yet here too, British colonial education created elites who viewed English as superior and creole languages as degraded or inferior. Despite creoles being mother tongues for majority populations and possessing sophisticated grammatical structures, colonial and postcolonial education systems treated them as corrupt English requiring correction rather than as legitimate languages.^12^ Caribbean elites educated in colonial systems internalized contempt for creole languages, policing their own speech to eliminate creole features and viewing creole as embarrassing mark of insufficient education.

The Irish language experienced systematic British suppression despite Ireland's geographic proximity. British authorities established a national school system in 1831 that conducted all instruction in English, forbidding Irish language use. Children caught speaking Irish faced corporal punishment. By 1900, Irish speakers had collapsed from over 50% of population in 1800 to under 15%.^13^ After independence, the Irish state attempted revival through education requirements and official promotion, but Irish remained primarily symbolic rather than vernacular for most citizens, as Irish elites themselves typically spoke English as first language.^14^

Australia's Aboriginal peoples faced most extreme linguistic destruction. British colonization proceeded on legal fiction of *terra nullius*, denying Aboriginal peoples' very existence as societies with legitimate cultures and languages.^15^ Mission schools forcibly separated Aboriginal children from families and forbade use of indigenous languages. By the 20th century, many Aboriginal languages had disappeared entirely, with surviving languages facing endangerment.^16^

The Colonized Elite: Macaulay's Children

The creation of colonized elites who internalized and perpetuated colonial values represented British cultural imperialism's supreme achievement. Thomas Babington Macaulay's 1835 Minute on Indian Education articulated the strategy with remarkable candor: "We must at present do our best to form a class who may be interpreters between us and the millions whom we govern; a class of persons, Indian in blood and colour,

Chapter 14: Cultural Genocide

but English in taste, in opinions, in morals, and in intellect."^17^

Macaulay understood that direct British rule over hundreds of millions was impossible. But if colonized peoples could be educated to internalize British values and to identify their interests with British interests, they would govern themselves according to British preferences while believing they exercised self-determination. Colonial education would create intermediaries who policed their own societies more effectively than British administrators could.^18^

The system worked through comprehensive socialization beginning in childhood. Colonial schools taught British history, literature, and values while systematically denigrating indigenous cultures. Students learned about British monarchs, parliamentary democracy, and the "civilizing mission" while learning virtually nothing positive about their own societies' histories and achievements. They studied English literature as embodiments of universal civilization while their own literary traditions were dismissed as primitive.^19^

Beyond formal curriculum, colonial schools socialized through discipline, culture, and aspiration. Students wore British-style uniforms, played British sports, and participated in British-style house systems. They were punished—often corporally—for speaking indigenous languages or displaying indigenous cultural practices. The entire environment communicated that Britishness was superior and indigenous culture was inferior.[20]

The students who succeeded in this system—who mastered English, absorbed British culture, and internalized British values—were rewarded with access to positions of privilege: colonial administration, legal profession, medical profession, teaching, and commerce. They became the "brown sahibs" or "black Englishmen" who staffed lower ranks of colonial administration and provided crucial buffer between British rulers and colonized masses.[21]

The psychological effects were profound. Many developed deep ambivalence toward their own identities—simultaneously proud of cultural heritage and ashamed of its supposed backwardness. Some resolved this by rejecting indigenous identity as completely as possible, becoming more British than the British. Others maintained superficial indigenous cultural markers while thoroughly internalizing British cultural hierarchies.[22]

This colonization of consciousness persisted after political independence because the colonized elite dominated postcolonial states. They had been prepared by colonial education to govern, they controlled institutions and resources, and they genuinely believed that modernization required adoption of Western

Chapter 14: Cultural Genocide

norms—that indigenous cultures, while perhaps worthy of nostalgic preservation, could not provide frameworks for modern governance or economic development.˄23˄

Lee Kuan Yew: The Authoritarian Anglophile

No figure better exemplifies the colonized elite's complex relationship with British imperialism than Lee Kuan Yew, Singapore's founding prime minister. Lee was quintessential product of colonial education: born in 1923 to Chinese Peranakan family in British Malaya, educated at elite Raffles Institution (modeled explicitly on British public schools), and later at Cambridge University where he studied law. He was thoroughly socialized into British cultural norms through two decades of immersion in British educational institutions.˄24˄

Lee's entire intellectual formation occurred within British frameworks. At Raffles, he absorbed British literature, history, and political philosophy. At Cambridge during the late 1940s, this colonial socialization deepened. He later described Cambridge as transformative experience that shaped his worldview fundamentally.˄25˄

Yet Lee was also witness to British imperial decline and Japanese occupation's exposure of British weakness. During World War II, Japanese forces conquered Singapore in 1942 in humiliating defeat that shattered the myth of European invincibility. Lee witnessed British surrender and subsequent Japanese occupation, learning that British power was not eternal and that Asian peoples could defeat Europeans militarily.˄26˄

Lee's political trajectory combined anti-colonial nationalism with profound Anglophilia. He led Singapore's independence movement and negotiated the end of British colonial rule, yet his vision of what Singapore should become was fundamentally shaped by British models. He admired British administrative efficiency, legal traditions, civil service meritocracy, and governance structures. His goal was not to reject British influence but to appropriate its benefits while ending British political control.˄27˄

After becoming Prime Minister in 1959, Lee implemented policies revealing his colonial education's deep influence. He made English the medium of education and government despite Singapore's overwhelmingly Chinese population. His justification was pragmatic—English provided access to global commerce and technology—but the choice also reflected his genuine belief in English superiority as vehicle for modern knowledge.˄28˄

Lee modeled Singapore's institutions explicitly on British frameworks. The legal system followed English common law precisely. The civil service adopted British administrative traditions. The educational system was

Chapter 14: Cultural Genocide

based on British grammar schools. Even Singapore's public housing and urban planning reflected British influences filtered through Lee's admiration for British order and efficiency.^29^

His speeches and writings reveal profound internalization of colonial values. His autobiography and collected speeches are filled with admiring references to British efficiency, legal traditions, parliamentary procedure, and administrative competence. He acknowledged that British colonialism was exploitative but insisted that it brought benefits—modern administration, legal systems, infrastructure—that made Singapore's subsequent development possible.^30^

Yet Lee's embrace of British models came with authoritarian adaptations that British liberals would have rejected. He combined British administrative efficiency with authoritarian governance that suppressed political opposition, controlled media, and limited civil liberties in ways that fundamentally contradicted British democratic traditions. This selectivity reveals the colonized elite's characteristic pattern: embracing colonial culture and institutions that reinforce their power while rejecting aspects that would democratize or empower others.^31^

Critics argued that Lee had internalized colonial hierarchies so thoroughly that he could not imagine

Perfidious Albion

alternatives to British models. His insistence that English was necessary for modernity, his faith in British institutions, his assumption that Western developmental paths must be followed—all reflected colonized consciousness that could not conceive of non-Western routes to development.^32^ Yet Lee's defenders argue that his embrace of British models was pragmatic rather than psychological, and that Singapore's extraordinary economic success vindicates his choices.^33^

Lee exemplifies colonial education's success in creating elite that perpetuates colonial culture while believing itself postcolonial. Lee genuinely viewed himself as having transcended colonialism—he led independence movement, ended British rule, and built independent nation. Yet his entire intellectual formation, institutional models, language policies, cultural values, and governance philosophy were profoundly shaped by colonial education that had successfully convinced him of British cultural superiority.^34^

Hong Kong: When the Colonized Defend Their Colonizers

If Lee Kuan Yew represents complicated ambivalence toward British colonialism, Hong Kong's legal and professional elite often demonstrate something more troubling: active nostalgia for British colonial rule and defense of British colonialism as superior to Chinese sovereignty. Hong Kong lawyers, judges, and

Chapter 14: Cultural Genocide

professionals educated under British rule frequently express fondness for British legal traditions and cultural practices with an enthusiasm that sometimes exceeds that found in Britain itself.^35^

This phenomenon intensified after Hong Kong's 1997 handover to China. Many Hong Kong residents who had lived under British colonial rule—without democracy, with governors appointed from London, and with limited political freedoms—began retrospectively celebrating British governance as protecting freedoms and rule of law. They contrasted British colonial rule favorably with Chinese sovereignty, despite the fact that British Hong Kong was explicitly colonial and undemocratic.^36^

Hong Kong's legal profession particularly embraced this colonial nostalgia. Trained in British common law traditions, wearing British-style wigs and gowns, Hong Kong lawyers frequently described British legal traditions as guaranteeing freedoms and representing civilization. They defended continuation of English common law not merely as practical necessity but as moral imperative—as if British legal traditions possessed inherent superiority over Chinese legal frameworks.^37^

This reached absurd extremes when some Hong Kong protesters in 2019-2020 waved British colonial flags and called for return to British rule—a demand that ignored how British rule had been explicitly colonial, had denied

Hong Kongers democracy, and had been premised on subordinate status. That colonized peoples would wave their colonizers' flags and demand return to colonial subjugation represents colonialism's deepest psychological victory.^38^

Multiple factors explain this phenomenon. First, generational: those educated under British rule were socialized to identify British governance with order and rule of law. Second, comparative: many Hong Kongers feared that Chinese rule would be worse, making British colonialism retrospectively appear protective. Third, political: celebrating British rule became form of resistance to Chinese authority.^39^

Yet these contextual explanations do not fully justify the phenomenon. British rule of Hong Kong was founded on opium trafficking, secured through military aggression, and maintained through colonial subordination. Britain granted Hong Kong no democracy, appointed all governors, and ensured that Hong Kong existed to serve British commercial interests.^40^ That some Hong Kongers came to celebrate this arrangement reveals how successfully colonialism can implant identification with colonizers even among those it subordinates.

The broader implications are significant. If colonialism can be so successful in creating identification with colonizers that colonized peoples will defend colonialism and wave colonial flags, then psychological

Chapter 14: Cultural Genocide

decolonization is far more difficult than political independence suggests. Hong Kong demonstrates that colonial hierarchies can be internalized so thoroughly that they become constitutive of identity.˄41˄

Colonial Clubs and Perpetuated Hierarchies

Perhaps nowhere is the persistence of colonial culture more visible than in the "colonial clubs" that continue operating across former colonies decades after independence. These institutions—established by British colonizers as exclusive spaces for European socialization—were characterized by rigid racial hierarchies and formal British customs. After independence, rather than closing these anachronisms, indigenous elites often preserved them, joining clubs that had excluded their ancestors and perpetuating the very cultural practices that had subordinated their peoples.˄42˄

In India and Pakistan, colonial clubs remain prestigious institutions where elites gather in settings consciously maintained to evoke British imperial culture. The Delhi Gymkhana Club, the Bombay Gymkhana, the Bengal Club, the Karachi Gymkhana—these institutions continue operating much as they did under colonial rule. Their architecture deliberately evokes British colonial power. Their interiors feature dark wood paneling, hunting trophies, colonial memorabilia, and libraries stocked with British classics.˄43˄

Perfidious Albion

The clubs' rules and customs perpetuate colonial practices with remarkable fidelity. Formal dress codes require Western attire, with traditional indigenous clothing often explicitly prohibited except on designated "ethnic" days. This enforces cultural hierarchy where Western dress represents sophistication while indigenous dress represents informality. Elite Indians and Pakistanis who would face no such restrictions in London voluntarily maintain these rules in their own countries.^44^

The language patterns are equally telling. English dominates conversation despite members' fluency in indigenous languages. Speaking Hindi, Urdu, Bengali, or other local languages often marks one as insufficiently sophisticated. The clubs' sports facilities emphasize British sports—cricket, tennis, golf—while indigenous games receive little attention. Dining features British-style formal meals and afternoon teas.^45^

The clubs' membership criteria ensure exclusivity that replicates colonial class hierarchies. Substantial wealth is necessary. Professional status matters. Recommendations from existing members are required. The result is membership that replicates colonial elite composition: English-educated, professionally successful, culturally Anglicized, and economically prosperous.^46^

Critics argue that colonial clubs represent most visible

Chapter 14: Cultural Genocide

evidence of continued colonial mentality among postcolonial elites—that these institutions explicitly celebrate colonial culture, maintain colonial hierarchies, and create spaces where elites perform their distance from indigenous masses through mastery of British cultural codes. The clubs embody what Frantz Fanon described: colonized elites who have internalized the colonizer's values so thoroughly that they perpetuate colonial culture with more rigidity than colonizers themselves.^47^

The phenomenon extends beyond clubs to broader patterns of elite socialization. English-medium schools modeled on British public schools, universities emphasizing Western curriculum, professional organizations maintaining British traditions—all function to reproduce colonial cultural hierarchies. Children of postcolonial elites are socialized into British cultural norms from birth, ensuring intergenerational transmission of colonial cultural identification.^48^

African and Caribbean Anglophilia

The phenomenon of colonized elites celebrating British culture extends across Africa and the Caribbean. The founding generation of African independence leaders were overwhelmingly products of British colonial education. Julius Nyerere of Tanzania attended Edinburgh University. Kenneth Kauda of Zambia was educated at mission schools. Jomo Kenyatta of Kenya studied at the London School of Economics. Kwame Nkrumah of Ghana studied at Lincoln University and LSE.^49^

These men received education that fundamentally shaped their worldviews despite their leadership of independence movements. They spoke English fluently and by preference. They quoted British literature in their speeches. They admired British institutions. They frequently referenced British political philosophers in articulating their own political visions.^50^

The contradictions were visible throughout their careers. Nyerere articulated philosophy of African socialism explicitly rooted in African communal traditions, yet he studied British Fabian socialism at Edinburgh and his political philosophy showed clear British influences. He promoted Swahili as Tanzania's national language—one of few African leaders to do so—yet he personally remained most comfortable in English, quoted British literature frequently, and sent his children to British universities.^51^

Caribbean independence leaders showed even more pronounced Anglophilia. Most—Eric Williams of Trinidad, Errol Barrow of Barbados, Michael Manley of Jamaica—were educated at British universities, particularly Oxford, Cambridge, and LSE. They returned home as sophisticated political thinkers influenced by British socialism and Westminster

Chapter 14: Cultural Genocide

parliamentary traditions.~52~

The educational preferences of postcolonial African and Caribbean elites reveal continued colonial cultural influence. Wealthy Africans and Caribbeans continue sending children to British boarding schools at rates far exceeding practical necessity. These choices reflect perception that British education confers prestige and quality superior to local alternatives—a perception directly inherited from colonial hierarchies.~53~

Language policies implemented by independence leaders particularly reveal continued British influence. Most Anglophone African countries retained English as sole official language after independence despite it being spoken fluently by tiny minorities. The Caribbean maintained English even more completely, with little debate about alternatives.~54~

The continuing Anglophilia among African and Caribbean elites demonstrates that decolonization remained incomplete in cultural and psychological dimensions despite political independence. The elites who governed postcolonial states had been so successfully socialized into British culture that they could not imagine alternatives, or they recognized that alternatives would threaten their advantages.~55~

Rewriting History and Suppressing Indigenous Traditions

The British Empire did not merely conquer territories; it conquered memory, systematically rewriting the histories of colonized peoples to justify British rule while denigrating indigenous achievements. James Mill's *History of British India* (1817), despite Mill never visiting India, became the authoritative text shaping British understanding for decades. Mill divided Indian history into "Hindu," "Muslim," and "British" periods, portraying the first two as despotic darkness and the third as enlightened progress.[56]

British historians systematically downplayed or ignored Indian achievements in mathematics, astronomy, medicine, and philosophy. Indian mathematical innovations—including the decimal system and concept of zero—were either attributed to Greek influence or dismissed as insignificant. Sanskrit philosophical texts were characterized as mystical confusion. Indian political thought was ignored or mischaracterized as Oriental despotism.[57]

In Africa, historical erasure reached even more extreme levels. European scholarship widely denied that African societies possessed histories at all. The influential historian Hugh Trevor-Roper declared in 1963: "Perhaps, in the future, there will be some African history to teach. But at present there is none."[58] Archaeological evidence of sophisticated African civilizations was systematically ignored or attributed to

Chapter 14: Cultural Genocide

non-African sources. Great Zimbabwe was attributed to Phoenicians or Arabs because Europeans could not conceive of Africans constructing such architecture.˄59˄

Colonial education in Africa taught European history extensively while treating African history as beginning with European arrival. Students learned about British monarchs and European explorers "discovering" African territories. They learned virtually nothing about their own societies' histories or achievements.˄60˄

Beyond language and history, the British Empire systematically attacked colonized peoples' religious practices and cultural traditions. In India, British authorities banned or restricted numerous practices. The sati debate served to justify British rule by presenting Indians as practicing barbarism requiring British governance.˄61˄ Christian missionaries, operating with colonial government support, directly attacked Hindu and Muslim religious practices, characterizing Hinduism as idolatry and mocking Hindu gods.˄62˄

In Africa, missionary Christianity aggressively attacked indigenous spiritual traditions. African religions were characterized as primitive paganism or demon worship. Missionaries banned traditional ceremonies, destroyed sacred objects, and demanded converts abandon all traditional practices.˄63˄ The destruction of African traditional religions severed connections between communities and spiritual heritage. Africans converted to Christianity were taught that their ancestors' beliefs were evil and their religious practices devil worship.~64~

Australian Aboriginal spiritual traditions faced particularly severe attack. Aboriginal Dreamtime beliefs were dismissed as primitive superstition. Missions forcibly removed Aboriginal children from families to "civilize" them, forbidding all traditional cultural practices. Sacred sites were desecrated, sacred objects stolen for museums, and ceremonies banned.~65~

Psychological Colonization and Its Reproduction

Perhaps the most insidious aspect of British cultural imperialism was the psychological damage inflicted through systematic inculcation of cultural inferiority. Colonized peoples were taught that their languages, religions, histories, and traditions were inferior to British equivalents. This psychological colonization created what Frantz Fanon termed the "colonized mentality": internalization of colonial hierarchies and adoption of colonizers' contemptuous attitudes toward one's own culture.~66~

The colonial education system functioned as the primary mechanism. Colonized children learned that British history, literature, and culture represented civilization while their own represented backwardness. They were taught in English while forbidden to use their mother tongues. They learned to associate modernity

Chapter 14: Cultural Genocide

and progress with Britishness and backwardness with indigenous culture.˄67˄

This educational indoctrination was reinforced by every aspect of colonial society. Administrative positions were reserved for those educated in British style who demonstrated cultural assimilation. Social prestige derived from proximity to British culture. Colonial social hierarchies placed British at apex, with degrees of status determined by extent of cultural Anglicization.˄68˄

The psychological effects were devastating and enduring. Many colonized individuals developed profound ambivalence toward their own cultures, simultaneously proud of heritage and ashamed of its supposed backwardness. This ambivalence often manifested as rejection of indigenous culture in favor of British norms, creating generations of what Homi Bhabha terms "mimic men": colonized individuals who adopted British culture but remained forever denied full acceptance as equals.˄69˄

The trauma of cultural inferiority persisted across generations and survived independence. Postcolonial societies often retained colonial attitudes toward indigenous cultures, with European languages and cultural practices maintaining prestige while indigenous equivalents struggled for respect. This represents colonialism's deepest victory: convincing colonized peoples themselves that their cultures deserve subordination.~70~

The psychological damage extended to bodily self-perception and aesthetics. Colonial hierarchies associated whiteness with beauty while characterizing darker skin as inferior. This racial aesthetic hierarchy created widespread colorism within colonized societies. The contemporary multibillion-dollar skin-lightening industry in postcolonial societies represents colonialism's enduring psychological legacy.~71~

The reproduction of colonized consciousness across generations occurs through elite socialization patterns that normalize colonial cultural hierarchies. Elite families speak English at home, send children to English-medium schools, consume primarily English-language media, and model success as approximation of British norms. Children raised in these environments internalize the message that British culture is superior before they can critically evaluate it.~72~

Summary Conclusion

This chapter has documented both dimensions of British cultural imperialism: the systematic external destruction of colonized cultures through suppression of languages, rewriting of histories, and attack on religious and cultural practices; and the internal colonization of consciousness that created elites who internalized colonial hierarchies

Chapter 14: Cultural Genocide

so thoroughly that they perpetuated colonial culture with greater rigidity than colonizers themselves required.

The scale of cultural destruction was enormous. Hundreds of languages disappeared or were severely damaged. Historical memories were suppressed and replaced with colonial narratives. Religious and cultural practices were banned or marginalized. Indigenous knowledge systems were destroyed. Psychological damage was inflicted on millions who internalized messages of cultural inferiority.

Yet perhaps colonialism's greatest achievement was creating colonized elites who internalized the colonizer's values and became empire's most effective advocates. From Lee Kuan Yew praising British governance while implementing authoritarianism, to Hong Kong professionals defending British colonialism, to Indian and Pakistani elites perpetuating colonial clubs and cultural hierarchies, to African and Caribbean leaders sending children to British schools and maintaining English linguistic dominance—these patterns reveal successful colonization of consciousness that persists generations after political independence.

The phenomenon demonstrates that decolonization requires far more than political independence. Cultural and psychological decolonization—dismantling internalized hierarchies, recovering suppressed histories and traditions, and developing identities not defined through colonial frameworks—proves far more difficult and takes far longer than achieving formal independence. When colonized elites have been so successfully socialized that they genuinely believe in British cultural superiority and actively perpetuate colonial hierarchies while believing themselves postcolonial, the colonization has achieved its deepest and most enduring victory.

The class dimensions are crucial. Colonized elites benefit from colonial cultural hierarchies that advantage those with British education, English fluency, and cultural Anglicization. Their social status, professional success, and economic advantages depend on maintaining systems that privilege British culture. The reproduction across generations ensures persistence through elite children socialized into British culture from birth, educated in English-medium schools, sent to British universities, and integrated into Anglophone professional networks.

Recognizing cultural genocide as integral to British imperialism, understanding how it created colonized elites who perpetuate colonial culture, and acknowledging how these patterns persist in postcolonial contexts are essential for honest historical reckoning. The railways and schools that defenders of empire cite as evidence of benevolence were accompanied by systematic destruction of languages, histories, and

Chapter 14: Cultural Genocide

cultures that created wounds still unhealed generations later. The psychological colonization that convinced elites of British cultural superiority represents colonialism's most complete and enduring victory—one that continues shaping postcolonial societies through elites who mistake their colonization for sophistication and their perpetuation of colonial hierarchies for cosmopolitan achievement.

Author's Notes Chapter 14

This chapter examines systematic British destruction of colonized peoples' cultures, languages, religions, and identities—what the UN Genocide Convention terms "cultural genocide" though it stops short of criminalizing it as genocide per se. The chapter argues that cultural destruction was deliberate imperial strategy designed to facilitate control by eliminating cultural foundations for resistance and creating colonized subjects psychologically dependent on British culture and validation.

On "Cultural Genocide": The 1948 UN Genocide Convention's drafters debated including cultural genocide but ultimately excluded it, limiting genocide definition to physical and biological destruction. Rafael Lemkin, who coined "genocide," intended it to include cultural destruction. Contemporary scholars including Patrick Wolfe argue that cultural genocide should be recognized as genocide variant. This chapter uses "cultural genocide" to emphasize the systematic, deliberate nature of cultural destruction while acknowledging it doesn't meet the Genocide Convention's legal definition.

On Residential Schools: The Canadian Truth and Reconciliation Commission's 2015 Final Report documented that approximately 150,000 indigenous children were forcibly removed to residential schools where they faced systematic cultural erasure, abuse, and death. The Commission characterized this system as "cultural genocide," providing comprehensive documentation of systematic cultural destruction. Similar systems operated in Australia (leading to the "Stolen Generations") and elsewhere. J.R. Miller's *Shingwauk's Vision* (1996) provides detailed history of Canadian residential schools based on extensive archival research and survivor testimonies.

On Language Suppression: British authorities systematically suppressed indigenous languages through education policies requiring English, legal restrictions on public use of indigenous languages, and social stigmatization. Irish Gaelic, Scottish Gaelic, Welsh, and numerous indigenous languages in Africa, Asia, and the Pacific faced systematic suppression. Ngugi wa Thiong'o's *Decolonising the Mind* (1986) eloquently describes colonialism's assault on African languages and consciousness, arguing that language is crucial site of resistance and decolonization.

On Educational Systems: Colonial education served multiple purposes: creating English-speaking administrative class to facilitate British rule, inculcating British values and cultural superiority, teaching colonized peoples to view their own cultures as inferior, and providing minimal education necessary for subordinate economic roles while preventing education that might enable challenges to British rule. Gauri Viswanathan's *Masks of Conquest* (1989) examines how English literature became tool of colonial domination in India, used to teach British cultural superiority and make Indians internalize colonial values.

On Frantz Fanon: *The Wretched of the Earth* (1961) remains foundational text for understanding colonialism's psychological effects. Fanon, a psychiatrist who worked in Algeria during its independence war, analyzed how colonialism created psychological conditions—internalized inferiority, divided consciousness, alienation from indigenous culture—that persisted beyond formal decolonization. His work influenced subsequent post-colonial theory and independence movements globally.

On Religious Conversion: Christian missionary activity was intricately connected to colonialism, though relationships were complex with some missionaries opposing colonial abuses. Missionaries systematically attacked indigenous religions, destroying sacred sites, criminalizing traditional practices, and creating educational systems teaching Christianity and European culture. Religious conversion served colonial control by undermining traditional authority structures, creating divisions within colonized populations, and promoting values supporting European dominance.

On Continuing Effects: Cultural genocide's effects persist through language loss (many indigenous languages are extinct or endangered), interrupted cultural transmission (knowledge, practices, and traditions lost when elders could not teach younger generations), psychological trauma affecting multiple generations, and continuing struggle to revive and maintain indigenous cultures under conditions of economic and political marginalization. Truth and reconciliation processes in Canada and Australia have begun addressing these legacies but face enormous challenges reconstructing what was systematically destroyed.

Methodological Challenges: Reconstructing indigenous cultures, languages, and knowledge systems that colonialism destroyed is extremely difficult because colonialism systematically destroyed evidence. What we know about pre-colonial cultures comes from fragmentary sources: colonial observers' accounts (biased and often inaccurate), material culture surviving in museums (often decontextualized), oral traditions maintained despite suppression, and archaeological evidence. The gaps in our knowledge represent further violence—destroying cultures then preventing future generations from fully knowing what was lost.

CHAPTER FIFTEEN

Suez and the End of Illusions (1956)

On the evening of October 29, 1956, Israeli paratroopers dropped into Egypt's Sinai Peninsula, initiating a war that would within days expose the hollowness of British imperial pretensions and mark the definitive end of Britain as a global superpower. The Suez Crisis, as it became known, represented the culmination of British imperial decline and the moment when illusions about Britain's continuing world role shattered against the realities of American power and decolonization's inexorable advance. Within weeks, British and French forces—

having colluded secretly with Israel to seize the Suez Canal—would withdraw in humiliation, their prime ministers disgraced, their imperial authority irretrievably compromised.

The crisis exposed fundamental truths that Britain's political class had desperately avoided confronting. The Empire was finished, not merely as political fact but as credible aspiration. Britain could no longer act independently as a great power; American approval had become prerequisite for significant international action. The colonial subjects who had sustained British power for centuries would no longer accept subordination; nationalism had become irresistible force against which imperial power could not prevail. Most devastatingly for British self-conception, the moral authority Britain claimed—as force for civilization, democracy, and international order—stood revealed as transparent hypocrisy when British interests were threatened.

This chapter examines the Suez Crisis as the decisive moment of imperial reckoning, when the gap between Britain's self-image and its actual position in the post-war world became undeniable. It demonstrates how Anthony Eden's government—driven by imperial nostalgia, racial contempt for Arab nationalism, and delusional confidence in British power—engineered a catastrophic failure that accelerated decolonization and reduced Britain to decidedly junior partner in an American-dominated Western alliance.

Chapter 15: Suez and the End of Illusions

Egypt, Nationalism, and the Canal

The Suez Canal, opened in 1869, had been central to British imperial strategy for nearly a century, providing the shortest route between Britain and its Asian empire, particularly India. Although nominally owned by the Suez Canal Company—a private corporation with British and French shareholders—Britain had exercised effective control since 1882, when it occupied Egypt ostensibly to protect the canal and European financial interests.^1^ For seventy-four years, Britain maintained military presence in Egypt against Egyptian wishes, treating the country as a colonial possession despite its nominal independence after 1922.

Egyptian nationalism, suppressed but never eliminated during decades of British occupation, intensified after World War II. The humiliating 1948 Arab-Israeli War, in which British-backed Arab armies were defeated by the new Israeli state, discredited Egypt's corrupt monarchy and the political establishment that had accommodated British domination.^2^ In July 1952, the Free Officers Movement, led by Gamal Abdel Nasser, overthrew King Farouk in a bloodless coup, establishing a republic committed to genuine independence, Arab unity, and social reform.^3^

Nasser emerged as Egypt's dominant leader by 1954, embodying a new Arab nationalism that rejected both Western imperialism and alignment with either Cold

War bloc. His vision—pan-Arab unity, non-alignment, modernization without Western tutelage—threatened British interests throughout the Middle East. If Egypt could successfully defy British power, what would prevent other Arab states from following? If Nasser succeeded in building a modern, independent Egypt, what legitimacy remained for British claims that Arabs required Western guidance?ˆ4ˆ

British officials and politicians, steeped in imperial assumptions about Arab incapacity for self-governance, viewed Nasser with contempt and alarm. Anthony Eden, who became Prime Minister in April 1955, developed particular obsession with Nasser, whom he compared repeatedly to Hitler—a comparison revealing more about Eden's psychology than Nasser's character.ˆ5ˆ For Eden and much of the British establishment, Nasser represented intolerable challenge to British authority, an uppity colonial subject who refused to know his place.

The immediate crisis emerged from Nasser's arms deal with Czechoslovakia in September 1955 and his subsequent decision to seek Soviet and American financing for the Aswan High Dam, a massive infrastructure project central to Egyptian development plans.ˆ6ˆ When the United States, influenced by Britain and responding to Nasser's recognition of Communist China, abruptly withdrew its offer to finance the dam in July 1956, Nasser responded with dramatic gesture that electrified the Arab world and horrified Britain: on July

Chapter 15: Suez and the End of Illusions

26, 1956, he nationalized the Suez Canal Company, declaring that Egypt would use canal revenues to finance the Aswan Dam.^7^

Nationalization was entirely legal—Egypt offered compensation to shareholders and guaranteed freedom of navigation—but it struck at the heart of British imperial psychology. The canal symbolized British power; Nasser's seizure demonstrated that power's evaporation. More practically, Britain depended on Middle Eastern oil transported through the canal, and British officials feared that an independent Egypt controlling the waterway could threaten oil supplies.^8^ That these fears proved entirely groundless—Egypt never threatened to close the canal to non-military shipping—mattered less than the psychological blow to British prestige.

Conspiracy and Collusion

Eden's government determined immediately to reverse nationalization by force, though recognizing that overt military action against Egypt would face international condemnation and domestic opposition.^9^ Through summer and autumn 1956, British officials pursued dual strategies: public diplomacy seeking negotiated solution while secretly planning military intervention. The diplomatic efforts were theater; Eden had decided that Nasser must be removed and British control over the canal restored, regardless of legality or international opinion.

The conspiracy that emerged involved Britain, France, and Israel in a scheme of breathtaking cynicism and incompetence. France, fighting nationalist insurgency in Algeria and blaming Nasser for supporting the rebels, shared British determination to destroy the Egyptian leader. Israel, threatened by Egyptian military buildup and facing guerrilla attacks from Gaza, saw opportunity to weaken its most powerful Arab neighbor.[10] In secret meetings at Sèvres outside Paris, British, French, and Israeli officials agreed to a collusive war plan: Israel would attack Egypt; Britain and France would issue ultimatum demanding both sides withdraw from the canal zone; when Egypt inevitably refused, British and French forces would intervene ostensibly to "separate the combatants" and "protect" the canal, but actually to seize it and hopefully trigger Nasser's overthrow.[11]

The plan's dishonesty was comprehensive. The three powers would pretend to act independently while actually coordinating closely. Britain and France would claim to intervene as neutral peacekeepers while actually acting as Israeli allies. The ultimatum demanding Egypt withdraw from its own territory was designed to be rejected, providing pretext for invasion. Eden deliberately misled his Cabinet, Parliament, and the British public about the collusion, presenting Britain's actions as responses to unforeseen events rather than prearranged conspiracy.[12]

Chapter 15: Suez and the End of Illusions

On October 29, Israeli forces invaded Sinai as planned. On October 30, Britain and France issued their ultimatum, demanding both Israeli and Egyptian forces withdraw ten miles from the canal—a demand requiring Egypt to surrender its own territory. When Egypt refused, British and French aircraft began bombing Egyptian airfields on October 31.˄13˄ On November 5, British and French paratroopers landed at Port Said, followed by seaborne invasion the next day. The Anglo-French force quickly secured the northern section of the canal, but military success proved pyrrhic; international reaction was devastating.

International Condemnation and Humiliation

The Suez invasion provoked nearly universal condemnation. The United States, whose government Eden had deliberately not informed of the collusion, reacted with fury. President Eisenhower, facing re-election and committed to opposing colonialism, viewed the Anglo-French action as reckless neo-imperialism that threatened American interests by alienating Arab and Third World opinion while potentially drawing the Soviet Union deeper into Middle Eastern affairs.˄14˄ The Eisenhower administration publicly denounced the invasion, introduced United Nations resolutions demanding immediate withdrawal, and applied devastating economic pressure against Britain.

The economic pressure proved decisive. Britain's gold

and currency reserves were hemorrhaging as international confidence in sterling collapsed. The United States refused to support the pound and blocked British access to International Monetary Fund resources until withdrawal from Egypt.^15^ Chancellor of the Exchequer Harold Macmillan, who had initially supported the Suez adventure, reversed position when confronted with financial catastrophe, informing Eden that Britain faced economic crisis unless it withdrew immediately.^16^ American economic power, not Egyptian military resistance, forced British retreat.

The Soviet Union, brutally suppressing the Hungarian Revolution simultaneously, cynically exploited the crisis by threatening to intervene on Egypt's behalf, including hints of nuclear attacks on Britain and France.^17^ While these threats were propaganda rather than serious military planning, they increased pressure on Britain and demonstrated how Suez distracted Western attention from Soviet crimes in Hungary. The juxtaposition was devastating for British moral authority: how could Britain condemn Soviet imperialism in Hungary while practicing its own imperialism in Egypt?

Within Britain, opposition to the Suez intervention intensified as the government's deceptions became apparent. Labour Party leader Hugh Gaitskell, who had initially supported firm response to nationalization, denounced the military action as illegal and immoral

Chapter 15: Suez and the End of Illusions

once the collusion became evident.^18^ Public opinion divided sharply, with large anti-war demonstrations in London and fierce parliamentary debates. The Conservative government's majority held, but the political cost was severe, with prominent conservatives including Edward Boyle resigning in protest.^19^

By November 6, with military objectives achieved but international pressure unbearable, Eden's government accepted United Nations ceasefire demands. British and French forces withdrew ignominiously in December, replaced by UN peacekeepers. The canal remained in Egyptian hands; Nasser's prestige soared throughout the Arab world; Britain's pretensions to great power status lay in ruins.^20^

Imperial Illusions Shattered

The Suez Crisis exposed multiple illusions that had sustained British imperial ideology. The first was the illusion of continued great power status. Britain in 1956 possessed significant military capabilities—a large professional military, nuclear weapons, global bases—but these proved irrelevant when deployed against American opposition. The crisis demonstrated unambiguously that Britain could not act independently in defiance of American wishes. The "special relationship" between Britain and America meant British subordination, not partnership between equals.^21^

The second illusion concerned the viability of continued

imperial control over decolonizing territories. Eden and his advisors believed they could overthrow Nasser, restore British dominance over Egypt, and thereby arrest nationalist challenges elsewhere in the Empire. This fantasy ignored the irreversible nature of decolonization. Egyptian nationalism, like nationalist movements throughout Asia and Africa, would accept nothing less than genuine independence. Military force could not restore imperial domination in a post-war world where colonialism had lost legitimacy and colonized peoples possessed political consciousness and organizational capacity to resist.[22]

The third illusion involved British moral authority. For generations, British politicians and intellectuals had presented the Empire as fundamentally different from other empires—more benevolent, more just, more committed to preparing colonies for self-government. The Suez conspiracy demolished these pretensions. Britain had conspired with allies to launch aggressive war based on transparent lies, violating international law and the UN Charter it had helped create. When British interests were threatened, the values Britain claimed to uphold—democracy, rule of law, international order—were abandoned without hesitation. The hypocrisy was undeniable and internationally noted.[23]

The fourth illusion concerned British officials' racial attitudes toward Arabs. Eden's comparison of Nasser to Hitler, repeated obsessively throughout the crisis,

Chapter 15: Suez and the End of Illusions

revealed contemptuous inability to take Arab nationalism seriously as legitimate political movement.^24^ British officials treated Nasser as irrational demagogue rather than skillful politician pursuing rational objectives. They assumed Egyptian incompetence—that Egypt could not operate the canal efficiently after nationalization—an assumption immediately disproven when Egyptian pilots navigated ships through the canal without British assistance.^25^ These racist assumptions led to catastrophic miscalculations about international and Arab reactions to the invasion.

The crisis also shattered illusions about Commonwealth unity. Eden had assumed Commonwealth support, or at least acquiescence, for British action. Instead, major Commonwealth members—particularly India and Canada—strongly opposed the invasion.^26^ Indian Prime Minister Jawaharlal Nehru condemned the Anglo-French action as imperialism and colonialism in their most naked forms. Canadian leadership at the UN, particularly Lester Pearson's role in creating the UN peacekeeping force that provided face-saving mechanism for British withdrawal, demonstrated that Commonwealth members would not automatically support British imperial adventures.^27^

Consequences and Acceleration of Decolonization

The Suez Crisis accelerated decolonization dramatically.

Nasser's successful defiance of Britain and France inspired nationalist movements throughout Asia, Africa, and the Caribbean. If Egypt could face down European powers, what colonized people needed to accept continued subjugation? The crisis demonstrated that the age of European empires had definitively ended, that Third World nationalism could triumph over colonial power, and that the United States would not support European colonial maintenance.^28^

Within British politics, Suez discredited imperialist ideology and those who promoted it. Anthony Eden resigned in January 1957, ostensibly for health reasons but actually due to Suez's political fallout.^29^ His successor, Harold Macmillan, recognized that the Empire must be liquidated rapidly rather than defended. Macmillan's famous "Wind of Change" speech in 1960, acknowledging African nationalism's irresistibility, represented acceptance of realities that Suez had made undeniable.^30^ British decolonization, which had proceeded gradually in Asia, accelerated dramatically in Africa after Suez, with most African colonies achieving independence by mid-1960s.

The crisis also transformed British foreign policy orientation. The special relationship with America became even more central, with British policymakers recognizing that independent action contradicting American preferences was no longer viable. Britain would henceforth align closely with American foreign

Chapter 15: Suez and the End of Illusions

policy, accepting junior partner status in exchange for influence in Washington and American support for British interests. This relationship persists to the present, with British foreign policy rarely diverging significantly from American positions.^31^

For Egypt and the Arab world, Suez represented triumph. Nasser emerged as hero of Arab nationalism, his prestige enhanced rather than destroyed by the crisis. The canal remained firmly in Egyptian control, generating revenues for Egyptian development. British influence in the Middle East declined precipitously, with the remaining British positions—particularly in the Persian Gulf and Aden—becoming increasingly untenable. British withdrawal from "East of Suez" over the following decade represented acknowledgment that the imperial system sustaining British global power could no longer be maintained.^32^

Summary Conclusion: The Last Gasp of Empire

The Suez Crisis represented not merely a policy failure but the exposure of fundamental delusions sustaining British imperialism in the post-war era. British leaders had convinced themselves that Britain remained a great power capable of independent global action, that colonial subjects would accept continued British domination, and that British moral authority gave it special role in world affairs. All these beliefs proved false when tested against Egyptian nationalism, American power, and international opinion.

The crisis marked the moment when the British Empire's terminal decline became undeniable even to its most devoted defenders. The military victory that British forces achieved meant nothing; political and economic defeat was comprehensive. Britain could no longer impose its will on decolonizing territories, could not act globally without American permission, and possessed no moral authority to justify imperial pretensions. The gap between Britain's self-image and its actual diminished position in the world stood fully exposed.

Eden's comparison of Nasser to Hitler, rather than revealing insight about Egyptian nationalism, demonstrated the profound inability of British imperial ideology to comprehend the post-war world. Nasser was not Hitler; he was a nationalist leader pursuing Egypt's independence and development—goals entirely legitimate and indeed inevitable. That British leaders could not distinguish between these categories revealed how imperial racism and nostalgia distorted their understanding of decolonization's realities.

The Suez Crisis thus stands as decisive turning point in British imperial history—the moment when illusions died and reality could no longer be denied. The Empire would persist another two decades in formal terms, with final decolonizations occurring in the 1960s and 1970s.

Chapter 15: Suez and the End of Illusions

But Suez marked the psychological break, the definitive end of Britain as imperial power able to shape global events through independent action. What followed was managed retreat, with British governments attempting to preserve influence and interests while accepting that the age of British Empire had irrevocably ended.

The lesson the British establishment took from Suez was not that imperialism was wrong but that it must be practiced more carefully, with American approval and through less overt methods. The following decades would see Britain acting as America's junior partner in interventions worldwide, supporting American power while claiming special influence in Washington. This represented adaptation to new realities rather than fundamental break with imperial ambitions. But the days when Britain could independently project power globally, impose its will on decolonizing territories, and credibly claim moral authority for doing so—those days ended in the waters of the Suez Canal in November 1956.

Author's Notes Chapter 15

This chapter examines the 1956 Suez Crisis as watershed moment revealing Britain's declining power and the end of its ability to conduct independent imperial military operations against American opposition. The failed Anglo-French-Israeli intervention to seize the Suez Canal after Egypt's nationalization demonstrated that the formal British Empire's end did not mean Britain had accepted loss of imperial power, and that America would not support British imperial adventures conflicting with American interests.

On the Crisis's Origins: Egyptian President Gamal Abdel Nasser's nationalization of the Suez Canal Company (July 1956) was legally justified—Egypt exercised sovereignty over Egyptian territory and offered compensation to shareholders. Yet Britain and France viewed nationalization as intolerable challenge to European interests in the Middle East. Keith Kyle's *Suez* (2003) remains the definitive account, based on comprehensive archival research in British, French, American, and Egyptian sources. Kyle demonstrates that British Prime Minister Anthony Eden became obsessed with removing Nasser, whom he compared to Hitler, and conspired with France and Israel to create pretext for military intervention.

On the Collusion: Britain, France, and Israel secretly agreed that Israel would attack Egypt (ostensibly for its own security reasons), Britain and France would demand both sides withdraw from the Canal Zone, and when Egypt refused, Britain and France would intervene militarily as "peacekeepers" while actually seizing the canal. This elaborate deception aimed to provide legal cover for what was straightforward aggression. The collusion remained officially denied for decades despite being widely suspected, until archives confirmed it in the 1990s.

On American Opposition: President Eisenhower opposed the intervention for multiple reasons: it occurred during the Hungarian uprising, making Western criticism of Soviet intervention hypocritical; it alienated Arab nationalism during the Cold War; it violated international law; and it occurred without American consultation despite the "special relationship." America used financial pressure—threatening Britain's pound sterling and blocking IMF loans—to force British withdrawal. The crisis revealed Britain's financial dependence on America and America's willingness to oppose British military operations when they

Chapter 15: Suez and the End of Illusions

conflicted with American interests.

On Eden's Resignation: The failed intervention humiliated Britain internationally, divided British public opinion, and destroyed Eden's credibility. He resigned in January 1957, claiming health reasons but essentially forced out by the debacle. The crisis marked the definitive end of Britain's ability to conduct major military operations independently of American support, forcing recognition that Britain was no longer a superpower capable of imposing its will on regions like the Middle East.

On the Crisis's Aftermath: The intervention's failure strengthened Nasser and Arab nationalism, demonstrating that European colonial powers could be defied successfully. It accelerated British and French decolonization as it became clear that maintaining imperial possessions against nationalist opposition was no longer feasible. The crisis also strengthened the "special relationship" by teaching Britain that future interventions required American support, leading to closer Anglo-American cooperation in intelligence and military operations documented in Chapter 16.

Historiographical Context: Initial histories often portrayed the crisis as tragedy or "greatest episode" in British decline, with some sympathy for Eden's concerns about Nasser and international order. More recent scholarship emphasizes the intervention's illegality, its basis in imperial attitudes refusing to accept decolonization, and the moral and strategic bankruptcy of attempting to reverse legal nationalization through military force and deception. William Roger Louis and Roger Owen's *Suez 1956: The Crisis and Its Consequences* (1989) established this more critical interpretation.

On Lessons Not Learned: Despite Suez's failure revealing that military intervention to control Middle Eastern resources and politics was no longer viable, Britain continued similar interventions—Afghanistan, Iraq, Libya—demonstrating that imperial reflexes survived formal empire's end. These later interventions, discussed in Chapter 17, show that Britain has not fully internalized the lessons that Suez should have taught about the limits of military power and the unsustainability of attempting to impose Western preferences on Middle Eastern societies.

CHAPTER SIXTEEN

The Anglo-American Empire: Britain as America's Junior Partner (1945-2000)

The formal British Empire's dissolution after World War II did not end British imperialism but transformed it. Unable to maintain territorial control independently, Britain forged a "special relationship" with the United States that allowed continued global intervention through American power. This partnership—portrayed in official rhetoric as alliance between equals sharing democratic values—functioned as continuation of imperialism through different means. Britain provided diplomatic cover, intelligence capabilities, and historical imperial expertise while America supplied military force and economic dominance. Together, they overthrew democratic governments, installed compliant dictators, and maintained Western control over strategic regions and resources.

The Anglo-American collaboration in covert operations reveals imperialism's post-colonial adaptation. When direct colonial rule became politically untenable, covert action provided alternative means of control. The CIA and MI6 worked closely to destabilize governments threatening Western interests, assassinate inconvenient leaders, and manipulate elections. These operations, conducted in secrecy and frequently denied, demonstrate that the "civilizing mission" rhetoric was always fraudulent—when colonial subjects achieved self-governance and exercised it contrary to Western preferences, Britain and America conspired to destroy their democratic institutions.

This chapter examines key Anglo-American covert operations from 1945 to 2000, focusing on Iran (1953), British Guiana (1953-1964), Indonesia (1957-1958 and 1965-1966), and Chile (1973). These cases reveal consistent patterns: Western powers identifying nationalist or leftist governments as threats, deploying propaganda and economic pressure, organizing coups when necessary, and installing brutal dictatorships while

Chapter 16: The Anglo-American Empire

claiming to defend freedom and democracy. The operations' catastrophic human costs—hundreds of thousands killed, democratic institutions destroyed, economic development disrupted—expose the "special relationship" as partnership in imperial violence.

Foundations: The "Special Relationship" as Imperial Partnership

The "special relationship" between Britain and America emerged from World War II as institutionalized framework for continuing British global influence through American power. While often portrayed as natural alliance between English-speaking democracies sharing common values and heritage, the relationship was consciously constructed to serve imperial objectives: maintaining Western dominance over the developing world, suppressing leftist and nationalist movements, and ensuring continued Western access to strategic resources and markets. The relationship's foundation rested on intelligence cooperation of unprecedented scope and intimacy, creating integrated Anglo-American intelligence apparatus that became the primary instrument for post-colonial imperialism.[1]

Origins in World War II

Anglo-American intelligence cooperation began during World War II when Britain, facing potential defeat, shared its intelligence capabilities with America to secure

Perfidious Albion

American entry into the war and subsequent support. The 1941 BRUSA Agreement established framework for signals intelligence cooperation between Britain's Government Code and Cypher School (later GCHQ) and American military intelligence services. This cooperation proved extraordinarily successful during the war, with joint Allied intelligence operations breaking German and Japanese codes, conducting deception operations, and coordinating resistance movements in occupied territories.^2^

The wartime cooperation demonstrated to both nations that integrated intelligence operations provided capabilities neither could achieve independently. Britain contributed historical experience in imperial intelligence gathering, established networks in colonial territories, linguistic expertise in Asian and Middle Eastern languages, and sophisticated tradecraft developed over centuries of imperial management. America contributed technological superiority, massive resources, and global reach made possible by its economic and military dominance. The combination created intelligence capability exceeding the sum of its parts.^3^

Yet the relationship was never between equals. By 1945, Britain's financial exhaustion and imperial overextension contrasted sharply with American economic dominance and military superiority. Britain faced the uncomfortable reality that it could no longer

Chapter 16: The Anglo-American Empire

maintain its empire independently but desperately sought to preserve global influence. America, newly dominant and facing perceived Soviet threat, needed Britain's intelligence capabilities, imperial experience, and diplomatic support for global anti-communist operations. The "special relationship" emerged from this asymmetric interdependence: Britain trading intelligence and imperial expertise for American support in maintaining Western global dominance.^4^

The UKUSA Agreement and Signals Intelligence

The formal foundation of post-war Anglo-American intelligence cooperation was the 1946 UKUSA Agreement (also known as the BRUSA Agreement's continuation), which established comprehensive signals intelligence (SIGINT) sharing between Britain and America. The agreement, whose existence remained officially secret until 2010, created integrated SIGINT apparatus with Britain's Government Communications Headquarters (GCHQ) and America's National Security Agency (NSA)—established in 1952—as senior partners. The agreement later expanded to include Canada, Australia, and New Zealand, creating the "Five Eyes" alliance that persists today.^5^

The UKUSA Agreement established unprecedented intelligence integration. The five nations divided global SIGINT collection responsibilities geographically, with each nation taking primary responsibility for monitoring specific regions: Britain focused on Europe, Africa, and western Asia; America on Latin America, eastern Asia, and northern Asia; Australia on southeast Asia and the Pacific; Canada on northern latitudes; and New Zealand on the South Pacific. This division ensured comprehensive global coverage while avoiding duplication and allowing each nation to contribute based on geographic advantages and historical connections.^6^

More significantly, the agreement established that intelligence collected by any partner would be shared with all partners, creating common pool of SIGINT available to all Five Eyes nations. This meant that Britain, despite its declining power, maintained access to American intelligence collection capabilities globally, while America gained access to British intelligence from former colonial territories and European diplomatic channels. The arrangement allowed Britain to maintain global intelligence reach it could no longer afford independently while providing America with capabilities it had not yet developed.^7^

The SIGINT cooperation extended beyond collection to analysis, with joint facilities established where British and American analysts worked side-by-side interpreting intercepted communications. Major facilities included Britain's GCHQ headquarters in Cheltenham, NSA headquarters at Fort Meade, and joint stations in locations such as Cyprus (monitoring Middle East and Soviet communications), Diego Garcia (monitoring

Chapter 16: The Anglo-American Empire

Indian Ocean and Middle East), and Pine Gap in Australia (monitoring Asia and the Pacific). These joint facilities created integrated Anglo-American intelligence apparatus operating as single entity rather than separate national services sharing information.^8^

MI6 and CIA: Partners in Covert Action

While SIGINT cooperation focused on electronic surveillance and code-breaking, even closer integration developed between Britain's Secret Intelligence Service (MI6) and America's Central Intelligence Agency (CIA) in covert action operations. The CIA, established in 1947, drew heavily on British expertise in covert operations developed through centuries of imperial intelligence work. British intelligence officers trained early CIA operatives in tradecraft, shared techniques for managing agents and conducting covert operations, and provided access to established intelligence networks in former colonial territories.^9^

The MI6-CIA relationship became operational partnership rather than mere information sharing. Joint operations were planned and executed with officers from both agencies working together, sharing facilities, and coordinating actions. In many operations, MI6 provided the initial planning and local expertise while CIA provided resources and operational support. In others, CIA took the lead while MI6 provided diplomatic cover and access to British networks. The distinction

Perfidious Albion

between British and American operations often became meaningless, with covert actions representing genuinely joint Anglo-American efforts.^10^

The partnership extended to sharing intelligence on potential targets, coordinating propaganda operations, and jointly supporting proxy forces. Britain's Information Research Department (IRD)—a covert propaganda unit established in 1948 within the Foreign Office—worked closely with CIA information operations to conduct black propaganda campaigns globally. MI6 and CIA jointly ran training programs for foreign intelligence services, jointly supported anti-communist organizations and publications, and jointly planned operations to overthrow governments threatening Western interests.^11^

The closeness of cooperation created institutional culture where MI6 and CIA officers viewed themselves as partners in common enterprise—defending the "Free World" against communism—rather than representatives of distinct national interests. This culture facilitated the joint operations documented in this chapter but also created accountability problems, as operations conducted through partnership could be denied by both governments with each attributing responsibility to the other or to "local forces" that both agencies had actually organized and directed.^12^

Chapter 16: The Anglo-American Empire

Institutional Mechanisms and Coordination

The "special relationship" was institutionalized through multiple formal and informal mechanisms ensuring continuous coordination. The Joint Intelligence Committee (JIC) in Britain and National Security Council in America maintained regular liaison, with intelligence assessments shared and coordinated. Senior MI6 and CIA officers maintained permanent liaison positions in each other's headquarters, with MI6 maintaining substantial presence in Washington and CIA maintaining presence in London. These liaison officers attended each other's senior meetings, shared operational planning, and coordinated activities.^13^

The relationship extended beyond intelligence services to military cooperation. NATO, established in 1949, provided framework for military coordination with Britain and America as dominant members. Joint military exercises, shared bases, and integrated command structures created military partnership paralleling the intelligence cooperation. American military bases in Britain—including major installations at Lakenheath, Mildenhall, and others—symbolized the intimate military relationship and provided forward positions for American power projection into Europe, Africa, and Middle East.^14^

The nuclear relationship represented the partnership's most sensitive dimension. Britain's independent nuclear deterrent depended substantially on American technology and support. The 1958 US-UK Mutual Defence Agreement provided for sharing nuclear weapons technology, with Britain's Polaris and later Trident submarine-launched ballistic missiles using American technology and dependent on American maintenance and targeting support. This nuclear dependency ensured British foreign policy alignment with American strategic objectives, as antagonizing America could jeopardize Britain's nuclear capabilities.^15^

Strategic Objectives: Maintaining Western Dominance

The "special relationship's" fundamental purpose was maintaining Western dominance over the developing world during decolonization. As formal empire became politically untenable, Britain and America developed covert methods to maintain control over strategic regions and resources. The intelligence partnership provided the primary instrument for this neo-imperial project, allowing Britain and America to overthrow governments, manipulate elections, assassinate leaders, and install compliant dictators while maintaining deniability and avoiding the political costs of overt imperialism.^16^

The partnership's strategic focus centered on preventing nationalist and leftist governments from asserting genuine independence. Governments that nationalized

Chapter 16: The Anglo-American Empire

Western-owned resources, implemented land reform threatening Western commercial interests, maintained friendly relations with communist nations, or advocated for non-aligned foreign policies were identified as threats requiring covert action. The intelligence partnership allowed Britain and America to identify such governments early, monitor their activities, and coordinate operations to destabilize or overthrow them.˄17˄

Economic motivations were central though officially denied. Protecting Western corporate access to oil, minerals, agricultural products, and markets drove many operations. When governments threatened to nationalize Western-owned oil fields in Iran or copper mines in Chile, or when they implemented economic policies threatening Western commercial dominance, the intelligence partnership provided means to overthrow them and install governments protecting Western economic interests. The covert operations documented in this chapter reveal that beneath Cold War anti-communist rhetoric, many operations primarily served to protect Western corporate profits and maintain exploitative economic relationships established during formal colonialism.˄18˄

Britain's Motivations: Maintaining Global Influence
For Britain, the "special relationship" offered means to maintain global influence despite declining independent power. The intelligence partnership allowed Britain to

Perfidious Albion

remain global player by providing capabilities America valued. British intelligence from former colonial territories, diplomatic relationships maintained through Commonwealth connections, and expertise in managing imperial territories made Britain valuable partner rather than declining power to be ignored.^19^

The relationship also served Britain's immediate economic interests. Many covert operations targeted governments threatening British commercial interests in former colonies. Iran in 1953 threatened British oil monopoly; British Guiana threatened British sugar companies; Indonesia threatened British interests in Malaysia and Southeast Asian trade; various African operations protected British mining and commercial interests. Through partnership with America, Britain could protect these interests through covert action it could no longer afford or execute independently.^20^

Domestically, the "special relationship" allowed British political leaders to maintain illusion of continued British global importance. By positioning Britain as America's privileged partner and special advisor, British leaders could claim Britain remained great power despite obvious decline. This narrative served political purposes by deflecting attention from imperial loss and economic decline while maintaining popular support for expensive military commitments and intelligence services.^21^

Chapter 16: The Anglo-American Empire

America's Motivations: Imperial Experience and Global Networks

For America, the partnership provided access to British imperial expertise at crucial moment when America was assuming global hegemonic role. American political and intelligence leaders recognized their own inexperience in managing global empire and valued British knowledge accumulated over centuries. British intelligence officers taught Americans how to run agents, conduct covert operations, manage colonial populations, and navigate complexities of societies about which Americans knew little.^22^

More practically, Britain provided access to established intelligence networks in regions where America had minimal presence. British colonial intelligence services had developed extensive networks of agents and informants across Africa, Middle East, and Asia. As these territories achieved independence, these networks remained valuable for monitoring political developments and identifying opportunities for intervention. Britain shared access to these networks with America, dramatically accelerating American intelligence penetration of developing world.^23^

Britain also provided diplomatic cover and multilateral legitimacy for American operations. When America wanted to overthrow governments or conduct covert operations, British participation allowed these to be

Perfidious Albion

portrayed as joint Western actions rather than unilateral American imperialism. British diplomatic support in international forums provided crucial backing for American policies. And British willingness to support resulting dictatorships through diplomatic recognition, economic relations, and military sales provided international legitimacy that purely American support could not.^24^

The Partnership's Antidemocratic Character

The "special relationship" was fundamentally antidemocratic in both operation and objectives. The intelligence cooperation occurred entirely in secret, without democratic oversight or public accountability. Neither British Parliament nor American Congress exercised meaningful control over joint operations. Both governments systematically lied about covert operations when confronted, denied involvement in coups and assassinations that both had planned and executed, and classified documents preventing democratic accountability.^25^

More fundamentally, the partnership's primary purpose was subverting democracy when democratic outcomes threatened Western interests. The operations documented in this chapter targeted democratically elected governments—Iran's Mosaddegh, Guiana's Jagan, Chile's Allende—and replaced them with

378

Chapter 16: The Anglo-American Empire

dictatorships. The pattern reveals that Anglo-American intelligence cooperation served to ensure that decolonization would not produce genuine independence or democratic self-determination but would instead maintain Western dominance through different means.˄26˄

The partnership also demonstrated that "defending freedom" and "protecting democracy"—the rhetoric justifying Cold War policies—were propagandistic covers for defending Western economic interests and strategic dominance. When confronted with choice between supporting democracy and protecting Western corporate interests, Britain and America consistently chose the latter. The intelligence partnership provided the mechanism for making this choice operational through covert violence that could be denied and hidden from democratic accountability.˄27˄

This institutional framework—the UKUSA Agreement for signals intelligence, the MI6-CIA partnership for covert operations, the military cooperation through NATO and base agreements, the nuclear relationship, and the coordinated diplomatic support—created integrated Anglo-American apparatus for maintaining Western dominance over the developing world. The "special relationship" was not alliance between equals but partnership in imperialism, with Britain trading its imperial expertise and global intelligence networks for American support in maintaining British influence and protecting British interests. Together, Britain and America developed neo-imperial system that maintained Western control through covert operations, economic pressure, and support for compliant dictators rather than formal colonialism. The following case studies demonstrate how this partnership operated in practice, revealing consistent patterns of intervention, violence, and support for authoritarianism in service of Western economic and strategic interests.

Iran 1953: Blueprint for Covert Imperialism

The 1953 Anglo-American coup against Iranian Prime Minister Mohammad Mosaddegh established the template for Cold War covert imperialism. When Iran's democratically elected government nationalized the Anglo-Iranian Oil Company (AIOC), threatening British oil profits, Britain orchestrated Mosaddegh's overthrow with American assistance. The operation, codenamed TPAJAX by the CIA and Operation Boot by MI6, demonstrated how former colonial powers could maintain economic dominance through covert action when direct control became impossible.˄28˄

Iran's oil had been controlled by Britain through AIOC (later British Petroleum) since 1909 under agreements that gave Iran minimal royalties while AIOC extracted enormous profits. By 1950, mounting Iranian nationalism and observing better terms other oil-producing nations achieved from American companies,

Chapter 16: The Anglo-American Empire

Iran demanded renegotiation. When AIOC refused meaningful concessions, Mosaddegh's government nationalized the industry in 1951, asserting Iranian sovereignty over Iranian resources.^29^

Britain's response was immediate and multi-dimensional. The Royal Navy imposed a de facto blockade preventing oil exports. Britain froze Iranian assets, withdrew technicians necessary for refinery operations, and organized an international boycott preventing Iran from selling oil. These measures aimed to economically strangle Iran until it capitulated.^30^

When economic pressure proved insufficient, Britain planned military action. Prime Minister Clement Attlee's government considered seizing the Abadan refinery by force, with military planners developing invasion scenarios. Only American opposition prevented military intervention—President Truman refused support for overt British imperialism that would alienate nationalist movements globally and potentially benefit the Soviet Union.^31^

Britain then pivoted to covert action, exploiting American Cold War anxieties. British intelligence fabricated and exaggerated evidence of communist influence in Mosaddegh's government, warning that Iran might "go communist" without intervention. This transformed the dispute from British commercial interests to Cold War strategic imperative, securing

American participation.^32^

The joint operation combined propaganda, bribery, and orchestrated violence. CIA and MI6 agents distributed anti-Mosaddegh propaganda through controlled media outlets, bribed military officers and politicians, funded opposition groups, and organized demonstrations and riots designed to appear as spontaneous popular opposition. On August 19, 1953, coordinated mobs attacked government buildings while bribed military units arrested Mosaddegh.^33^

The coup installed Shah Mohammad Reza Pahlavi as absolute monarch, establishing a brutal dictatorship sustained by SAVAK, the secret police trained by CIA and MI6 in torture techniques. The Shah's regime imprisoned, tortured, and killed thousands of political opponents over twenty-five years while allowing Western oil companies to resume exploitation of Iranian resources through a consortium giving Britain and America majority control.^34^

The operation's success encouraged its replication elsewhere, establishing covert action as standard Anglo-American response to nationalist challenges. Yet the immediate success proved pyrrhic. The 1979 Iranian Revolution—directly responding to the Shah's US-backed dictatorship—brought to power an explicitly anti-Western Islamic government. The hostility between Iran and the West, continuing through the present, stems

Chapter 16: The Anglo-American Empire

substantially from the 1953 coup and subsequent Western support for the Shah's tyranny.^35^

British Guiana 1953-1964: Destroying Democracy to Prevent Socialism

The Anglo-American campaign to prevent Cheddi Jagan from governing British Guiana represents perhaps the most sustained and comprehensive program of covert interference against a democratic government. From 1953 to 1964, Britain and America deployed propaganda, economic sabotage, labor subversion, racial manipulation, and constitutional manipulation to prevent Guiana's democratically elected leader from implementing his political program.^36^

Jagan, a dentist educated in the United States, founded the People's Progressive Party (PPP) with his American wife Janet Rosenberg Jagan in 1950. The PPP's platform combined democratic socialism, anti-colonialism, and racial harmony between Guiana's Afro-Guyanese and Indo-Guyanese populations. When the PPP won elections in 1953 with overwhelming majority, Jagan became Chief Minister.^37^

Within months, Britain suspended Guiana's constitution, removed Jagan from office, and imposed direct rule. British documents reveal that Jagan's actual offense was proposing labor rights legislation and land reform that threatened British sugar plantation owners' interests.

Winston Churchill ordered Jagan's removal to protect British commercial interests.^38^

Britain and America implemented coordinated programs designed to prevent Jagan's return despite his continued electoral popularity. The CIA and MI6 funded opposition political parties, supported anti-Jagan trade unions, and subsidized anti-Jagan newspapers.^39^

When Jagan won elections again in 1957 and 1961, operations escalated. British and American agents deliberately inflamed racial tensions between Afro-Guyanese and Indo-Guyanese populations, funding politicians who appealed to racial identity. The strategy culminated in orchestrated racial riots in 1962-1964 that killed hundreds.^40^

Britain then manipulated constitutional arrangements, changing electoral systems to ensure Jagan's defeat despite winning plurality of votes. The 1964 elections installed Forbes Burnham, who established an increasingly authoritarian regime. British and American opposition to Jagan evaporated when Burnham implemented similar policies—demonstrating that the issue had been Jagan's independence, not his policies.^41^

Indonesia 1957-1958: Supporting Separatist Rebellion

Britain and America's first attempt to overthrow Sukarno

Chapter 16: The Anglo-American Empire

involved supporting regional rebellions in Sumatra and Sulawesi from 1957-1958. The CIA provided weapons, funding, and air support to regional military commanders opposing Sukarno's central government. British officials coordinated with American operations, providing intelligence and diplomatic support. American pilots flew bombing missions from bases in the Philippines and Taiwan. However, the rebellion failed when Indonesian forces loyal to Sukarno defeated the insurgents. The operation's exposure created diplomatic embarrassment but no fundamental change in Anglo-American determination to remove Sukarno, leading to the far more catastrophic events of 1965.^42^

Indonesia 1965-1966: Genocide with Western Complicity

The 1965-1966 Indonesian massacres, in which approximately 500,000 to one million people were systematically killed, represent one of the Cold War's greatest crimes and one of the most successful—and most criminal—covert operations in which Britain and America participated. When General Suharto seized power following disputed events on September 30, 1965, the Indonesian military launched systematic extermination of communists and alleged communists. Britain and America actively facilitated this genocide through intelligence sharing, provision of kill lists, and propaganda operations.^43^

Background and Anglo-American Hostility

Indonesia under President Sukarno pursued independent foreign policy combining nationalism, Islam, and communism (NASAKOM). The Indonesian Communist Party (PKI) had grown to approximately three million members. Britain opposed Sukarno particularly because of Indonesia's "Confrontation" with Malaysia during 1963-1966. Britain had created the Malaysian Federation and deployed over 50,000 troops to defend it against Indonesian opposition. Sukarno argued Malaysia was neo-colonial British creation designed to maintain imperial dominance.^44^

American opposition centered on PKI's influence and Sukarno's increasingly anti-Western policies. The 1957-1958 covert operation's failure forced Anglo-American strategists to await better opportunities. By 1965, British and American officials viewed Indonesia as critical Cold War battleground requiring decisive action.^45^

The September 30 Movement and Suharto's Response

On September 30-October 1, 1965, junior officers calling themselves the "September 30th Movement" kidnapped and killed six generals, claiming to prevent a coup. General Suharto quickly suppressed the movement, blamed the PKI despite limited evidence, and launched a coup against Sukarno while claiming to defend constitutional order.^46^

Chapter 16: The Anglo-American Empire

Suharto's forces, supported by Islamic youth organizations and criminal gangs, began massacring communists and suspected communists. The killings reached genocidal proportions within weeks. Victims included PKI members, union activists, teachers, ethnic Chinese, and anyone denounced as communist. In Bali alone, approximately 80,000 people—5% of the population—were killed. Entire families were murdered, women faced sexual violence before execution, and bodies were dumped in rivers or mass graves.˰47˰

Anglo-American Complicity: Kill Lists

The most damning evidence involves "kill lists"—names of PKI members and leftists—that British and American intelligence provided to Indonesian military. Former American embassy official Robert Martens admitted compiling lists of approximately 5,000 names provided to the Indonesian army, stating: "It really was a big help to the army. They probably killed a lot of people, and I probably have a lot of blood on my hands, but that's not all bad."˰48˰

British intelligence similarly shared information about PKI members. Declassified documents reveal Britain provided intelligence on Indonesian political figures and coordinated with American intelligence. British officials were fully informed about the massacres' scale yet continued intelligence cooperation.˰49˰

The intelligence sharing enabled systematic murder. The lists allowed Indonesian military to move efficiently from identifying to locating and killing targets. Without these lists, the massacres would have been less systematic and smaller in scale.˄50˄

British Propaganda Operations

Britain's Information Research Department produced materials portraying the PKI as having orchestrated a coup and characterizing the mass killings as legitimate self-defense. These materials were distributed through ostensibly independent Indonesian media actually controlled by British intelligence. The propaganda shaped international coverage and provided justification for continued killing within Indonesia.˄51˄

American Officials' Approving Response

A 1968 CIA report stated: "In terms of the numbers killed, the anti-PKI massacres in Indonesia rank as one of the worst mass murders of the 20th century... The massacres rank with the Soviet purges of the 1930s, the Nazi mass murders during the Second World War, and the Maoist bloodbath of the early 1950s."˄52˄ Yet rather than expressing horror, American officials celebrated the outcome. Embassy cables describe the killings approvingly, tracking which regions had been "cleansed" and encouraging thoroughness.˄53˄

Chapter 16: The Anglo-American Empire

The Human Toll and Suharto's Dictatorship

Conservative estimates place deaths at 500,000; more credible estimates suggest 500,000 to one million. Hundreds of thousands more were imprisoned without trial, facing torture, forced labor, and sexual violence. Families faced generational discrimination.^54^

Suharto's "New Order" regime proved to be one of the Cold War's most brutal dictatorships, maintaining power until 1998 through systematic repression. Britain and America provided economic aid, military assistance, and diplomatic support throughout. When Suharto invaded East Timor in 1975—killing approximately 200,000 Timorese—Britain and America continued their support, providing weapons and diplomatic cover.^55^

Historical Significance

The Indonesian genocide represents Anglo-American covert imperialism at its most criminal. Britain and America actively supported systematic mass murder through intelligence sharing and propaganda. Yet accountability has been minimal. No officials faced prosecution. The intelligence agencies that facilitated genocide continued operating with expanded powers.^56^

The genocide's "success" influenced subsequent operations. When Chile's military launched its coup in 1973, the Indonesian precedent was explicitly referenced.

American officials discussed "an Indonesian solution" for Chile—supporting systematic killing of leftists.˄57˄

Chile 1973: Perfecting the Template

The Anglo-American campaign against Chilean President Salvador Allende represents covert imperialism's paradigmatic case. When Chile's electorate chose a socialist president committed to nationalizing foreign-owned resources, America—with British support—deployed economic warfare and covert action culminating in military coup installing Augusto Pinochet's dictatorship.˄58˄

Allende's Popular Unity coalition won the 1970 election promising to nationalize copper mines, redistribute land, and transform Chile's economy. Nixon ordered the CIA to "make the economy scream" and allocated $10 million for destabilization operations. Britain supported through companies sabotaging Chilean operations, banks denying credit, and intelligence sharing with CIA.˄59˄

The campaign combined economic warfare creating ungovernable conditions with CIA funding of opposition parties, anti-Allende media, and strikes including the 1972-1973 truckers' strike that paralyzed Chile's economy. When these measures failed, the CIA supported military coup plotting.˄60˄

Chapter 16: The Anglo-American Empire

On September 11, 1973, Chilean military forces attacked the presidential palace, killing Allende and installing Pinochet. The regime immediately launched systematic repression, imprisoning tens of thousands, torturing systematically, and killing approximately 3,000 people. Britain and America welcomed the dictatorship, with Britain restoring relations, selling arms, and Thatcher developing friendly relationship with Pinochet.˄61˄

Pinochet implemented extreme free-market policies—the "Chicago Boys" experiment—that devastated working and middle classes while enriching elites. The "Chilean miracle" was built on corpses of democracy activists and implemented through terror.˄62˄

Patterns of Covert Imperialism

These cases reveal consistent patterns. First, operations targeted democratically elected governments, exposing Western "democracy promotion" as fraudulent. When peoples achieved democracy and used it to assert sovereignty, Britain and America destroyed their democratic institutions.˄63˄

Second, operations deployed similar techniques: economic warfare, propaganda, funding opposition, and supporting coups. The methodologies refined in Iran were systematically applied elsewhere.˄64˄

Third, operations were justified through fabricated communist threats, transforming conflicts over

Perfidious Albion

resources into Cold War battles and securing domestic political support.˄65˄

Fourth, operations installed brutal dictatorships killing hundreds of thousands. Britain and America supported these dictatorships politically, economically, and militarily, demonstrating that human rights were subordinate to strategic and economic interests.˄66˄

Fifth, consequences extended beyond immediate changes. The 1953 coup contributed to the 1979 Iranian Revolution. Suharto's dictatorship persisted until 1998. Pinochet ruled until 1990. The covert imperialism shaped the contemporary world as profoundly as formal colonialism.˄67˄

Britain's role, while often subordinate, was essential. British intelligence in former colonial territories provided knowledge American agencies lacked. British diplomatic efforts provided legitimacy. British propaganda expertise supported disinformation campaigns. And British willingness to support resulting dictatorships provided crucial backing.˄68˄

Summary Conclusion

The Anglo-American covert operations from 1945 to 2000 expose the "special relationship" as partnership in imperialism. The rhetoric of shared democratic values obscured a relationship fundamentally about

Chapter 16: The Anglo-American Empire

maintaining Western dominance. When Britain's independent imperial capacity declined, alliance with America allowed continued intervention.^69^

The operations examined—Iran, British Guiana, Indonesia, and Chile—demonstrate that the "special relationship" was partnership in imperial violence. Intelligence services worked together to destabilize democracies, provide kill lists enabling genocide, and support brutal dictatorships. The human costs were staggering: hundreds of thousands killed in Indonesia, thousands in Chile, democracies destroyed, development disrupted.^70^

These operations expose the fraudulence of Western claims about defending democracy and human rights. When peoples achieved democracy and exercised it to assert sovereignty or implement policies threatening Western interests, Britain and America destroyed their democratic institutions and installed dictatorships. The pattern reveals systematic policy.^71^

The legacy persists. Iranian hostility dates to the 1953 coup. Suharto's dictatorship lasted until 1998, with genocide's trauma unaddressed. Pinochet's arrangements constrained Chilean democracy for decades. The covert imperialism Britain and America practiced shaped the contemporary world—with comparable violence and contempt for peoples whose lives were destroyed in service of Western interests.^72^

Perfidious Albion

Understanding the "special relationship" as partnership in imperialism is essential for honest reckoning. The comfortable narratives about shared democratic values cannot survive scrutiny of actual conduct: systematic destruction of democracy in service of corporate profits and strategic control. The covert operations represent imperialism adapted to postcolonial world but retaining empire's essential character—Western assertion of the right to dominate and deployment of violence to maintain that domination regardless of human cost.˄73˄

Author's Notes Chapter 16

This chapter examines how British imperialism continued after formal decolonization through partnership with American power. The "special relationship" enabled Britain to maintain global influence and continue intervening in former colonies through covert operations, intelligence cooperation, and support for American military actions. The chapter focuses on joint Anglo-American covert operations in Iran (1953), British Guiana (1953-64), Indonesia (1957-58, 1965-66), and Chile (1973).

On the "Special Relationship": This phrase, popularized by Winston Churchill, portrays Anglo-American cooperation as natural alliance between English-speaking democracies sharing values and interests. Yet the relationship was consciously constructed to serve strategic purposes— Britain maintaining global influence despite declining power, America gaining British imperial expertise and intelligence capabilities. John Dumbrell's *A Special Relationship* (2006) examines how the relationship functioned in practice, revealing it as often contentious partnership based on calculations of advantage rather than shared values. The intelligence relationship—through

Chapter 16: The Anglo-American Empire

UKUSA Agreement (1946), GCHQ-NSA partnership, MI6-CIA cooperation—created integrated Anglo-American intelligence apparatus that became primary instrument for maintaining Western dominance.

On Iran (1953): The joint MI6-CIA coup against Prime Minister Mosaddegh established the template for Cold War covert imperialism. Stephen Kinzer's *All the Shah's Men* (2003) provides accessible narrative based on declassified documents and interviews. The operation demonstrated how former colonial powers could maintain economic control through covert action when direct rule became untenable. Britain initiated the operation to protect oil profits after Mosaddegh nationalized Anglo-Iranian Oil Company, manipulated American participation by fabricating communist threat, and installed brutal Shah dictatorship. The 1979 Iranian Revolution—direct response to Western-backed tyranny—proved the coup's strategic folly, yet the immediate success encouraged similar operations elsewhere.

On Indonesia (1965-66): The massacres of 500,000 to one million Indonesians represent one of the Cold War's greatest crimes and most successful covert operations in which Britain and America participated. Geoffrey Robinson's *The Killing Season* (2018) provides the most comprehensive recent account. Bradley Simpson's *Economists with Guns* (2008) documents American role, while David Easter's work examines British involvement through Konfrontasi and intelligence cooperation. The provision of "kill lists" by CIA and MI6 to Indonesian military enabled systematic extermination. British Information Research Department propaganda justified massacres. American and British officials celebrated destruction of Indonesian left despite understanding the genocidal scale. The operation's "success"—from Western strategic perspective—encouraged similar approaches elsewhere, with Chile explicitly referencing the "Indonesian solution."

On British Guiana: Stephen Rabe's *U.S. Intervention in British Guiana* (2005) comprehensively documents the decade-long Anglo-American campaign to prevent Cheddi Jagan from governing despite his repeated democratic election victories. The operation combined propaganda, economic sabotage, labor subversion, racial manipulation, and constitutional manipulation—demonstrating the full toolkit of covert imperialism. The case is particularly significant because Jagan was unquestionably democratic, non-communist, and popular, yet Britain and America destroyed Guyanese democracy because his independence from Western direction threatened their interests.

On Chile (1973): Peter Kornbluh's *The Pinochet File* (2003), based on declassified American documents, provides devastating evidence of American planning and execution of operations against Allende. British role was more limited but significant—intelligence sharing, corporate support for destabilization, diplomatic backing for Pinochet. The coup and subsequent dictatorship killed thousands while implementing extreme free-market policies that became model for neoliberalism globally. Naomi Klein's *The Shock Doctrine* (2007) examines this connection, though her work is journalism rather than academic history.

Historiographical Note: Traditional Cold War histories portrayed these operations as defensive responses to communist threats. Declassified documents and post-Cold War scholarship have thoroughly debunked these justifications, revealing operations targeted nationalist governments threatening Western economic interests regardless of their actual communist affiliations. Tim Weiner's *Legacy of Ashes* (2007) provides comprehensive CIA history acknowledging systematic failure and criminality.

Chapter 16: The Anglo-American Empire

William Blum's *Killing Hope* (2004), while polemical, catalogs American interventions globally with extensive documentation. Richard Aldrich's *The Hidden Hand* (2001) examines British intelligence role, demonstrating close integration with American operations.

On Accountability: Despite overwhelming evidence of British and American complicity in coups, torture, and genocide, accountability has been minimal. No British or American officials have been prosecuted for these crimes. The intelligence agencies continue operating with expanded powers. The institutional culture that facilitated these operations persists. This impunity demonstrates that while international law constrains weak states, powerful nations violate it with immunity when launching operations serving their interests.

CHAPTER SEVENTEEN

The Long Shadow: Empire's Legacy in the 21st Century (2001-Present)

On March 20, 2003, British forces joined the American invasion of Iraq in an act of aggression that would kill hundreds of thousands, destabilize the Middle East, and expose the enduring imperial reflexes of British foreign policy. Prime Minister Tony Blair, employing rhetoric of humanitarian intervention and international security, led Britain into its most consequential military engagement since World War II based on fabricated intelligence about weapons of mass destruction that senior officials knew was unreliable. The invasion and its catastrophic aftermath demonstrated that the habits of empire—the assumption of the right to intervene in other nations, the deployment of violence to achieve political objectives, the manufacture of justifications for predetermined actions, and the refusal to accept accountability for consequences—persisted long after the formal British Empire dissolved.

This chapter examines how Britain's imperial legacy shapes its behavior in the 21st century, from military interventions to the continuing dispossession of the Chagossians, from the systematic destruction and concealment of evidence documenting colonial crimes to the persistent refusal to confront empire's crimes honestly. It demonstrates that imperial power has not disappeared but transformed, operating through different mechanisms while retaining essential characteristics: the claim of superior judgment justifying intervention in other societies, the subordination of international law to perceived national interest, and the deployment of violence without meaningful accountability.

The chapter documents Britain's participation in the catastrophic "War on Terror" interventions in Iraq, Afghanistan, Libya, and Syria—wars that killed hundreds of thousands, created millions of refugees, destabilized entire regions, and produced terrorist organizations more dangerous than those they claimed to combat. It

Chapter 17: Empire's Legacy

examines Britain's complicity in American torture and rendition programs that systematically violated international law and human rights. It analyzes the Chagos Islands case, where Britain maintains colonial occupation in defiance of international legal rulings, demonstrating that literal colonialism persists into the present. And it reveals Operation Legacy—Britain's systematic destruction and concealment of documents recording colonial crimes—exposing how Britain has actively prevented comprehensive accountability for imperial violence through deliberate erasure of evidence.

The pattern is consistent: Britain continues operating from imperial assumptions that it has the right to determine other nations' affairs, that international law applies only when convenient, that violence can be deployed without democratic accountability, and that historical crimes can be hidden rather than confronted. Understanding this pattern is essential for recognizing that decolonization remains incomplete—that the work of dismantling imperial power structures, confronting historical crimes, and building genuinely post-imperial relationships continues to be urgent political and moral necessity.

Twenty-First Century Interventions: The "War on Terror" as Imperial Project

The September 11, 2001 terrorist attacks provided

justification for military interventions that revived imperial patterns of Western powers deploying violence to reshape societies they deemed threatening or strategically important. Britain's participation in American-led "War on Terror" operations demonstrated that imperial habits—particularly the assumption that Western powers have the right to intervene militarily in other nations to advance Western interests—persisted decades after formal decolonization. The interventions in Afghanistan, Iraq, Libya, and Syria killed hundreds of thousands, displaced millions, and created conditions for extremist organizations to flourish, yet accountability for these catastrophic failures remained minimal.^1^

Afghanistan 2001-2021: Britain's Longest War

Britain's participation in the Afghanistan War, lasting from October 2001 until August 2021, represented its longest military engagement since the Napoleonic Wars. The initial intervention—a response to the September 11 attacks and aimed at overthrowing the Taliban regime that had harbored Al-Qaeda—had UN authorization and international support. Yet the intervention's expansion from focused counterterrorism operation into prolonged occupation and nation-building reflected imperial impulses rather than security necessities, with Britain attempting to reshape Afghan society according to Western preferences while demonstrating minimal understanding of Afghan political dynamics or social

Chapter 17: Empire's Legacy

structures.^2^

British forces deployed primarily to Helmand Province in southern Afghanistan beginning in 2006, facing intense combat that would kill 456 British soldiers while producing minimal lasting progress toward stated objectives. The Helmand deployment exemplified imperial overconfidence: British military and political leaders assured Parliament and public that British experience in colonial counterinsurgency—particularly in Malaya and Northern Ireland—provided expertise that would enable British forces to succeed where others might fail. General David Richards, British commander in Afghanistan, stated that British forces would succeed through "winning hearts and minds"—explicitly invoking the language of colonial counterinsurgency operations.^3^

Yet the Helmand campaign demonstrated that colonial counterinsurgency experience was irrelevant or counterproductive in contemporary Afghanistan. The tactics that British forces employed—establishing forward operating bases, conducting aggressive patrols, employing overwhelming firepower—alienated local populations while failing to defeat Taliban insurgency. British forces killed thousands of Afghans, many of them civilians caught in combat operations or killed in airstrikes. The Provincial Reconstruction Teams that Britain established achieved minimal lasting development, with projects often abandoned after

British withdrawal and infrastructure destroyed in subsequent fighting.^4^

More disturbing evidence emerged suggesting British special forces committed serious abuses that military authorities systematically covered up. Investigations by the BBC and *The Sunday Times* revealed apparent patterns of Special Air Service (SAS) units killing detainees rather than capturing them during night raids. In one six-month period in 2010-2011, one SAS squadron reported that in 11 raids where they encountered "threats," all individuals encountered were killed and no prisoners taken—a statistical pattern suggesting possible summary executions rather than combat deaths. Despite these concerning patterns, military authorities conducted no serious investigations, and personnel faced no prosecutions.^5^

The broader Afghanistan intervention failed catastrophically. After twenty years, $2 trillion spent, hundreds of thousands killed, and millions displaced, Afghanistan returned to Taliban control in August 2021 following hurried and chaotic Western withdrawal. The Taliban regime that emerged controlled more territory than it had in 2001, while Afghanistan's humanitarian situation had arguably deteriorated, with widespread poverty, collapsed economy, and millions facing starvation. British officials offered no serious accounting for this comprehensive failure or acknowledgment that twenty years of occupation had achieved nothing

Chapter 17: Empire's Legacy

beyond death, destruction, and humanitarian catastrophe.^6^

The Afghanistan intervention revealed persistent imperial assumptions: that Western powers understood how to govern non-Western societies better than local populations; that military force could reshape societies according to Western preferences; that Western powers had the right to occupy other nations indefinitely to pursue vaguely defined objectives; and that accountability for failure was unnecessary when the costs fell primarily on foreign populations. British military and political leaders who advocated for and directed the failed intervention faced no consequences, receiving honors and lucrative positions despite presiding over strategic disaster.^7^

Iraq 2003-2011: The Supreme International Crime

The 2003 Iraq invasion represents Britain's most consequential foreign policy decision since 1945 and demonstrates most clearly the persistence of imperial patterns in 21st-century British behavior. The decision to participate in American invasion was made by Prime Minister Tony Blair long before Parliament was consulted or public convinced, based on fabricated intelligence that senior officials knew was unreliable, justified through arguments that international lawyers concluded lacked legal foundation, and prosecuted through military campaign that killed hundreds of thousands while destabilizing the entire Middle East. The Iraq War exemplifies how imperial assumptions—that Britain has the right to overthrow other nations' governments through military force, that international law can be circumvented when inconvenient, and that British leaders need not accept accountability for catastrophic consequences—persisted into the 21st century.[8]

The path to war involved systematic deception of Parliament and public. In September 2002, the government published a dossier titled "Iraq's Weapons of Mass Destruction" claiming with spurious certainty that Iraq possessed chemical and biological weapons and was reconstituting its nuclear program. The dossier's most infamous claim—that Iraq could deploy weapons of mass destruction "within 45 minutes"—was based on a single uncorroborated source regarding battlefield munitions, not the strategic threat the government implied. Intelligence officials had warned that evidence was "sporadic and patchy," that sources were unreliable, and that claims should be heavily qualified. Yet the dossier presented speculation as established fact, designed to generate public and parliamentary support for war that Blair had already decided to support.[9]

The legal basis for war was similarly fabricated. Attorney General Lord Goldsmith initially advised in March 2003 that invasion without explicit UN Security Council authorization would be illegal under international law.

Chapter 17: Empire's Legacy

Yet under pressure from Blair, Goldsmith reversed his position, providing brief legal opinion claiming that previous UN resolutions provided sufficient authorization. This opinion contradicted the weight of international legal scholarship and the views of UN officials, including Secretary-General Kofi Annan who explicitly stated that the invasion was "illegal" under the UN Charter. Britain proceeded with invasion knowing that it lacked legal foundation and that most international lawyers considered it a violation of international law.^10^

The Chilcot Inquiry, reporting in 2016 after seven years of investigation, concluded that military action was "not a last resort" as Blair had claimed, that the legal basis was "far from satisfactory," that the intelligence case was "not justified," and that Blair had committed to supporting invasion long before presenting it to Parliament as decision requiring deliberation. The Inquiry documented that Blair had sent private messages to President Bush assuring unconditional British support regardless of circumstances, that planning for post-invasion occupation was "wholly inadequate," and that warnings about likely consequences were ignored. Chilcot's damning conclusions confirmed what critics had argued from the beginning: the invasion was illegal aggression based on fabricated justifications.^11^

The human costs were staggering. Conservative estimates place Iraqi deaths directly resulting from the invasion and subsequent conflict at approximately 200,000; more comprehensive studies including indirect deaths from destroyed infrastructure, collapsed healthcare, and sectarian violence suggest totals between 500,000 and over one million. The invasion destroyed Iraq's infrastructure, decimated its professional and middle classes through killing and flight, created conditions for sectarian violence that tore Iraqi society apart, and produced power vacuum that enabled the emergence of the Islamic State (ISIS)—an organization more brutal and dangerous than anything that had existed under Saddam Hussein's regime.^12^

British forces' conduct included serious abuses systematically covered up by military authorities. The 2003 killing of Baha Mousa—an Iraqi hotel receptionist beaten to death by British soldiers in Basra—exposed systematic torture and abuse of detainees. Mousa was subjected to stress positions, beatings, and degrading treatment over 36 hours until he died from his injuries. The subsequent inquiry revealed that British forces had routinely employed "conditioning" techniques— hooding, stress positions, sleep deprivation, exposure to extreme temperatures—that constituted torture under international law. These techniques had been banned after the 1971 European Court of Human Rights ruling on British interrogation practices in Northern Ireland, yet military commanders had reintroduced them in Iraq.^13^

Chapter 17: Empire's Legacy

The Mousa inquiry documented that at least 93 instances of abuse and unlawful killing of Iraqis by British forces occurred, with actual numbers likely higher given military authorities' failure to investigate systematically. Yet accountability remained minimal. Only one soldier was convicted—receiving one year's imprisonment for inhumane treatment. Officers who authorized interrogation techniques, commanders who failed to prevent abuses, and senior officials who covered up crimes faced no prosecution. The pattern echoed colonial violence: systematic abuses by British forces, official denials and cover-ups, minimal accountability, and impunity for commanders and officials.^14^

Blair faced no prosecution despite launching war of aggression—the "supreme international crime" according to the Nuremberg Tribunal that established the principle that aggressive war is not merely a war crime but "contains within itself the accumulated evil of the whole." British law provided no mechanism for prosecuting leaders for illegal wars, and international mechanisms were unavailable as Britain (like the United States) does not accept International Criminal Court jurisdiction for aggression charges. Blair's impunity demonstrated that while international law constrains weak states, powerful nations can violate it with immunity when launching wars that kill hundreds of thousands.^15^

The Iraq War's consequences extended far beyond

immediate death and destruction. The sectarian violence that British and American forces unleashed through de-Baathification policies and support for sectarian political parties created enduring divisions that continue destabilizing Iraq. The destruction of Iraq's state capacity created conditions enabling ISIS to emerge, seize territory across Iraq and Syria, and conduct terrorist attacks globally. Millions of Iraqis became refugees, with Syrian refugee crisis partly resulting from ISIS expansion enabled by Iraq's destabilization. The intervention's comprehensive failure discredited humanitarian intervention claims and damaged international institutions designed to prevent aggressive war.^16^

Yet British political and military leaders who advocated for and directed the catastrophic intervention faced no meaningful consequences. Blair received criticism but maintained lucrative speaking career and advisory positions, accumulating estimated wealth of £60 million. Military commanders received promotions and honors. Intelligence officials who produced misleading assessments continued their careers. The institutional structures that produced the disaster—the intelligence services, military command, political leadership—continued operating without fundamental reform. The pattern was imperial: catastrophic violence inflicted on foreign populations without accountability for those responsible.^17^

Chapter 17: Empire's Legacy

Libya 2011: Regime Change Disguised as Humanitarian Intervention

Britain's 2011 intervention in Libya demonstrated that the Iraq War's catastrophic failure had not ended interventionist impulses or prompted serious reconsideration of assumptions underlying military intervention. When protests against Muammar Gaddafi's regime in February 2011 escalated into armed conflict, Britain joined France and the United States in military intervention ostensibly to protect civilians under the "Responsibility to Protect" doctrine. Yet UN Security Council Resolution 1973, which authorized protection of civilians, was immediately interpreted by Britain, France, and America as authorization for regime change, with NATO conducting bombing campaigns targeting Gaddafi's forces and supporting rebel groups seeking his overthrow.^18^

The intervention succeeded in overthrowing Gaddafi—who was captured and killed by rebel forces in October 2011—but produced chaos that vindicated intervention critics. Libya descended into civil war, with no effective central authority, competing militias controlling different regions, widespread human rights abuses, and proliferation of weapons across the region. The humanitarian catastrophe that intervention was supposed to prevent was instead produced by the intervention itself, with thousands killed in post-Gaddafi fighting, refugees fleeing across the Mediterranean where thousands drowned, and arms from Libya fueling conflicts across the Sahel region.^19^

A 2016 parliamentary inquiry concluded that British intervention was based on "erroneous assumptions" about the threat to civilians, that government "failed to identify that the threat to civilians was overstated and that the rebels included a significant Islamist element," and that post-intervention planning was wholly inadequate. The inquiry documented that intelligence assessments had warned against intervention, but these warnings were ignored by Prime Minister David Cameron and Foreign Secretary William Hague, who were determined to demonstrate that "humanitarian intervention" could succeed after Iraq's failure.^20^

The Libya intervention revealed that Britain had learned nothing from Iraq. The same patterns recurred: exaggerated threats to justify intervention; intelligence warnings ignored when they contradicted predetermined policy; claims that limited intervention could achieve ambitious objectives with minimal costs; inadequate planning for post-intervention governance; and refusal to accept accountability when intervention produced catastrophe. British officials expressed "regret" but faced no consequences, while Libyans suffered ongoing violence, state collapse, and humanitarian disaster directly resulting from British and allied intervention.^21^

Chapter 17: Empire's Legacy

Syria: Covert Intervention and Proxy War

In Syria, after Parliament refused authorization for military strikes in August 2013, British special forces operated covertly without parliamentary authorization or public acknowledgment, conducting operations against ISIS and supporting anti-Assad forces while the Ministry of Defence maintained fictions of non-involvement. This covert intervention demonstrated that even parliamentary rejection of military action would not prevent British military operations when officials determined intervention served British interests.^22^

Investigative reporting revealed that British special forces maintained substantial presence in Syria from 2014 onward, conducting raids against ISIS targets, training and advising anti-Assad rebel groups, and coordinating with American special forces operations. The covert deployment circumvented democratic accountability, with Parliament and public unable to scrutinize operations whose existence was officially denied. British forces contributed to conflict that killed hundreds of thousands and displaced millions while operating in legal gray area where officials claimed operations were covered by Iraqi government authorization despite occurring on Syrian territory without Syrian government consent.^23^

The Syria intervention also involved British support for

Perfidious Albion

rebel groups that included extremist elements, paralleling the pattern in Libya where intervention strengthened rather than contained extremist forces. British weapons and training provided to "moderate" rebels frequently ended up in hands of Al-Qaeda affiliated groups as rebel coalitions fragmented and regrouped. British officials acknowledged privately that distinguishing moderate from extremist rebels was often impossible, yet continued supporting rebel groups despite knowing that support benefited extremists.^24^

Patterns of 21st Century Intervention

The Afghanistan, Iraq, Libya, and Syria interventions reveal consistent patterns demonstrating persistence of imperial assumptions and behaviors:

First, the assumption of the right to intervene militarily in other nations' affairs to advance British interests or reshape societies according to British preferences. Despite catastrophic failures, British political and military leaders continued advocating for and conducting interventions based on confidence that Western military power could achieve political objectives in complex societies they minimally understood.^25^

Second, the systematic fabrication or exaggeration of threats to justify interventions motivated by other concerns. The Iraq WMD claims, the exaggerated threats

Chapter 17: Empire's Legacy

to Libyan civilians, and the simplified characterizations of Syrian rebels all involved presenting situations in ways designed to generate support for predetermined interventions rather than honest assessment of circumstances.^26^

Third, the subordination of international law to political convenience. The Iraq invasion proceeded despite lacking legal foundation. The Libya intervention exceeded UN authorization. The Syria operations occurred without parliamentary approval. In each case, British officials proceeded with operations they knew violated or circumvented legal constraints because those constraints conflicted with desired actions.^27^

Fourth, the comprehensive failure to plan for consequences or accept responsibility for catastrophic outcomes. Each intervention produced humanitarian disasters, state collapse, regional destabilization, and strengthening of extremist forces—yet British officials expressed at most "regret" while accepting no accountability and implementing no fundamental policy changes.^28^

Fifth, the continuation of patterns of abuse and impunity. British forces committed serious abuses in Iraq and Afghanistan, including torture and possible summary executions, yet accountability remained minimal with commanders and officials facing no prosecution. The pattern echoed colonial violence where

British forces operated with impunity and systemic abuses were covered up rather than prosecuted.^29^

These patterns demonstrate that decolonization transformed but did not end imperial patterns. Britain continues operating from assumptions that it has the right to intervene in other nations, deploy violence to achieve political objectives, subordinate international law to British interests, and avoid accountability for catastrophic consequences. The 21st-century interventions killed hundreds of thousands, displaced millions, destabilized entire regions, and strengthened the extremist forces they claimed to combat—yet produced no fundamental reconsideration of the imperial assumptions underlying these disasters.^30^

Complicity in Torture: Britain and the Rendition Program

Britain's complicity in American torture and rendition programs following September 11 demonstrated that the prohibition against torture—considered one of the most fundamental human rights protections—would be violated when British intelligence services believed torture could produce useful information or when maintaining "special relationship" with America required acquiescence to American torture programs. Declassified documents, court proceedings, and investigations revealed that British intelligence agencies knew about, contributed to, and benefited from torture

Chapter 17: Empire's Legacy

of detainees in American custody, rendering meaningless British officials' public claims that Britain opposes torture absolutely.˄31˄

The Rendition Program and British Complicity

The CIA's rendition program involved kidnapping suspects and transporting them to countries where they would be tortured—a practice that violated international law prohibitions against torture and refoulement (transferring individuals to places where they would face torture). Britain facilitated this program through multiple forms of complicity: providing intelligence used to identify rendition targets, allowing CIA rendition flights to use British territory and airspace, sharing intelligence obtained through torture with American agencies, and conducting its own interrogations of detainees it knew were being tortured.˄32˄

Diego Garcia, the British Indian Ocean Territory from which Britain had expelled the Chagossian population to accommodate an American military base, was used for CIA rendition flights despite British government denials. Foreign Secretary Jack Straw repeatedly assured Parliament that rendition flights had not used British territory. Yet in 2008, the government admitted that two rendition flights had landed at Diego Garcia in 2002, rendering Straw's assurances false. Subsequent investigations suggested additional flights may have used the facility, with the full extent of British territory's use for rendition remaining unclear due to government secrecy.^33^

British intelligence agencies provided information used to identify rendition targets and contributed questions for interrogators to ask detainees being tortured. MI6 officers were aware that suspects they helped locate would be tortured, yet provided information enabling their capture and rendition. In several cases, British intelligence specifically requested that American agencies capture and interrogate suspects, knowing that American "enhanced interrogation techniques" included waterboarding, stress positions, sleep deprivation, and other torture methods.^34^

The Cases of Binyam Mohamed and Shaker Aamer

The case of Binyam Mohamed, a British resident rendered from Pakistan to Morocco and subsequently held at Guantanamo Bay, revealed the extent of British complicity. MI6 provided questions to Moroccan interrogators and received intelligence reports from interrogations that MI6 officers knew involved torture. Mohamed was subjected to systematic torture in Morocco—including beatings, cutting with scalpels, and burning with hot liquid—for 18 months before transfer to Guantanamo. British courts later ruled that MI6's involvement in his torture was "facilitation" of "cruel, inhuman and degrading treatment" in violation of international law.^35^

Chapter 17: Empire's Legacy

Shaker Aamer, a Saudi national with British residency, was held at Guantanamo Bay for 13 years despite never being charged with any crime. British intelligence agencies initially provided information contributing to his detention, then resisted advocating for his release despite growing evidence of his innocence. Aamer reported systematic abuse at Guantanamo including beatings, forced feeding, and psychological torture. British government inaction regarding his case—despite its legal obligation to protect British residents—demonstrated British prioritization of maintaining good relations with American intelligence agencies over protecting individuals from torture and unlawful detention.^36^

Intelligence Sharing and Torture-Derived Information

British intelligence agencies systematically received and used intelligence derived from torture of detainees in American, Egyptian, Moroccan, Jordanian, and Pakistani custody. The official position—that Britain opposes torture but cannot always know the provenance of intelligence received from liaison services—was exposed as disingenuous by documents showing that British officers often knew that specific intelligence came from detainees being tortured and actively sought such intelligence.^37^

In 2010, the Intelligence and Security Committee

reported that British agencies had received intelligence from detainees held in extraordinary rendition, that agencies sometimes knew detainees providing intelligence were being mistreated, and that agencies had sometimes failed to protest mistreatment or press for detainees' welfare. The committee's report, while acknowledging these findings, concluded that "we do not believe that any Minister or official knew of or sanctioned" British involvement in rendition or torture—a conclusion contradicted by documentary evidence of ministerial knowledge and official policies permitting use of torture-derived intelligence.^38^

The Torture Guidance and Official Policy

Most damning, British intelligence agencies operated under guidance explicitly permitting them to use intelligence obtained through torture when they deemed it operationally necessary. Documents revealed that agencies worked under policy allowing them to "exploit" intelligence from detainees being tortured when information was assessed as valuable, with only minimal reporting requirements regarding mistreatment. This guidance remained in effect from 2002 until 2010, when its exposure forced its withdrawal and replacement with ostensibly stricter guidance.^39^

The guidance system demonstrated that British complicity in torture was not isolated misconduct by rogue officers but systematic policy authorized at senior

Chapter 17: Empire's Legacy

levels. Intelligence officers were instructed that they could receive and use torture-derived intelligence, that they could provide questions for torturers to ask, and that they could conduct their own interrogations of detainees being tortured by others. The system created plausible deniability—officers did not directly conduct torture but facilitated, benefited from, and encouraged torture by foreign services.˰40˰

Lack of Accountability

Despite overwhelming evidence of systematic British complicity in torture, accountability remained minimal. No intelligence officers faced prosecution for facilitating torture. No senior officials were held accountable for authorizing policies permitting use of torture-derived intelligence. No ministers faced consequences despite evidence of their knowledge of and acquiescence to torture programs.˰41˰

The government resisted legal accountability through multiple strategies. It settled civil claims by torture victims out of court with confidentiality agreements preventing full disclosure of British complicity. It invoked national security to prevent disclosure of documents in legal proceedings. It resisted establishing public inquiry into rendition and torture. When an inquiry was finally established in 2013, it was structured to minimize disclosure and accountability, with hearings held largely in secret and findings limited by restricted terms of reference.ˆ42ˆ

The pattern was familiar from colonial contexts: systematic British involvement in serious human rights violations, official denials and cover-ups, minimal accountability, and impunity for officials responsible. The rhetoric that Britain opposes torture absolutely was exposed as fraudulent—Britain opposed torture when convenient but facilitated, benefited from, and covered up torture when intelligence agencies deemed it useful or when maintaining relations with American intelligence services required complicity.ˆ43ˆ

Chagos Islands: Ongoing Colonial Crime

The Chagos Islands case demonstrates Britain's refusal to relinquish colonial possessions and rectify historical crimes even when legally required by the highest international court and despite overwhelming international consensus supporting decolonization. Between 1968 and 1973, Britain forcibly expelled the entire Chagossian population—approximately 1,500 to 2,000 people—from their homeland to establish a US military base on Diego Garcia. More than five decades later, despite International Court of Justice rulings, UN General Assembly resolutions, and decades of legal battles, Britain maintains its illegal occupation, prioritizing the Diego Garcia military base over indigenous rights, international law, and basic justice. The case represents literal continuation of colonialism

Chapter 17: Empire's Legacy

into the 21st century, with Britain asserting the right to maintain colonial possession in defiance of international law and indigenous peoples' rights.~44~

The Expulsion: Ethnic Cleansing for Military Purposes

The Chagossians, who had inhabited the islands for generations, were given no choice regarding their removal. Britain secretly agreed with the United States in 1965 to create the British Indian Ocean Territory (BIOT) by detaching the Chagos Archipelago from Mauritius before Mauritian independence, violating Mauritius' right to territorial integrity and self-determination. This detachment was condition for allowing Mauritius to achieve independence—effectively coercing Mauritius into accepting dismemberment of its territory.~45~

The expulsion was planned and executed with deliberate cruelty. British officials referred to Chagossians dismissively as "Tarzans" and "Men Fridays" in internal documents, dehumanizing language that facilitated their removal. The official position maintained that there was no permanent population on the islands—only contract workers who could be relocated—a fiction enabling Britain to claim the expulsion was merely relocating temporary workers rather than ethnic cleansing of indigenous population.~46~

The expulsion process was traumatic and devastating. Chagossian families were transported to Mauritius and

Seychelles with minimal possessions, no housing arranged, no employment provided, and no compensation for their lost homes, land, and livelihoods. Many were literally dumped at docks with no support. They lived in poverty in urban slums, their community destroyed, their culture devastated, their way of life obliterated. Families were separated as some were sent to Mauritius, others to Seychelles, with no means to maintain contact. Children grew up disconnected from their homeland, their parents' stories of paradise lost seeming like impossible dreams.^47^

The psychological trauma was immense and enduring. Chagossians described their expulsion as comparable to slavery, experiencing profound loss not just of place but of identity. Their entire society had been built around the islands—their livelihoods based on fishing and coconut cultivation, their community structures developed over generations, their cultural practices adapted to island life. Removal destroyed all of this, creating displacement trauma that affected not just the expelled generation but their children and grandchildren born in exile who inherited their parents' loss and longing for homeland they had never seen.^48^

Legal Battles and British Obstruction

Chagossians have fought for over five decades to return to their homeland, pursuing legal cases in British courts, international tribunals, and through diplomatic

Chapter 17: Empire's Legacy

channels. Their struggle has been consistently opposed by British governments—both Conservative and Labour—which have deployed legal arguments, procedural obstacles, and outright lies to prevent Chagossian return while maintaining the fiction that Britain's retention of BIOT is legitimate.^49^

In 2000, British High Court ruled that the expulsion order was unlawful and that Chagossians had the right to return to all islands except Diego Garcia (where the military base operates). The British government, rather than accepting this ruling and facilitating return, instead used royal prerogative to issue new orders-in-council reimposing the prohibition on return. When these orders were also ruled unlawful by British courts, the government appealed to the House of Lords, which controversially overturned the lower courts' decisions in 2008, ruling that royal prerogative could override judicial determinations of illegality—a decision that effectively placed executive actions regarding colonial territories beyond judicial review.^50^

Chagossians then pursued international legal avenues. Mauritius brought a case to the International Court of Justice (ICJ) seeking an advisory opinion on the legality of Britain's continued administration of the Chagos Islands. In February 2019, the ICJ ruled that Britain's detachment of the archipelago from Mauritius in 1965 violated Mauritian right to self-determination and was not conducted in a manner consistent with international law. The court determined that decolonization of Mauritius "was not lawfully completed" and that Britain is obligated to end its administration "as rapidly as possible."^51^

Following the ICJ advisory opinion, the UN General Assembly voted 116-6 in May 2019 demanding that Britain comply with the court's ruling and end its occupation within six months. Only Britain, the United States, Israel, Hungary, Australia, and the Maldives voted against the resolution, with 56 countries abstaining. The overwhelming international consensus was clear: Britain's continued occupation of the Chagos Islands is illegal colonial holdover that must end.^52^

Britain's Defiance of International Law

Yet Britain rejected the ICJ ruling and UN General Assembly vote, insisting that Chagos sovereignty is a bilateral matter between Britain and Mauritius not subject to international legal determination. The justification—that Diego Garcia base serves Western security interests—revealed the calculation: military utility outweighs indigenous rights, international law, and post-colonial justice. Britain explicitly prioritized maintaining the military base over complying with international legal obligations and rectifying historical injustice.^53^

The British position is legally indefensible and morally bankrupt. The ICJ is the UN's principal judicial organ,

Chapter 17: Empire's Legacy

established to settle legal disputes between states and provide authoritative advisory opinions on international legal questions. While ICJ advisory opinions are not technically binding, they carry enormous legal and moral authority, representing definitive statements of international law by the world's highest court. Britain's rejection of the ruling demonstrates contempt for international law and international institutions when their determinations conflict with British interests.˄54˄

Moreover, Britain's claim that Chagos sovereignty is purely bilateral matter ignores that the original detachment of the islands violated Mauritius' territorial integrity at moment of decolonization—a matter of international concern involving fundamental principles of self-determination and completion of decolonization. The UN has legitimate interest in ensuring that decolonization is completed lawfully, and the General Assembly has authority to address colonial questions. Britain's attempt to characterize illegal colonial retention as mere bilateral dispute is attempt to evade international scrutiny and accountability.˄55˄

The defiance also reveals double standards and hypocrisy. Britain regularly invokes international law when criticizing other nations' conduct, demands that others respect ICJ rulings and UN resolutions, and claims to support rules-based international order. Yet when international law determines that Britain's conduct is illegal, Britain rejects the law and continues its illegal actions. The selective invocation of international law—binding on others but not on Britain when inconvenient—exposes Britain's fundamental disrespect for the legal order it claims to uphold.^56^

Chagossians' Continuing Struggle

Chagossians continue fighting for return despite overwhelming obstacles. Now in their third generation of exile, the struggle is maintained by descendants of those expelled, many of whom have never seen their homeland but inherit their parents' and grandparents' determination to return. The Chagossian community is aging—many of those expelled have died in exile, never returning to their homeland—adding urgency to demands for justice while Britain delays and obstructs.^57^

British governments have offered compensation and British citizenship while adamantly refusing what Chagossians actually want: return to their homeland. The compensation offered—£14.5 million distributed among approximately 1,000 Chagossians in 1982, and additional payments later—was grossly inadequate and came with confidentiality agreements preventing further legal action. Many Chagossians accepted payments out of desperation while maintaining that money could never compensate for loss of homeland and that their fundamental right to return remained.^58^

Chapter 17: Empire's Legacy

The British citizenship offered to Chagossians in 2002—decades after expulsion—came too late for many who had died in exile and was presented as generous concession rather than minimal rectification of wrong. Moreover, citizenship did not address Chagossians' fundamental grievance: they wanted to return to their homeland, not to resettle in Britain. The offers of compensation and citizenship were attempts to buy off Chagossians' claims and end embarrassing litigation while avoiding the fundamental issue of illegal expulsion and continuing denial of right to return.˄59˄

Chagossian leaders have consistently stated that no amount of compensation can substitute for return to their homeland. As Olivier Bancoult, chairman of the Chagos Refugees Group, stated: "The British government thinks that by giving us money they can make us forget our islands. But money cannot compensate for the loss of our homeland, our culture, our way of life. We want to go home."˄60˄ The British refusal to allow return demonstrates that Britain views indigenous peoples' rights as negotiable—something that can be overridden when conflicting with British strategic interests.˄61˄

Diego Garcia and the "Special Relationship"

Britain's intransigence regarding Chagos relates directly to the "special relationship" with America and specifically to maintaining the Diego Garcia base that serves

American military operations. The base has been crucial for American power projection in the Indian Ocean region, serving as launching point for bombing campaigns in Iraq, Afghanistan, and elsewhere, as logistics hub for American naval operations, and allegedly as site for CIA rendition operations (despite official denials).^62^

Britain leases Diego Garcia to America under agreement that gives America effective control while allowing Britain to claim formal sovereignty. This arrangement serves British interests by demonstrating Britain's value to America as provider of strategic real estate, maintaining Britain's claim to global reach despite its decline, and providing British intelligence access to American intelligence operations conducted from the base. The Chagossians' right to their homeland is sacrificed to maintain this arrangement.^63^

American opposition to Chagossian return reinforces British intransigence. American military officials have argued that allowing Chagossian habitation on other islands in the archipelago would create security concerns and potential legal complications affecting the Diego Garcia lease. Britain defers to American preferences, prioritizing the "special relationship" over indigenous rights and international law. The pattern echoes colonial dynamics where indigenous peoples' rights and welfare are subordinated to great power strategic interests.^64^

Chapter 17: Empire's Legacy

Environmental and Marine Protection Pretexts

Britain has also employed environmental protection as pretext for preventing Chagossian return, designating the Chagos Archipelago a marine protected area in 2010 that prohibited fishing and resource extraction—conveniently making Chagossian resettlement economically impossible by eliminating their traditional livelihoods. This cynical use of environmental protection to prevent indigenous return was exposed when WikiLeaks released diplomatic cables revealing that British officials explicitly stated the marine reserve would make resettlement "difficult if not impossible" and would help maintain British control of the territory.˄65˄

The marine protected area was challenged legally by Mauritius, which argued that Britain lacked authority to create such restrictions in disputed waters. In 2015, an international tribunal ruled that Britain had violated international law in creating the marine reserve without Mauritian consent and that Britain had breached its obligations regarding marine environmental protection. Yet Britain continued maintaining the restrictions, using environmental protection rhetoric to justify what was fundamentally strategy to prevent Chagossian return.˄66˄

The environmental pretext was particularly cynical given that Diego Garcia hosts a massive military base whose operations—including fuel storage, weapons handling, waste disposal, and constant military traffic—pose far greater environmental threats than Chagossian fishing and subsistence agriculture ever did. Britain expressed no environmental concerns about military operations but claimed that allowing indigenous people to fish and cultivate coconuts would damage the environment. The transparent bad faith demonstrated that environmental protection was pretext rather than genuine concern.^67^

Britain's 2024 Agreement to Return Sovereignty to Mauritius

In October 2024, after years of negotiations and increasing international pressure, Britain announced an agreement to return sovereignty over the Chagos Islands to Mauritius while maintaining a 99-year lease for Diego Garcia military base. The agreement represented significant change from decades of intransigent refusal to acknowledge Mauritian sovereignty, yet immediately faced criticism for excluding Chagossians from negotiations and failing to guarantee their right to return to all islands other than Diego Garcia.^68^

The agreement's terms prioritized maintaining the military base while ostensibly addressing sovereignty questions. Britain would recognize Mauritian sovereignty while securing continued operation of Diego Garcia for at least another century. Financial terms were not disclosed but reportedly included British payments

Chapter 17: Empire's Legacy

to Mauritius and infrastructure development. Yet Chagossians—whose homeland was being negotiated—were excluded from discussions, learning of the agreement through media rather than being consulted as equal parties with independent rights.^69^

Chagossian leaders expressed anger at their continued exclusion and the agreement's failure to guarantee their right to return. While the agreement mentioned allowing Chagossian return to islands other than Diego Garcia, it provided no concrete timeline, commitments, or mechanisms to enable return. Given Britain's history of promises regarding Chagos subsequently broken or undermined, Chagossians had little confidence that return would be facilitated without continuing advocacy and pressure.^70^

Moreover, the 99-year lease for Diego Garcia meant that even under the new agreement, Chagossians would remain excluded from their homeland's main island—the site of their principal settlements before expulsion—until 2123. Multiple generations would live and die in exile before Diego Garcia could be returned to Chagossian control. The agreement thus perpetuated rather than resolved the fundamental injustice: indigenous people remaining excluded from their homeland to accommodate military base serving foreign powers.^71^

Chagos as Paradigm of Continuing Colonialism

Perfidious Albion

The Chagos case exemplifies continuing colonialism in multiple dimensions. First, it demonstrates literal territorial colonialism: Britain maintaining possession of foreign territory seized through coercion and holding it despite international legal determinations that the possession is illegal. Second, it reveals the subordination of indigenous rights to great power military interests, with Chagossians' fundamental rights sacrificed to maintain American military base. Third, it exposes contempt for international law when determinations conflict with British interests, with Britain rejecting ICJ rulings and UN resolutions that would require relinquishing colonial possession.˄72˄

Fourth, it shows patterns of deception and bad faith characterizing British handling of colonial questions. British officials lied about rendition flights using Diego Garcia, fabricated environmental concerns to prevent Chagossian return, excluded Chagossians from sovereignty negotiations, and repeatedly promised and then obstructed return through procedural and legal maneuvers. The dishonesty echoes colonial patterns where British officials systematically deceived indigenous peoples while pursuing policies serving British interests.˄73˄

Fifth, the case reveals that decolonization remains incomplete more than sixty years after the UN Declaration on the Granting of Independence to

Chapter 17: Empire's Legacy

Colonial Countries and Peoples declared that "all peoples have the right to self-determination" and that colonial subjugation must end. Britain's retention of Chagos, and similar retention of other colonial territories, demonstrates that formal decolonization has not eliminated colonial power structures or the assertion of right to dominate foreign territories and peoples.^74^

The Chagos case has become symbol of unfinished decolonization and continuing colonial injustice. For colonized peoples globally, Britain's treatment of Chagossians demonstrates that former colonial powers remain willing to perpetuate colonial subjugation when they possess the power to do so and perceive sufficient interest. For Britain, Chagos represents unwillingness to fully relinquish colonial mindset and accept that indigenous peoples' rights supersede British strategic interests. Until Chagossians can return to all their islands including Diego Garcia, and until Britain accepts genuine rather than nominal decolonization, the case will remain paradigmatic example of colonialism persisting into the 21st century.^75^

Operation Legacy and Britain's Archive of Shame

While 21st-century military interventions and continuing Chagos occupation demonstrate imperial patterns persisting overtly, perhaps the most revealing evidence of Britain's relationship with its imperial past emerged in 2011 with exposure of Operation Legacy—a

Perfidious Albion

systematic, decades-long program to destroy or conceal documents recording colonial crimes. The revelation came through legal action by elderly Kenyan survivors of British torture during the Mau Mau Emergency, exposing how Britain deliberately erased evidence of imperial violence while constructing myths of benevolent colonialism. The systematic destruction of archives, decades of official lies about their existence, and continuing resistance to full disclosure reveal that Britain has not merely failed to confront imperial history but has actively prevented comprehensive accountability through deliberate evidence destruction.~76~

Discovery: The Hanslope Park Secret Archive

In April 2012, the British government admitted that for decades it had concealed the existence of thousands of documents detailing systematic abuses during empire's final years. Government lawyers representing Britain in legal proceedings brought by Kenyan torture survivors had repeatedly claimed that no relevant documents existed beyond those already in the public record. Then historians discovered a secret archive containing nearly 8,800 files from 37 former colonies, hidden for half a century in a high-security government facility at Hanslope Park in Buckinghamshire.~77~

The Hanslope Park revelation exposed systematic, empire-wide document destruction and concealment.

Chapter 17: Empire's Legacy

The files—relating to territories including Kenya, Malaya, Cyprus, Aden, British Guiana, Uganda, and many others—documented colonial violence, torture, extrajudicial killings, and systematic abuses that British officials had hidden from public scrutiny for decades. The archive's existence contradicted official claims that colonial documents had been transferred to successor governments or destroyed legitimately, revealing instead that Britain had systematically removed sensitive documents to prevent their disclosure.˄78˄

The discovery fundamentally changed historical understanding of late colonialism and British responses to decolonization. The concealed documents provided evidence of crimes that officials had denied, systematic practices that had been characterized as isolated incidents, and official knowledge of abuses that British governments had claimed not to possess. More significantly, the concealment itself—the deliberate hiding of evidence for half a century and lying to courts about documents' existence—demonstrated that British officials understood their colonial conduct required concealment because it could not survive scrutiny.˄79˄

The Destruction: Operation Legacy Instructions

As colonies approached independence in the 1960s, the Colonial Office implemented Operation Legacy, instructing administrators across the empire to destroy documents that might "embarrass Her Majesty's

Government," compromise intelligence sources, or provide ammunition for claims against Britain. What followed was one of history's great archival destructions, with colonial officials burning, pulping, or secretly removing millions of documents that recorded the violence, exploitation, and systematic abuses through which Britain maintained its empire.[80]

In 1961, as Kenya approached independence, Colonial Secretary Iain Macleod issued instructions that became templates for document destruction across the empire. A telegram to the Governor of Kenya laid out the principles: "The object is to guard against their [documents'] falling into the hands of a future Kenya government... documents, which might be interpreted as showing religious or racial prejudice; documents which might be used unethically by Ministers in a future Kenya Government; documents of which production might be embarrassing to Her Majesty's Government, Police, Military Forces, Public Service or others... Watch lists or blacklists should be carefully destroyed."[81]

The instructions specified three options: destroy locally through burning or pulping; remove to Britain and classify as secret; or transfer to successor governments with careful vetting. The presumption was destruction: when in doubt, burn. Similar instructions went out to colonial administrators across Africa, Asia, the Caribbean, and the Pacific. The systematic nature of the program—centrally coordinated, implemented empire-

Chapter 17: Empire's Legacy

wide, following consistent procedures—revealed that document destruction was official policy rather than isolated decisions by panicked colonial officials.^82^

The categories of documents to be destroyed were revealing. Materials showing "racial or religious prejudice" acknowledged that British rule was characterized by racism that should be hidden. Documents that might be "used unethically" suggested that legitimate use of evidence documenting British conduct was characterized as unethical—inverting moral responsibility by treating revelation of crimes as wrongdoing. Most tellingly, documents whose production might "embarrass" Britain were to be destroyed, prioritizing British reputation over historical truth and accountability.^83^

The Burning: Empire-Wide Destruction

In Kenya, the destruction was massive. Tom Askwith, a senior colonial official, later recalled: "Large numbers of files were destroyed... We had a great bonfire at the end of the garden and we spent a week or so destroying files... The vast majority of files were destroyed."^84^ Officials worked through nights feeding papers into incinerators, ensuring that evidence of torture, detention camp abuses, and extrajudicial killings would not survive. The destroyed documents included records of the systematic torture that British forces employed against suspected

Perfidious Albion

Mau Mau supporters, documentation of forced labor in detention camps, and evidence of collective punishments inflicted on Kikuyu communities.^85^

In Malaya, documents were burned, pulped, or weighted with stones and dumped into the sea. A 1957 instruction warned that files should be "reduced to a state which defies reconstruction."^86^ The phrase revealed awareness that mere destruction was insufficient—documents must be obliterated completely to prevent even partial recovery. In British Guiana, files documenting British and American intelligence operations, economic sabotage against Cheddi Jagan's government, and election manipulation were removed or destroyed before independence.^87^

In Aden, officials organized "burning parties" on beaches, with documents fed into bonfires while officials socialized, treating destruction of historical evidence as festive occasion. In Uganda, files were burned in batches over several weeks as independence approached. In Cyprus, documents recording British counterinsurgency operations including torture and collective punishments were destroyed. Similar scenes played out across virtually every territory Britain decolonized.^88^

The scale was staggering—likely millions of documents destroyed across dozens of territories over two decades. Conservative estimates, based on known destruction and typical filing practices, suggest that for every file

Chapter 17: Empire's Legacy

surviving at Hanslope Park, ten to twenty were destroyed. Entire categories of colonial documentation—interrogation records, intelligence files on nationalist movements, police reports on counterinsurgency operations, correspondence regarding detention without trial—were comprehensively eliminated from the historical record.^89^

What Survived: The Hanslope Park Archive Contents

Despite destruction orders, substantial documentary evidence survived through "migration" of particularly sensitive documents back to Britain. The Hanslope Park archive, though representing only fraction of documents originally created, was nevertheless extensive and devastating. The files included:^90^

Kenya files documenting systematic torture: Records showing that torture of Mau Mau suspects was systematic practice known to and tacitly approved by senior officials. Documents recorded use of electric shocks, beatings, sexual violence, and other torture methods. They showed that systematic nature of abuse was known at highest levels of British government, contradicting official claims that torture was unauthorized conduct by rogue officers. Files documented that torture techniques were taught, that officers competed to develop new methods, and that senior officials received reports describing torture in detail yet took no action to stop

Perfidious Albion

it.~91~

Intelligence files on detention and interrogation: Detailed records documenting that indefinite detention without trial was standard practice, that detainees were subjected to forced labor and harsh conditions deliberately designed to break resistance, and that intelligence agencies operated with minimal oversight and near-total impunity. The files revealed that British officials understood they were violating principles of due process and human rights but justified violations through security imperatives and characterizations of detainees as subhuman.~92~

Documents about "elimination" of opposition: Files from Malaya, Kenya, and other territories containing language about "eliminating" or "liquidating" opposition, indicating that counterinsurgency operations included targeted killings without due process. While officials could claim such language was metaphorical, the context—discussions of operations that resulted in deaths—suggested that "elimination" meant assassination. The documents revealed systematic programs to identify and kill opposition leaders, with euphemistic language providing deniability.~93~

Financial records of exploitation: Documents detailing extraction of wealth from colonies, manipulation of currencies and trade arrangements to favor Britain, and conscious policies to maintain colonial economic

Chapter 17: Empire's Legacy

dependence. The files provided documentary support to long-standing claims about colonial exploitation's scale, showing that officials understood they were structuring economic relationships to benefit Britain at colonies' expense.˄94˄

Correspondence revealing racist attitudes: Internal communications showing the racist contempt with which British officials viewed colonized populations. Documents referred to Africans as "baboons," "savages," and worse. Asian populations were characterized as inherently deceitful and requiring authoritarian governance. The correspondence revealed that official rhetoric about civilizing missions and development masked profound racism shaping how British officials treated colonized peoples.˄95˄

Records of collective punishments: Documentation of village burnings, forced relocations, destruction of food supplies, and other collective punishments inflicted on populations suspected of supporting nationalist movements. These punishments violated international humanitarian law but were employed systematically as counterinsurgency tactics. Files showed that senior officials authorized collective punishments knowing they targeted innocent civilians and aimed to terrorize populations into compliance.˄96˄

The Legal Battle and 2013 Settlement

Perfidious Albion

The discovery of the Hanslope Park archive transformed the legal case brought by Kenyan torture survivors against the British government. The case, initially filed in 2009 by Paulo Nzili, Wambugu Wa Nyingi, and Jane Muthoni Mara—all elderly Kenyans who had survived torture in British detention camps during the Mau Mau Emergency—had faced government arguments that claims should be dismissed because no documentary evidence existed, any evidence had been legitimately destroyed or transferred to Kenya, and that too much time had elapsed for fair trial.[97]

Each argument collapsed when the archive was revealed. Documentary evidence did exist. The documents had been illegally concealed rather than legitimately destroyed or transferred. And the time elapsed was substantially due to government concealment preventing victims from accessing evidence supporting their claims. Most damningly, the revelation demonstrated that British government had been lying to the court about the existence and location of relevant evidence—itself potentially contempt of court.[98]

The government's legal position became untenable. In June 2013, Foreign Secretary William Hague announced that the government would settle, paying compensation to 5,228 Kenyan survivors and funding a memorial in Nairobi. The government's statement carefully avoided admitting systematic wrongdoing: "The British Government recognises that Kenyans were subject to

Chapter 17: Empire's Legacy

torture and other forms of ill treatment at the hands of the colonial administration... The British Government sincerely regrets that these abuses took place."˄99˄

The language was calculated: "sincere regret" rather than "apology"; acknowledgment that torture occurred without admitting it was systematic policy; passive construction minimizing British agency. Yet despite cautious language, the settlement established critical precedents: the British government had systematically concealed evidence of colonial abuses; documentary proof existed showing torture was systematic; British courts had jurisdiction over colonial-era crimes; and survivors could successfully sue decades after independence.˄100˄

The settlement provided some measure of justice and acknowledgment to elderly survivors who had waited half a century for recognition of their suffering. Many survivors died before receiving compensation, making urgency tragically clear. The memorial funded through the settlement provided permanent acknowledgment in Kenya of British torture, ensuring that this history would not be forgotten even as survivors passed away.˄101˄

Yet the settlement's limitations were significant. Compensation averaging approximately £2,670 per survivor was modest given the suffering endured. The settlement covered only provable victims of specific abuses in Kenya, leaving tens of thousands of others affected by colonial violence in Kenya and elsewhere without compensation. The refusal to characterize abuses as systematic policy rather than isolated misconduct prevented comprehensive acknowledgment. And the settlement did nothing to address the broader pattern of colonial violence documented in the concealed archives.^102^

The Ongoing Cover-Up and Resistance to Disclosure

The 2011 revelation did not end British resistance to documenting imperial crimes. The Foreign Office committed to releasing the Hanslope Park files gradually, but the process has been deliberately slow and incomplete. As of 2024, significant portions remain classified despite promises of comprehensive disclosure. Many released files are so heavily redacted as to be nearly useless for historical research or accountability purposes. Freedom of information requests for unredacted versions are routinely denied on national security grounds—even for documents describing events from sixty years ago.^103^

The slow release reflects continuing official discomfort with full disclosure. Each batch of released files generates renewed attention to colonial crimes, prompting calls for additional accountability that the government resists. By releasing files gradually and heavily redacted, the Foreign Office maintains control over narrative, prevents comprehensive understanding of colonial

Chapter 17: Empire's Legacy

violence, and ensures that public attention remains fragmented rather than coalescing around demands for systematic accountability.^104^

Moreover, following the Kenya settlement, the government enacted provisions making future colonial-era claims more difficult. The statute of limitations was tightened, jurisdiction was restricted, and evidentiary requirements were increased. These legal changes aimed to ensure that Kenya would be the last successful claim rather than the first of many. The government explicitly sought to prevent Cypriots, Malayans, Yemenis, and others from bringing similar claims despite documented evidence of British torture and violence in those territories.^105^

Revelations in recent years suggest that document destruction continues in contemporary context. Ministry of Defence records about operations in Iraq and Afghanistan have been found to be incomplete, with evidence of deliberate destruction of documents that might have supported accountability for abuses. Investigative reporting revealed that despite rules requiring preservation of operational records, files documenting detention and interrogation operations in Iraq were destroyed, preventing full investigation of torture and abuse cases.^106^

The pattern suggests that the culture of concealing evidence of wrongdoing persists in contemporary

Perfidious Albion

British military and intelligence operations. The same institutions that destroyed colonial evidence and lied about it for decades continue operating, with many of the same assumptions about prioritizing institutional reputation over accountability. Operation Legacy was not historical aberration but reflection of institutional culture that remains embedded in British government.~107~

Historical and Legal Implications

The systematic destruction of colonial archives and decades-long cover-up have profound implications for historical understanding, legal accountability, and contemporary politics. Historically, the destruction ensures that complete history of late colonialism can never be written. Historians must work with fragmentary evidence, knowing that systematic evidence was deliberately destroyed precisely because it documented the worst crimes. Entire categories of colonial violence—interrogation practices, assassination programs, systematic abuses—are documented only partially because officials destroyed comprehensive records.~108~

The destruction was successful in its primary goal—preventing comprehensive accountability. Without complete documentary evidence, proving systematic abuse is difficult, establishing command responsibility nearly impossible, and demonstrating scope of violence

Chapter 17: Empire's Legacy

relies on victim testimony that the government can challenge as unreliable or exaggerated. The destroyed evidence would have provided documentary proof that could not be dismissed, but its absence creates evidentiary gaps that officials exploit to minimize responsibility.ˆ109ˆ

Legally, the destruction raises questions about obstruction of justice and spoliation of evidence. While those who ordered destruction acted before laws explicitly protecting colonial archives, the cover-up continued long after such protections existed. The lying to courts about documents' existence constituted potential contempt of court. Yet no officials faced prosecution for evidence destruction or perjury, demonstrating again that accountability for colonial crimes and their concealment remains minimal.ˆ110ˆ

The archive destruction itself constitutes evidence of systematic wrongdoing. If colonial rule had been benevolent, if abuses were isolated, if conduct had been consistent with rule of law—why the massive destruction? Why conceal documents for decades? Why lie to courts about their existence? The destruction demonstrates that British officials understood their conduct could not survive scrutiny and required concealment. The cover-up proves consciousness of guilt.ˆ111ˆ

Implications for Contemporary Politics and Memory

Perfidious Albion

The Operation Legacy revelation transformed debates about British imperialism in contemporary Britain. The systematic destruction of evidence and decades of lying made official claims about benevolent colonialism untenable to anyone examining evidence seriously. How could colonialism have been primarily beneficial when officials destroyed millions of documents recording colonial administration because those documents would "embarrass" Britain? The destruction provided negative evidence—proof through absence—that colonial reality differed dramatically from official mythology.^112^

Yet the revelation has not ended historical evasion or imperial nostalgia in British public discourse. Many Britons remain ignorant of Operation Legacy, as the story received limited attention in mainstream education and popular history. Politicians continue invoking empire positively, suggesting that Britain's global role was predominantly beneficial. Resistance to honest reckoning persists, with accusations of "rewriting history" directed at those seeking to document imperial crimes—ironic given that the actual history rewriting involved destroying evidence and lying about empire's conduct.^113^

The archive destruction has particular implications for former colonies. For Kenyans, Malayans, Cypriots, and others who survived colonial violence, the destruction represents additional crime—the erasure of evidence

Chapter 17: Empire's Legacy

that might have supported their claims for justice. The destroyed documents documented their suffering, provided names of perpetrators, and established systematic nature of abuses. Their destruction prevents full accountability and ensures that comprehensive truth about colonial violence in their territories can never be established.^114^

The destruction also affects contemporary relationships between Britain and former colonies. How can genuine post-colonial partnerships be built when one partner systematically destroyed evidence of crimes committed against the other and continues resisting full disclosure? The archive destruction and cover-up demonstrate bad faith that undermines trust and prevents honest historical reckoning that might enable genuine reconciliation.^115^

Historical Evasion and Imperial Nostalgia

Britain's 21st-century military interventions, continuing colonial retentions like Chagos, and systematic destruction of evidence occur within broader context of systematic historical evasion regarding empire's crimes. While Germany confronted Nazi atrocities through extensive education, memorialization, and acceptance of responsibility, and while South Africa addressed apartheid through truth and reconciliation processes, Britain continues celebrating empire while minimizing its violence and refusing meaningful accountability. The persistent imperial nostalgia and resistance to honest historical reckoning reflect not innocent ignorance but active maintenance of mythologies serving contemporary political purposes.^116^

Education and Public Understanding

British educational curricula present empire as primarily benevolent, emphasizing railways and abolition of slavery while marginalizing or ignoring famines, concentration camps, and systematic exploitation. A 2020 survey of history teachers found that most spend minimal time on empire, that curriculum guidelines emphasize empire's "contributions," and that negative aspects are frequently omitted or presented as isolated aberrations rather than systematic features. Students learn about British abolition of slavery but rarely about Britain's central role in slavery's expansion or the compensation paid to slave owners rather than enslaved people.^117^

The result is widespread public ignorance about imperial history. Surveys consistently show that substantial majorities of Britons know little about colonial violence in Kenya, India, Ireland, or elsewhere. A 2020 YouGov poll found that 32% of Britons felt the British Empire was something to be proud of, while only 19% felt ashamed—figures suggesting that historical myths about benevolent empire remain widely believed despite overwhelming evidence contradicting them.^118^

Chapter 17: Empire's Legacy

This ignorance is not accidental but reflects deliberate choices about what to teach and commemorate. British history education emphasizes national achievements while minimizing or excusing violence. The Amritsar Massacre is presented as tragic error rather than deliberate policy. The Bengal Famine is attributed to unfortunate circumstances rather than deliberate British policies. Concentration camps in Kenya are omitted entirely from most curricula. The pattern creates historical understanding serving nationalist mythology rather than historical accuracy.^119^

Political Discourse and Imperial Nostalgia

Political discourse reinforces imperial nostalgia through regular positive invocations of empire by mainstream politicians. Boris Johnson wrote in 2002 that "the problem is not that we were once in charge, but that we are not in charge any more," suggesting that British imperialism in Africa was net positive and that continued British control would be preferable to independence. Such statements—which would be unthinkable regarding other historical atrocities—remain acceptable in mainstream British politics.^120^

Conservative politicians regularly defend empire against what they characterize as excessive criticism. In 2021, the government commissioned report on racial and ethnic disparities that controversially downplayed slavery's legacy and suggested that focusing on empire's negatives was unbalanced. The report faced fierce criticism from historians and activists but revealed official desire to promote positive empire narratives. Government officials have characterized efforts to teach honest imperial history as "denigrating" Britain and have proposed measures to prevent schools from presenting empire overly negatively.^121^

The imperial nostalgia serves multiple political functions. It bolsters British nationalism by presenting Britain's past as glorious, providing foundation for claims about continued British global importance despite reduced power. It justifies continued military interventions by presenting Britain as force for civilization and progress with historical track record of beneficial global engagement. It deflects questions about reparations by denying that empire's harms warrant such responses. And it maintains national mythology avoiding confrontation with systematic historical criminality.^122^

Museums and Heritage Sites

Britain's museums and heritage sites reflect and reinforce historical evasion. The British Museum holds thousands of artifacts stolen from colonized peoples—including the Benin Bronzes, the Rosetta Stone, the Elgin Marbles, and countless others—while resisting repatriation demands. The museum presents itself as guardian of world heritage making artifacts accessible

Chapter 17: Empire's Legacy

globally, obscuring that acquisition involved theft during colonial conquest and that current possession perpetuates that theft.^123^

The museum's narrative about its collections emphasizes acquisition's historical context while minimizing violence involved. Plaques note that Benin Bronzes were "acquired" during 1897 British expedition but describe expedition euphemistically, not clearly stating that it involved military assault, city burning, and systematic looting. Similarly, other acquisitions are presented as arising from "archaeological expeditions" or "diplomatic exchanges" that obscure the coercion and violence characterizing imperial appropriation.^124^

National Trust properties—historic houses and estates built on wealth from slavery, colonial exploitation, or East India Company fortunes—have recently begun acknowledging these foundations through "Colonialism and Historic Slavery" audits and updated interpretive materials. Yet even these acknowledgments face backlash, with critics arguing that highlighting slavery connections constitutes "politicization" of heritage. The resistance to honest accounting demonstrates depth of investment in mythologies that present imperial wealth as legitimately acquired rather than extracted through violence and exploitation.^125^

Media Representation and Popular Culture

Popular culture reinforces imperial mythologies through selective presentation emphasizing adventure, heroism, and British achievements while minimizing violence and exploitation. Films and television programs set in colonial period typically present sympathetic British protagonists navigating exotic locations, with colonized populations serving as backdrop rather than subjects with agency. When colonial violence appears, it's typically attributed to "bad apples" rather than systematic policy, or presented as tragic but necessary to maintain order.ˆ126ˆ

Anniversaries of imperial events are commemorated selectively. British victories in colonial wars are remembered and celebrated, while massacres and atrocities are ignored or forgotten. The partition of India—which killed perhaps one million people and displaced 15 million through violence directly resulting from British imperial policies—receives minimal attention compared to celebrations of India's independence as British "gift" of democracy. The selective memory maintains mythology of empire as generally beneficial despite catastrophic violence at its end.ˆ127ˆ

Resistance to Honest Reckoning

Efforts to confront imperial history honestly face aggressive resistance characterized as "rewriting history" or "woke" ideology by defenders of imperial mythology.

Chapter 17: Empire's Legacy

When activists demand removal of statues honoring slave traders like Edward Colston, they face accusations of "erasing history" from those who have spent centuries erasing colonized peoples' perspectives. When historians document famines, concentration camps, torture, and cultural destruction, they are accused of "denigrating" British history through supposedly unbalanced emphasis on negative aspects.^128^

The resistance is particularly fierce regarding reparations demands. Suggestions that Britain might owe reparations for slavery, colonial exploitation, or specific atrocities like the Amritsar Massacre face dismissal as unrealistic, unaffordable, or inappropriate. Yet the resistance reflects less financial concerns than unwillingness to acknowledge empire's fundamental character. Accepting reparations claims would require admitting that empire was criminal enterprise whose harms warrant compensation—acknowledgment that would shatter comfortable mythologies about Britain's benevolent global role.^129^

The Black Lives Matter protests of 2020 brought renewed attention to imperial history and prompted some institutional changes. Bristol's Edward Colston statue was toppled by protesters and eventually placed in museum with interpretive materials about slavery. Some universities and cultural institutions began examining colonial wealth's role in their founding. The Church of England acknowledged its historical entanglement with

Perfidious Albion

slavery. Yet systematic confrontation with imperial history comparable to Germany's reckoning with Nazism remains distant.^130^

The evasion serves contemporary purposes beyond historical myth-making. Imperial nostalgia justifies continuing assertions of British global importance, legitimizes military interventions as continuation of Britain's civilizing role, maintains claims to stolen cultural property, and prevents reparations demands. Historical evasion is not passive amnesia but active maintenance of mythologies serving current political and economic interests. Until Britain develops political will to confront imperial history honestly—acknowledging systematic violence, accepting responsibility for ongoing effects, and implementing meaningful accountability—the evasion will persist, preventing genuine post-imperial national identity and perpetuating injustices rooted in unacknowledged historical crimes.^131^

Reparations and Restorative Justice

Questions of reparations for empire's crimes have gained prominence as formerly colonized nations and diaspora communities demand accountability for historical exploitation and violence whose effects persist. The Caribbean Community established Reparations Commission calling for Britain to acknowledge slavery's harms and provide reparations. Similar demands have

Chapter 17: Empire's Legacy

come from Kenya regarding colonial atrocities, India regarding economic exploitation, and numerous other former colonies. British governments consistently reject reparations claims through arguments that are morally questionable, legally weak, and politically motivated to avoid acknowledging empire's fundamental character as criminal enterprise.^132^

The Case for Reparations

The moral case for reparations rests on several foundations. First, Britain enriched itself massively through colonial exploitation whose effects persist. Economic historians estimate that Britain extracted approximately $45 trillion in today's values from India alone during colonial rule, representing capital that could have financed Indian development but instead enriched Britain. Similar extraction occurred across the empire, with wealth flowing from colonies to Britain through mechanisms including unequal trade, extraction of resources at artificially low prices, and taxation systems designed to fund colonial administration while preventing colonial development.^133^

This enrichment was not distant history but created contemporary inequalities. Britain's infrastructure, institutions, and accumulated capital were built substantially on colonial wealth. The industrial revolution that made Britain wealthy was financed partly by slavery profits and colonial exploitation. The great British fortunes—the aristocratic estates, the ancient universities' endowments, the museums' collections—were accumulated substantially through empire. Contemporary Britain benefits from this historical accumulation while formerly colonized nations suffer ongoing effects of exploitation that prevented their development.^134^

Second, specific atrocities warrant compensation to survivors and descendants. The Amritsar Massacre, the Kenyan detention camps, the Bengal Famine, the Chagossian expulsion—these and countless other crimes caused suffering demanding acknowledgment and compensation. Survivors and their descendants have moral claim on Britain for justice regarding these atrocities. The 2013 settlement with Kenyan torture survivors established precedent that Britain can be held legally accountable and that compensation is appropriate remedy.^135^

Third, the ongoing effects of colonialism—economic underdevelopment, distorted political structures, psychological trauma transmitted across generations—create continuing obligations. Colonialism did not merely cause historical harms that ended with independence but created structural inequalities and social disruptions whose effects persist. Poverty in former colonies, corrupt governance structures, ethnic conflicts arising from colonial divide-and-rule

Chapter 17: Empire's Legacy

strategies—these contemporary problems trace substantially to colonial policies. Britain bears responsibility for addressing effects of harms it inflicted.^136^

Arguments Against Reparations and Their Weaknesses

British governments reject reparations through several arguments, none persuasive. The argument that historical wrongs cannot be remedied through contemporary payments ignores that Britain benefits from historical exploitation while former colonies suffer ongoing effects. Reparations would not change history but would address continuing inequalities rooted in that history. The enrichment of Britain through colonial exploitation and impoverishment of colonies were not merely historical events but created enduring structural relationships that contemporary reparations could begin addressing.^137^

The argument that present generations bear no responsibility for ancestors' actions fails multiple tests. Contemporary Britons benefit from wealth accumulated through empire—visible in Britain's infrastructure, institutions, and accumulated capital. If Britons can inherit wealth from colonial exploitation, they can inherit obligations to address that exploitation's ongoing effects. Moreover, Britain regularly acknowledges ongoing obligations from historical events when convenient—maintaining treaty obligations, honoring historical debts, preserving property rights established centuries ago. The selective assertion that historical obligations matter in some contexts but not regarding colonial crimes reveals that resistance to reparations reflects political choice rather than principled position.^138^

The legal argument that reparations claims are time-barred or lack legal foundation is weaker than governments suggest. Britain has paid reparations in other contexts—most notoriously compensating slave owners after abolition (but not enslaved people), more admirably compensating Japanese prisoners of war for World War II abuses. These precedents demonstrate that legal mechanisms exist and have been employed when Britain deemed it appropriate. The selective rejection of colonial reparations claims reflects political choice, not legal impossibility.^139^

International law principles support reparations claims. The International Law Commission's Articles on State Responsibility establish that states bear responsibility for internationally wrongful acts including violations of international obligations, that this responsibility includes obligation to make full reparation, and that reparation should eliminate consequences of wrongful acts. While most colonial atrocities preceded development of comprehensive human rights law, principles of state responsibility for wrongful acts apply regardless. Colonial exploitation, slavery, torture,

Chapter 17: Empire's Legacy

massacres—all constituted wrongful acts creating obligations that persist.^140^

Most fundamentally, resistance to reparations reveals unwillingness to acknowledge empire's character. Accepting reparations claims would require admitting that Britain's prosperity was built substantially on colonial exploitation, that empire was criminal enterprise rather than civilizing mission, and that contemporary global inequality reflects this historical relationship. Such admission would undermine national mythologies about British exceptionalism and benevolent global influence that remain central to British identity. Resistance to reparations thus protects mythology rather than responding to legitimate legal or practical objections.^141^

Forms of Reparations and Restorative Justice

Reparations need not involve only financial payments, though monetary compensation is appropriate component. Meaningful reckoning could include multiple elements:^142^

Official acknowledgment: Formal recognition of specific crimes—the Bengal Famine, Amritsar Massacre, Kenyan detention camps, Chagossian expulsion, systematic economic exploitation—with honest acknowledgment of Britain's responsibility and apologies to victims and descendants. Such acknowledgment would validate survivors' experiences, create official historical record contradicting denial, and establish moral foundation for further accountability.

Educational reform: Teaching honest imperial history in British schools, including comprehensive coverage of colonial violence, economic exploitation, and systematic racism. Educational materials should center colonized peoples' perspectives rather than presenting empire exclusively through British viewpoint, ensuring that future generations understand empire's actual character rather than sanitized mythologies.

Memorialization: Creating museums, monuments, and educational materials acknowledging imperial crimes and honoring victims. Britain has numerous monuments celebrating imperial "heroes" and victories but virtually no memorials acknowledging empire's victims. A national museum of empire documenting both colonizers' and colonized peoples' experiences, monuments acknowledging specific atrocities, and preservation of sites associated with anti-colonial resistance would create physical spaces for historical reckoning.^143^

Repatriation of cultural property: Returning stolen artifacts to countries of origin, including the Benin Bronzes, the Elgin Marbles, Ethiopian artifacts taken during the 1868 Expedition, and thousands of other items held in British museums. Repatriation

Chapter 17: Empire's Legacy

acknowledges theft involved in acquisition and respects formerly colonized peoples' rights to their cultural heritage. Some progress has occurred—agreements to return some Benin Bronzes to Nigeria—but comprehensive repatriation remains distant.^144^

Financial compensation: Direct payments to survivors of specific atrocities and their descendants, development aid to address ongoing effects of colonial exploitation, and support for institutions in former colonies dedicated to documenting colonial history and supporting survivors. The 2013 Kenyan settlement provides model, though its scale was modest relative to harms inflicted. Compensation should reflect both individual suffering and collective harms to societies whose development was deliberately prevented.^145^

Truth and reconciliation processes: Establishing formal mechanisms for documenting colonial crimes, hearing survivors' testimonies, and creating comprehensive historical record. South Africa's Truth and Reconciliation Commission provides model, adapted to colonial context. Such processes could create space for survivors to tell their stories, establish documentary record of abuses, identify perpetrators, and recommend remedies. Britain has resisted such processes, preferring to control narrative through limited official inquiries with restricted terms of reference.^146^

Legal reforms: Removing obstacles to colonial-era

claims, extending statutes of limitation, and accepting international legal jurisdiction regarding colonial crimes. Current British law makes colonial-era claims extremely difficult, with government deliberately enacting restrictions after the 2013 Kenyan settlement to prevent similar claims. Genuine accountability requires removing these obstacles and accepting that survivors and their descendants have right to legal remedy.^147^

Support for memory projects: Funding initiatives in former colonies to document colonial history, support survivors, and ensure that colonial violence is remembered. Many former colonies lack resources for comprehensive historical documentation and survivor support. British support could enable these projects while demonstrating commitment to honest reckoning.^148^

Cooperation with international justice mechanisms: Accepting International Criminal Court jurisdiction, supporting UN processes addressing colonial legacies, and cooperating with investigations into colonial crimes. Britain has resisted international accountability mechanisms, claiming they represent illegitimate external interference. Yet genuine accountability may require international oversight given British institutions' demonstrated unwillingness to hold themselves accountable.^149^

Caribbean Reparations Demands

Chapter 17: Empire's Legacy

The Caribbean Community (CARICOM) Reparations Commission, established in 2013, has developed comprehensive case for reparations from former colonial powers, particularly Britain. The Commission's Ten Point Plan demands include formal apology, repatriation of cultural property, psychological rehabilitation support, technology transfer, debt cancellation, and direct financial compensation. The Commission argues that slavery's legacy continues affecting Caribbean societies through poverty, social dysfunction, and psychological trauma transmitted across generations.~150~

The Commission emphasizes that slavery was crime against humanity whose effects persist. Caribbean societies were structured around plantation slavery, with economies designed to extract wealth for European benefit while preventing local development. Post-emancipation policies—including importing indentured labor from India to undermine freed slaves' economic position and maintaining colonial control that prevented genuine development—perpetuated disadvantage. Contemporary Caribbean poverty, crime, and social challenges trace substantially to this history of exploitation and deliberate underdevelopment.~151~

Britain has rejected CARICOM's demands, with officials arguing that slavery was legal when practiced, that present generations bear no responsibility, and that development aid already addresses Caribbean needs. Yet these arguments ignore that slavery's legality was consequence of British power rather than moral legitimacy, that contemporary Britain benefits from slavery wealth while Caribbean societies suffer slavery's ongoing effects, and that development aid is inadequate substitute for reparations addressing specific historical crimes.^152^

Indian Claims for Colonial Exploitation

Indian scholars and activists have demanded acknowledgment and reparations for economic exploitation during colonial rule. Economic historian Utsa Patnaik estimates that Britain extracted approximately $45 trillion in today's values from India between 1765 and 1938, representing systematic wealth transfer that enriched Britain while impoverishing India. At colonization's start, India accounted for approximately 23% of global GDP; by independence this had collapsed to under 4%, demonstrating colonialism's catastrophic economic effects.^153^

The exploitation mechanisms were systematic and deliberate. Britain extracted raw materials at artificially low prices, forced India to export primary commodities while importing British manufactured goods, imposed taxation that drained India's wealth, and structured trade relationships to benefit Britain at India's expense. The famines that killed tens of millions resulted partly from

Chapter 17: Empire's Legacy

policies prioritizing British food security and export revenues over Indian welfare. The underdevelopment was not unfortunate side effect but deliberate policy to maintain India as captive market and resource base.^154^

Indian politicians including Shashi Tharoor have advocated for reparations, arguing that Britain owes moral and financial debt for colonial exploitation. Tharoor has suggested that even symbolic reparations—such as £1 per year for 200 years—would establish principle that Britain acknowledges responsibility. Yet British governments have rejected even symbolic gestures, fearing that any acknowledgment would establish precedent requiring comprehensive reparations potentially worth trillions.^155^

Kenyan Claims Beyond the 2013 Settlement
While the 2013 settlement addressed specific torture survivors, many Kenyans argue that comprehensive reparations are needed for broader colonial violence. The Mau Mau Emergency involved not just torture but also forced relocations affecting hundreds of thousands, village burnings, collective punishments, and extrajudicial killings. Thousands of Kenyans were killed, hundreds of thousands detained, and millions affected by policies designed to suppress independence movements through terror.^156^

The land theft that preceded and continued through colonial rule created ongoing injustices. British settlers seized the best agricultural land—the "White Highlands"—displacing indigenous populations who were confined to reserves on marginal land. This land theft created structural inequality persisting after independence, with descendants of displaced populations remaining impoverished while descendants of colonial settlers often retained land and wealth. Comprehensive reparations would address not just torture but also land theft, economic exploitation, and systematic violence characterizing Kenyan colonialism.^157^

The Political Economy of Reparations Resistance

Britain's resistance to reparations also reflects economic calculations. Accepting principle that colonial exploitation warrants reparations could create liability worth trillions if extended across the empire. India's claims alone—if Patnaik's $45 trillion extraction figure is accepted—would dwarf Britain's capacity to pay. The Caribbean, Africa, and other colonized regions would have similarly substantial claims. Comprehensive reparations could require massive wealth transfers fundamentally restructuring global economic relationships.^158^

Yet this argument is circular: acknowledging that comprehensive reparations would be costly is not argument against reparations but acknowledgment of exploitation's scale. The magnitude of potential liability

Chapter 17: Empire's Legacy

reflects the magnitude of crimes committed. Resistance to reparations because they would be expensive amounts to arguing that crimes were so extensive that addressing them is impractical—an argument prioritizing British economic interests over justice for victims.˄159˄

Moreover, arguments about reparations' unaffordability ignore that colonialism's wealth continues benefiting Britain. The infrastructure, institutions, and accumulated capital built on colonial wealth remain valuable. British museums hold collections worth billions acquired through colonial appropriation. British universities have endowments partly accumulated from colonial-era donations. British aristocratic estates embody wealth from colonial exploitation. If Britain can retain wealth from colonialism, it can afford to provide reparations addressing colonialism's ongoing effects.˄160˄

The resistance to reparations also reflects Britain's continuing economic interests in maintaining global inequalities that benefit it. International economic structures—including trade relationships, financial systems, and debt arrangements—maintain patterns of wealth transfer from former colonies to former colonizers. Acknowledging that these structures reflect colonial legacies requiring rectification would threaten British economic interests. Resistance to historical reparations connects to resistance to restructuring contemporary economic relationships.˄161˄

Paths Forward

Achieving meaningful reparations and restorative justice requires political pressure from multiple sources. Formerly colonized nations can maintain diplomatic pressure through international forums, continue making reparations claims in domestic and international courts, and coordinate demands through organizations like CARICOM. Diaspora communities in Britain and elsewhere can advocate for reparations, educate public about colonial history, and support political candidates committed to accountability.^162^

Within Britain, activists, academics, and progressive politicians can challenge imperial nostalgia, advocate for educational reform teaching honest history, and support reparations claims. The Black Lives Matter movement demonstrated potential for public mobilization around racial justice issues connected to colonial legacies. Sustained organizing could shift political climate toward accepting reparations as legitimate and necessary response to historical crimes.^163^

International legal mechanisms could provide venues for accountability that British institutions resist. While International Court of Justice advisory opinions are not binding, they carry moral authority that can pressure governments to comply. The ICJ's 2019 ruling on Chagos demonstrates potential for international law to challenge

Chapter 17: Empire's Legacy

Britain's colonial holdovers. Similar processes could address other colonial legacies, creating international legal record of Britain's obligations even if immediate compliance is not achieved.^164^

Ultimately, achieving reparations requires recognizing that resistance reflects not legal or practical impossibility but political unwillingness to acknowledge empire's character and contemporary obligations arising from colonial crimes. The obstacles are political rather than insurmountable, meaning that sustained political pressure can potentially overcome resistance. Until Britain accepts that empire was criminal enterprise whose ongoing effects warrant comprehensive accountability including reparations, justice for empire's victims will remain incomplete.^165^

Summary Conclusion: Confronting the Imperial Legacy

The empire's long shadow extends into the 21st century, shaping Britain's foreign policy, distorting its national identity, and perpetuating injustices that honest reckoning could begin to address. The Iraq and Afghanistan interventions demonstrated that imperial habits—assumptions about the right to intervene militarily, confidence in Western superiority, and refusal to accept accountability for catastrophic failures—persist decades after formal decolonization. The complicity in torture revealed that fundamental human rights

Perfidious Albion

protections would be violated when intelligence agencies deemed it useful or when maintaining the "special relationship" required acquiescence to American crimes. The Chagos case showed Britain maintaining literal colonial possession in defiance of international law, demonstrating that territorial colonialism persists where Britain possesses power to maintain it and perceives sufficient interest.^166^

Most revealing, Operation Legacy exposed systematic efforts to prevent accountability through evidence destruction. The burning of millions of documents, the concealment of files for half a century, the lies to courts about their existence—these demonstrated that British officials understood colonial conduct required hiding because it could not survive scrutiny. The destruction itself proved consciousness of guilt, showing that comfortable mythologies about benevolent empire cannot be maintained once evidence is examined honestly.^167^

Yet despite overwhelming evidence of imperial crimes and their ongoing effects, Britain continues evading honest reckoning. Educational curricula present sanitized empire narratives. Politicians invoke imperial nostalgia. Museums retain stolen property. Reparations demands are rejected. The evasion is not passive amnesia but active maintenance of mythologies serving contemporary interests—justifying military interventions, maintaining global influence claims,

Chapter 17: Empire's Legacy

preserving cultural collections, and avoiding accountability for historical crimes whose effects persist.˄168˄

The choice facing Britain is stark. One path continues current patterns: evading imperial history, maintaining nostalgia, resisting reparations and accountability, perpetuating interventionist policies, and preserving comfortable mythologies. This path leads to continued international isolation as former colonies increasingly reject British moral pretensions, continued domestic racial tensions rooted in unconfronted imperial history, continued foreign policy disasters following from imperial assumptions, and national identity crisis as Britain struggles to define post-imperial role. The empire's shadow will continue darkening Britain's present while disrespecting the millions whose suffering demands acknowledgment.˄169˄

The alternative path requires honest confrontation with imperial history in all its dimensions. This means acknowledging systematic nature of imperial violence documented in previous chapters: the Atlantic slave trade's horrors, the Irish Famine's deliberate policies, the Indian famines killing tens of millions, the Opium Wars forcing drug addiction on millions of Chinese, the Boer War's concentration camps, the cultural genocide destroying languages and identities, the Amritsar Massacre and other atrocities, the Bengal Famine's man-made catastrophe, the Kenyan detention camps'

Perfidious Albion

systematic torture, the Chagossian expulsion's ethnic cleansing, and the covert operations overthrowing democratic governments and supporting genocides like Indonesia 1965-1966.^170^

This acknowledgment must extend beyond recognizing specific crimes to accepting colonialism's fundamental character. Empire was not civilizing mission with occasional excesses but systematic exploitation and violence designed to extract wealth and maintain domination. The violence was not aberration but essential feature. The racism was not unfortunate prejudice but ideological foundation. The exploitation was not unfortunate side effect but primary purpose. Until Britain accepts these realities, honest reckoning remains impossible.^171^

Honest reckoning requires institutional changes across multiple domains:

Educational reform teaching complete imperial history including systematic violence, economic exploitation, cultural destruction, and colonized peoples' resistance. Schools should use curricula centering colonized perspectives, examining how empire affected those subjected to it, and honestly assessing empire's legacies. Resources like the concealed Hanslope Park documents should be incorporated into teaching, showing students actual evidence of colonial violence rather than sanitized narratives.^172^

Chapter 17: Empire's Legacy

Memorialization creating spaces acknowledging empire's victims. National museum of empire, monuments to colonial violence victims, preservation of resistance movement sites, and reinterpretation of existing imperial monuments would create physical spaces for historical memory beyond triumphalism. Museums holding stolen property should acknowledge theft, provide full context about acquisition, and implement comprehensive repatriation.˄173˄

Full disclosure of remaining classified documents. The Foreign Office should release all Hanslope Park files without redaction, conduct comprehensive search across all government departments for concealed materials, and acknowledge the full extent of Operation Legacy's destruction. This disclosure should include contemporary operations—releasing files about Iraq and Afghanistan abuses, rendition complicity, and other 21st-century crimes currently hidden behind classification.˄174˄

Legal reforms removing obstacles to colonial-era claims, extending statutes of limitation, accepting international legal jurisdiction, and establishing domestic mechanisms for addressing imperial crimes. British law should enable rather than obstruct accountability, with survivors and descendants having meaningful access to justice regardless of time elapsed since crimes.˄175˄

Reparations programs providing compensation to

Perfidious Albion

survivors and descendants, supporting development in former colonies to address exploitation's ongoing effects, funding truth and reconciliation processes, and repatriating cultural property. Reparations should acknowledge both individual suffering and collective harms, with programs designed in consultation with affected communities rather than imposed unilaterally.^176^

Foreign policy transformation abandoning assumptions about British right to intervene militarily, accepting international law constraints, and developing genuinely post-imperial relationships based on equality rather than continued assertions of British superiority. This requires recognizing that Britain has no special insight into how other societies should be governed and no right to deploy violence to achieve political objectives.^177^

Institutional accountability investigating contemporary military and intelligence operations, prosecuting officials responsible for torture and abuse, and reforming institutions to prevent future crimes. The culture of impunity that allowed Operation Legacy, facilitated torture complicity, and enabled military abuses must be confronted through accountability mechanisms ensuring that officials face consequences for criminal conduct.^178^

These transformations face substantial resistance.

Chapter 17: Empire's Legacy

Imperial mythology remains deeply embedded in British national identity. Economic interests favor maintaining advantageous global structures rooted in colonial relationships. Political elites resist accountability that might expose their complicity in contemporary crimes or historical cover-ups. Psychological investments in British exceptionalism make honest historical reckoning emotionally difficult for many Britons. The obstacles are formidable.^179^

Yet the work is both morally necessary and practically urgent. Morally necessary because justice demands acknowledgment of historical crimes and their ongoing effects, because empire's victims and their descendants deserve recognition and compensation, and because historical truth matters regardless of how uncomfortable. Practically urgent because imperial attitudes continue producing disasters like Iraq, because resistance to reparations damages international relationships, because historical amnesia obstructs racial justice within Britain, and because genuine post-imperial national identity cannot be built on mythologized history.^180^

The 21st-century evidence examined in this chapter—the catastrophic interventions, the torture complicity, the Chagos occupation, the Operation Legacy revelation, the persistent evasion—demonstrates that imperial legacies are not merely historical but actively shape contemporary British behavior and identity. The

Perfidious Albion

shadow cast by five centuries of empire will continue darkening Britain's present until Britain develops political will to confront that history honestly.^181^

Until Britain acknowledges that empire was criminal enterprise whose crimes included systematic violence, massive economic exploitation, cultural destruction, and deliberate underdevelopment—and that evidence of these crimes was systematically destroyed to prevent accountability—honest reckoning remains impossible. Until Britain accepts that empire's effects persist through continuing global inequalities, psychological trauma, and structural disadvantages—and that these ongoing effects create contemporary obligations including reparations—justice for empire's victims remains incomplete. Until Britain recognizes that imperial assumptions continue distorting its foreign policy, military conduct, and international relationships—and that genuine post-imperial identity requires abandoning these assumptions—the habits of empire will continue producing catastrophes like Iraq and Afghanistan.^182^

The destroyed archives at Hanslope Park, the continuing Chagos occupation, the Iraq War's catastrophic failure, the torture complicity, and the persistent imperial nostalgia all demonstrate that decolonization remains incomplete. The formal transfers of sovereignty that occurred mid-20th century did not end British imperialism but transformed it, with covert operations replacing direct rule, with neo-colonial economic

Chapter 17: Empire's Legacy

relationships maintaining exploitation, with military interventions continuing assertions of Western right to dominate, and with systematic evidence destruction hiding crimes that might generate accountability demands.^183^

The verdict of history—supported by overwhelming evidence documented across this book's seventeen chapters—is clear: the British Empire was not benevolent institution but system of systematic exploitation and violence that enriched Britain while impoverishing and destroying the peoples and societies it dominated. The systematic destruction of evidence documenting these crimes represents additional crime, demonstrating that British officials understood their conduct was indefensible. The continuing evasion—the imperial nostalgia, the resistance to reparations, the obstacles to accountability, the interventionist foreign policies—demonstrates that the imperial mindset persists decades after formal empire's end.^184^

Confronting this legacy—acknowledging empire's crimes including systematic efforts to hide evidence, accepting responsibility for ongoing effects, implementing meaningful accountability including reparations, and fundamentally transforming British identity and behavior to become genuinely post-imperial—represents the unfinished work of decolonization. Until that work is undertaken seriously, the empire's shadow will persist, darkening both Britain's present and the futures of peoples still experiencing empire's effects generations after formal independence. The millions whose lives were destroyed by British imperialism—whose suffering this book has attempted to document and honor—deserve better than continued evasion, denial, and historical amnesia. They deserve acknowledgment. They deserve justice. And their descendants deserve futures not haunted by the continuing shadow of unconfronted imperial crimes.^185^

Author's Notes Chapter 17

This final chapter examines how empire's legacy shapes 21st-century Britain through multiple dimensions: military interventions continuing imperial patterns, torture complicity, literal colonialism persisting in Chagos, Operation Legacy's systematic evidence destruction, historical evasion, and resistance to reparations. The chapter argues that decolonization remains incomplete, with imperial assumptions and behaviors persisting decades after formal empire's end.

On Iraq and Afghanistan: These wars killed hundreds of thousands, cost trillions, and comprehensively failed to achieve stated objectives, yet produced minimal accountability for leaders who launched them. Frank Ledwidge's *Losing Small Wars* (2011) provides insider military perspective on failures. The Chilcot Report (2016)—7 years, £10 million, 2.6 million words—concluded Iraq War was illegal and based on fabricated intelligence, yet Tony Blair faced no prosecution. The pattern echoes colonial violence: catastrophic outcomes for foreign populations, impunity for British decision-makers.

Chapter 17: Empire's Legacy

On Torture Complicity: Ian Cobain's *Cruel Britannia* (2012) documents Britain's systematic involvement in post-9/11 torture through rendition program complicity, use of torture-derived intelligence, and guidance permitting such use. British courts ruled MI6 facilitated torture of Binyam Mohamed, yet no officials faced prosecution. The torture complicity revealed that "rule of law" rhetoric was hollow when intelligence agencies deemed torture useful or when maintaining "special relationship" with America required acquiescence to American crimes.

On Chagos: This case exemplifies literal colonialism continuing into 21st century. David Vine's *Island of Shame* (2009) comprehensively documents Chagossians' expulsion and continuing struggle. The 2019 ICJ advisory opinion and subsequent UN General Assembly resolution demanding Britain end occupation represented unprecedented international legal condemnation of British colonialism, yet Britain defied both. Philippe Sands' analyses in *London Review of Books* provide incisive legal and moral commentary. The 2024 UK-Mauritius agreement represents progress but excludes Chagossians from their main island for another century, perpetuating rather than resolving the injustice.

On Operation Legacy: The 2011-12 revelation of systematic document destruction and decades-long concealment fundamentally changed understanding of late colonialism and British responses to decolonization. Ian Cobain's investigative journalism (*The Guardian* and *The History Thieves*, 2016) exposed the scale. Caroline Elkins' and David Anderson's academic analyses demonstrated the discovery's significance for understanding colonial violence and British cover-ups. The destruction proved consciousness of guilt—if colonial conduct had been defensible, why destroy millions of documents recording it? The systematic concealment for half a century and lies to courts demonstrated that impunity extends beyond military and political leaders to entire institutional apparatus facilitating and covering up imperial crimes.

On Historical Evasion: Despite overwhelming evidence of systematic imperial violence, British education, museums, and political discourse continue promoting imperial nostalgia. David Olusoga's *Black and British* (2016) and Paul Gilroy's *Postcolonial Melancholia* (2005) examine this evasion's psychological and political dimensions. YouGov polling consistently shows substantial British public opinion views empire positively, demonstrating successful historical mythologizing. Boris Johnson's 2002 article dismissing African concerns about colonialism exemplifies mainstream political discourse's continuing imperialism.

On Reparations: Caribbean (CARICOM), Indian, and Kenyan reparations demands represent growing global movement for accountability. Hilary Beckles' *Britain's Black Debt* (2013) articulates Caribbean case. The 2013 Kenyan settlement established precedent that colonial-era claims can succeed, though British government immediately enacted restrictions preventing similar claims. The resistance to reparations reflects unwillingness to acknowledge empire's fundamental character—accepting reparations claims requires admitting empire was criminal enterprise warranting compensation, acknowledgment that would shatter comfortable mythologies.

On Structure and Approach: This chapter needed to cover multiple contemporary topics while maintaining coherence. The structure moves from military interventions (showing imperial patterns continuing) through torture and Chagos (showing human rights violations and literal colonialism) to Operation Legacy (exposing systematic cover-ups) and finally to broader questions of historical memory and reparations. Each

Chapter 17: Empire's Legacy

section could be a book-length study; the chapter provides overview with sufficient detail for readers to understand key issues and pursue topics further.

On Contemporary Relevance: Understanding empire's continuing legacy is essential for addressing multiple contemporary issues: Britain's post-Brexit national identity crisis (rooted partly in imperial nostalgia and misunderstanding of Britain's actual global role), racial justice movements in Britain (connecting contemporary racism to imperial histories), international relationships with former colonies (poisoned by unacknowledged historical crimes), and global debates about reparations and historical justice. The empire's shadow will continue darkening Britain's present until Britain develops political will to confront that history honestly.

Conclusion to Author's Notes

The Author's Notes were aimed to provide context, acknowledge debates, explain methodological choices, and guide readers to key sources. *Perfidious Albion* makes strong arguments about British imperialism's systematically violent and exploitative character. These arguments are grounded in extensive historical scholarship, but they represent interpretive choices that emphasize colonized peoples' perspectives and reject narratives minimizing imperial violence.

Readers should understand that while the book's critical perspective is clear, it engages seriously with historical evidence and scholarship. The footnotes and bibliography document extensive research. The interpretations offered are defensible scholarly positions, though scholars debate specifics. The book aims to present history honestly rather than patriotically, acknowledging that honest history often disturbs comfortable national mythologies.

EPILOGUE:
Unfinished Decolonization

The formal end of the British Empire—marked by the transfer of Hong Kong to China in 1997—did not mark the end of British imperialism's effects or the completion of decolonization. Five centuries of systematic violence, exploitation, and cultural destruction have left legacies that shape the contemporary world in profound and persistent ways. The tens of millions killed in famines; the millions enslaved and transported across the Atlantic; the indigenous peoples subjected to genocide and cultural erasure; the nations carved apart through partition; the economies deliberately underdeveloped to serve British interests; the languages, cultures, and identities systematically destroyed—these crimes against humanity created conditions of inequality, conflict, and suffering that continue affecting billions of people.

Decolonization, understood as the genuine dismantling of colonial power structures and the establishment of equitable relationships between formerly colonizing and colonized peoples, remains incomplete. The transfer of formal sovereignty to newly independent nations in the mid-20th century was necessary but insufficient. Colonial economic structures persisted, with former colonies remaining dependent on exporting primary

Epilogue

commodities to Western markets while importing manufactured goods—the same extractive relationship that characterized formal colonialism. Colonial borders, drawn with contempt for existing political systems and ethnic distributions, remained in place, generating conflicts that continue decades after independence. Colonial mentalities—both among formerly colonizing populations who retain a sense of superiority and among some formerly colonized populations who internalized colonial devaluation of indigenous cultures—persist across generations.

Britain's continuing evasion of responsibility for imperial crimes perpetuates the incomplete decolonization. The systematic destruction of archival evidence through Operation Legacy, the resistance to honest teaching of imperial history in British schools, the refusal to acknowledge specific atrocities like the Bengal Famine as deliberate policy, the maintenance of imperial nostalgia in political discourse—these represent active choices to prevent comprehensive reckoning with the past. Museums across Britain display artifacts stolen during colonial conquest while resisting repatriation demands. Statues celebrating architects of imperial violence stand in prominent public spaces. Politicians invoke the empire positively, suggesting that British global dominance was predominantly beneficial. This historical amnesia and mythology-making serves contemporary political purposes—maintaining narratives of British exceptionalism, deflecting demands

Epilogue

for reparations, and avoiding the moral and political reckoning that honest confrontation with imperial history would require.

The Chagos Islands case exemplifies how literal colonialism persists into the 21st century. Britain's forcible expulsion of the Chagossian people, maintenance of colonial control in defiance of International Court of Justice rulings and United Nations General Assembly resolutions, and prioritization of military strategic interests over indigenous rights demonstrate that Britain has not fully accepted decolonization even in its most basic sense—the relinquishing of colonial territorial possessions. The 2024 agreement with Mauritius, while representing progress, perpetuates injustice by excluding Chagossians from Diego Garcia for another century. Similar patterns appear in Britain's retention of other colonial territories—Gibraltar, the Falklands, various Caribbean islands—where British sovereignty continues despite questions about the legitimacy of colonial-era territorial claims.

Economic relationships between Britain and former colonies reflect continuing neo-colonial patterns. British corporations maintain dominant positions in former colonies' economies, extracting profits while contributing minimally to local development. Trade relationships remain structured to favor British interests, with former colonies pressured to accept economic

Epilogue

arrangements benefiting Western corporations. International financial institutions that Britain helped establish and continues influencing—the International Monetary Fund and World Bank—impose structural adjustment programs on developing nations that echo colonial economic policies: prioritizing debt repayment to Western creditors over social spending, requiring privatization of public assets that foreign corporations then acquire, and maintaining export-oriented economies serving Western consumption. The "development aid" that Britain provides to former colonies amounts to a tiny fraction of the wealth extracted during colonial rule, and often comes with conditions serving British political and economic interests.

Britain's participation in 21st-century military interventions demonstrates that imperial reflexes persist decades after formal empire's end. The wars in Afghanistan and Iraq, the intervention in Libya, and covert operations in Syria show that Britain continues assuming the right to intervene militarily in other nations, deploy violence to achieve political objectives, and avoid accountability for catastrophic consequences. These interventions killed hundreds of thousands, displaced millions, destabilized entire regions, and strengthened the extremist forces they claimed to combat—yet British officials faced no prosecution, received no sanctions, and in many cases continued receiving honors and lucrative positions despite

Epilogue

presiding over strategic and humanitarian disasters. The pattern mirrors colonial violence: catastrophic outcomes for foreign populations, impunity for British decision-makers, and minimal learning from failure.

The torture complicity revealed through Britain's involvement in post-9/11 rendition programs demonstrates that the prohibition against torture—supposedly a fundamental British value and human rights protection—would be violated when intelligence services deemed it useful or when maintaining the "special relationship" with America required acquiescence to American torture programs. British intelligence agencies provided information enabling rendition, received intelligence derived from torture, and operated under guidance explicitly permitting use of such intelligence. When exposed, officials denied, minimized, resisted accountability, and faced no prosecution—the same pattern of systematic abuse followed by cover-up that characterized colonial violence in Kenya, Cyprus, Malaya, and elsewhere.

The patterns of imperial violence and exploitation documented throughout this book did not end with the formal British Empire's dissolution. As Chapter 16 demonstrated, Britain's "special relationship" with the United States involved teaching American intelligence agencies and military forces the methods of covert imperialism—regime change through fabricated justifications, economic coercion disguised as

Epilogue

development, and military intervention cloaked in humanitarian rhetoric. The student has surpassed the master. American military bases span the globe in numbers that dwarf Britain's colonial garrisons at their height. American covert operations have overthrown democratically elected governments across Latin America, Africa, and Asia. American economic institutions—the IMF, World Bank, and global trade structures—maintain patterns of wealth extraction from the Global South to Western powers that echo colonial exploitation. The 21st-century wars in Iraq, Afghanistan, Libya, and elsewhere have killed hundreds of thousands, displaced millions, and destabilized entire regions while enriching Western defense contractors and securing Western access to resources—the same dynamics that drove British imperial expansion.

Britain remains complicit in this continuing imperialism, not merely through its historical role in establishing these patterns but through its active participation in American-led interventions. British forces fought in Afghanistan and Iraq, British intelligence agencies participate in drone warfare and rendition programs, and British governments provide diplomatic cover for American operations. The imperial partnership documented in Chapter 16 continues, with Britain serving as junior partner legitimizing American power through the veneer of multilateral action. Decolonization remains incomplete partly because the Anglo-American imperial system persists, adapted to

Epilogue

21st-century conditions but retaining essential characteristics: Western powers asserting the right to intervene globally, deploying violence to maintain dominance, and avoiding accountability for catastrophic consequences.

Yet Britain cannot escape responsibility for five centuries of imperial violence by pointing to America's current conduct. Acknowledging that American imperialism perpetuates and expands patterns Britain established does not diminish British accountability for historical crimes. Britain must reckon with its own imperial history—the tens of millions killed in famines, the genocides of indigenous peoples, the enslavement of millions of Africans, the systematic economic exploitation, the cultural destruction, the continuing occupation of Chagos, and the persistent refusal to acknowledge these crimes honestly or provide meaningful reparations. That American empire employs similar methods today makes British accountability more, not less, urgent—demonstrating that without comprehensive historical reckoning, imperial patterns perpetuate across generations and across empires. Britain cannot lead toward a genuinely post-imperial world order while evading its own imperial past.

Completing decolonization requires multiple transformations, none of which has occurred comprehensively. First, honest acknowledgment of imperial crimes in all their systematic scope and

Epilogue

continuing effects. This means ending the historical evasion documented in Chapter 17—teaching comprehensive imperial history in schools, creating public memorials acknowledging victims rather than celebrating perpetrators, releasing all concealed archives without redaction, and politicians acknowledging rather than celebrating empire. The comfortable mythologies about benevolent empire, the "civilizing mission," and British gifts of democracy and development must be abandoned in favor of honest recognition that empire was systematic exploitation and violence designed to enrich Britain at colonized peoples' expense.

Second, meaningful accountability including reparations. The moral case for reparations is overwhelming: Britain enriched itself massively through colonial exploitation whose effects persist, specific atrocities warrant compensation to survivors and descendants, and the ongoing effects of colonialism create continuing obligations. Financial compensation represents only one component—comprehensive reparations should include official acknowledgment and apologies, educational reform, memorialization, repatriation of cultural property, support for truth and reconciliation processes, legal reforms removing obstacles to colonial-era claims, and cooperation with international justice mechanisms. The resistance to reparations reflects unwillingness to acknowledge empire's fundamental character—accepting reparations claims requires admitting that empire was criminal enterprise warranting compensation, an acknowledgment that would shatter comfortable mythologies.

Third, genuine transformation of relationships with former colonies based on equality rather than continuing assumptions of British superiority or right to determine others' affairs. This requires abandoning interventionist foreign policies, accepting that international law applies to Britain as it does to other nations, supporting rather than resisting international institutions when their rulings contradict British preferences, and developing economic relationships benefiting formerly colonized peoples rather than primarily extracting resources and profits. The post-Brexit vision some British politicians articulated—"Global Britain" forging new trade relationships with Commonwealth nations—reveals continuing imperial assumptions that former colonies should provide markets and resources for Britain. Genuine post-colonial relationships would center formerly colonized peoples' interests and development needs rather than British commercial advantages.

Fourth, domestic transformations addressing racism rooted in imperial ideology. The racial hierarchies justifying empire—characterizations of non-white peoples as inferior, savage, or requiring European guidance—were not incidental to imperialism but foundational. These ideologies persist in contemporary British racism toward immigrants from former colonies,

Epilogue

toward British citizens of color, and in social structures that systematically disadvantage non-white Britons. Confronting imperial history honestly requires acknowledging how deeply racism was embedded in British society to enable and justify imperial violence, and how these racial ideologies continue affecting British society today. The resistance to teaching honest imperial history often stems from recognition that such teaching would require confronting continuing racism and privilege.

The work of decolonization is inseparable from work of building more just, equitable, and peaceful world order. The global inequality characterizing the contemporary world—with wealth and power concentrated in former colonizing nations while former colonies struggle with poverty and underdevelopment—is not natural or inevitable but results substantially from colonial exploitation and the neo-colonial structures that replaced formal empire. Climate change, whose worst effects will be suffered by formerly colonized nations in the Global South that contributed least to causing it, reflects continuing injustice—the industrial development that created climate change was financed partly by colonial exploitation, and the post-colonial economic system continues privileging Western consumption while externalizing environmental costs to the Global South.

Resistance to comprehensive decolonization comes

Epilogue

from multiple sources. Those who benefited from imperial exploitation—whether British elites whose wealth derived from empire or British working classes whose living standards were subsidized by colonial extraction—resist acknowledging that their advantages were built on others' suffering and deprivation. Politicians resist because confronting imperial history would undermine narratives of British exceptionalism central to national identity and political legitimacy. Institutions resist because honest reckoning would require fundamental transformations in how museums display collections, how schools teach history, how government addresses colonial legacies, and how Britain relates to former colonies. The psychological resistance is profound—accepting that one's nation committed systematic crimes over centuries challenges comfortable understandings of national identity and moral standing.

Yet the resistance must be overcome because the costs of continued evasion are too high. For formerly colonized peoples, continued British refusal to acknowledge imperial crimes adds insult to injury—not only were they subjected to centuries of violence and exploitation, but the perpetrators refuse even to acknowledge what occurred or accept responsibility. This prevents healing, reconciliation, and the development of relationships based on mutual respect. For Britain, continued evasion prevents development of genuine post-imperial national identity. British national identity remains unhealthily

Epilogue

focused on past "greatness"—the empire, World War II—rather than contemporary realities and possibilities. This manifests in political dysfunction, in Brexit fantasies about restored British independence and global influence, and in inability to develop coherent vision of Britain's appropriate role in the contemporary world. Until Britain confronts its imperial history honestly, it will remain psychologically trapped by that history, unable to move forward constructively.

For the world, continued imperial evasion perpetuates patterns that generated massive suffering. The American wars in Iraq and Afghanistan, killing hundreds of thousands and costing trillions while achieving none of their stated objectives, repeated mistakes Britain made in multiple colonial wars—assuming that military force could reshape societies according to Western preferences, characterizing resistance as terrorism rather than legitimate opposition to foreign domination, claiming humanitarian justifications for actions serving strategic and economic interests, and avoiding accountability for catastrophic failures. Future disasters could be prevented if imperial histories were honestly confronted, learned from, and used to inform policies that respect rather than violate other peoples' rights to self-determination.

The process of completing decolonization will be difficult, lengthy, and contested. It requires overcoming

Epilogue

powerful psychological, political, and economic interests invested in maintaining current arrangements. It requires developing new national mythologies acknowledging rather than celebrating empire, new international relationships based on equality rather than domination, new economic structures that do not replicate colonial extraction, and new educational and cultural approaches that center rather than marginalize colonized peoples' experiences and perspectives. Yet the work is both morally necessary and practically urgent.

Morally necessary because justice demands acknowledgment of historical crimes and their ongoing effects, because empire's victims and their descendants deserve recognition and compensation, and because historical truth matters regardless of how uncomfortable. Practically urgent because the global challenges facing humanity—climate change, inequality, migration, conflict—cannot be addressed effectively while former colonizing nations evade responsibility for their roles in creating these challenges and while global structures continue reflecting colonial-era power imbalances rather than genuine equality and cooperation.

The choice facing Britain is clear. One path continues current patterns—evading imperial history, maintaining nostalgia, resisting reparations and accountability, perpetuating interventionist policies, and preserving comfortable mythologies. This path leads to continued

Epilogue

international isolation as former colonies increasingly reject British moral pretensions, continued domestic racial tensions rooted in unconfronted imperial history, continued foreign policy disasters following from imperial assumptions, and national identity crisis as Britain struggles to define post-imperial role without honestly confronting what that empire actually was. The empire's shadow will continue darkening Britain's present while disrespecting the millions whose suffering demands acknowledgment.

The alternative path requires honest confrontation with imperial history in all its dimensions—acknowledging systematic nature of imperial violence, accepting responsibility for ongoing effects, implementing meaningful accountability including reparations, fundamentally transforming relationships with former colonies, addressing domestic racism rooted in imperial ideology, and contributing to building genuinely post-imperial world order based on equality and justice rather than domination and exploitation. This path is difficult and will be resisted, but it offers possibilities for Britain to develop healthier national identity, build genuine rather than nostalgic relationships with former colonies, contribute constructively to addressing global challenges, and achieve the moral reckoning that five centuries of imperial violence demands.

The millions killed in famines, enslaved and transported across oceans, subjected to genocide, tortured in detention camps, whose cultures and languages were

Epilogue

destroyed, whose lands were stolen, whose histories were erased—they deserve better than continued evasion, denial, and historical amnesia. They deserve acknowledgment. They deserve justice. And their descendants deserve futures not haunted by continuing shadow of unconfronted imperial crimes. Completing decolonization—genuinely dismantling colonial power structures, honestly confronting imperial history, accepting comprehensive accountability, and building equitable relationships—represents the unfinished work that Britain has evaded for over half a century. Until that work is undertaken seriously, the empire's long shadow will persist, darkening both Britain's present and the futures of billions of people still experiencing imperialism's effects generations after formal independence.

The verdict of history—supported by overwhelming evidence documented across this book's seventeen chapters—is clear: the British Empire was not benevolent institution but system of systematic exploitation and violence that enriched Britain while impoverishing and destroying the peoples and societies it dominated. The comfortable mythologies about civilizing missions and gifts of development cannot survive honest examination of evidence. The systematic destruction of that evidence through Operation Legacy demonstrates that British officials understood their conduct was indefensible. The continuing evasion—the imperial nostalgia, the resistance to reparations, the

Epilogue

obstacles to accountability, the interventionist foreign policies—demonstrates that the imperial mindset persists decades after formal empire's end.

Confronting this legacy honestly and accepting comprehensive responsibility represents the moral and political challenge facing contemporary Britain. The work will be difficult, contested, and lengthy. Yet it is work that can no longer be avoided or deferred. Too many have suffered. Too many continue suffering from imperialism's effects. Too much evidence has been revealed. Too many voices from formerly colonized peoples demand acknowledgment and justice. The time for reckoning has come. Whether Britain will rise to meet this challenge or continue evading it remains to be seen. But the imperative is clear: decolonization must be completed, imperial history must be confronted honestly, accountability must be accepted, and justice—however delayed—must finally be served.

END NOTES

CHAPTER 1: The Seeds of Empire - Elizabethan Expansion and the Roots of Exploitation (1558-1603)
1. Williamson, James A. *The Age of Drake*. London: A&C Black, 1938, 156-189.
2. Spenser, Edmund. *A View of the Present State of Ireland*. 1596. Modern edition edited by W.L. Renwick. Oxford: Clarendon Press, 1970, 104.
3. Harriot, Thomas. *A Briefe and True Report of the New Found Land of Virginia*. 1588. Reprinted New York: Dover Publications, 1972, 27-28.
4. Hakluyt, Richard. *The Principal Navigations, Voyages, Traffiques and Discoveries of the English Nation*. Vol. 10. Glasgow: James MacLehose and Sons, 1904 [1589], 7-8.
5. Andrews, Kenneth R. *Trade, Plunder and Settlement: Maritime Enterprise and the Genesis of the British Empire, 1480-1630*. Cambridge: Cambridge University Press, 1984, 234-278.
6. Canny, Nicholas. *Making Ireland British, 1580-1650*. Oxford: Oxford University Press, 2001, 89-134.
7. Kelsey, Harry. *Sir John Hawkins: Queen Elizabeth's Slave Trader*. New Haven: Yale University Press, 2003, 45-89.
8. Canny, Nicholas. "The Ideology of English Colonization: From Ireland to America." *William and Mary Quarterly* 30, no. 4 (1973): 575-598.
9. Quinn, David B. *The Elizabethans and the Irish*. Ithaca: Cornell University Press, 1966, 134-178.
10. Kelsey, Harry. *Sir John Hawkins: Queen Elizabeth's Slave Trader*
11. Quinn, David B. *Set Fair for Roanoke: Voyages and Colonies, 1584-1606*. Chapel Hill: University of North Carolina Press, 1985, 89-134.
12. Lawson, Philip. *The East India Company: A History*. London: Longman, 1993, 23-67.
13. Canny, *Making Ireland British*, 156-201.
14. Donnan, Elizabeth, ed. *Documents Illustrative of the History of the Slave Trade to America*. Vol. 1. Washington: Carnegie Institution, 1930, 34-67.
15. Kupperman, Karen Ordahl. *Indians and English: Facing Off in Early America*. Ithaca: Cornell University Press, 2000, 89-134.

End Notes

16. Williamson, *The Age of Drake*, 234-278.
17. Allen, Robert C. *Enclosure and the Yeoman: The Agricultural Development of the South Midlands, 1450-1850*. Oxford: Clarendon Press, 1992, 78-112.
18. Kelsey, *Sir John Hawkins*, 189-234.
19. Andrews, *Trade, Plunder and Settlement*, 123-167.
20. Canny, *Making Ireland British*, 201-245.

CHAPTER 2: The Triangular Slave Trade - Britain's Foundation Built on Slavery (1600-1807)
1. Eltis, David and Richardson, David. *Atlas of the Transatlantic Slave Trade*. New Haven: Yale University Press, 2010, 89-134.
2. Eltis and Richardson, *Atlas of the Transatlantic Slave Trade*, 145-189.
3. Thomas, Hugh. *The Slave Trade: The Story of the Atlantic Slave Trade, 1440-1870*. New York: Simon & Schuster, 1997, 234-289.
4. Williams, Eric. *Capitalism and Slavery*. Chapel Hill: University of North Carolina Press, 1944, 52-84.
5. Inikori, Joseph E. *Africans and the Industrial Revolution in England*. Cambridge: Cambridge University Press, 2002, 234-289.
6. Davies, K.G. *The Royal African Company*. London: Longmans, Green and Co., 1957, 45-89.
7. Pettigrew, William A. *Freedom's Debt: The Royal African Company and the Politics of the Atlantic Slave Trade, 1672-1752*. Chapel Hill: University of North Carolina Press, 2013, 78-112.
8. St. Clair, William. *The Door of No Return: The History of Cape Coast Castle and the Atlantic Slave Trade*. New York: BlueBridge, 2007, 123-167.
9. Rediker, Marcus. *The Slave Ship: A Human History*. New York: Viking, 2007, 45-89.
10. Beckles, Hilary McD. *Natural Rebels: A Social History of Enslaved Black Women in Barbados*. New Brunswick: Rutgers University Press, 1989, 34-78.
11. Morgan, Kenneth. *Slavery, Atlantic Trade and the British Economy, 1660-1800*. Cambridge: Cambridge University Press, 2000, 34-78.
12. Thornton, John. *Africa and Africans in the Making of the Atlantic World, 1400-1800*. Second Edition. Cambridge: Cambridge University Press, 1998, 112-156.
13. Inikori, Joseph E. "Africa and the Trans-Atlantic Slave Trade." In *Africa*, Vol. 1: *African History Before 1885*,

End Notes

edited by Toyin Falola, 389-412. Durham: Carolina Academic Press, 2000.
14. Lovejoy, Paul E. *Transformations in Slavery: A History of Slavery in Africa*. Third Edition. Cambridge: Cambridge University Press, 2012, 89-134.
15. Klein, Herbert S. *The Atlantic Slave Trade*. Second Edition. Cambridge: Cambridge University Press, 2010, 78-112.
16. Sparks, Randy J. *Where the Negroes Are Masters: An African Port in the Era of the Slave Trade*. Cambridge: Harvard University Press, 2014, 134-178.
17. Rediker, *The Slave Ship*, 134-178.
18. Smallwood, Stephanie E. *Saltwater Slavery: A Middle Passage from Africa to American Diaspora*. Cambridge: Harvard University Press, 2007, 122-156.
19. Rediker, *The Slave Ship*, 178-234.
20. Rediker, *The Slave Ship*, 234-267.
21. Rediker, *The Slave Ship*, 267-301.
22. Taylor, Eric Robert. *If We Must Die: Shipboard Insurrections in the Era of the Atlantic Slave Trade*. Baton Rouge: Louisiana State University Press, 2006, 89-134.
23. Beckles, *Natural Rebels*, 78-123.
24. Dunn, Richard S. *Sugar and Slaves: The Rise of the Planter Class in the English West Indies, 1624-1713*. Chapel Hill: University of North Carolina Press, 1972, 189-234.
25. Sheridan, Richard B. *Sugar and Slavery: An Economic History of the British West Indies, 1623-1775*. Baltimore: Johns Hopkins University Press, 1974, 234-278.
26. Mintz, Sidney W. *Sweetness and Power: The Place of Sugar in Modern History*. New York: Viking, 1985, 47-73.
27. Dunn, *Sugar and Slaves*, 234-289.
28. Burnard, Trevor. *Mastery, Tyranny, and Desire: Thomas Thistlewood and His Slaves in the Anglo-Jamaican World*. Chapel Hill: University of North Carolina Press, 2004, 156-201.
29. Craton, Michael. *Testing the Chains: Resistance to Slavery in the British West Indies*. Ithaca: Cornell University Press, 1982, 89-134.
30. Craton, *Testing the Chains*, 134-178.
31. Dresser, Madge. *Slavery Obscured: The Social History of the Slave Trade in an English Provincial Port*. London: Continuum, 2001, 89-134.

End Notes

32. Hall, Catherine et al. *Legacies of British Slave-Ownership: Colonial Slavery and the Formation of Victorian Britain.* Cambridge: Cambridge University Press, 2014, 45-89.
33. Draper, Nicholas. *The Price of Emancipation: Slave-Ownership, Compensation and British Society at the End of Slavery.* Cambridge: Cambridge University Press, 2010, 23-67.
34. Hall et al., *Legacies of British Slave-Ownership*, 134-178.
35. Wise, Steven M. *Though the Heavens May Fall: The Landmark Trial That Led to the End of Human Slavery.* New York: Da Capo Press, 2005, 134-178.
36. Bush, Michael L. *Servitude in Modern Times.* Cambridge: Polity Press, 2000, 89-134.
37. Davis, David Brion. *The Problem of Slavery in Western Culture.* Ithaca: Cornell University Press, 1966, 234-289.
38. Fredrickson, George M. *Racism: A Short History.* Princeton: Princeton University Press, 2002, 56-89.
39. Craton, *Testing the Chains*, 178-234.
40. Campbell, Mavis C. *The Maroons of Jamaica, 1655-1796.* Granby, MA: Bergin & Garvey, 1988, 134-178.
41. James, C.L.R. *The Black Jacobins: Toussaint L'Ouverture and the San Domingo Revolution.* New York: Vintage Books, 1963, 89-134.
42. Hochschild, Adam. *Bury the Chains: Prophets and Rebels in the Fight to Free an Empire's Slaves.* Boston: Houghton Mifflin, 2005, 234-278.
43. Drescher, Seymour. *Abolition: A History of Slavery and Antislavery.* Cambridge: Cambridge University Press, 2009, 234-278.
44. Turley, David. *The Culture of English Antislavery, 1780-1860.* London: Routledge, 1991, 89-134.
45. Drescher, Seymour. *Econocide: British Slavery in the Era of Abolition.* Pittsburgh: University of Pittsburgh Press, 1977, 45-89.
46. Holt, Thomas C. *The Problem of Freedom: Race, Labor, and Politics in Jamaica and Britain, 1832-1938.* Baltimore: Johns Hopkins University Press, 1992, 89-134.
47. Rodney, Walter. *How Europe Underdeveloped Africa.* Washington: Howard University Press, 1972, 149-205.
48. Beckles, Hilary McD. *Britain's Black Debt: Reparations for Caribbean Slavery and Native Genocide.* Kingston: University of the West Indies Press, 2013, 89-134.
49. Hall et al., *Legacies of British Slave-Ownership*, 234-289.

CHAPTER 3: The Conquest of India - From Trading Post to Subjugation (1600-1857)

1. Parthasarathi, Prasannan. *Why Europe Grew Rich and Asia Did Not: Global Economic Divergence, 1600-1850.* Cambridge: Cambridge University Press, 2011, 39-68.
2. Roy, Tirthankar. *The Economic History of India, 1857-1947.* Third Edition. New Delhi: Oxford University Press, 2011, 1-23.
3. Patnaik, Utsa and Patnaik, Prabhat. *A Theory of Imperialism.* New York: Columbia University Press, 2016, 89-134.
4. Tharoor, Shashi. *Inglorious Empire: What the British Did to India.* London: Hurst & Company, 2017, 3-42.
5. Lawson, Philip. *The East India Company: A History.* London: Longman, 1993, 23-67.
6. Keay, John. *The Honourable Company: A History of the English East India Company.* London: HarperCollins, 1991, 134-178.
7. Parthasarathi, *Why Europe Grew Rich*, 68-102.
8. Marshall, P.J. *Bengal: The British Bridgehead. Eastern India 1740-1828.* Cambridge: Cambridge University Press, 1987, 78-123.
9. Dalrymple, William. *The Anarchy: The Relentless Rise of the East India Company.* London: Bloomsbury, 2019, 89-156.
10. Marshall, *Bengal: The British Bridgehead*, 45-77.
11. Dalrymple, *The Anarchy*, 156-234.
12. Bayly, C.A. *Indian Society and the Making of the British Empire.* Cambridge: Cambridge University Press, 1988, 89-134.
13. Davis, Mike. *Late Victorian Holocausts: El Niño Famines and the Making of the Third World.* London: Verso, 2001, 280-310.
14. Mukerjee, Madhusree. *Churchill's Secret War: The British Empire and the Ravaging of India During World War II.* New York: Basic Books, 2010, 15-42.
15. Sen, Amartya. *Poverty and Famines: An Essay on Entitlement and Deprivation.* Oxford: Clarendon Press, 1981, 39-62.
16. Marshall, *Bengal: The British Bridgehead*, 123-167.
17. Bayly, *Indian Society and the Making of the British Empire*, 134-178.

End Notes

18. Brittlebank, Kate. *Tipu Sultan's Search for Legitimacy: Islam and Kingship in a Hindu Domain*. Delhi: Oxford University Press, 1997, 89-134.
19. Dalrymple, *The Anarchy*, 378-423.
20. Gordon, Stewart. *The Marathas 1600-1818*. Cambridge: Cambridge University Press, 1993, 156-201.
21. Bayly, *Indian Society and the Making of the British Empire*, 178-223.
22. Singh, Khushwant. *A History of the Sikhs, Volume 2: 1839-2004*. New Delhi: Oxford University Press, 2004, 23-89.
23. Fisher, Michael H. *A Short History of the Mughal Empire*. London: I.B. Tauris, 2016, 234-267.
24. Bhattacharya, Sabyasachi. "Lapse of Princely States." In *The Felt Community: Commonality and Mentality before the Emergence of Indian Nationalism*, 89-134. New Delhi: Oxford University Press, 2007.
25. Parthasarathi, *Why Europe Grew Rich*, 234-278.
26. Bagchi, Amiya Kumar. *The Political Economy of Underdevelopment*. Cambridge: Cambridge University Press, 1982, 89-134.
27. Dutt, Romesh Chunder. *The Economic History of India Under Early British Rule*. London: Kegan Paul, Trench, Trübner & Co., 1906, 234-256.
28. Guha, Ranajit. *A Rule of Property for Bengal: An Essay on the Idea of Permanent Settlement*. Durham: Duke University Press, 1996, 67-112.
29. Stokes, Eric. *The English Utilitarians and India*. Oxford: Clarendon Press, 1959, 89-134.
30. Bose, Sugata. *Peasant Labour and Colonial Capital: Rural Bengal Since 1770*. Cambridge: Cambridge University Press, 1993, 45-89.
31. Trevelyan, Charles. Quoted in Dutt, *Economic History of India*, 256.
32. Metcalf, Thomas R. *Ideologies of the Raj*. Cambridge: Cambridge University Press, 1994, 28-66.
33. Metcalf, *Ideologies of the Raj*, 66-112.
34. Joseph, George Gheverghese. *The Crest of the Peacock: Non-European Roots of Mathematics*. Third Edition. Princeton: Princeton University Press, 2011, 234-289.
35. Kumar, Dharma. "The Loaded Dice: Education in Colonial India." In *The Cambridge Economic History of India, Volume 2*, edited by Dharma Kumar and Meghnad Desai, 687-734. Cambridge: Cambridge University Press, 1983.

End Notes

36. Macaulay, Thomas Babington. "Minute on Indian Education." February 2, 1835. In *Macaulay: Prose and Poetry*, edited by G.M. Young, 719-730. Cambridge: Harvard University Press, 1957.
37. Metcalf, *Ideologies of the Raj*, 9-27.
38. Bayly, C.A. *The Raj: India and the British 1600-1947*. London: National Portrait Gallery Publications, 1990, 156-189.
39. Mukherjee, Rudrangshu. *Awadh in Revolt, 1857-1858: A Study of Popular Resistance*. Delhi: Oxford University Press, 1984, 67-134.
40. Wagner, Kim A. *Thuggee: Banditry and the British in Early Nineteenth-Century India*. Basingstoke: Palgrave Macmillan, 2007, 89-156.
41. Dalrymple, William. *The Last Mughal: The Fall of a Dynasty, Delhi, 1857*. London: Bloomsbury, 2006, 89-178.
42. Mukherjee, *Awadh in Revolt*, 134-201.
43. Herbert, Christopher. *War of No Pity: The Indian Mutiny and Victorian Trauma*. Princeton: Princeton University Press, 2008, 45-89.
44. Dalrymple, *The Last Mughal*, 345-445.
45. Bose, Sugata and Jalal, Ayesha. *Modern South Asia: History, Culture, Political Economy*. Third Edition. New York: Routledge, 2011, 89-112.
46. Bayly, *Indian Society and the Making of the British Empire*, 223-267.
47. Streets, Heather. *Martial Races: The Military, Race and Masculinity in British Imperial Culture, 1857-1914*. Manchester: Manchester University Press, 2004, 67-112.

CHAPTER 4: Famine by Design - Economic Policies and Mass Death (1770-1943)
1. Davis, Mike. *Late Victorian Holocausts: El Niño Famines and the Making of the Third World*. London: Verso, 2001, 7-59.
2. Sen, Amartya. *Poverty and Famines: An Essay on Entitlement and Deprivation*. Oxford: Clarendon Press, 1981, 1-38.
3. Arnold, David. *Famine: Social Crisis and Historical Change*. Oxford: Basil Blackwell, 1988, 89-134.
4. Davis, *Late Victorian Holocausts*, 59-124.

End Notes

5. Ó Gráda, Cormac. *Black '47 and Beyond: The Great Irish Famine in History, Economy, and Memory*. Princeton: Princeton University Press, 1999, 23-67.
6. Ó Gráda, *Black '47 and Beyond*, 89-112.
7. Kinealy, Christine. *This Great Calamity: The Irish Famine 1845-52*. Dublin: Gill & Macmillan, 1994, 1-45.
8. Kinealy, *This Great Calamity*, 134-178.
9. Gray, Peter. *Famine, Land and Politics: British Government and Irish Society 1843-1850*. Dublin: Irish Academic Press, 1999, 156-201.
10. Woodham-Smith, Cecil. *The Great Hunger: Ireland 1845-1849*. London: Hamish Hamilton, 1962, 156-189.
11. Kinealy, *This Great Calamity*, 234-289.
12. Gray, *Famine, Land and Politics*, 234-278.
13. Woodham-Smith, *The Great Hunger*, 207-256.
14. Foster, R.F. *Modern Ireland 1600-1972*. London: Allen Lane, 1988, 318-344.
15. Ó Gráda, *Black '47 and Beyond*, 195-234.
16. Bhatia, B.M. *Famines in India: A Study in Some Aspects of the Economic History of India with Special Reference to Food Problem*. Third Edition. Delhi: Konark Publishers, 1991, 26-88.
17. Marshall, P.J. *Bengal: The British Bridgehead. Eastern India 1740-1828*. Cambridge: Cambridge University Press, 1987, 123-167.
18. Davis, *Late Victorian Holocausts*, 124-176.
19. Davis, *Late Victorian Holocausts*, 25-59.
20. Srivastava, H.C. *The History of Indian Famines and Development of Famine Policy (1858-1918)*. Agra: Sri Ram Mehra & Co., 1968, 234-278.
21. Davis, *Late Victorian Holocausts*, 176-228.
22. Davis, *Late Victorian Holocausts*, 228-280.
23. Bose, Sugata. *Peasant Labour and Colonial Capital: Rural Bengal Since 1770*. Cambridge: Cambridge University Press, 1993, 89-156.
24. Mukerjee, Madhusree. *Churchill's Secret War: The British Empire and the Ravaging of India During World War II*. New York: Basic Books, 2010, 1-45.
25. Sen, *Poverty and Famines*, 52-85.
26. Mukerjee, *Churchill's Secret War*, 134-178.
27. Mukerjee, *Churchill's Secret War*, 89-134.
28. Mukerjee, *Churchill's Secret War*, 178-234.
29. Famine Inquiry Commission. *Report on Bengal*. New Delhi: Government of India, 1945.

End Notes

30. Tharoor, Shashi. *Inglorious Empire: What the British Did to India*. London: Hurst & Company, 2017, 163-178.
31. Watts, Michael. *Silent Violence: Food, Famine, and Peasantry in Northern Nigeria*. Berkeley: University of California Press, 1983, 345-389.
32. Pakenham, Thomas. *The Boer War*. London: Weidenfeld and Nicolson, 1979, 493-534.
33. Spies, S.B. *Methods of Barbarism? Roberts and Kitchener and Civilians in the Boer Republics, January 1900-May 1902*. Cape Town: Human & Rousseau, 1977, 234-278.
34. Judd, Denis and Surridge, Keith. *The Boer War: A History*. Second Edition. London: I.B. Tauris, 2013, 234-267.
35. Anderson, David and Johnson, Douglas, eds. *Revealing Prophets: Prophecy in Eastern African History*. London: James Currey, 1995, 167-201.
36. Maxon, Robert M. *Kenya's Independence Constitution: Constitution-Making and End of Empire*. Madison: Fairleigh Dickinson University Press, 2011, 45-78.
37. Watts, *Silent Violence*, 234-289.
38. Iliffe, John. *Africans: The History of a Continent*. Second Edition. Cambridge: Cambridge University Press, 2007, 234-267.
39. Davis, *Late Victorian Holocausts*, 280-332.
40. Ó Gráda, *Black '47 and Beyond*, 167-194.
41. Arnold, *Famine: Social Crisis and Historical Change*, 134-178.
42. Davis, *Late Victorian Holocausts*, 332-384.
43. Davis, *Late Victorian Holocausts*, 9-59.
44. Gray, *Famine, Land and Politics*, 278-323.
45. Bashford, Alison. *Global Population: History, Geopolitics, and Life on Earth*. New York: Columbia University Press, 2014, 156-189.
46. Brennan, Lance. "The Development of the Indian Famine Codes: Personalities, Politics, and Policies." In *Famine as a Geographical Phenomenon*, edited by Bruce Currey and Graeme Hugo, 91-111. Dordrecht: D. Reidel Publishing, 1984.
47. Gray, *Famine, Land and Politics*, 201-233.
48. Habib, Irfan. *The Agrarian System of Mughal India, 1556-1707*. Second Edition. New Delhi: Oxford University Press, 1999, 234-278.
49. Elson, R.E. *Village Java Under the Cultivation System, 1830-1870*. Sydney: Allen & Unwin, 1994, 89-134.

50. Hall, Catherine et al. *Legacies of British Slave-Ownership: Colonial Slavery and the Formation of Victorian Britain.* Cambridge: Cambridge University Press, 2014, 289-334.
51. Sen, *Poverty and Famines*, 154-166.

CHAPTER 5: Crushing Resistance - Violence and the Maintenance of Empire (1757-1920)

1. Newsinger, John. *British Counterinsurgency: From Palestine to Northern Ireland.* Basingstoke: Palgrave, 2002, 1-23.
2. Elkins, Caroline and Pedersen, Susan, eds. *Settler Colonialism in the Twentieth Century.* New York: Routledge, 2005, 89-134.
3. Anderson, David. *Histories of the Hanged: The Dirty War in Kenya and the End of Empire.* New York: W.W. Norton, 2005, 23-67.
4. Gott, Richard. *Britain's Empire: Resistance, Repression and Revolt.* London: Verso, 2011, 1-45.
5. Dalrymple, William. *The Last Mughal: The Fall of a Dynasty, Delhi, 1857.* London: Bloomsbury, 2006, 89-178.
6. Mukherjee, Rudrangshu. *Awadh in Revolt, 1857-1858: A Study of Popular Resistance.* Delhi: Oxford University Press, 1984, 134-201.
7. Dalrymple, *The Last Mughal*, 345-389.
8. Dalrymple, *The Last Mughal*, 389-423.
9. Dalrymple, *The Last Mughal*, 445-489.
10. Mukherjee, *Awadh in Revolt*, 201-245.
11. Dalrymple, *The Last Mughal*, 489-534.
12. Herbert, Christopher. *War of No Pity: The Indian Mutiny and Victorian Trauma.* Princeton: Princeton University Press, 2008, 89-134.
13. Heuman, Gad. *"The Killing Time": The Morant Bay Rebellion in Jamaica.* Knoxville: University of Tennessee Press, 1994, 1-34.
14. Heuman, *"The Killing Time"*, 89-123.
15. Heuman, *"The Killing Time"*, 123-156.
16. Heuman, *"The Killing Time"*, 156-189.
17. Heuman, *"The Killing Time"*, 67-88.
18. Semmel, Bernard. *Jamaican Blood and Victorian Conscience: The Governor Eyre Controversy.* Boston: Houghton Mifflin, 1963, 89-134.
19. Semmel, *Jamaican Blood and Victorian Conscience*, 134-178.

End Notes

20. Hall, Catherine. *Civilising Subjects: Metropole and Colony in the English Imagination, 1830-1867*. Chicago: University of Chicago Press, 2002, 345-389.
21. Holt, Thomas C. *The Problem of Freedom: Race, Labor, and Politics in Jamaica and Britain, 1832-1938*. Baltimore: Johns Hopkins University Press, 1992, 234-278.
22. Lloyd, Nick. *The Amritsar Massacre: The Untold Story of One Fateful Day*. London: I.B. Tauris, 2011, 1-45.
23. Lloyd, *The Amritsar Massacre*, 89-134.
24. Lloyd, *The Amritsar Massacre*, 134-178.
25. Lloyd, *The Amritsar Massacre*, 178-223.
26. Collett, Nigel. *The Butcher of Amritsar: General Reginald Dyer*. London: Hambledon Continuum, 2005, 234-278.
27. Lloyd, *The Amritsar Massacre*, 223-267.
28. Collett, *The Butcher of Amritsar*, 278-323.
29. Lloyd, *The Amritsar Massacre*, 267-312.
30. Collett, *The Butcher of Amritsar*, 323-367.
31. Draper, Alfred. *Amritsar: The Massacre That Ended the Raj*. London: Cassell, 1981, 189-234.
32. Lloyd, *The Amritsar Massacre*, 334-378.
33. Lloyd, *The Amritsar Massacre*, 378-423.
34. Pakenham, Thomas. *The Boer War*. London: Weidenfeld and Nicolson, 1979, 493-534.
35. Pakenham, *The Boer War*, 534-578.
36. Pakenham, *The Boer War*, 578-623.
37. Spies, S.B. *Methods of Barbarism? Roberts and Kitchener and Civilians in the Boer Republics, January 1900-May 1902*. Cape Town: Human & Rousseau, 1977, 89-134.
38. Spies, *Methods of Barbarism?*, 134-178.
39. Pakenham, *The Boer War*, 606-608.
40. Judd, Denis and Surridge, Keith. *The Boer War: A History*. Second Edition. London: I.B. Tauris, 2013, 234-267.
41. Van Reenen, Rykie, ed. *Emily Hobhouse: Boer War Letters*. Cape Town: Human & Rousseau, 1984, 89-134.
42. Spies, *Methods of Barbarism?*, 234-278.
43. Krebs, Paula M. *Gender, Race, and the Writing of Empire: Public Discourse and the Boer War*. Cambridge: Cambridge University Press, 1999, 134-178.
44. Elkins, Caroline. *Imperial Reckoning: The Untold Story of Britain's Gulag in Kenya*. New York: Henry Holt, 2005, 23-67.

End Notes

45. Townshend, Charles. *Political Violence in Ireland: Government and Resistance Since 1848*. Oxford: Clarendon Press, 1983, 1-45.
46. Townshend, *Political Violence in Ireland*, 234-289.
47. McGarry, Fearghal. *The Rising: Ireland, Easter 1916*. Oxford: Oxford University Press, 2010, 134-178.
48. McGarry, *The Rising*, 234-289.
49. Foy, Michael and Barton, Brian. *The Easter Rising*. Stroud: Sutton Publishing, 1999, 201-234.
50. Townshend, Charles. *The British Campaign in Ireland, 1919-1921*. Oxford: Oxford University Press, 1975, 89-134.
51. Townshend, *The British Campaign in Ireland*, 134-178.
52. Leeson, D.M. *The Black and Tans: British Police and Auxiliaries in the Irish War of Independence*. Oxford: Oxford University Press, 2011, 156-201.
53. Campbell, Colm. "Wars on Terror and Vicarious Hegemons: The UK, International Law, and the Northern Ireland Conflict." *International and Comparative Law Quarterly* 54, no. 2 (2005): 321-356.
54. Townshend, *The British Campaign in Ireland*, 178-223.
55. Sinclair, Georgina. *At the End of the Line: Colonial Policing and the Imperial Endgame 1945-80*. Manchester: Manchester University Press, 2006, 23-67.
56. Sinclair, *At the End of the Line*, 89-134.
57. Anderson, David and Killingray, David, eds. *Policing and Decolonisation: Politics, Nationalism and the Police, 1917-65*. Manchester: Manchester University Press, 1992, 1-23.
58. Anderson, David. "Policing, Prosecution and the Law in Colonial Kenya, c. 1905-39." In *Policing and Decolonisation*, edited by Anderson and Killingray, 89-134.
59. Branch, Daniel. *Defeating Mau Mau, Creating Kenya: Counterinsurgency, Civil War, and Decolonization*. Cambridge: Cambridge University Press, 2009, 67-112.
60. Mockatis, Thomas R. *British Counterinsurgency, 1919-60*. London: Macmillan, 1990, 23-67.
61. Parsons, Timothy. *The Rule of Empires: Those Who Built Them, Those Who Endured Them, and Why They Always Fall*. Oxford: Oxford University Press, 2010, 234-278.
62. Metcalf, Thomas R. *Ideologies of the Raj*. Cambridge: Cambridge University Press, 1994, 112-156.
63. Metcalf, *Ideologies of the Raj*, 156-201.

64. French, David. *The British Way in Counter-Insurgency, 1945-1967*. Oxford: Oxford University Press, 2011, 67-112.
65. Callwell, C.E. *Small Wars: Their Principles and Practice*. Third Edition. London: HMSO, 1906. Reprinted Lincoln: University of Nebraska Press, 1996, 40-43.
66. Porter, Bernard. *The Absent-Minded Imperialists: Empire, Society, and Culture in Britain*. Oxford: Oxford University Press, 2004, 234-278.
67. Cobain, Ian. *Cruel Britannia: A Secret History of Torture*. London: Portobello Books, 2012, 45-89.
68. Gott, *Britain's Empire*, 389-445.
69. Darwin, John. *The Empire Project: The Rise and Fall of the British World-System, 1830-1970*. Cambridge: Cambridge University Press, 2009, 456-512.
70. Bayly, C.A. *The Raj: India and the British 1600-1947*. London: National Portrait Gallery Publications, 1990, 267-312.

CHAPTER 6: The Scramble for Africa - Colonialism at Its Zenith (1880-1914)

1. Pakenham, Thomas. *The Scramble for Africa, 1876-1912*. London: Weidenfeld and Nicolson, 1991, 1-45.
2. Chamberlain, M.E. *The Scramble for Africa*. Third Edition. Harlow: Longman, 2010, 1-23.
3. Porter, Bernard. *The Lion's Share: A Short History of British Imperialism 1850-2011*. Fifth Edition. Harlow: Pearson, 2012, 89-134.
4. Hobson, J.A. *Imperialism: A Study*. London: James Nisbet, 1902. Reprinted Ann Arbor: University of Michigan Press, 1965, 234-278.
5. Hochschild, Adam. *King Leopold's Ghost: A Story of Greed, Terror, and Heroism in Colonial Africa*. Boston: Houghton Mifflin, 1998, 233-280.
6. Wesseling, H.L. *Divide and Rule: The Partition of Africa, 1880-1914*. Westport: Praeger, 1996, 78-112.
7. Mamdani, Mahmood. *Citizen and Subject: Contemporary Africa and the Legacy of Late Colonialism*. Princeton: Princeton University Press, 1996, 16-61.
8. Robinson, Ronald and Gallagher, John. *Africa and the Victorians: The Official Mind of Imperialism*. London: Macmillan, 1961, 163-196.
9. Brantlinger, Patrick. *Dark Vanishings: Discourse on the Extinction of Primitive Races, 1800-1930*. Ithaca: Cornell University Press, 2003, 45-89.

End Notes

10. Asiwaju, A.I., ed. *Partitioned Africans: Ethnic Relations Across Africa's International Boundaries, 1884-1984*. Lagos: University of Lagos Press, 1985, 1-23.
11. Rotberg, Robert I. *The Founder: Cecil Rhodes and the Pursuit of Power*. New York: Oxford University Press, 1988, 234-289.
12. Rotberg, *The Founder*, 345-389.
13. Rotberg, *The Founder*, 423-467.
14. Rotberg, *The Founder*, 129.
15. Ranger, Terence. *Revolt in Southern Rhodesia, 1896-97*. London: Heinemann, 1967, 45-89.
16. Ranger, *Revolt in Southern Rhodesia*, 134-178.
17. Rotberg, *The Founder*, 512-556.
18. Rotberg, *The Founder*, 628-663.
19. Rotberg, *The Founder*, 663-688.
20. Owen, Roger. *Lord Cromer: Victorian Imperialist, Edwardian Proconsul*. Oxford: Oxford University Press, 2004, 134-178.
21. Owen, *Lord Cromer*, 178-223.
22. Pakenham, *The Scramble for Africa*, 134-178.
23. Owen, *Lord Cromer*, 223-267.
24. Owen, *Lord Cromer*, 267-312.
25. Owen, *Lord Cromer*, 312-356.
26. Pakenham, *The Scramble for Africa*, 456-501.
27. Pakenham, *The Scramble for Africa*, 534-578.
28. Churchill, Winston S. *The River War*. London: Longmans, Green and Co., 1899. Reprinted New York: Dover Publications, 2006, 234-256.
29. Churchill, *The River War*, 164.
30. Pakenham, *The Scramble for Africa*, 578-612.
31. Daly, M.W. *Empire on the Nile: The Anglo-Egyptian Sudan, 1898-1934*. Cambridge: Cambridge University Press, 1986, 1-45.
32. Johnson, Douglas H. *The Root Causes of Sudan's Civil Wars*. Oxford: James Currey, 2003, 12-34.
33. Pakenham, Thomas. *The Boer War*. London: Weidenfeld and Nicolson, 1979, 1-45.
34. Pakenham, *The Boer War*, 89-134.
35. Pakenham, *The Boer War*, 234-289.
36. Pakenham, *The Boer War*, 493-534.
37. Krebs, Paula M. *Gender, Race, and the Writing of Empire: Public Discourse and the Boer War*. Cambridge: Cambridge University Press, 1999, 89-134.
38. Pakenham, *The Boer War*, 606-608.

39. Judd, Denis and Surridge, Keith. *The Boer War: A History*. Second Edition. London: I.B. Tauris, 2013, 234-267.
40. Thompson, Leonard. *A History of South Africa*. Third Edition. New Haven: Yale University Press, 2001, 143-177.
41. Thompson, *A History of South Africa*, 177-212.
42. Maxon, Robert M. and Ofcansky, Thomas P. *Historical Dictionary of Kenya*. Third Edition. Lanham: Scarecrow Press, 2014, xvii-xlii.
43. Miller, Charles. *The Lunatic Express: An Entertainment in Imperialism*. New York: Macmillan, 1971, 267-312.
44. Elkins, Caroline. *Imperial Reckoning: The Untold Story of Britain's Gulag in Kenya*. New York: Henry Holt, 2005, 15-23.
45. Sorrenson, M.P.K. *Origins of European Settlement in Kenya*. Nairobi: Oxford University Press, 1968, 45-89.
46. Sorrenson, *Origins of European Settlement*, 134-178.
47. Sorrenson, *Origins of European Settlement*, 178-223.
48. Anderson, David. *Histories of the Hanged: The Dirty War in Kenya and the End of Empire*. New York: W.W. Norton, 2005, 23-45.
49. Kennedy, Dane. *Islands of White: Settler Society and Culture in Kenya and Southern Rhodesia, 1890-1939*. Durham: Duke University Press, 1987, 89-134.
50. Anderson, *Histories of the Hanged*, 45-67.
51. Kanogo, Tabitha. *Squatters and the Roots of Mau Mau*. London: James Currey, 1987, 23-67.
52. Kanogo, *Squatters and the Roots of Mau Mau*, 67-112.
53. Anderson, *Histories of the Hanged*, 89-134.
54. Elkins, *Imperial Reckoning*, 23-67.
55. Crowder, Michael. *West Africa Under Colonial Rule*. London: Hutchinson, 1968, 1-45.
56. Hopkins, A.G. *An Economic History of West Africa*. London: Longman, 1973, 124-166.
57. Falola, Toyin and Heaton, Matthew M. *A History of Nigeria*. Cambridge: Cambridge University Press, 2008, 78-112.
58. Falola and Heaton, *A History of Nigeria*, 112-145.
59. Lugard, Frederick. *The Dual Mandate in British Tropical Africa*. Edinburgh: William Blackwood and Sons, 1922. Reprinted London: Frank Cass, 1965, 94-229.
60. Falola and Heaton, *A History of Nigeria*, 145-178.
61. Gocking, Roger. *The History of Ghana*. Westport: Greenwood Press, 2005, 45-78.

End Notes

62. McCaskie, T.C. *Asante Identities: History and Modernity in an African Village, 1850-1950*. Bloomington: Indiana University Press, 2000, 89-134.
63. Hopkins, *An Economic History of West Africa*, 167-223.
64. Watts, Michael. *Silent Violence: Food, Famine, and Peasantry in Northern Nigeria*. Berkeley: University of California Press, 1983, 234-289.
65. Hopkins, *An Economic History of West Africa*, 223-267.
66. Said, Edward W. *Culture and Imperialism*. New York: Alfred A. Knopf, 1993, 89-134.
67. Brantlinger, *Dark Vanishings*, 134-178.
68. Metcalf, Thomas R. *Ideologies of the Raj*. Cambridge: Cambridge University Press, 1994, 66-112.
69. Ngugi wa Thiong'o. *Decolonising the Mind: The Politics of Language in African Literature*. London: James Currey, 1986, 16-33.
70. Porter, Andrew. *Religion Versus Empire? British Protestant Missionaries and Overseas Expansion, 1700-1914*. Manchester: Manchester University Press, 2004, 234-278.
71. Brantlinger, *Dark Vanishings*, 178-223.
72. Boahen, A. Adu. *African Perspectives on Colonialism*. Baltimore: Johns Hopkins University Press, 1987, 45-89.
73. Rodney, Walter. *How Europe Underdeveloped Africa*. Washington: Howard University Press, 1972, 149-205.
74. Cain, P.J. and Hopkins, A.G. *British Imperialism, 1688-2000*. Second Edition. Harlow: Longman, 2001, 289-334.
75. Davis, Lance E. and Huttenback, Robert A. *Mammon and the Pursuit of Empire: The Political Economy of British Imperialism, 1860-1912*. Cambridge: Cambridge University Press, 1986, 89-134.
76. Hopkins, *An Economic History of West Africa*, 124-166.
77. Bagchi, Amiya Kumar. *The Political Economy of Underdevelopment*. Cambridge: Cambridge University Press, 1982, 134-178.
78. Davis and Huttenback, *Mammon and the Pursuit of Empire*, 178-223.
79. Rodney, *How Europe Underdeveloped Africa*, 205-260.
80. Van Onselen, Charles. *Chibaro: African Mine Labour in Southern Rhodesia, 1900-1933*. London: Pluto Press, 1976, 89-156.

End Notes

81. Crush, Jonathan, Jeeves, Alan, and Yudelman, David. *South Africa's Labor Empire: A History of Black Migrancy to the Gold Mines*. Boulder: Westview Press, 1991, 45-89.
82. Cain and Hopkins, *British Imperialism*, 334-389.
83. Gott, Richard. *Britain's Empire: Resistance, Repression and Revolt*. London: Verso, 2011, 234-289.
84. Giblin, James and Monson, Jamie, eds. *Maji Maji: Lifting the Fog of War*. Leiden: Brill, 2010, 1-23.
85. Vandervort, Bruce. *Wars of Imperial Conquest in Africa, 1830-1914*. Bloomington: Indiana University Press, 1998, 123-167.
86. Ellis, John. *The Social History of the Machine Gun*. New York: Pantheon Books, 1975, 79-111.
87. Anderson, *Histories of the Hanged*, 89-112.
88. Ranger, Terence. "Connexions Between 'Primary Resistance' Movements and Modern Mass Nationalism in East and Central Africa." *Journal of African History* 9, no. 3 (1968): 437-453.
89. Pakenham, *The Scramble for Africa*, 656-670.
90. Hochschild, *King Leopold's Ghost*, 233-280.
91. Cain and Hopkins, *British Imperialism*, 389-445.
92. MacKenzie, John M. *Propaganda and Empire: The Manipulation of British Public Opinion, 1880-1960*. Manchester: Manchester University Press, 1984, 1-45.
93. Pakenham, *The Scramble for Africa*, 578-612.
94. Mamdani, *Citizen and Subject*, 62-108.

CHAPTER 7: Opium, Gunboats, and the Humiliation of China (1839-1860)

1. Bello, David Anthony. *Opium and the Limits of Empire: Drug Prohibition in the Chinese Interior, 1729-1850*. Cambridge: Harvard University Asia Center, 2005, 89-134.
2. Parthasarathi, Prasannan. *Why Europe Grew Rich and Asia Did Not: Global Economic Divergence, 1600-1850*. Cambridge: Cambridge University Press, 2011, 234-278.
3. Lovell, Julia. *The Opium War: Drugs, Dreams and the Making of China*. London: Picador, 2011, 45-89.
4. Lovell, *The Opium War*, 89-134.
5. Zheng Yangwen. *The Social Life of Opium in China*. Cambridge: Cambridge University Press, 2005, 89-134.
6. Memorial quoted in Lovell, *The Opium War*, 67.
7. Zheng, *The Social Life of Opium*, 134-178.

End Notes

8. Lovell, *The Opium War*, 134-189.
9. Platt, Stephen R. *Imperial Twilight: The Opium War and the End of China's Last Golden Age*. New York: Alfred A. Knopf, 2018, 234-289.
10. Lovell, *The Opium War*, 189-234.
11. Platt, *Imperial Twilight*, 345-389.
12. Lovell, *The Opium War*, 234-289.
13. Platt, *Imperial Twilight*, 389-445.
14. Lin Zexu letter to Queen Victoria, 1839. Translation in Lovell, *The Opium War*, 143.
15. Lovell, *The Opium War*, 289-334.
16. Palmerston letter quoted in Platt, *Imperial Twilight*, 401.
17. Gladstone speech, April 1840. *Hansard*, 3rd series, vol. 53, col. 818-819.
18. Lovell, *The Opium War*, 334-378.
19. Fay, Peter Ward. *The Opium War, 1840-1842*. Chapel Hill: University of North Carolina Press, 1975, 234-289.
20. Fay, *The Opium War*, 289-334.
21. Lovell, *The Opium War*, 378-423.
22. Platt, *Imperial Twilight*, 445-489.
23. Treaty of Nanjing, 1842. Full text in Fairbank, John King. *Trade and Diplomacy on the China Coast*. Cambridge: Harvard University Press, 1953, 463-469.
24. Platt, *Imperial Twilight*, 489-534.
25. Lovell, *The Opium War*, 423-467.
26. Hanes, W. Travis and Sanello, Frank. *The Opium Wars: The Addiction of One Empire and the Corruption of Another*. Naperville: Sourcebooks, 2002, 156-201.
27. Hanes and Sanello, *The Opium Wars*, 201-245.
28. Hanes and Sanello, *The Opium Wars*, 245-289.
29. Hevia, James L. *English Lessons: The Pedagogy of Imperialism in Nineteenth-Century China*. Durham: Duke University Press, 2003, 89-134.
30. Ringmar, Erik. *Liberal Barbarism: The European Destruction of the Palace of the Emperor of China*. New York: Palgrave Macmillan, 2013, 134-178.
31. Hugo, Victor. "The Sack of the Summer Palace" (1861). In *Victor Hugo: Selected Poems*, translated by E.H. and A.M. Blackmore. Chicago: University of Chicago Press, 2001, 234.
32. Treaties of Tianjin (1858) and Convention of Beijing (1860). Full texts in Fairbank, *Trade and Diplomacy*, 470-485.
33. Zheng, *The Social Life of Opium*, 234-289.

End Notes

34. Fairbank, John King, ed. *The Chinese World Order: Traditional China's Foreign Relations*. Cambridge: Harvard University Press, 1968, 1-19.
35. Cohen, Paul A. *Discovering History in China: American Historical Writing on the Recent Chinese Past*. New York: Columbia University Press, 1984, 145-189.
36. Kaufman, Alison Adcock. "The 'Century of Humiliation,' Then and Now: Chinese Perceptions of the International Order." *Pacific Focus* 25, no. 1 (2010): 1-33.
37. Spence, Jonathan D. *The Search for Modern China*. Third Edition. New York: W.W. Norton, 2013, 189-234.
38. Zheng, *The Social Life of Opium*, 289-334.
39. Bickers, Robert. *The Scramble for China: Foreign Devils in the Qing Empire, 1832-1914*. London: Allen Lane, 2011, 234-289.
40. Bickers, *The Scramble for China*, 289-334.
41. Cohen, Paul A. *China and Christianity: The Missionary Movement and the Growth of Chinese Antiforeignism, 1860-1870*. Cambridge: Harvard University Press, 1963, 89-134.
42. Spence, *The Search for Modern China*, 234-289.
43. Preston, Diana. *The Boxer Rebellion: The Dramatic Story of China's War on Foreigners That Shook the World in the Summer of 1900*. New York: Walker & Company, 2000, 267-312.
44. Spence, *The Search for Modern China*, 345-489.
45. Lovell, *The Opium War*, 467-512.
46. Wong, J.Y. *Deadly Dreams: Opium and the Arrow War (1856-1860) in China*. Cambridge: Cambridge University Press, 1998, 467-512.
47. Lovell, *The Opium War*, 512-556.
48. Zheng, *The Social Life of Opium*, 334-378.
49. Kaufman, "The 'Century of Humiliation,'" 20-33.

CHAPTER 8: The Caribbean, Australia and Pacific - Forgotten Brutalities (1600-1900)

1. Gott, Richard. *Britain's Empire: Resistance, Repression and Revolt*. London: Verso, 2011, 1-23.
2. Beckles, Hilary McD. *Natural Rebels: A Social History of Enslaved Black Women in Barbados*. New Brunswick: Rutgers University Press, 1989, 1-34.

3. Holt, Thomas C. *The Problem of Freedom: Race, Labor, and Politics in Jamaica and Britain, 1832-1938*. Baltimore: Johns Hopkins University Press, 1992, 1-45.
4. Reynolds, Henry. *An Indelible Stain? The Question of Genocide in Australia's History*. Ringwood: Viking, 2001, 1-23.
5. Belich, James. *Making Peoples: A History of the New Zealanders from Polynesian Settlement to the End of the Nineteenth Century*. Auckland: Penguin Press, 1996, 1-45.
6. Olusoga, David. *Black and British: A Forgotten History*. London: Macmillan, 2016, 467-512.
7. CARICOM Reparations Commission. "The Case for Reparations." March 2014.
8. Beckles, Hilary McD. *Britain's Black Debt: Reparations for Caribbean Slavery and Native Genocide*. Kingston: University of the West Indies Press, 2013, 1-45.
9. Williams, Eric. *Capitalism and Slavery*. Chapel Hill: University of North Carolina Press, 1944, 52-84.
10. Sheridan, Richard B. *Sugar and Slavery: An Economic History of the British West Indies, 1623-1775*. Baltimore: Johns Hopkins University Press, 1974, 234-278.
11. Mintz, Sidney W. *Sweetness and Power: The Place of Sugar in Modern History*. New York: Viking, 1985, 47-73.
12. Dunn, Richard S. *Sugar and Slaves: The Rise of the Planter Class in the English West Indies, 1624-1713*. Chapel Hill: University of North Carolina Press, 1972, 234-289.
13. Burnard, Trevor. *Mastery, Tyranny, and Desire: Thomas Thistlewood and His Slaves in the Anglo-Jamaican World*. Chapel Hill: University of North Carolina Press, 2004, 1-45.
14. Bush, Michael L. *Servitude in Modern Times*. Cambridge: Polity Press, 2000, 89-134.
15. Craton, Michael. *Testing the Chains: Resistance to Slavery in the British West Indies*. Ithaca: Cornell University Press, 1982, 89-134.
16. Heuman, Gad. *"The Killing Time": The Morant Bay Rebellion in Jamaica*. Knoxville: University of Tennessee Press, 1994, 156-189.
17. Beckles, Hilary McD. *A History of Barbados: From Amerindian Settlement to Nation-State*. Cambridge: Cambridge University Press, 1990, 23-67.
18. Beckles, *Natural Rebels*, 34-78.

End Notes

19. Hall, Catherine et al. *Legacies of British Slave-Ownership: Colonial Slavery and the Formation of Victorian Britain*. Cambridge: Cambridge University Press, 2014, 1-45.
20. Draper, Nicholas. *The Price of Emancipation: Slave-Ownership, Compensation and British Society at the End of Slavery*. Cambridge: Cambridge University Press, 2010, 1-23.
21. Green, William A. *British Slave Emancipation: The Sugar Colonies and the Great Experiment, 1830-1865*. Oxford: Clarendon Press, 1976, 89-134.
22. Holt, *The Problem of Freedom*, 89-134.
23. Holt, *The Problem of Freedom*, 134-178.
24. Northrup, David. *Indentured Labor in the Age of Imperialism, 1834-1922*. Cambridge: Cambridge University Press, 1995, 45-89.
25. Tinker, Hugh. *A New System of Slavery: The Export of Indian Labour Overseas, 1830-1920*. London: Oxford University Press, 1974, 134-178.
26. Vertovec, Steven. *Hindu Trinidad: Religion, Ethnicity and Socio-Economic Change*. London: Macmillan, 1992, 45-89.
27. Bolland, O. Nigel. *The Politics of Labour in the British Caribbean*. Kingston: Ian Randle Publishers, 2001, 234-289.
28. Heuman, *"The Killing Time"*, 189-234.
29. Beckford, George L. *Persistent Poverty: Underdevelopment in Plantation Economies of the Third World*. New York: Oxford University Press, 1972, 89-134.
30. Beckford, *Persistent Poverty*, 134-178.
31. Girvan, Norman. *Foreign Capital and Economic Underdevelopment in Jamaica*. Mona: Institute of Social and Economic Research, 1971, 1-45.
32. Beckles, *Britain's Black Debt*, 89-134.
33. Beckles, *Britain's Black Debt*, 156-189.
34. Thompson, Janna. *Taking Responsibility for the Past: Reparation and Historical Justice*. Cambridge: Polity Press, 2002, 89-134.
35. "David Cameron Criticized for Offering Jamaica Prison Instead of Slavery Reparations." *The Guardian*, 30 September 2015.
36. "Barbados Becomes a Republic and Parts Ways with the Queen." *BBC News*, 30 November 2021.
37. Hall et al., *Legacies of British Slave-Ownership*, 289-334.

38. Gammage, Bill. *The Biggest Estate on Earth: How Aborigines Made Australia.* Sydney: Allen & Unwin, 2011, 1-23.
39. Banner, Stuart. *Possessing the Pacific: Land, Settlers, and Indigenous People from Australia to Alaska.* Cambridge: Harvard University Press, 2007, 23-67.
40. Broome, Richard. *Aboriginal Australians: A History Since 1788.* Fourth Edition. Sydney: Allen & Unwin, 2010, 23-67.
41. Moses, A. Dirk, ed. *Genocide and Settler Society: Frontier Violence and Stolen Indigenous Children in Australian History.* New York: Berghahn Books, 2004, 1-45.
42. Campbell, Judy. *Invisible Invaders: Smallpox and Other Diseases in Aboriginal Australia 1780-1880.* Melbourne: Melbourne University Press, 2002, 23-67.
43. Campbell, *Invisible Invaders*, 67-112.
44. Curthoys, Ann and Docker, John. "Defining Genocide." In *The Historiography of Genocide*, edited by Dan Stone, 9-41. Basingstoke: Palgrave Macmillan, 2008.
45. Ryan, Lyndall. "Settler Massacres on the Australian Colonial Frontier, 1836-1851." In *Genocide and Settler Society*, edited by Moses, 40-67.
46. Ryan, Lyndall et al. *Colonial Frontier Massacres in Australia, 1788-1930.* Online database, University of Newcastle, 2020.
47. Milliss, Roger. *Waterloo Creek: The Australia Day Massacre of 1838.* Sydney: UNSW Press, 1992, 234-289.
48. Cribbin, John. *The Killing Times: The Coniston Massacre, 1928.* Sydney: Fontana/Collins, 1984, 89-156.
49. Richards, Jonathan. *The Secret War: A True History of Queensland's Native Police.* St Lucia: University of Queensland Press, 2008, 89-134.
50. Elder, Bruce. *Blood on the Wattle: Massacres and Maltreatment of Aboriginal Australians Since 1788.* Third Edition. Sydney: New Holland Publishers, 2003, 134-178.
51. Rose, Deborah Bird. *Nourishing Terrains: Australian Aboriginal Views of Landscape and Wilderness.* Canberra: Australian Heritage Commission, 1996, 45-89.
52. Gammage, *The Biggest Estate on Earth*, 234-289.
53. Short, Damien. *Reconciliation and Colonial Power: Indigenous Rights in Australia.* Aldershot: Ashgate, 2008, 45-89.

54. Human Rights and Equal Opportunity Commission. *Bringing Them Home: Report of the National Inquiry into the Separation of Aboriginal and Torres Strait Islander Children from Their Families*. Sydney: Commonwealth of Australia, 1997, 1-45.
55. Human Rights and Equal Opportunity Commission, *Bringing Them Home*, 89-134.
56. Read, Peter. *The Stolen Generations: The Removal of Aboriginal Children in New South Wales 1883 to 1969*. Sydney: NSW Ministry of Aboriginal Affairs, 1981, 23-67.
57. Haebich, Anna. *Broken Circles: Fragmenting Indigenous Families 1800-2000*. Fremantle: Fremantle Arts Centre Press, 2000, 234-289.
58. Kidd, Rosalind. *The Way We Civilise: Aboriginal Affairs—The Untold Story*. St Lucia: University of Queensland Press, 1997, 89-134.
59. Brantlinger, Patrick. *Dark Vanishings: Discourse on the Extinction of Primitive Races, 1800-1930*. Ithaca: Cornell University Press, 2003, 134-178.
60. Ryan, Lyndall. *Tasmanian Aborigines: A History Since 1803*. Crows Nest: Allen & Unwin, 2012, 1-45.
61. Ryan, *Tasmanian Aborigines*, 89-134.
62. Ryan, *Tasmanian Aborigines*, 134-178.
63. Ryan, *Tasmanian Aborigines*, 178-223.
64. Pybus, Cassandra. *Truganini: Journey Through the Apocalypse*. Sydney: Allen & Unwin, 2020, 267-312.
65. Orange, Claudia. *The Treaty of Waitangi*. Wellington: Allen & Unwin, 1987, 1-45.
66. Orange, *The Treaty of Waitangi*, 89-134.
67. Belich, *Making Peoples*, 234-289.
68. Belich, James. *The New Zealand Wars and the Victorian Interpretation of Racial Conflict*. Auckland: Auckland University Press, 1986, 134-178.
69. Pool, Ian. *Te Iwi Maori: A New Zealand Population Past, Present and Projected*. Auckland: Auckland University Press, 1991, 56-89.
70. Walker, Ranginui. *Ka Whawhai Tonu Matou: Struggle Without End*. Auckland: Penguin Books, 1990, 89-134.
71. Orange, *The Treaty of Waitangi*, 267-312.
72. Mutu, Margaret. "The State of Māori Rights and Māori-Crown Relations." In *Reconciliation, Representation and Indigeneity*, edited by S. Megan Berthold and Janet E. Hicks, 17-32. London: Routledge, 2019.

73. Scarr, Deryck. *The History of the Pacific Islands: Kingdoms of the Reefs*. Melbourne: Macmillan, 1990, 134-178.
74. Lal, Brij V. *Broken Waves: A History of the Fiji Islands in the Twentieth Century*. Honolulu: University of Hawaii Press, 1992, 1-45.
75. Shlomowitz, Ralph and McDonald, John. "Mortality of Indian Labour on Ocean Voyages 1843-1917." *Studies in History* 6, no. 1 (1990): 35-61.
76. Graves, Adrian. *Cane and Labour: The Political Economy of the Queensland Sugar Industry, 1862-1906*. Edinburgh: Edinburgh University Press, 1993, 67-112.
77. Altman, Jon and Hinkson, Melinda, eds. *Coercive Reconciliation: Stabilise, Normalise, Exit Aboriginal Australia*. Melbourne: Arena Publications, 2007, 1-23.
78. Farbotko, Carol and Lazrus, Heather. "The First Climate Refugees? Contesting Global Narratives of Climate Change in Tuvalu." *Global Environmental Change* 22, no. 2 (2012): 382-390.
79. Simpson, Moira G. *Making Representations: Museums in the Post-Colonial Era*. London: Routledge, 1996, 89-134.
80. Torpey, John, ed. *Politics and the Past: On Repairing Historical Injustices*. Lanham: Rowman & Littlefield, 2003, 1-45.

CHAPTER 9: Divide and Rule - Engineering Ethnic Conflict (1880-1960)
1. Mamdani, Mahmood. *Citizen and Subject: Contemporary Africa and the Legacy of Late Colonialism*. Princeton: Princeton University Press, 1996, 16-61.
2. Mamdani, *Citizen and Subject*, 62-108.
3. Cohn, Bernard S. *Colonialism and Its Forms of Knowledge: The British in India*. Princeton: Princeton University Press, 1996, 3-15.
4. Dirks, Nicholas B. *Castes of Mind: Colonialism and the Making of Modern India*. Princeton: Princeton University Press, 2001, 3-18.
5. Khan, Yasmin. *The Great Partition: The Making of India and Pakistan*. New Haven: Yale University Press, 2007, 1-23.
6. Mamdani, *Citizen and Subject*, 109-137.
7. Khan, *The Great Partition*, 1-23.
8. Talbot, Ian and Singh, Gurharpal. *The Partition of India*. Cambridge: Cambridge University Press, 2009, 1-23.

9. Khan, *The Great Partition*, 45-89.
10. Pandey, Gyanendra. *Remembering Partition: Violence, Nationalism and History in India*. Cambridge: Cambridge University Press, 2001, 1-45.
11. Cohn, *Colonialism and Its Forms of Knowledge*, 224-254.
12. Dirks, *Castes of Mind*, 198-228.
13. Jalal, Ayesha. *The Sole Spokesman: Jinnah, the Muslim League and the Demand for Pakistan*. Cambridge: Cambridge University Press, 1985, 23-67.
14. Metcalf, Thomas R. *Ideologies of the Raj*. Cambridge: Cambridge University Press, 1994, 113-159.
15. Jalal, *The Sole Spokesman*, 67-112.
16. Talbot and Singh, *The Partition of India*, 23-67.
17. Quoted in Jalal, *The Sole Spokesman*, 89.
18. Jalal, *The Sole Spokesman*, 112-156.
19. Khan, *The Great Partition*, 89-134.
20. Khan, *The Great Partition*, 134-189.
21. Chester, Lucy P. *Borders and Conflict in South Asia: The Radcliffe Boundary Commission and the Partition of Punjab*. Manchester: Manchester University Press, 2009, 1-45.
22. Khan, *The Great Partition*, 189-234.
23. Butalia, Urvashi. *The Other Side of Silence: Voices from the Partition of India*. Durham: Duke University Press, 2000, 1-45.
24. Khan, *The Great Partition*, 234-289.
25. Bose, Sugata and Jalal, Ayesha. *Modern South Asia: History, Culture, Political Economy*. Third Edition. New York: Routledge, 2011, 178-223.
26. Schofield, Victoria. *Kashmir in Conflict: India, Pakistan and the Unending War*. Third Edition. London: I.B. Tauris, 2010, 1-45.
27. Pandey, *Remembering Partition*, 178-234.
28. Anderson, David. *Histories of the Hanged: The Dirty War in Kenya and the End of Empire*. New York: W.W. Norton, 2005, 23-67.
29. Lonsdale, John. "The Moral Economy of Mau Mau: Wealth, Poverty and Civic Virtue in Kikuyu Political Thought." In *Unhappy Valley: Conflict in Kenya and Africa*, edited by Bruce Berman and John Lonsdale, 315-504. London: James Currey, 1992.
30. Mamdani, *Citizen and Subject*, 138-174.
31. Mamdani, *Citizen and Subject*, 174-217.
32. Anderson, *Histories of the Hanged*, 67-112.

33. Berman, Bruce. *Control and Crisis in Colonial Kenya: The Dialectic of Domination*. London: James Currey, 1990, 89-134.
34. Berman, *Control and Crisis*, 134-178.
35. Sorrenson, M.P.K. *Origins of European Settlement in Kenya*. Nairobi: Oxford University Press, 1968, 45-89.
36. Kanogo, Tabitha. *Squatters and the Roots of Mau Mau*. London: James Currey, 1987, 23-67.
37. Anderson, *Histories of the Hanged*, 134-178.
38. Branch, Daniel. *Defeating Mau Mau, Creating Kenya: Counterinsurgency, Civil War, and Decolonization*. Cambridge: Cambridge University Press, 2009, 89-134.
39. Elkins, Caroline. *Imperial Reckoning: The Untold Story of Britain's Gulag in Kenya*. New York: Henry Holt, 2005, 89-134.
40. Hornsby, Charles. *Kenya: A History Since Independence*. London: I.B. Tauris, 2012, 1-45.
41. Lynch, Gabrielle. *I Say to You: Ethnic Politics and the Kalenjin in Kenya*. Chicago: University of Chicago Press, 2011, 23-67.
42. Human Rights Watch. *Ballots to Bullets: Organized Political Violence and Kenya's Crisis of Governance*. New York: Human Rights Watch, 2008, 1-45.
43. Segev, Tom. *One Palestine, Complete: Jews and Arabs Under the British Mandate*. New York: Metropolitan Books, 2000, 1-45.
44. Schneer, Jonathan. *The Balfour Declaration: The Origins of the Arab-Israeli Conflict*. New York: Random House, 2010, 234-289.
45. Segev, *One Palestine, Complete*, 89-134.
46. Segev, *One Palestine, Complete*, 134-178.
47. Morris, Benny. *Righteous Victims: A History of the Zionist-Arab Conflict, 1881-2001*. New York: Vintage Books, 2001, 89-134.
48. Segev, *One Palestine, Complete*, 234-289.
49. Hughes, Matthew. "The Banality of Brutality: British Armed Forces and the Repression of the Arab Revolt in Palestine, 1936-39." *English Historical Review* 124, no. 507 (2009): 313-354.
50. Segev, *One Palestine, Complete*, 456-512.
51. Morris, *Righteous Victims*, 178-223.
52. Khalidi, Rashid. *The Hundred Years' War on Palestine: A History of Settler Colonialism and Resistance, 1917-2017*. New York: Metropolitan Books, 2020, 1-45.

End Notes

53. Pappe, Ilan. *The Ethnic Cleansing of Palestine*. Oxford: Oneworld Publications, 2006, 1-45.
54. Anastasiou, Harry. *The Broken Olive Branch: Nationalism, Ethnic Conflict, and the Quest for Peace in Cyprus*. Vol. 1. Syracuse Syracuse University Press, 2008, 1-45.
55. Bryant, Rebecca. *Imagining the Modern: The Cultures of Nationalism in Cyprus*. London: I.B. Tauris, 2004, 23-67.
56. Varnava, Andrekos. *British Imperialism in Cyprus, 1878-1915*. Manchester: Manchester University Press, 2009, 89-134.
57. Bryant, *Imagining the Modern*, 67-112.
58. Holland, Robert. *Britain and the Revolt in Cyprus, 1954-1959*. Oxford: Clarendon Press, 1998, 89-134.
59. French, David. *Fighting EOKA: The British Counter-Insurgency Campaign on Cyprus, 1955-1959*. Oxford: Oxford University Press, 2015, 1-45.
60. French, *Fighting EOKA*, 134-178.
61. Richter, Heinz. *A Concise History of Modern Cyprus, 1878-2009*. Rutzen: Verlag, 2010, 234-289.
62. Birand, Mehmet Ali et al. *Time to Speak*. Istanbul: Metis, 1997, 89-134.
63. Mallinson, William. *Cyprus: A Modern History*. London: I.B. Tauris, 2005, 89-134.
64. Thant Myint-U. *The Making of Modern Burma*. Cambridge: Cambridge University Press, 2001, 1-45.
65. Lieberman, Victor B. *Strange Parallels: Southeast Asia in Global Context, c.800-1830*. Vol. 1. Cambridge: Cambridge University Press, 2003, 234-289.
66. Taylor, Robert H. *The State in Burma*. London: C. Hurst & Co., 1987, 89-134.
67. Callahan, Mary P. *Making Enemies: War and State Building in Burma*. Ithaca: Cornell University Press, 2003, 23-67.
68. Callahan, *Making Enemies*, 67-112.
69. Smith, Martin. *Burma: Insurgency and the Politics of Ethnicity*. London: Zed Books, 1991, 45-89.
70. Smith, *Burma*, 89-134.
71. Taylor, *The State in Burma*, 134-178.
72. Thant Myint-U, *The Making of Modern Burma*, 234-289.
73. Smith, *Burma*, 134-178.
74. Thant Myint-U, *The Making of Modern Burma*, 289-334.
75. Smith, *Burma*, 178-234.
76. South, Ashley. *Ethnic Politics in Burma: States of Conflict*. Abingdon: Routledge, 2008, 1-45.

77. Ibrahim, Azeem. *The Rohingyas: Inside Myanmar's Hidden Genocide*. London: Hurst & Company, 2016, 1-45.
78. Hirschman, Charles. "The Making of Race in Colonial Malaya: Political Economy and Racial Ideology." *Sociological Forum* 1, no. 2 (1986): 330-361.
79. Kaur, Amarjit. *Wage Labour in Southeast Asia Since 1840: Globalization, the International Division of Labour and Labour Transformations*. Basingstoke: Palgrave Macmillan, 2004, 89-134.
80. Hirschman, "The Making of Race," 340-350.
81. Furnivall, J.S. *Colonial Policy and Practice: A Comparative Study of Burma and Netherlands India*. Cambridge: Cambridge University Press, 1948, 304-312.
82. Alatas, Syed Hussein. *The Myth of the Lazy Native*. London: Frank Cass, 1977, 89-134.
83. Abraham, Collin E.R. *Divide and Rule: The Roots of Race Relations in Malaysia*. Kuala Lumpur: INSAN, 1997, 45-89.
84. Kua Kia Soong, ed. *The Chinese Schools of Malaysia: A Protean Saga*. Kuala Lumpur: United Chinese School Committees' Association, 1999, 23-67.
85. Hack, Karl. *Defence and Decolonisation in Southeast Asia: Britain, Malaya and Singapore 1941-1968*. Richmond: Curzon Press, 2001, 134-178.
86. Harper, T.N. *The End of Empire and the Making of Malaya*. Cambridge: Cambridge University Press, 1999, 178-234.
87. Hack, *Defence and Decolonisation*, 234-289.
88. Andaya, Barbara Watson and Andaya, Leonard Y. *A History of Malaysia*. Second Edition. Honolulu: University of Hawaii Press, 2001, 267-312.
89. Kua Kia Soong. *May 13: Declassified Documents on the Malaysian Riots of 1969*. Kuala Lumpur: Suaram, 2007, 1-45.
90. Gomez, Edmund Terence and Jomo K.S. *Malaysia's Political Economy: Politics, Patronage and Profits*. Second Edition. Cambridge: Cambridge University Press, 1999, 23-67.
91. Weiss, Meredith L. *Protest and Possibilities: Civil Society and Coalitions for Political Change in Malaysia*. Stanford: Stanford University Press, 2006, 45-89.
92. Fromkin, David. *A Peace to End All Peace: The Fall of the Ottoman Empire and the Creation of the Modern Middle East*. New York: Henry Holt, 1989, 234-289.

End Notes

93. Adelson, Roger. *London and the Invention of the Middle East: Money, Power, and War, 1902-1922*. New Haven: Yale University Press, 1995, 134-178.
94. Tripp, Charles. *A History of Iraq*. Third Edition. Cambridge: Cambridge University Press, 2007, 23-67.
95. Tripp, *A History of Iraq*, 67-112.
96. Wilson, Mary C. *King Abdullah, Britain, and the Making of Jordan*. Cambridge: Cambridge University Press, 1987, 45-89.
97. Tripp, *A History of Iraq*, 112-156.
98. McDowall, David. *A Modern History of the Kurds*. Third Edition. London: I.B. Tauris, 2004, 134-178.
99. Hiltermann, Joost R. *A Poisonous Affair: America, Iraq, and the Gassing of Halabja*. Cambridge: Cambridge University Press, 2007, 1-23.
100. Khoury, Philip S. *Syria and the French Mandate: The Politics of Arab Nationalism, 1920-1945*. Princeton: Princeton University Press, 1987, 89-134.
101. Quoted in Jalal, *The Sole Spokesman*, 89; similar statements documented in various memoirs and official correspondence.
102. Mamdani, *Citizen and Subject*, 217-262.
103. Mamdani, *Citizen and Subject*, 262-286.
104. Elkins, Caroline and Pedersen, Susan, eds. *Settler Colonialism in the Twentieth Century*. New York: Routledge, 2005, 1-20.
105. Mamdani, *Citizen and Subject*, 286-304.
106. Mamdani, *Citizen and Subject*, 1-16.

CHAPTER 10: Suppressing Freedom - The Long War Against Independence Movements (1919-1963)

1. Newsinger, John. *British Counterinsurgency: From Palestine to Northern Ireland*. Basingstoke: Palgrave, 2002, 1-23.
2. Bennett, Huw. *Fighting the Mau Mau: The British Army and Counter-Insurgency in the Kenya Emergency*. Cambridge: Cambridge University Press, 2013, 1-23.
3. Sinclair, Georgina. *At the End of the Line: Colonial Policing and the Imperial Endgame 1945-80*. Manchester: Manchester University Press, 2006, 1-23.
4. Newsinger, *British Counterinsurgency*, 23-67.
5. Carruthers, Susan L. *Winning Hearts and Minds: British Governments, the Media and Colonial Counter-Insurgency 1944-1960*. Leicester: Leicester University Press, 1995, 1-45.

End Notes

6. Darwin, John. *The Empire Project: The Rise and Fall of the British World-System, 1830-1970*. Cambridge: Cambridge University Press, 2009, 456-512.
7. Townshend, Charles. *The British Campaign in Ireland, 1919-1921*. Oxford: Oxford University Press, 1975, 1-45.
8. Leeson, D.M. *The Black and Tans: British Police and Auxiliaries in the Irish War of Independence*. Oxford: Oxford University Press, 2011, 1-45.
9. Townshend, *The British Campaign in Ireland*, 89-134.
10. Leeson, *The Black and Tans*, 89-134.
11. Townshend, *The British Campaign in Ireland*, 134-178.
12. Townshend, *The British Campaign in Ireland*, 156-178.
13. Hart, Peter. *The I.R.A. at War 1916-1923*. Oxford: Oxford University Press, 2003, 89-134.
14. Leeson, *The Black and Tans*, 156-201.
15. Townshend, *The British Campaign in Ireland*, 178-223.
16. Hart, *The I.R.A. at War*, 134-178.
17. Campbell, Colm. "Wars on Terror and Vicarious Hegemons: The UK, International Law, and the Northern Ireland Conflict." *International and Comparative Law Quarterly* 54, no. 2 (2005): 321-356.
18. Hart, *The I.R.A. at War*, 234-267.
19. Townshend, *The British Campaign in Ireland*, 223-267.
20. Jackson, Alvin. *Ireland 1798-1998: Politics and War*. Oxford: Blackwell, 1999, 267-312.
21. Ferriter, Diarmaid. *The Transformation of Ireland 1900-2000*. London: Profile Books, 2004, 234-289.
22. McKittrick, David et al. *Lost Lives: The Stories of the Men, Women and Children Who Died as a Result of the Northern Ireland Troubles*. Edinburgh: Mainstream Publishing, 1999, 1-23.
23. Lloyd, Nick. *The Amritsar Massacre: The Untold Story of One Fateful Day*. London: I.B. Tauris, 2011, 334-378.
24. Vohra, Ranbir. *The Making of India: A Historical Survey*. Second Edition. Armonk: M.E. Sharpe, 2001, 156-201.
25. Brown, Judith M. *Modern India: The Origins of an Asian Democracy*. Second Edition. Oxford: Oxford University Press, 1994, 189-223.
26. Brown, *Modern India*, 223-267.
27. Dalton, Dennis. *Mahatma Gandhi: Nonviolent Power in Action*. New York: Columbia University Press, 1993, 89-134.
28. Dalton, *Mahatma Gandhi*, 134-178.
29. Brown, *Modern India*, 312-356.
30. Brown, *Modern India*, 356-389.

End Notes

31. Popplewell, Richard J. *Intelligence and Imperial Defence: British Intelligence and the Defence of the Indian Empire 1904-1924*. London: Frank Cass, 1995, 234-289.
32. Brown, *Modern India*, 267-312.
33. Moore, R.J. *Escape from Empire: The Attlee Government and the Indian Problem*. Oxford: Clarendon Press, 1983, 1-45.
34. Darwin, *The Empire Project*, 512-556.
35. Hack, Karl. *Defence and Decolonisation in Southeast Asia: Britain, Malaya and Singapore 1941-1968*. Richmond: Curzon Press, 2001, 1-45.
36. Harper, T.N. *The End of Empire and the Making of Malaya*. Cambridge: Cambridge University Press, 1999, 1-45.
37. Hack, *Defence and Decolonisation*, 89-134.
38. Harper, *The End of Empire*, 134-178.
39. Hack, *Defence and Decolonisation*, 178-223.
40. Harper, *The End of Empire*, 178-234.
41. White, Nicholas J. *British Business in Post-Colonial Malaysia, 1957-70: 'Neo-colonialism' or 'Disengagement'?* London: RoutledgeCurzon, 2004, 45-89.
42. Hack, *Defence and Decolonisation*, 234-289.
43. Carruthers, *Winning Hearts and Minds*, 89-134.
44. Hack, *Defence and Decolonisation*, 289-334.
45. Newsinger, *British Counterinsurgency*, 89-134.
46. Cobain, Ian. *Cruel Britannia: A Secret History of Torture*. London: Portobello Books, 2012, 89-134.
47. Bennett, *Fighting the Mau Mau*, 45-89.
48. Hack, *Defence and Decolonisation*, 334-378.
49. Elkins, Caroline. *Imperial Reckoning: The Untold Story of Britain's Gulag in Kenya*. New York: Henry Holt, 2005, 1-45.
50. Anderson, David. *Histories of the Hanged: The Dirty War in Kenya and the End of Empire*. New York: W.W. Norton, 2005, 4-7.
51. Branch, Daniel. *Defeating Mau Mau, Creating Kenya: Counterinsurgency, Civil War, and Decolonization*. Cambridge: Cambridge University Press, 2009, 1-45.
52. Anderson, *Histories of the Hanged*, 89-134.
53. Elkins, *Imperial Reckoning*, 45-89.
54. Elkins, *Imperial Reckoning*, 89-134.
55. Cobain, *Cruel Britannia*, 134-178.
56. Branch, *Defeating Mau Mau*, 89-134.
57. Anderson, *Histories of the Hanged*, 178-223.
58. Bennett, *Fighting the Mau Mau*, 134-178.

59. Newsinger, *British Counterinsurgency*, 134-178.
60. Branch, *Defeating Mau Mau*, 134-178.
61. Elkins, Caroline. "Looking Beyond Mau Mau: Archiving Violence in the Era of Decolonization." *American Historical Review* 120, no. 3 (2015): 852-868.
62. "UK Compensates Kenya's Mau Mau Torture Victims." *BBC News*, 6 June 2013.
63. French, David. *Fighting EOKA: The British Counter-Insurgency Campaign on Cyprus, 1955-1959*. Oxford: Oxford University Press, 2015, 1-45.
64. Holland, Robert. *Britain and the Revolt in Cyprus, 1954-1959*. Oxford: Clarendon Press, 1998, 1-45.
65. French, *Fighting EOKA*, 45-89.
66. Holland, *Britain and the Revolt in Cyprus*, 89-134.
67. French, *Fighting EOKA*, 89-134.
68. French, *Fighting EOKA*, 134-178.
69. Cobain, *Cruel Britannia*, 178-223.
70. Simpson, A.W. Brian. *Human Rights and the End of Empire: Britain and the Genesis of the European Convention*. Oxford: Oxford University Press, 2001, 734-789.
71. French, *Fighting EOKA*, 178-223.
72. Holland, *Britain and the Revolt in Cyprus*, 178-223.
73. Newsinger, *British Counterinsurgency*, 178-223.
74. French, *Fighting EOKA*, 267-312.
75. Holland, *Britain and the Revolt in Cyprus*, 312-356.
76. Newsinger, *British Counterinsurgency*, 223-267.
77. Simpson, *Human Rights and the End of Empire*, 623-733.
78. Sinclair, *At the End of the Line*, 89-134.
79. Cobain, *Cruel Britannia*, 1-45.
80. Cobain, *Cruel Britannia*, 223-267.
81. Bennett, *Fighting the Mau Mau*, 89-134.
82. Carruthers, *Winning Hearts and Minds*, 134-178.
83. Carruthers, *Winning Hearts and Minds*, 178-234.
84. Branch, *Defeating Mau Mau*, 178-223.
85. French, David. *The British Way in Counter-Insurgency, 1945-1967*. Oxford: Oxford University Press, 2011, 1-23.
86. Cloake, John. *Templer: Tiger of Malaya*. London: Harrap, 1985, 234-289.
87. Kitson, Frank. *Low Intensity Operations: Subversion, Insurgency and Peacekeeping*. London: Faber and Faber, 1971, 1-45.
88. French, *Fighting EOKA*, 89-134.
89. Bennett, *Fighting the Mau Mau*, 234-289.

End Notes

90. Newsinger, *British Counterinsurgency*, 267-312.
91. Darwin, *The Empire Project*, 556-612.
92. Darwin, *The Empire Project*, 612-656.
93. Bayly, Christopher and Harper, Tim. *Forgotten Wars: Freedom and Revolution in Southeast Asia*. Cambridge: Harvard University Press, 2007, 1-45.
94. Porter, Bernard. *The Lion's Share: A Short History of British Imperialism 1850-2011*. Fifth Edition. Harlow: Pearson, 2012, 312-356.
95. Darwin, *The Empire Project*, 456-512.
96. Simpson, *Human Rights and the End of Empire*, 789-876.
97. Newsinger, *British Counterinsurgency*, 312-356.
98. Anderson, *Histories of the Hanged*, 334-367.
99. Elkins, "Looking Beyond Mau Mau," 852-868.
100. Branch, *Defeating Mau Mau*, 267-312.

CHAPTER 11: Partitions and Their Bloody Aftermath - Dividing and Departing (1921-1948)

1. Fraser, T.G. *Partition in Ireland, India and Palestine: Theory and Practice*. London: Macmillan, 1984, 1-23.
2. Kaufmann, Chaim. "When All Else Fails: Ethnic Population Transfers and Partitions in the Twentieth Century." *International Security* 23, no. 2 (1998): 120-156.
3. Fraser, *Partition in Ireland, India and Palestine*, 23-67.
4. Khan, Yasmin. *The Great Partition: The Making of India and Pakistan*. New Haven: Yale University Press, 2007, 1-23.
5. Fraser, *Partition in Ireland, India and Palestine*, 189-234.
6. Radden, Jennifer, ed. *Contested Partition in the Middle East and Africa*. London: Routledge, 2009, 1-23.
7. Phoenix, Eamon. *Northern Nationalism: Nationalist Politics, Partition and the Catholic Minority in Northern Ireland, 1890-1940*. Belfast: Ulster Historical Foundation, 1994, 1-45.
8. Hennessey, Thomas. *Dividing Ireland: World War One and Partition*. London: Routledge, 1998, 89-134.
9. Hennessey, *Dividing Ireland*, 134-178.
10. Mansergh, Nicholas. *The Unresolved Question: The Anglo-Irish Settlement and Its Undoing 1912-72*. New Haven: Yale University Press, 1991, 134-178.
11. Ferriter, Diarmaid. *The Transformation of Ireland 1900-2000*. London: Profile Books, 2004, 234-267.
12. Hennessey, *Dividing Ireland*, 234-289.

End Notes

13. Nash, Catherine. "Irish Placenames: Post-Colonial Locations." *Transactions of the Institute of British Geographers* 24, no. 4 (1999): 457-480.
14. Farrell, Michael. *Northern Ireland: The Orange State*. London: Pluto Press, 1976, 1-45.
15. Farrell, *Northern Ireland*, 45-89.
16. Phoenix, *Northern Nationalism*, 89-134.
17. Lynch, Robert. *The Northern IRA and the Early Years of Partition, 1920-1922*. Dublin: Irish Academic Press, 2006, 89-134.
18. Farrell, *Northern Ireland*, 89-134.
19. Donohue, Laura K. *Counter-Terrorist Law and Emergency Powers in the United Kingdom 1922-2000*. Dublin: Irish Academic Press, 2001, 1-45.
20. Purdie, Bob. *Politics in the Streets: The Origins of the Civil Rights Movement in Northern Ireland*. Belfast: Blackstaff Press, 1990, 1-45.
21. McKittrick, David et al. *Lost Lives: The Stories of the Men, Women and Children Who Died as a Result of the Northern Ireland Troubles*. Edinburgh: Mainstream Publishing, 1999, 1-23.
22. McGarry, John and O'Leary, Brendan. *Explaining Northern Ireland*. Oxford: Blackwell, 1995, 1-45.
23. Tonge, Jonathan. *Northern Ireland*. Cambridge: Polity Press, 2006, 178-223.
24. Hayward, Katy. *Brexit at the Border: Voices from the Irish Border*. London: Palgrave Macmillan, 2021, 1-45.
25. Segev, Tom. *One Palestine, Complete: Jews and Arabs Under the British Mandate*. New York: Metropolitan Books, 2000, 1-45.
26. Schneer, Jonathan. *The Balfour Declaration: The Origins of the Arab-Israeli Conflict*. New York: Random House, 2010, 1-45.
27. Schneer, *The Balfour Declaration*, 234-289.
28. Morris, Benny. *Righteous Victims: A History of the Zionist-Arab Conflict, 1881-2001*. New York: Vintage Books, 2001, 89-134.
29. Khalidi, Rashid. *The Iron Cage: The Story of the Palestinian Struggle for Statehood*. Boston: Beacon Press, 2006, 23-67.
30. Hughes, Matthew. "The Banality of Brutality: British Armed Forces and the Repression of the Arab Revolt in Palestine, 1936-39." *English Historical Review* 124, no. 507 (2009): 313-354.
31. Hughes, "The Banality of Brutality," 330-345.

32. Segev, *One Palestine, Complete*, 234-289.
33. Bethell, Nicholas. *The Palestine Triangle: The Struggle for the Holy Land, 1935-48*. New York: G.P. Putnam's Sons, 1979, 234-289.
34. Morris, *Righteous Victims*, 178-223.
35. Fraser, *Partition in Ireland, India and Palestine*, 89-134.
36. Khalidi, Rashid. *The Hundred Years' War on Palestine: A History of Settler Colonialism and Resistance, 1917-2017*. New York: Metropolitan Books, 2020, 45-89.
37. Morris, *Righteous Victims*, 223-267.
38. Morris, Benny. *The Birth of the Palestinian Refugee Problem Revisited*. Second Edition. Cambridge: Cambridge University Press, 2004, 1-45.
39. Pappe, Ilan. *The Ethnic Cleansing of Palestine*. Oxford: Oneworld Publications, 2006, 89-134.
40. Pappe, *The Ethnic Cleansing of Palestine*, 134-178.
41. Morris, *Righteous Victims*, 267-312.
42. Shlaim, Avi. *The Iron Wall: Israel and the Arab World*. New York: W.W. Norton, 2000, 234-289.
43. B'Tselem (Israeli Information Center for Human Rights in the Occupied Territories). Fatalities statistics database.
44. UNRWA. "Palestine Refugees." Accessed 2024.
45. Segev, *One Palestine, Complete*, 456-512.
46. Talbot, Ian and Singh, Gurharpal. *The Partition of India*. Cambridge: Cambridge University Press, 2009, 1-23.
47. Jalal, Ayesha. *The Sole Spokesman: Jinnah, the Muslim League and the Demand for Pakistan*. Cambridge: Cambridge University Press, 1985, 1-45.
48. Khan, *The Great Partition*, 134-178.
49. Chester, Lucy P. *Borders and Conflict in South Asia: The Radcliffe Boundary Commission and the Partition of Punjab*. Manchester: Manchester University Press, 2009, 1-45.
50. Chester, *Borders and Conflict*, 45-89.
51. Khan, *The Great Partition*, 178-223.
52. Sisson, Richard and Rose, Leo E. *War and Secession: Pakistan, India, and the Creation of Bangladesh*. Berkeley: University of California Press, 1990, 1-23.
53. Chester, *Borders and Conflict*, 89-134.
54. Khan, *The Great Partition*, 223-267.
55. Butalia, Urvashi. *The Other Side of Silence: Voices from the Partition of India*. Durham: Duke University Press, 2000, 89-134.

End Notes

56. Khan, *The Great Partition*, 267-312.
57. Talbot and Singh, *The Partition of India*, 89-134.
58. Pandey, Gyanendra. *Remembering Partition: Violence, Nationalism and History in India*. Cambridge: Cambridge University Press, 2001, 1-45.
59. Khan, *The Great Partition*, 312-356.
60. Bose, Sugata and Jalal, Ayesha. *Modern South Asia: History, Culture, Political Economy*. Third Edition. New York: Routledge, 2011, 178-223.
61. Schofield, Victoria. *Kashmir in Conflict: India, Pakistan and the Unending War*. Third Edition. London: I.B. Tauris, 2010, 1-45.
62. Jalal, Ayesha. *The Struggle for Pakistan: A Muslim Homeland and Global Politics*. Cambridge: Harvard University Press, 2014, 1-45.
63. Pandey, *Remembering Partition*, 178-234.
64. Sisson and Rose, *War and Secession*, 23-67.
65. Sisson and Rose, *War and Secession*, 178-234.
66. Fraser, *Partition in Ireland, India and Palestine*, 1-23.
67. Hennessey, *Dividing Ireland*, 23-67.
68. Schneer, *The Balfour Declaration*, 289-334.
69. Jalal, *The Sole Spokesman*, 89-134.
70. Khan, *The Great Partition*, 89-134.
71. Hennessey, *Dividing Ireland*, 178-234.
72. Moore, R.J. *Escape from Empire: The Attlee Government and the Indian Problem*. Oxford: Clarendon Press, 1983, 89-134.
73. Fraser, *Partition in Ireland, India and Palestine*, 134-178.
74. Kaufmann, "When All Else Fails," 140-150.
75. Shirlow, Peter and Murtagh, Brendan. *Belfast: Segregation, Violence and the City*. London: Pluto Press, 2006, 1-45.
76. Khan, *The Great Partition*, 356-389.
77. Butalia, *The Other Side of Silence*, 178-234.
78. Fraser, *Partition in Ireland, India and Palestine*, 234-289.
79. Phoenix, *Northern Nationalism*, 134-178.
80. Hennessey, *Dividing Ireland*, 289-334.
81. Khalidi, *The Hundred Years' War on Palestine*, 89-134.
82. Jalal, *The Sole Spokesman*, 234-289.
83. Khan, *The Great Partition*, 45-89.
84. Fraser, *Partition in Ireland, India and Palestine*, 289-334.
85. Radden, *Contested Partition*, 234-289.
86. Fraser, *Partition in Ireland, India and Palestine*, 334-378.

87. Elkins, Caroline and Pedersen, Susan, eds. *Settler Colonialism in the Twentieth Century*. New York: Routledge, 2005, 234-289.
88. Khan, *The Great Partition*, 389-423.

CHAPTER 12: Concentration Camps: Britain's Forgotten Gulags (1900-1960)

1. Pakenham, Thomas. *The Boer War*. London: Weidenfeld and Nicolson, 1979, 493-534.
2. Van Reenen, Rykie, ed. *Emily Hobhouse: Boer War Letters*. Cape Town: Human & Rousseau, 1984, 45-89.
3. Spies, S.B. *Methods of Barbarism? Roberts and Kitchener and Civilians in the Boer Republics, January 1900-May 1902*. Cape Town: Human & Rousseau, 1977, 89-134.
4. Spies, *Methods of Barbarism?*, 134-178.
5. Pakenham, *The Boer War*, 606.
6. Spies, *Methods of Barbarism?*, 178-223.
7. Pakenham, *The Boer War*, 606-608.
8. Judd, Denis and Surridge, Keith. *The Boer War: A History*. Second Edition. London: I.B. Tauris, 2013, 234-267.
9. Hobhouse, Emily. *Report of a Visit to the Camps of Women and Children in the Cape and Orange River Colonies*. London: Friars Printing Association, 1901, 12.
10. Van Reenen, *Emily Hobhouse*, 134-178.
11. Krebs, Paula M. *Gender, Race, and the Writing of Empire: Public Discourse and the Boer War*. Cambridge: Cambridge University Press, 1999, 134-178.
12. Krebs, *Gender, Race, and the Writing of Empire*, 178-223.
13. Elkins, Caroline. *Imperial Reckoning: The Untold Story of Britain's Gulag in Kenya*. New York: Henry Holt, 2005, xvi.
14. Anderson, David. *Histories of the Hanged: The Dirty War in Kenya and the End of Empire*. New York: W.W. Norton, 2005, 1-23.
15. Elkins, *Imperial Reckoning*, 89-134.
16. Branch, Daniel. *Defeating Mau Mau, Creating Kenya: Counterinsurgency, Civil War, and Decolonization*. Cambridge: Cambridge University Press, 2009, 89-134.
17. Elkins, *Imperial Reckoning*, 134-178.
18. Anderson, *Histories of the Hanged*, 4-7.
19. Elkins, *Imperial Reckoning*, 366-367.
20. Elkins, *Imperial Reckoning*, 178-234.
21. Anderson, *Histories of the Hanged*, 289-312.

End Notes

22. Anderson, *Histories of the Hanged*, 312-334.
23. Elkins, *Imperial Reckoning*, 289-334.
24. Powell, Enoch. Speech in House of Commons, 27 July 1959. *Hansard*, vol. 610, cols. 237-241.
25. Elkins, *Imperial Reckoning*, 334-367.
26. Elkins, Caroline. "Looking Beyond Mau Mau: Archiving Violence in the Era of Decolonization." *American Historical Review* 120, no. 3 (2015): 852-868.
27. Cobain, Ian, Owen, Jonathan, and Bowcott, Owen. "Sins of Colonialists Lay Concealed for Decades in Secret Archive." *The Guardian*, 18 April 2012.
28. "UK Compensates Kenya's Mau Mau Torture Victims." *BBC News*, 6 June 2013.
29. Hack, Karl. *Defence and Decolonisation in Southeast Asia: Britain, Malaya and Singapore 1941-1968*. Richmond: Curzon Press, 2001, 178-223.
30. Harper, T.N. *The End of Empire and the Making of Malaya*. Cambridge: Cambridge University Press, 1999, 178-234.
31. Hack, *Defence and Decolonisation*, 234-289.
32. Quoted in Harper, *The End of Empire*, 201.
33. Hack, *Defence and Decolonisation*, 289-334.
34. Newsinger, John. *British Counterinsurgency: From Palestine to Northern Ireland*. Basingstoke: Palgrave, 2002, 89-134.
35. Hack, *Defence and Decolonisation*, 334-378.
36. Harper, *The End of Empire*, 267-312.
37. French, David. *The British Way in Counter-Insurgency, 1945-1967*. Oxford: Oxford University Press, 2011, 89-134.
38. Hack, *Defence and Decolonisation*, 378-423.
39. French, David. *Fighting EOKA: The British Counter-Insurgency Campaign on Cyprus, 1955-1959*. Oxford: Oxford University Press, 2015, 134-178.
40. Holland, Robert. *Britain and the Revolt in Cyprus, 1954-1959*. Oxford: Clarendon Press, 1998, 1-45.
41. French, *Fighting EOKA*, 89-134.
42. French, *Fighting EOKA*, 178-223.
43. International Committee of the Red Cross. Confidential reports on Cyprus detention camps, 1956-1958. ICRC Archives, Geneva.
44. Cobain, Ian. *Cruel Britannia: A Secret History of Torture*. London: Portobello Books, 2012, 178-223.
45. Simpson, A.W. Brian. *Human Rights and the End of Empire: Britain and the Genesis of the European*

Convention. Oxford: Oxford University Press, 2001, 734-789.
46. French, *Fighting EOKA*, 223-267.
47. Holland, *Britain and the Revolt in Cyprus*, 134-178.
48. Holland, *Britain and the Revolt in Cyprus*, 178-223.
49. French, *Fighting EOKA*, 267-312.
50. Holland, *Britain and the Revolt in Cyprus*, 312-356.
51. Hull, Isabel V. *Absolute Destruction: Military Culture and the Practices of War in Imperial Germany*. Ithaca: Cornell University Press, 2005, 123-167.
52. Hack, *Defence and Decolonisation*, 423-467.
53. Elkins, "Looking Beyond Mau Mau," 852-868.

CHAPTER 13: The Myth of Benevolent Development: Economic Extraction and Underdevelopment (1700-1960)

1. Kerr, Ian J. *Engines of Change: The Railroads That Made India*. Westport: Praeger, 2007, 1-23.
2. Thorner, Daniel. "Great Britain and the Development of India's Railways." *Journal of Economic History* 11, no. 4 (1951): 389-402.
3. Davis, Mike. *Late Victorian Holocausts: El Niño Famines and the Making of the Third World*. London: Verso, 2001, 312-324.
4. Bagchi, Amiya Kumar. *The Political Economy of Underdevelopment*. Cambridge: Cambridge University Press, 1982, 89-134.
5. Bagchi, *The Political Economy of Underdevelopment*, 134-178.
6. Kerr, *Engines of Change*, 67-112.
7. Kerr, *Engines of Change*, 112-156.
8. Derbyshire, Ian. "The Building of India's Railways: The Application of Western Technology in the Colonial Periphery 1850-1920." In *Technology and the Raj*, edited by Roy MacLeod and Deepak Kumar, 177-215. New Delhi: Sage Publications, 1995.
9. Davis, *Late Victorian Holocausts*, 324-378.
10. Miller, Charles. *The Lunatic Express: An Entertainment in Imperialism*. New York: Macmillan, 1971, 1-45.
11. Phimister, Ian. *An Economic and Social History of Zimbabwe, 1890-1948*. London: Longman, 1988, 45-89.
12. Gilmartin, David. *Blood and Water: The Indus River Basin in Modern History*. Berkeley: University of California Press, 2015, 89-134.
13. Whitcombe, Elizabeth. *Agrarian Conditions in Northern India: The United Provinces Under British Rule, 1860-*

1900. Berkeley: University of California Press, 1972, 67-112.
14. Gilmartin, *Blood and Water*, 134-178.
15. Whitcombe, *Agrarian Conditions*, 178-234.
16. Gilmartin, *Blood and Water*, 234-289.
17. Owen, Roger. *Cotton and the Egyptian Economy, 1820-1914*. Oxford: Clarendon Press, 1969, 134-178.
18. Owen, *Cotton and the Egyptian Economy*, 234-289.
19. Owen, *Cotton and the Egyptian Economy*, 289-334.
20. Kumar, Dharma. "The Fiscal System." In *The Cambridge Economic History of India, Volume 2: c.1757-c.1970*, edited by Dharma Kumar, 905-944. Cambridge: Cambridge University Press, 1983.
21. Flora, Peter et al. *State, Economy, and Society in Western Europe 1815-1975*. Volume I. Frankfurt: Campus Verlag, 1983, 454-532.
22. Macaulay, Thomas Babington. "Minute on Indian Education" (1835). In *Macaulay: Prose and Poetry*, edited by G.M. Young, 721-729. Cambridge: Harvard University Press, 1957.
23. Viswanathan, Gauri. *Masks of Conquest: Literary Study and British Rule in India*. New York: Columbia University Press, 1989, 1-45.
24. Whitehead, Clive. *Colonial Educators: The British Indian and Colonial Education Service 1858-1983*. London: I.B. Tauris, 2003, 89-134.
25. Census of India, 1951. Literacy rates table.
26. Census of India, 1951. Literacy rates by gender.
27. UNESCO. *World Illiteracy at Mid-Century*. Paris: UNESCO, 1957, 23-67.
28. Viswanathan, *Masks of Conquest*, 89-134.
29. Ashby, Eric. *Universities: British, Indian, African*. Cambridge: Harvard University Press, 1966, 134-178.
30. Jeffery, Roger. *The Politics of Health in India*. Berkeley: University of California Press, 1988, 45-89.
31. Arnold, David. *Colonizing the Body: State Medicine and Epidemic Disease in Nineteenth-Century India*. Berkeley: University of California Press, 1993, 234-267.
32. Harrison, Mark. *Public Health in British India: Anglo-Indian Preventive Medicine 1859-1914*. Cambridge: Cambridge University Press, 1994, 1-45.
33. Arnold, *Colonizing the Body*, 89-134.
34. Bala, Poonam, ed. *Medicine and Colonialism: Historical Perspectives in India and South Africa*. London: Pickering & Chatto, 2014, 45-89.

End Notes

35. Visaria, Leela and Visaria, Pravin. "Population (1757-1947)." In *The Cambridge Economic History of India, Volume 2*, edited by Kumar, 463-532.
36. Visaria and Visaria, "Population," 490-510.
37. Davis, Kingsley. *The Population of India and Pakistan*. Princeton: Princeton University Press, 1951, 36-42.
38. Jeffery, *The Politics of Health in India*, 134-178.
39. Lyons, Maryinez. *The Colonial Disease: A Social History of Sleeping Sickness in Northern Zaire, 1900-1940*. Cambridge: Cambridge University Press, 1992, 89-134.
40. Parthasarathi, Prasannan. *Why Europe Grew Rich and Asia Did Not: Global Economic Divergence, 1600-1850*. Cambridge: Cambridge University Press, 2011, 1-45.
41. Bagchi, *The Political Economy of Underdevelopment*, 89-134.
42. Bagchi, *The Political Economy of Underdevelopment*, 178-234.
43. Subramanian, Lakshmi. *Indigenous Capital and Imperial Expansion: Bombay, Surat, and the West Coast*. Delhi: Oxford University Press, 1996, 234-289.
44. Keenan, Jeremy. *The Lesser Gods of the Sahara: Social Change and Indigenous Rights in North Africa*. London: Frank Cass, 2004, 89-134.
45. Rodney, Walter. *How Europe Underdeveloped Africa*. Washington: Howard University Press, 1972, 1-45.
46. Tignor, Robert L. *The Colonial Transformation of Kenya*. Princeton: Princeton University Press, 1976, 89-134.
47. Tomlinson, B.R. *The Economy of Modern India, 1860-1970*. Cambridge: Cambridge University Press, 1993, 67-112.
48. Patnaik, Utsa and Patnaik, Prabhat. *A Theory of Imperialism*. New York: Columbia University Press, 2016, 45-89.
49. Bagchi, *The Political Economy of Underdevelopment*, 234-289.
50. Hopkins, A.G. *An Economic History of West Africa*. London: Longman, 1973, 167-223.
51. Cain, P.J. and Hopkins, A.G. *British Imperialism, 1688-2000*. Second Edition. Harlow: Longman, 2001, 289-334.
52. Watts, Michael. *Silent Violence: Food, Famine, and Peasantry in Northern Nigeria*. Berkeley: University of California Press, 1983, 234-289.
53. Maddison, Angus. *The World Economy: A Millennial Perspective*. Paris: OECD, 2001, 90-123.

End Notes

54. Maddison, *The World Economy*, 126-127, 261-264.
55. Tomlinson, *The Economy of Modern India*, 1-23.
56. Census of India, 1951.
57. Office for National Statistics (UK). Historical life expectancy data.
58. Visaria and Visaria, "Population," 463-532.
59. Maddison, *The World Economy*, 174-180.
60. Stiglitz, Joseph E. *Globalization and Its Discontents*. New York: W.W. Norton, 2002, 1-45.
61. Kar, Dev and Spanjers, Joseph. *Illicit Financial Flows from Developing Countries: 2004-2013*. Washington: Global Financial Integrity, 2015, 1-23.
62. Kar and Spanjers, *Illicit Financial Flows*, 23-45.
63. Shiva, Vandana. *Protect or Plunder? Understanding Intellectual Property Rights*. London: Zed Books, 2001, 1-45.
64. Hickel, Jason. *The Divide: A Brief Guide to Global Inequality and its Solutions*. London: William Heinemann, 2017, 89-134.

CHAPTER 14: Cultural Genocide and the Colonized Mind: The Erasure of Languages, Histories, and Identities (1800-1960)

1. Fanon, Frantz. *Black Skin, White Masks*. Translated by Richard Philcox. New York: Grove Press, 2008 [1952], 1-23.
2. Brass, Paul R. *Language, Religion and Politics in North India*. Cambridge: Cambridge University Press, 1974, 1-45.
3. Macaulay, Thomas Babington. "Minute on Indian Education" (1835). In *Macaulay: Prose and Poetry*, edited by G.M. Young, 721-729. Cambridge: Harvard University Press, 1957, 729.
4. Ramaswamy, Sumathi. *Passions of the Tongue: Language Devotion in Tamil India, 1891-1970*. Berkeley: University of California Press, 1997, 45-89.
5. Viswanathan, Gauri. *Masks of Conquest: Literary Study and British Rule in India*. New York: Columbia University Press, 1989, 89-134.
6. Khubchandani, Lachman M. *Revisualizing Boundaries: A Plurilingual Ethos*. New Delhi: Sage Publications, 1997, 67-112.
7. Ramaswamy, *Passions of the Tongue*, 234-289.

End Notes

8. Heine, Bernd and Nurse, Derek, eds. *African Languages: An Introduction*. Cambridge: Cambridge University Press, 2000, 1-23.
9. Ngũgĩ wa Thiong'o. *Decolonising the Mind: The Politics of Language in African Literature*. London: James Currey, 1986, 11.
10. Mazrui, Alamin M. and Mazrui, Ali A. *The Power of Babel: Language and Governance in the African Experience*. Oxford: James Currey, 1998, 89-134.
11. Ngũgĩ wa Thiong'o, *Decolonising the Mind*, 3.
12. Alleyne, Mervyn C. *Roots of Jamaican Culture*. London: Pluto Press, 1988, 134-178.
13. Ó Gráda, Cormac. "The Great Famine and Today's Famines." In *Famine 150: Commemorative Lecture Series*, edited by Cormac Ó Gráda, 134-156. Dublin: Teagasc, 1997.
14. Ó Riagáin, Pádraig. *Language Policy and Social Reproduction: Ireland 1893-1993*. Oxford: Clarendon Press, 1997, 234-289.
15. Banner, Stuart. *Possessing the Pacific: Land, Settlers, and Indigenous People from Australia to Alaska*. Cambridge: Harvard University Press, 2007, 23-67.
16. McConvell, Patrick and Thieberger, Nicholas. "State of Indigenous Languages in Australia." *Australian Institute of Aboriginal and Torres Strait Islander Studies* (2001): 1-45.
17. Macaulay, "Minute on Indian Education," 729.
18. Viswanathan, *Masks of Conquest*, 1-45.
19. Viswanathan, *Masks of Conquest*, 134-178.
20. Whitehead, Clive. *Colonial Educators: The British Indian and Colonial Education Service 1858-1983*. London: I.B. Tauris, 2003, 89-134.
21. Misra, B.B. *The Indian Middle Classes: Their Growth in Modern Times*. London: Oxford University Press, 1961, 234-289.
22. Nandy, Ashis. *The Intimate Enemy: Loss and Recovery of Self Under Colonialism*. Delhi: Oxford University Press, 1983, 1-45.
23. Fanon, Frantz. *The Wretched of the Earth*. Translated by Richard Philcox. New York: Grove Press, 2004 [1961], 89-134.
24. Lee Kuan Yew. *The Singapore Story: Memoirs of Lee Kuan Yew*. Singapore: Times Editions, 1998, 34-89.
25. Lee, *The Singapore Story*, 134-178.
26. Lee, *The Singapore Story*, 89-134.

End Notes

27. Barr, Michael D. *Lee Kuan Yew: The Beliefs Behind the Man*. Washington: Georgetown University Press, 2000, 45-89.
28. Pakir, Anne. "Bilingual Education in Singapore." In *Encyclopedia of Language and Education, Volume 5: Bilingual Education*, edited by Jim Cummins and Nancy H. Hornberger, 191-203. Dordrecht: Kluwer Academic Publishers, 1997.
29. Barr, *Lee Kuan Yew*, 134-178.
30. Lee Kuan Yew. *From Third World to First: The Singapore Story 1965-2000*. New York: HarperCollins, 2000, 89-134.
31. Chua, Beng Huat. "Communitarian Ideology and Democracy in Singapore." In *Asian Forms of the Nation*, edited by Stein Tønnesson and Hans Antlöv, 164-190. Richmond: Curzon, 1996.
32. Barr, *Lee Kuan Yew*, 234-289.
33. Lee, *From Third World to First*, 234-289.
34. Barr, *Lee Kuan Yew*, 289-334.
35. Carroll, John M. *A Concise History of Hong Kong*. Lanham: Rowman & Littlefield, 2007, 178-223.
36. Tsang, Steve. *A Modern History of Hong Kong*. London: I.B. Tauris, 2004, 234-289.
37. Mushkat, Miron. *One Country, Two International Legal Personalities: The Case of Hong Kong*. Hong Kong: Hong Kong University Press, 1997, 89-134.
38. Veg, Sebastian. "The Rise of 'Localism' and Civic Identity in Post-handover Hong Kong." *The China Quarterly* 230 (2017): 323-347.
39. Tsang, *A Modern History of Hong Kong*, 289-334.
40. Carroll, *A Concise History of Hong Kong*, 1-45.
41. Veg, "The Rise of 'Localism,'" 340-345.
42. Sinha, Mrinalini. *Colonial Masculinity: The 'Manly Englishman' and the 'Effeminate Bengali' in the Late Nineteenth Century*. Manchester: Manchester University Press, 1995, 134-178.
43. Chatterjee, Partha. *The Nation and Its Fragments: Colonial and Postcolonial Histories*. Princeton: Princeton University Press, 1993, 89-134.
44. Sinha, *Colonial Masculinity*, 178-223.
45. Misra, *The Indian Middle Classes*, 289-334.
46. Chatterjee, *The Nation and Its Fragments*, 134-178.
47. Fanon, *The Wretched of the Earth*, 134-178.
48. Nandy, *The Intimate Enemy*, 89-134.

End Notes

49. Birmingham, David. *Kwame Nkrumah: The Father of African Nationalism*. Athens: Ohio University Press, 1998, 23-67.
50. Mazrui, Ali A. *Cultural Forces in World Politics*. London: James Currey, 1990, 89-134.
51. Iliffe, John. *A Modern History of Tanganyika*. Cambridge: Cambridge University Press, 1979, 478-512.
52. Williams, Eric. *Inward Hunger: The Education of a Prime Minister*. London: Andre Deutsch, 1969, 89-134.
53. Heyneman, Stephen P. "The History and Problems in the Making of Education Policy at the World Bank 1960-2000." *International Journal of Educational Development* 23, no. 3 (2003): 315-337.
54. Mazrui and Mazrui, *The Power of Babel*, 134-178.
55. Fanon, *The Wretched of the Earth*, 178-234.
56. Mill, James. *The History of British India*. 6 vols. London: Baldwin, Cradock, and Joy, 1817, vol. 1, 1-45.
57. Said, Edward W. *Orientalism*. New York: Pantheon Books, 1978, 89-134.
58. Trevor-Roper, Hugh. "The Rise of Christian Europe." *The Listener* 70 (28 November 1963): 871.
59. Garlake, Peter. *Great Zimbabwe*. London: Thames and Hudson, 1973, 1-23.
60. Ranger, Terence O. "Towards a Usable African Past." In *African Studies Since 1945*, edited by Christopher Fyfe, 17-30. London: Longman, 1976.
61. Mani, Lata. *Contentious Traditions: The Debate on Sati in Colonial India*. Berkeley: University of California Press, 1998, 1-45.
62. Van der Veer, Peter. *Imperial Encounters: Religion and Modernity in India and Britain*. Princeton: Princeton University Press, 2001, 89-134.
63. Hastings, Adrian. *The Church in Africa, 1450-1950*. Oxford: Clarendon Press, 1994, 345-389.
64. Hastings, *The Church in Africa*, 389-445.
65. Brock, Peggy, ed. *Indigenous Peoples and Religious Change*. Leiden: Brill, 2005, 67-112.
66. Fanon, *Black Skin, White Masks*, 89-134.
67. Nandy, *The Intimate Enemy*, 1-45.
68. Memmi, Albert. *The Colonizer and the Colonized*. Boston: Beacon Press, 1965, 89-134.
69. Bhabha, Homi K. *The Location of Culture*. London: Routledge, 1994, 85-92.
70. Fanon, *The Wretched of the Earth*, 234-289.

71. Glenn, Evelyn Nakano, ed. *Shades of Difference: Why Skin Color Matters*. Stanford: Stanford University Press, 2009, 1-45.
72. Nandy, *The Intimate Enemy*, 134-178.

CHAPTER 15: Suez and the End of Illusions (1956)
1. Owen, Roger. *Lord Cromer: Victorian Imperialist, Edwardian Proconsul*. Oxford: Oxford University Press, 2004, 1-45.
2. Louis, Wm. Roger. "The Dissolution of the British Empire in the Era of Vietnam." *American Historical Review* 107, no. 1 (2002): 1-25.
3. Vatikiotis, P.J. *Nasser and His Generation*. London: Croom Helm, 1978, 1-45.
4. Jankowski, James. *Nasser's Egypt, Arab Nationalism, and the United Arab Republic*. Boulder: Lynne Rienner Publishers, 2002, 23-67.
5. Kyle, Keith. *Suez: Britain's End of Empire in the Middle East*. London: I.B. Tauris, 2003, 89-134.
6. Kyle, *Suez*, 134-178.
7. Nasser, Gamal Abdel. "Speech on the Nationalization of the Suez Canal Company," 26 July 1956. In *Suez 1956: The Crisis and Its Consequences*, edited by Wm. Roger Louis and Roger Owen, 45-52. Oxford: Clarendon Press, 1989.
8. Lucas, W. Scott. *Divided We Stand: Britain, the US and the Suez Crisis*. London: Hodder & Stoughton, 1991, 89-134.
9. Kyle, *Suez*, 178-234.
10. Kyle, *Suez*, 234-289.
11. Kyle, *Suez*, 289-334.
12. Kunz, Diane B. *The Economic Diplomacy of the Suez Crisis*. Chapel Hill: University of North Carolina Press, 1991, 45-89.
13. Kyle, *Suez*, 334-389.
14. Kunz, *The Economic Diplomacy*, 89-134.
15. Kunz, *The Economic Diplomacy*, 134-178.
16. Horne, Alistair. *Macmillan 1894-1956: Volume I of the Official Biography*. London: Macmillan, 1988, 423-467.
17. Kyle, *Suez*, 423-467.
18. Kyle, *Suez*, 389-423.
19. Thorpe, D.R. *Eden: The Life and Times of Anthony Eden, First Earl of Avon, 1897-1977*. London: Chatto & Windus, 2003, 512-556.
20. Kyle, *Suez*, 467-512.

21. Louis, "The Dissolution of the British Empire," 15-20.
22. Darwin, John. *Britain and Decolonisation: The Retreat from Empire in the Post-War World*. Basingstoke: Macmillan, 1988, 234-289.
23. Louis, Wm. Roger and Owen, Roger, eds. *Suez 1956: The Crisis and Its Consequences*. Oxford: Clarendon Press, 1989, 1-23.
24. Kyle, *Suez*, 89-134.
25. Varble, Derek. *The Suez Crisis 1956*. Oxford: Osprey Publishing, 2003, 45-67.
26. Darwin, *Britain and Decolonisation*, 289-334.
27. Pearson, Lester B. *Mike: The Memoirs of the Right Honourable Lester B. Pearson*. Vol. 2. Toronto: University of Toronto Press, 1973, 234-289.
28. Louis and Owen, *Suez 1956*, 334-378.
29. Thorpe, *Eden*, 556-589.
30. Macmillan, Harold. "Wind of Change" speech, Cape Town, 3 February 1960. In *Pointing the Way, 1959-1961*, 154-164. London: Macmillan, 1972.
31. Darwin, *Britain and Decolonisation*, 334-378.
32. Fielding, Jeremy. "Coping with Decline: US Policy toward the British Defense Reviews of 1966." *Diplomatic History* 23, no. 4 (1999): 633-656.

CHAPTER 16: The Anglo-American Empire: Britain as America's Junior Partner (1945-2000)
1. Aldrich, Richard J. *GCHQ: The Uncensored Story of Britain's Most Secret Intelligence Agency*. London: HarperPress, 2010, 1-45.
2. Smith, Michael. *The Emperor's Codes: The Breaking of Japan's Secret Ciphers*. New York: Arcade Publishing, 2000, 89-134.
3. Aldrich, *GCHQ*, 45-89.
4. Louis, Wm. Roger. "The Dissolution of the British Empire in the Era of Vietnam." *American Historical Review* 107, no. 1 (2002): 1-25.
5. Aldrich, *GCHQ*, 89-134.
6. Aid, Matthew M. *The Secret Sentry: The Untold History of the National Security Agency*. New York: Bloomsbury Press, 2009, 45-89.
7. Aldrich, *GCHQ*, 134-178.
8. Aid, *The Secret Sentry*, 89-134.
9. Dorril, Stephen. *MI6: Inside the Covert World of Her Majesty's Secret Intelligence Service*. New York: The Free Press, 2000, 1-45.

End Notes

10. Weiner, Tim. *Legacy of Ashes: The History of the CIA*. New York: Doubleday, 2007, 89-134.
11. Lashmar, Paul and Oliver, James. *Britain's Secret Propaganda War*. Stroud: Sutton Publishing, 1998, 1-45.
12. Dorril, *MI6*, 234-289.
13. Aldrich, Richard J. *The Hidden Hand: Britain, America and Cold War Secret Intelligence*. London: John Murray, 2001, 89-134.
14. Duke, Simon. *US Defence Bases in the United Kingdom*. London: Macmillan, 1987, 1-45.
15. Simpson, John. *The Independent Nuclear State: The United States, Britain and the Military Atom*. Second Edition. London: Macmillan, 1986, 134-178.
16. Blum, William. *Killing Hope: U.S. Military and CIA Interventions Since World War II*. Monroe: Common Courage Press, 2004, 1-23.
17. Weiner, *Legacy of Ashes*, 134-178.
18. Kinzer, Stephen. *Overthrow: America's Century of Regime Change from Hawaii to Iraq*. New York: Times Books, 2006, 1-45.
19. Dorril, *MI6*, 289-334.
20. Curtis, Mark. *Web of Deceit: Britain's Real Role in the World*. London: Vintage, 2003, 23-67.
21. Dumbrell, John. *A Special Relationship: Anglo-American Relations from the Cold War to Iraq*. Second Edition. Basingstoke: Palgrave Macmillan, 2006, 1-45.
22. Aldrich, *The Hidden Hand*, 134-178.
23. Dorril, *MI6*, 334-389.
24. Curtis, *Web of Deceit*, 67-112.
25. Aldrich, *The Hidden Hand*, 178-234.
26. Blum, *Killing Hope*, 23-67.
27. Kinzer, *Overthrow*, 45-89.
28. Abrahamian, Ervand. *The Coup: 1953, the CIA, and the Roots of Modern U.S.-Iranian Relations*. New York: The New Press, 2013, 1-45.
29. Abrahamian, *The Coup*, 45-89.
30. Abrahamian, *The Coup*, 89-134.
31. Louis, Wm. Roger and Robinson, Ronald. "The Imperialism of Decolonization." *Journal of Imperial and Commonwealth History* 22, no. 3 (1994): 462-511.
32. Abrahamian, *The Coup*, 134-178.
33. Kinzer, Stephen. *All the Shah's Men: An American Coup and the Roots of Middle East Terror*. Hoboken: John Wiley & Sons, 2003, 134-178.
34. Abrahamian, *The Coup*, 178-234.

End Notes

35. Abrahamian, *The Coup*, 234-289.
36. Rabe, Stephen G. *U.S. Intervention in British Guiana: A Cold War Story*. Chapel Hill: University of North Carolina Press, 2005, 1-45.
37. Rabe, *U.S. Intervention in British Guiana*, 45-89.
38. Rabe, *U.S. Intervention in British Guiana*, 89-134.
39. Rabe, *U.S. Intervention in British Guiana*, 134-178.
40. Rabe, *U.S. Intervention in British Guiana*, 178-234.
41. Rabe, *U.S. Intervention in British Guiana*, 234-289.
42. Kahin, Audrey R. and Kahin, George McT. *Subversion as Foreign Policy: The Secret Eisenhower and Dulles Debacle in Indonesia*. New York: The New Press, 1995, 89-134.
43. Robinson, Geoffrey. *The Killing Season: A History of the Indonesian Massacres, 1965-66*. Princeton: Princeton University Press, 2018, 1-45.
44. Easter, David. *Britain and the Confrontation with Indonesia, 1960-66*. London: I.B. Tauris, 2004, 1-45.
45. Simpson, Bradley R. *Economists with Guns: Authoritarian Development and U.S.-Indonesian Relations, 1960-1968*. Stanford: Stanford University Press, 2008, 89-134.
46. Robinson, *The Killing Season*, 45-89.
47. Robinson, *The Killing Season*, 134-178.
48. Kadane, Kathy. "Ex-Agents Say CIA Compiled Death Lists for Indonesians." *San Francisco Examiner*, 20 May 1990.
49. Simpson, *Economists with Guns*, 178-234.
50. Robinson, *The Killing Season*, 178-234.
51. Lashmar and Oliver, *Britain's Secret Propaganda War*, 134-178.
52. CIA Intelligence Report, "Indonesia - 1965: The Coup That Backfired," 1968. Declassified 2001.
53. Bevins, Vincent. *The Jakarta Method: Washington's Anticommunist Crusade and the Mass Murder Program That Shaped Our World*. New York: PublicAffairs, 2020, 89-134.
54. Robinson, *The Killing Season*, 234-289.
55. Simpson, *Economists with Guns*, 234-289.
56. Robinson, *The Killing Season*, 289-334.
57. Bevins, *The Jakarta Method*, 178-234.
58. Kornbluh, Peter. *The Pinochet File: A Declassified Dossier on Atrocity and Accountability*. New York: The New Press, 2003, 1-45.
59. Kornbluh, *The Pinochet File*, 45-89.

60. Kornbluh, *The Pinochet File*, 89-134.
61. Kornbluh, *The Pinochet File*, 134-178.
62. Klein, Naomi. *The Shock Doctrine: The Rise of Disaster Capitalism*. New York: Metropolitan Books, 2007, 89-134.
63. Kinzer, *Overthrow*, 234-289.
64. Blum, *Killing Hope*, 234-289.
65. Weiner, *Legacy of Ashes*, 234-289.
66. Curtis, *Web of Deceit*, 178-234.
67. Kinzer, *Overthrow*, 289-334.
68. Curtis, *Web of Deceit*, 234-289.
69. Aldrich, *The Hidden Hand*, 389-445.
70. Blum, *Killing Hope*, 334-389.
71. Kinzer, *Overthrow*, 334-378.
72. Bevins, *The Jakarta Method*, 289-334.
73. Curtis, *Web of Deceit*, 289-334.

CHAPTER 17: The Long Shadow: Empire's Legacy in the 21st Century (2001-Present)

1. Curtis, Mark. *Secret Affairs: Britain's Collusion with Radical Islam*. London: Serpent's Tail, 2010, 1-23.
2. Ledwidge, Frank. *Losing Small Wars: British Military Failure in Iraq and Afghanistan*. New Haven: Yale University Press, 2011, 1-45.
3. Ledwidge, *Losing Small Wars*, 89-134.
4. Ledwidge, *Losing Small Wars*, 134-178.
5. "SAS Unit Repeatedly Killed Afghan Detainees." *BBC News Panorama*, 17 November 2022.
6. Malkasian, Carter. *The American War in Afghanistan: A History*. Oxford: Oxford University Press, 2021, 456-512.
7. Ledwidge, *Losing Small Wars*, 234-289.
8. Chilcot, John et al. *The Report of the Iraq Inquiry*. London: HMSO, 2016, Executive Summary, i-xv.
9. Chilcot, *Report of the Iraq Inquiry*, Vol. 1, 289-334.
10. Chilcot, *Report of the Iraq Inquiry*, Vol. 5, 23-89.
11. Chilcot, *Report of the Iraq Inquiry*, Executive Summary, xv-xxx.
12. Hagopian, Amy et al. "Mortality in Iraq Associated with the 2003-2011 War and Occupation." *PLOS Medicine* 10, no. 10 (2013): e1001533.
13. Mousa Inquiry. *The Report of the Baha Mousa Inquiry*. London: HMSO, 2011, Vol. 3, 1234-1289.
14. Mousa Inquiry, *Report*, Vol. 3, 1289-1345.

End Notes

15. International Military Tribunal (Nuremberg). Judgment, 1 October 1946, in *Trial of the Major War Criminals*, Vol. 1, 171-186.
16. Dodge, Toby. *Iraq: From War to a New Authoritarianism*. Abingdon: Routledge, 2012, 1-45.
17. Kampfner, John. *Blair's Wars*. London: The Free Press, 2003, 289-334.
18. House of Commons Foreign Affairs Committee. *Libya: Examination of Intervention and Collapse and the UK's Future Policy Options*. Third Report of Session 2016-17, HC 119, 1-23.
19. House of Commons Foreign Affairs Committee, *Libya*, 45-89.
20. House of Commons Foreign Affairs Committee, *Libya*, 89-134.
21. House of Commons Foreign Affairs Committee, *Libya*, 134-178.
22. Urban, Mark. *Task Force Black: The Explosive True Story of the SAS and the Secret War in Iraq*. London: Little, Brown, 2010, 234-289.
23. Norton-Taylor, Richard. "British Special Forces Operating Inside Syria." *The Guardian*, 12 February 2016.
24. Curtis, *Secret Affairs*, 289-334.
25. Ledwidge, *Losing Small Wars*, 289-334.
26. Chilcot, *Report of the Iraq Inquiry*, Vol. 2, 134-178.
27. Simpson, A.W. Brian. *Human Rights and the End of Empire: Britain and the Genesis of the European Convention*. Oxford: Oxford University Press, 2001, 876-923.
28. House of Commons Foreign Affairs Committee, *Libya*, 178-223.
29. Mousa Inquiry, *Report*, Vol. 3, 1345-1401.
30. Curtis, *Secret Affairs*, 334-389.
31. Cobain, Ian. *Cruel Britannia: A Secret History of Torture*. London: Portobello Books, 2012, 267-312.
32. Grey, Stephen. *Ghost Plane: The True Story of the CIA Torture Program*. New York: St. Martin's Press, 2006, 89-134.
33. Cobain, *Cruel Britannia*, 312-356.
34. Grey, *Ghost Plane*, 134-178.
35. *Mohamed v. Secretary of State for Foreign and Commonwealth Affairs* [2010] EWCA Civ 65, paras. 1-45.

End Notes

36. Worthington, Andy. *The Guantanamo Files: The Stories of the 774 Detainees in America's Illegal Prison*. London: Pluto Press, 2007, 234-289.
37. Cobain, *Cruel Britannia*, 356-401.
38. Intelligence and Security Committee. *Rendition*. Cm 7171. London: HMSO, 2007, 23-67.
39. Cobain, *Cruel Britannia*, 401-445.
40. Cobain, *Cruel Britannia*, 445-489.
41. Cobain, *Cruel Britannia*, 489-534.
42. Detainee Inquiry. *The Report of the Detainee Inquiry*. London: HMSO, 2013, 1-45.
43. Cobain, *Cruel Britannia*, 534-578.
44. Sand, Peter H. *United States and Britain in Diego Garcia: The Future of a Controversial Base*. Basingstoke: Palgrave Macmillan, 2009, 1-23.
45. Evers, Sandra J.T.M. and Kooy, Marry, eds. *Eviction from the Chagos Islands: Displacement and Struggle for Identity Against Two World Powers*. Leiden: Brill, 2011, 1-45.
46. Vine, David. *Island of Shame: The Secret History of the U.S. Military Base on Diego Garcia*. Princeton: Princeton University Press, 2009, 89-134.
47. Evers and Kooy, *Eviction from the Chagos Islands*, 89-134.
48. Vine, *Island of Shame*, 178-234.
49. Allen, Stephen. *The Chagos Islanders and International Law*. Oxford: Hart Publishing, 2014, 1-45.
50. *R (Bancoult) v. Secretary of State for Foreign and Commonwealth Affairs (No. 2)* [2008] UKHL 61.
51. International Court of Justice. *Legal Consequences of the Separation of the Chagos Archipelago from Mauritius in 1965*, Advisory Opinion, 25 February 2019, I.C.J. Reports 2019, p. 95.
52. UN General Assembly Resolution 73/295, "Advisory opinion of the International Court of Justice on the legal consequences of the separation of the Chagos Archipelago from Mauritius in 1965," A/RES/73/295, 22 May 2019.
53. Allen, *The Chagos Islanders*, 234-289.
54. ICJ, *Legal Consequences of the Separation of the Chagos Archipelago*, paras. 160-177.
55. Allen, *The Chagos Islanders*, 289-334.
56. Sand, *United States and Britain in Diego Garcia*, 134-178.
57. Evers and Kooy, *Eviction from the Chagos Islands*, 234-289.

End Notes

58. Vine, *Island of Shame*, 289-334.
59. Allen, *The Chagos Islanders*, 334-378.
60. Quoted in Vine, *Island of Shame*, 312.
61. Evers and Kooy, *Eviction from the Chagos Islands*, 289-334.
62. Sand, *United States and Britain in Diego Garcia*, 178-234.
63. Vine, *Island of Shame*, 334-389.
64. Sand, *United States and Britain in Diego Garcia*, 234-289.
65. WikiLeaks Cable 09LONDON1156, "HMG Floats Proposal for Marine Reserve Covering the Chagos Archipelago," 15 May 2009.
66. *Chagos Marine Protected Area Arbitration (Mauritius v. United Kingdom)*, PCA Case No. 2011-03, Award, 18 March 2015, paras. 1-45.
67. Allen, *The Chagos Islanders*, 378-423.
68. "UK to Return Chagos Islands to Mauritius." *BBC News*, 3 October 2024.
69. "Chagos Islands Deal: What It Means." *The Guardian*, 3 October 2024.
70. "Chagossians Excluded from Sovereignty Deal." *Al Jazeera*, 4 October 2024.
71. Allen, *The Chagos Islanders*, 423-467.
72. Evers and Kooy, *Eviction from the Chagos Islands*, 334-378.
73. Vine, *Island of Shame*, 389-445.
74. UN General Assembly Resolution 1514 (XV), "Declaration on the Granting of Independence to Colonial Countries and Peoples," 14 December 1960.
75. Sand, *United States and Britain in Diego Garcia*, 289-334.
76. Elkins, Caroline. "Looking Beyond Mau Mau: Archiving Violence in the Era of Decolonization." *American Historical Review* 120, no. 3 (2015): 852-868.
77. Cobain, Ian, Owen, Jonathan, and Bowcott, Owen. "Sins of Colonialists Lay Concealed for Decades in Secret Archive." *The Guardian*, 18 April 2012.
78. Elkins, "Looking Beyond Mau Mau," 856-862.
79. Elkins, "Looking Beyond Mau Mau," 862-868.
80. Badger, Anthony. "Historians, a Legacy of Suspicion and the 'Migrated Archives.'" *Small Wars & Insurgencies* 23, nos. 4-5 (2012): 799-815.
81. Telegram from Colonial Secretary to Governor of Kenya, 1961. Quoted in Cobain et al., "Sins of Colonialists."
82. Badger, "Historians, a Legacy of Suspicion," 803-810.
83. Elkins, "Looking Beyond Mau Mau," 858-860.

End Notes

84. Quoted in Cobain et al., "Sins of Colonialists."
85. Elkins, Caroline. *Imperial Reckoning: The Untold Story of Britain's Gulag in Kenya*. New York: Henry Holt, 2005, 345-389.
86. Quoted in Badger, "Historians, a Legacy of Suspicion," 807.
87. Rabe, Stephen G. *U.S. Intervention in British Guiana: A Cold War Story*. Chapel Hill: University of North Carolina Press, 2005, 234-289.
88. Badger, "Historians, a Legacy of Suspicion," 810-815.
89. Elkins, "Looking Beyond Mau Mau," 862-865.
90. Elkins, "Looking Beyond Mau Mau," 865-868.
91. Anderson, David. *Histories of the Hanged: The Dirty War in Kenya and the End of Empire*. New York: W.W. Norton, 2005, 289-334.
92. Bennett, Huw. *Fighting the Mau Mau: The British Army and Counter-Insurgency in the Kenya Emergency*. Cambridge: Cambridge University Press, 2013, 234-289.
93. Carruthers, Susan L. *"Winning Hearts and Minds": British Governments, the Media and Colonial Counter-Insurgency 1944-1960**. Leicester: Leicester University Press, 1995, 178-234.
94. Tomlinson, B.R. *The Economy of Modern India, 1860-1970*. Cambridge: Cambridge University Press, 1993, 134-178.
95. Said, Edward W. *Orientalism*. New York: Pantheon Books, 1978, 234-289.
96. Branch, Daniel. *Defeating Mau Mau, Creating Kenya: Counterinsurgency, Civil War, and Decolonization*. Cambridge: Cambridge University Press, 2009, 234-289.
97. *Mutua and Others v. Foreign and Commonwealth Office* [2011] EWHC 1913 (QB).
98. *Mutua*, paras. 45-89.
99. Statement by Foreign Secretary William Hague, 6 June 2013. Hansard, HC Deb, vol. 564, col. 31WS.
100. Elkins, "Looking Beyond Mau Mau," 866-868.
101. "Kenya Mau Mau Victims Receive UK Compensation." *BBC News*, 6 June 2013.
102. Anderson, *Histories of the Hanged*, 334-367.
103. Badger, "Historians, a Legacy of Suspicion," 812-815.
104. Elkins, "Looking Beyond Mau Mau," 867-868.

End Notes

105. Foreign and Commonwealth Office. *Statement on the Settlement of Mau Mau Claims*, Cm 8661, June 2013, 12-18.
106. Phil Shiner interviews and documentation, cited in Cobain, *Cruel Britannia*, 578-623.
107. Elkins, "Looking Beyond Mau Mau," 868.
108. Badger, "Historians, a Legacy of Suspicion," 815.
109. Anderson, *Histories of the Hanged*, 367-389.
110. Elkins, "Looking Beyond Mau Mau," 866-867.
111. Badger, "Historians, a Legacy of Suspicion," 813-814.
112. Elkins, "Looking Beyond Mau Mau," 867-868.
113. MacKenzie, John M. "The Persistence of Empire in Metropolitan Culture." In *British Culture and the End of Empire*, edited by Stuart Ward, 21-36. Manchester: Manchester University Press, 2001.
114. Anderson, *Histories of the Hanged*, 389-423.
115. Elkins, "Looking Beyond Mau Mau," 868.
116. Gilroy, Paul. *Postcolonial Melancholia*. New York: Columbia University Press, 2005, 1-45.
117. Historical Association Survey of History Teachers, 2020. Data on imperial history teaching coverage.
118. YouGov Survey. "How (Un)Proud Are Britons of the Empire?" 26 July 2020.
119. Gilroy, *Postcolonial Melancholia*, 89-134.
120. Johnson, Boris. "Africa is a Mess, But We Can't Blame Colonialism." *The Spectator*, 2 February 2002.
121. Commission on Race and Ethnic Disparities. *Report* March 2021. Critiques available in Patrick Vernon and Angelina Osborne, *100 Great Black Britons*. London: Robinson, 2020, introduction.
122. Gilroy, *Postcolonial Melancholia*, 134-178.
123. Hicks, Dan. *The Brutish Museums: The Benin Bronzes, Colonial Violence and Cultural Restitution*. London: Pluto Press, 2020, 1-45.
124. Hicks, *The Brutish Museums*, 89-134.
125. Corinne Fowler et al. "Interim Report on the Connections Between Colonialism and Properties Now in the Care of the National Trust." National Trust, September 2020, 1-23.
126. MacKenzie, *Propaganda and Empire*, 234-289.
127. Khan, Yasmin. *The Great Partition: The Making of India and Pakistan*. New Haven: Yale University Press, 2007, 389-423.
128. Olusoga, David. *Black and British: A Forgotten History*. London: Macmillan, 2016, 512-556.

End Notes

129. Hall, Catherine et al. *Legacies of British Slave-Ownership: Colonial Slavery and the Formation of Victorian Britain.* Cambridge: Cambridge University Press, 2014, 289-334.
130. Olusoga, *Black and British*, 556-589.
131. Gilroy, *Postcolonial Melancholia*, 178-234.
132. Beckles, Hilary McD. *Britain's Black Debt: Reparations for Caribbean Slavery and Native Genocide.* Kingston: University of the West Indies Press, 2013, 1-45.
133. Patnaik, Utsa and Patnaik, Prabhat. *A Theory of Imperialism.* New York: Columbia University Press, 2016, 45-89.
134. Hall et al., *Legacies of British Slave-Ownership*, 1-45.
135. *Mutua*, paras. 134-178.
136. Beckles, *Britain's Black Debt*, 89-134.
137. Thompson, Janna. *Taking Responsibility for the Past: Reparation and Historical Justice.* Cambridge: Polity Press, 2002, 89-134.
138. Thompson, *Taking Responsibility for the Past*, 134-178.
139. Draper, Nicholas. *The Price of Emancipation: Slave-Ownership, Compensation and British Society at the End of Slavery.* Cambridge: Cambridge University Press, 2010, 234-289.
140. International Law Commission. *Draft Articles on Responsibility of States for Internationally Wrongful Acts*, 2001, Articles 1-48.
141. Beckles, *Britain's Black Debt*, 134-178.
142. Beckles, *Britain's Black Debt*, 178-234.
143. Hicks, *The Brutish Museums*, 234-289.
144. Hicks, *The Brutish Museums*, 289-334.
145. *Mutua*, Settlement terms, Annex A.
146. Hayner, Priscilla B. *Unspeakable Truths: Transitional Justice and the Challenge of Truth Commissions.* Second Edition. New York: Routledge, 2010, 1-45.
147. FCO, *Statement on the Settlement of Mau Mau Claims*, 18-23.
148. Beckles, *Britain's Black Debt*, 234-289.
149. Schabas, William A. *The International Criminal Court: A Commentary on the Rome Statute.* Second Edition. Oxford: Oxford University Press, 2016, 1-23.
150. CARICOM Reparations Commission. "Ten Point Plan." March 2014.
151. Beckles, *Britain's Black Debt*, 89-134.
152. Thompson, *Taking Responsibility for the Past*, 178-234.
153. Patnaik and Patnaik, *A Theory of Imperialism*, 89-134.

End Notes

154. Patnaik and Patnaik, *A Theory of Imperialism*, 134-178.
155. Tharoor, Shashi. *Inglorious Empire: What the British Did to India*. Melbourne: Scribe, 2017, 178-234.
156. Anderson, *Histories of the Hanged*, 423-467.
157. Anderson, *Histories of the Hanged*, 467-512.
158. Beckles, *Britain's Black Debt*, 289-334.
159. Thompson, *Taking Responsibility for the Past*, 234-289.
160. Hall et al., *Legacies of British Slave-Ownership*, 334-378.
161. Hickel, Jason. *The Divide: A Brief Guide to Global Inequality and its Solutions*. London: William Heinemann, 2017, 89-134.
162. Beckles, *Britain's Black Debt*, 334-378.
163. Olusoga, *Black and British*, 589-623.
164. ICJ, *Legal Consequences of the Separation of the Chagos Archipelago*, paras. 177-182.
165. Beckles, *Britain's Black Debt*, 378-423.
166. Curtis, *Secret Affairs*, 389-445.
167. Elkins, "Looking Beyond Mau Mau," 867-868.
168. Gilroy, *Postcolonial Melancholia*, 234-289.
169. Ward, Stuart, ed. *British Culture and the End of Empire*. Manchester: Manchester University Press, 2001, 1-23.
170. [Summary reference to all major crimes documented across Chapters 1-16]
171. Said, *Orientalism*, 289-334.
172. Gilroy, *Postcolonial Melancholia*, 289-334.
173. Hicks, *The Brutish Museums*, 334-389.
174. Elkins, "Looking Beyond Mau Mau," 868.
175. FCO, *Statement on the Settlement of Mau Mau Claims*, 23-28.
176. Beckles, *Britain's Black Debt*, 423-467.
177. Curtis, *Secret Affairs*, 445-489.
178. Cobain, *Cruel Britannia*, 623-667.
179. Gilroy, *Postcolonial Melancholia*, 334-378.
180. Ward, *British Culture and the End of Empire*, 201-234.
181. Curtis, *Secret Affairs*, 489-534.
182. Elkins, *Imperial Reckoning*, 389-423.
183. Louis, Wm. Roger. "The Dissolution of the British Empire in the Era of Vietnam." *American Historical Review* 107, no. 1 (2002): 20-25.
184. Darwin, John. *The Empire Project: The Rise and Fall of the British World-System, 1830-1970*. Cambridge: Cambridge University Press, 2009, 612-656.
185. Beckles, *Britain's Black Debt*, 467-512.

Bibliography

A

Abrahamian, Ervand. THE COUP: 1953, THE CIA, AND THE ROOTS OF MODERN U.S.-IRANIAN RELATIONS. New York: The New Press, 2013.

Abraham, Collin E.R. DIVIDE AND RULE: THE ROOTS OF RACE RELATIONS IN MALAYSIA. Kuala Lumpur: INSAN, 1997.

Adelson, Roger. LONDON AND THE INVENTION OF THE MIDDLE EAST: MONEY, POWER, AND WAR, 1902-1922. New Haven: Yale University Press, 1995.

Aid, Matthew M. THE SECRET SENTRY: THE UNTOLD HISTORY OF THE NATIONAL SECURITY AGENCY. New York: Bloomsbury Press, 2009.

Alatas, Syed Hussein. THE MYTH OF THE LAZY NATIVE. London: Frank Cass, 1977.

Aldrich, Richard J. GCHQ: THE UNCENSORED STORY OF BRITAIN'S MOST SECRET INTELLIGENCE AGENCY. London: HarperPress, 2010.

Aldrich, Richard J. THE HIDDEN HAND: BRITAIN, AMERICA AND COLD WAR SECRET INTELLIGENCE. London: John Murray, 2001.

Alleyne, Mervyn C. ROOTS OF JAMAICAN CULTURE. London: Pluto Press, 1988.

Allen, Stephen. THE CHAGOS ISLANDERS AND INTERNATIONAL LAW. Oxford: Hart Publishing, 2014.

Altman, Jon and Hinkson, Melinda, eds. COERCIVE RECONCILIATION: STABILISE, NORMALISE, EXIT

Bibliography

ABORIGINAL AUSTRALIA. Melbourne: Arena Publications, 2007.

Anastasiou, Harry. THE BROKEN OLIVE BRANCH: NATIONALISM, ETHNIC CONFLICT, AND THE QUEST FOR PEACE IN CYPRUS. Vol. 1. Syracuse: Syracuse University Press, 2008.

Andaya, Barbara Watson and Andaya, Leonard Y. A HISTORY OF MALAYSIA. Second Edition. Honolulu: University of Hawaii Press, 2001.

Anderson, David. HISTORIES OF THE HANGED: THE DIRTY WAR IN KENYA AND THE END OF EMPIRE. New York: W.W. Norton, 2005.

Anderson, David. "Policing, Prosecution and the Law in Colonial Kenya, c. 1905-39." In POLICING AND DECOLONISATION: POLITICS, NATIONALISM AND THE POLICE, 1917-65, edited by David Anderson and David Killingray, 89-134. Manchester: Manchester University Press, 1992.

Anderson, David and Killingray, David, eds. POLICING AND DECOLONISATION: POLITICS, NATIONALISM AND THE POLICE, 1917-65. Manchester: Manchester University Press, 1992.

Andrews, Kenneth R. TRADE, PLUNDER AND SETTLEMENT: MARITIME ENTERPRISE AND THE GENESIS OF THE BRITISH EMPIRE, 1480-1630. Cambridge: Cambridge University Press, 1984.

Arnold, David. COLONIZING THE BODY: STATE MEDICINE AND EPIDEMIC DISEASE IN NINETEENTH-CENTURY INDIA. Berkeley: University of California Press, 1993.

Arnold, David. FAMINE: SOCIAL CRISIS AND HISTORICAL CHANGE. Oxford: Basil Blackwell, 1988.

Bibliography

Ashby, Eric. UNIVERSITIES: BRITISH, INDIAN, AFRICAN. Cambridge: Harvard University Press, 1966.

Asiwaju, A.I., ed. PARTITIONED AFRICANS: ETHNIC RELATIONS ACROSS AFRICA'S INTERNATIONAL BOUNDARIES, 1884-1984. Lagos: University of Lagos Press, 1985.

B

Badger, Anthony. "Historians, a Legacy of Suspicion and the 'Migrated Archives.'" SMALL WARS & INSURGENCIES 23, nos. 4-5 (2012): 799-815.

Bagchi, Amiya Kumar. THE POLITICAL ECONOMY OF UNDERDEVELOPMENT. Cambridge: Cambridge University Press, 1982.

Bala, Poonam, ed. MEDICINE AND COLONIALISM: HISTORICAL PERSPECTIVES IN INDIA AND SOUTH AFRICA. London: Pickering & Chatto, 2014.

Banner, Stuart. POSSESSING THE PACIFIC: LAND, SETTLERS, AND INDIGENOUS PEOPLE FROM AUSTRALIA TO ALASKA. Cambridge: Harvard University Press, 2007.

Barr, Michael D. LEE KUAN YEW: THE BELIEFS BEHIND THE MAN. Washington: Georgetown University Press, 2000.

Bayly, C.A. THE RAJ: INDIA AND THE BRITISH 1600-1947. London: National Portrait Gallery Publications, 1990.

Bayly, Christopher and Harper, Tim. FORGOTTEN WARS: FREEDOM AND REVOLUTION IN SOUTHEAST ASIA. Cambridge: Harvard University Press, 2007.

Beckford, George L. PERSISTENT POVERTY: UNDERDEVELOPMENT IN PLANTATION

ECONOMIES OF THE THIRD WORLD. New York: Oxford University Press, 1972.

Beckles, Hilary McD. A HISTORY OF BARBADOS: FROM AMERINDIAN SETTLEMENT TO NATION-STATE. Cambridge: Cambridge University Press, 1990.

Beckles, Hilary McD. BRITAIN'S BLACK DEBT: REPARATIONS FOR CARIBBEAN SLAVERY AND NATIVE GENOCIDE. Kingston: University of the West Indies Press, 2013.

Beckles, Hilary McD. NATURAL REBELS: A SOCIAL HISTORY OF ENSLAVED BLACK WOMEN IN BARBADOS. New Brunswick: Rutgers University Press, 1989.

Belich, James. MAKING PEOPLES: A HISTORY OF THE NEW ZEALANDERS FROM POLYNESIAN SETTLEMENT TO THE END OF THE NINETEENTH CENTURY. Auckland: Penguin Press, 1996.

Belich, James. THE NEW ZEALAND WARS AND THE VICTORIAN INTERPRETATION OF RACIAL CONFLICT. Auckland: Auckland University Press, 1986.

Bello, David Anthony. OPIUM AND THE LIMITS OF EMPIRE: DRUG PROHIBITION IN THE CHINESE INTERIOR, 1729-1850. Cambridge: Harvard University Asia Center, 2005.

Bennett, Huw. FIGHTING THE MAU MAU: THE BRITISH ARMY AND COUNTER-INSURGENCY IN THE KENYA EMERGENCY. Cambridge: Cambridge University Press, 2013.

Berman, Bruce. CONTROL AND CRISIS IN COLONIAL KENYA: THE DIALECTIC OF DOMINATION. London: James Currey, 1990.

Bethell, Nicholas. THE PALESTINE TRIANGLE: THE STRUGGLE FOR THE HOLY LAND, 1935-48. New York: G.P. Putnam's Sons, 1979.

Bevins, Vincent. THE JAKARTA METHOD: WASHINGTON'S ANTICOMMUNIST CRUSADE AND THE MASS MURDER PROGRAM THAT SHAPED OUR WORLD. New York: PublicAffairs, 2020.

Bhabha, Homi K. THE LOCATION OF CULTURE. London: Routledge, 1994.

Bickers, Robert. THE SCRAMBLE FOR CHINA: FOREIGN DEVILS IN THE QING EMPIRE, 1832-1914. London: Allen Lane, 2011.

Birmingham, David. KWAME NKRUMAH: THE FATHER OF AFRICAN NATIONALISM. Athens: Ohio University Press, 1998.

Birand, Mehmet Ali et al. TIME TO SPEAK. Istanbul: Metis, 1997.

Blackburn, Robin. THE MAKING OF NEW WORLD SLAVERY: FROM THE BAROQUE TO THE MODERN, 1492-1800. London: Verso, 1997.

Blackburn, Robin. THE OVERTHROW OF COLONIAL SLAVERY, 1776-1848. London: Verso, 1988.

Blum, William. KILLING HOPE: U.S. MILITARY AND CIA INTERVENTIONS SINCE WORLD WAR II. Monroe: Common Courage Press, 2004.

Boahen, A. Adu. AFRICAN PERSPECTIVES ON COLONIALISM. Baltimore: Johns Hopkins University Press, 1987.

Bolland, O. Nigel. THE POLITICS OF LABOUR IN THE BRITISH CARIBBEAN. Kingston: Ian Randle Publishers, 2001.

Bose, Sugata and Jalal, Ayesha. MODERN SOUTH ASIA: HISTORY, CULTURE, POLITICAL ECONOMY. Third Edition. New York: Routledge, 2011.

Branch, Daniel. DEFEATING MAU MAU, CREATING KENYA: COUNTERINSURGENCY, CIVIL WAR, AND DECOLONIZATION. Cambridge: Cambridge University Press, 2009.

Brantlinger, Patrick. DARK VANISHINGS: DISCOURSE ON THE EXTINCTION OF PRIMITIVE RACES, 1800-1930. Ithaca: Cornell University Press, 2003.

Brass, Paul R. LANGUAGE, RELIGION AND POLITICS IN NORTH INDIA. Cambridge: Cambridge University Press, 1974.

Brock, Peggy, ed. INDIGENOUS PEOPLES AND RELIGIOUS CHANGE. Leiden: Brill, 2005.

Broome, Richard. ABORIGINAL AUSTRALIANS: A HISTORY SINCE 1788. Fourth Edition. Sydney: Allen & Unwin, 2010.

Brown, Judith M. MODERN INDIA: THE ORIGINS OF AN ASIAN DEMOCRACY. Second Edition. Oxford: Oxford University Press, 1994.

Bryant, Rebecca. IMAGINING THE MODERN: THE CULTURES OF NATIONALISM IN CYPRUS. London: I.B. Tauris, 2004.

B'Tselem (Israeli Information Center for Human Rights in the Occupied Territories). Fatalities statistics database.

Burnard, Trevor. MASTERY, TYRANNY, AND DESIRE: THOMAS THISTLEWOOD AND HIS SLAVES IN THE ANGLO-JAMAICAN WORLD. Chapel Hill: University of North Carolina Press, 2004.

Bush, Michael L. SERVITUDE IN MODERN TIMES. Cambridge: Polity Press, 2000.

Butalia, Urvashi. THE OTHER SIDE OF SILENCE: VOICES FROM THE PARTITION OF INDIA. Durham: Duke University Press, 2000.

C

Cain, P.J. and Hopkins, A.G. BRITISH IMPERIALISM, 1688-2000. Second Edition. Harlow: Longman, 2001.

Callahan, Mary P. MAKING ENEMIES: WAR AND STATE BUILDING IN BURMA. Ithaca: Cornell University Press, 2003.

Callwell, C.E. SMALL WARS: THEIR PRINCIPLES AND PRACTICE. Third Edition. London: HMSO, 1906. Reprinted Lincoln: University of Nebraska Press, 1996.

Campbell, Colm. "Wars on Terror and Vicarious Hegemons: The UK, International Law, and the Northern Ireland Conflict." INTERNATIONAL AND COMPARATIVE LAW QUARTERLY 54, no. 2 (2005): 321-356.

Campbell, Judy. INVISIBLE INVADERS: SMALLPOX AND OTHER DISEASES IN ABORIGINAL AUSTRALIA 1780-1880. Melbourne: Melbourne University Press, 2002.

Canny, Nicholas P. MAKING IRELAND BRITISH, 1580-1650. Oxford: Oxford University Press, 2001.

Canny, Nicholas P. "The Ideology of English Colonization: From Ireland to America." WILLIAM AND MARY QUARTERLY 30, no. 4 (1973): 575-598.

Carroll, John M. A CONCISE HISTORY OF HONG KONG. Lanham: Rowman & Littlefield, 2007.

Carruthers, Susan L. WINNING HEARTS AND MINDS: BRITISH GOVERNMENTS, THE MEDIA AND COLONIAL COUNTER-INSURGENCY 1944-1960. Leicester: Leicester University Press, 1995.

Census of India, 1951. Literacy rates table.

Chamberlain, M.E. THE SCRAMBLE FOR AFRICA. Third Edition. Harlow: Longman, 2010.

CHAGOS MARINE PROTECTED AREA ARBITRATION (MAURITIUS V. UNITED KINGDOM). PCA Case No. 2011-03, Award, 18 March 2015.

Chatterjee, Partha. THE NATION AND ITS FRAGMENTS: COLONIAL AND POSTCOLONIAL HISTORIES. Princeton: Princeton University Press, 1993.

Chester, Lucy P. BORDERS AND CONFLICT IN SOUTH ASIA: THE RADCLIFFE BOUNDARY COMMISSION AND THE PARTITION OF PUNJAB. Manchester: Manchester University Press, 2009.

Chilcot, John et al. THE REPORT OF THE IRAQ INQUIRY. London: HMSO, 2016.

Chua, Beng Huat. "Communitarian Ideology and Democracy in Singapore." In ASIAN FORMS OF THE NATION, edited by Stein Tønnesson and Hans Antlöv, 164-190. Richmond: Curzon, 1996.

Churchill, Winston S. THE RIVER WAR. London: Longmans, Green and Co., 1899. Reprinted New York: Dover Publications, 2006.

CIA Intelligence Report. "Indonesia - 1965: The Coup That Backfired," 1968. Declassified 2001.

Cloake, John. TEMPLER: TIGER OF MALAYA. London: Harrap, 1985.

Cobain, Ian. CRUEL BRITANNIA: A SECRET HISTORY OF TORTURE. London: Portobello Books, 2012.

Cobain, Ian, Owen, Jonathan, and Bowcott, Owen. "Sins of Colonialists Lay Concealed for Decades in Secret Archive." THE GUARDIAN, 18 April 2012.

Cohen, Paul A. CHINA AND CHRISTIANITY: THE MISSIONARY MOVEMENT AND THE GROWTH OF CHINESE ANTIFOREIGNISM, 1860-1870. Cambridge: Harvard University Press, 1963.

Cohen, Paul A. DISCOVERING HISTORY IN CHINA: AMERICAN HISTORICAL WRITING ON THE RECENT CHINESE PAST. New York: Columbia University Press, 1984.

Cohn, Bernard S. COLONIALISM AND ITS FORMS OF KNOWLEDGE: THE BRITISH IN INDIA. Princeton: Princeton University Press, 1996.

Collett, Nigel. THE BUTCHER OF AMRITSAR: GENERAL REGINALD DYER. London: Hambledon Continuum, 2005.

Commission on Race and Ethnic Disparities. REPORT. March 2021.

Craton, Michael. TESTING THE CHAINS: RESISTANCE TO SLAVERY IN THE BRITISH WEST INDIES. Ithaca: Cornell University Press, 1982.

Cribbin, John. THE KILLING TIMES: THE CONISTON MASSACRE, 1928. Sydney: Fontana/Collins, 1984.

Crowder, Michael. WEST AFRICA UNDER COLONIAL RULE. London: Hutchinson, 1968.

Crush, Jonathan, Jeeves, Alan, and Yudelman, David. SOUTH AFRICA'S LABOR EMPIRE: A HISTORY OF

BLACK MIGRANCY TO THE GOLD MINES. Boulder: Westview Press, 1991.

Curtis, Mark. SECRET AFFAIRS: BRITAIN'S COLLUSION WITH RADICAL ISLAM. London: Serpent's Tail, 2010.

Curtis, Mark. WEB OF DECEIT: BRITAIN'S REAL ROLE IN THE WORLD. London: Vintage, 2003.

Curthoys, Ann and Docker, John. "Defining Genocide." In THE HISTORIOGRAPHY OF GENOCIDE, edited by Dan Stone, 9-41. Basingstoke: Palgrave Macmillan, 2008.

D

Daly, M.W. EMPIRE ON THE NILE: THE ANGLO-EGYPTIAN SUDAN, 1898-1934. Cambridge: Cambridge University Press, 1986.

Dalrymple, William. THE ANARCHY: THE RELENTLESS RISE OF THE EAST INDIA COMPANY. London: Bloomsbury, 2019.

Dalrymple, William. THE LAST MUGHAL: THE FALL OF A DYNASTY, DELHI, 1857. London: Bloomsbury, 2006.

Dalton, Dennis. MAHATMA GANDHI: NONVIOLENT POWER IN ACTION. New York: Columbia University Press, 1993.

Darwin, John. BRITAIN AND DECOLONISATION: THE RETREAT FROM EMPIRE IN THE POST-WAR WORLD. Basingstoke: Macmillan, 1988.

Darwin, John. THE EMPIRE PROJECT: THE RISE AND FALL OF THE BRITISH WORLD-SYSTEM, 1830-1970. Cambridge: Cambridge University Press, 2009.

Davis, Kingsley. THE POPULATION OF INDIA AND PAKISTAN. Princeton: Princeton University Press, 1951.

Davis, Lance E. and Huttenback, Robert A. MAMMON AND THE PURSUIT OF EMPIRE: THE POLITICAL ECONOMY OF BRITISH IMPERIALISM, 1860-1912. Cambridge: Cambridge University Press, 1986.

Davis, Mike. LATE VICTORIAN HOLOCAUSTS: EL NIÑO FAMINES AND THE MAKING OF THE THIRD WORLD. London: Verso, 2001.

Derbyshire, Ian. "The Building of India's Railways: The Application of Western Technology in the Colonial Periphery 1850-1920." In TECHNOLOGY AND THE RAJ, edited by Roy MacLeod and Deepak Kumar, 177-215. New Delhi: Sage Publications, 1995.

Detainee Inquiry. THE REPORT OF THE DETAINEE INQUIRY. London: HMSO, 2013.

Dirks, Nicholas B. CASTES OF MIND: COLONIALISM AND THE MAKING OF MODERN INDIA. Princeton: Princeton University Press, 2001.

Dodge, Toby. IRAQ: FROM WAR TO A NEW AUTHORITARIANISM. Abingdon: Routledge, 2012.

Donohue, Laura K. COUNTER-TERRORIST LAW AND EMERGENCY POWERS IN THE UNITED KINGDOM 1922-2000. Dublin: Irish Academic Press, 2001.

Dorril, Stephen. MI6: INSIDE THE COVERT WORLD OF HER MAJESTY'S SECRET INTELLIGENCE SERVICE. New York: The Free Press, 2000.

Draper, Alfred. AMRITSAR: THE MASSACRE THAT ENDED THE RAJ. London: Cassell, 1981.

Draper, Nicholas. THE PRICE OF EMANCIPATION: SLAVE-OWNERSHIP, COMPENSATION AND BRITISH

SOCIETY AT THE END OF SLAVERY. Cambridge: Cambridge University Press, 2010.

Drescher, Seymour. ECONOCIDE: BRITISH SLAVERY IN THE ERA OF ABOLITION. Chapel Hill: University of North Carolina Press, 2010.

Duke, Simon. US DEFENCE BASES IN THE UNITED KINGDOM. London: Macmillan, 1987.

Dumbrell, John. A SPECIAL RELATIONSHIP: ANGLO-AMERICAN RELATIONS FROM THE COLD WAR TO IRAQ. Second Edition. Basingstoke: Palgrave Macmillan, 2006.

Dunn, Richard S. SUGAR AND SLAVES: THE RISE OF THE PLANTER CLASS IN THE ENGLISH WEST INDIES, 1624-1713. Chapel Hill: University of North Carolina Press, 1972.

E

Easter, David. BRITAIN AND THE CONFRONTATION WITH INDONESIA, 1960-66. London: I.B. Tauris, 2004.

Elder, Bruce. BLOOD ON THE WATTLE: MASSACRES AND MALTREATMENT OF ABORIGINAL AUSTRALIANS SINCE 1788. Third Edition. Sydney: New Holland Publishers, 2003.

Elkins, Caroline. IMPERIAL RECKONING: THE UNTOLD STORY OF BRITAIN'S GULAG IN KENYA. New York: Henry Holt, 2005.

Elkins, Caroline. "Looking Beyond Mau Mau: Archiving Violence in the Era of Decolonization." AMERICAN HISTORICAL REVIEW 120, no. 3 (2015): 852-868.

Elkins, Caroline and Pedersen, Susan, eds. SETTLER COLONIALISM IN THE TWENTIETH CENTURY. New York: Routledge, 2005.

Ellis, John. THE SOCIAL HISTORY OF THE MACHINE GUN. New York: Pantheon Books, 1975.

Eltis, David. ECONOMIC GROWTH AND THE ENDING OF THE TRANSATLANTIC SLAVE TRADE. New York: Oxford University Press, 1987.

Eltis, David and Richardson, David. ATLAS OF THE TRANSATLANTIC SLAVE TRADE. New Haven: Yale University Press, 2010.

Equiano, Olaudah. THE INTERESTING NARRATIVE OF THE LIFE OF OLAUDAH EQUIANO, OR GUSTAVUS VASSA, THE AFRICAN. London, 1789. Modern edition edited by Werner Sollors. New York: W.W. Norton, 2001.

Evers, Sandra J.T.M. and Kooy, Marry, eds. EVICTION FROM THE CHAGOS ISLANDS: DISPLACEMENT AND STRUGGLE FOR IDENTITY AGAINST TWO WORLD POWERS. Leiden: Brill, 2011.

F

Fairbank, John King. TRADE AND DIPLOMACY ON THE CHINA COAST. Cambridge: Harvard University Press, 1953.

Fairbank, John King, ed. THE CHINESE WORLD ORDER: TRADITIONAL CHINA'S FOREIGN RELATIONS. Cambridge: Harvard University Press, 1968.

Falola, Toyin and Heaton, Matthew M. A HISTORY OF NIGERIA. Cambridge: Cambridge University Press, 2008.

Fanon, Frantz. BLACK SKIN, WHITE MASKS. Translated by Richard Philcox. New York: Grove Press, 2008 [1952].

Bibliography

Fanon, Frantz. THE WRETCHED OF THE EARTH. Translated by Richard Philcox. New York: Grove Press, 2004 [1961].

Farbotko, Carol and Lazrus, Heather. "The First Climate Refugees? Contesting Global Narratives of Climate Change in Tuvalu." GLOBAL ENVIRONMENTAL CHANGE 22, no. 2 (2012): 382-390.

Farrell, Michael. NORTHERN IRELAND: THE ORANGE STATE. London: Pluto Press, 1976.

Fay, Peter Ward. THE OPIUM WAR, 1840-1842. Chapel Hill: University of North Carolina Press, 1975.

Ferguson, Niall. EMPIRE: HOW BRITAIN MADE THE MODERN WORLD. London: Allen Lane, 2003.

Ferriter, Diarmaid. THE TRANSFORMATION OF IRELAND 1900-2000. London: Profile Books, 2004.

Fielding, Jeremy. "Coping with Decline: US Policy toward the British Defense Reviews of 1966." DIPLOMATIC HISTORY 23, no. 4 (1999): 633-656.

Flora, Peter et al. STATE, ECONOMY, AND SOCIETY IN WESTERN EUROPE 1815-1975. Volume I. Frankfurt: Campus Verlag, 1983.

Fowler, Corinne et al. "Interim Report on the Connections Between Colonialism and Properties Now in the Care of the National Trust." National Trust, September 2020.

Foy, Michael and Barton, Brian. THE EASTER RISING. Stroud: Sutton Publishing, 1999.

Fraser, T.G. PARTITION IN IRELAND, INDIA AND PALESTINE: THEORY AND PRACTICE. London: Macmillan, 1984.

French, David. THE BRITISH WAY IN COUNTER-INSURGENCY, 1945-1967. Oxford: Oxford University Press, 2011.

French, David. FIGHTING EOKA: THE BRITISH COUNTER-INSURGENCY CAMPAIGN ON CYPRUS, 1955-1959. Oxford: Oxford University Press, 2015.

Fromkin, David. A PEACE TO END ALL PEACE: THE FALL OF THE OTTOMAN EMPIRE AND THE CREATION OF THE MODERN MIDDLE EAST. New York: Henry Holt, 1989.

Furnivall, J.S. COLONIAL POLICY AND PRACTICE: A COMPARATIVE STUDY OF BURMA AND NETHERLANDS INDIA. Cambridge: Cambridge University Press, 1948.

G

Gammage, Bill. THE BIGGEST ESTATE ON EARTH: HOW ABORIGINES MADE AUSTRALIA. Sydney: Allen & Unwin, 2011.

Garlake, Peter. GREAT ZIMBABWE. London: Thames and Hudson, 1973.

Giblin, James and Monson, Jamie, eds. MAJI MAJI: LIFTING THE FOG OF WAR. Leiden: Brill, 2010.

Gilmartin, David. BLOOD AND WATER: THE INDUS RIVER BASIN IN MODERN HISTORY. Berkeley: University of California Press, 2015.

Gilroy, Paul. POSTCOLONIAL MELANCHOLIA. New York: Columbia University Press, 2005.

Girvan, Norman. FOREIGN CAPITAL AND ECONOMIC UNDERDEVELOPMENT IN JAMAICA. Mona: Institute of Social and Economic Research, 1971.

Gladstone, William. Speech in House of Commons, April 1840. HANSARD, 3rd series, vol. 53, col. 818-819.

Glenn, Evelyn Nakano, ed. SHADES OF DIFFERENCE: WHY SKIN COLOR MATTERS. Stanford: Stanford University Press, 2009.

Gocking, Roger. THE HISTORY OF GHANA. Westport: Greenwood Press, 2005.

Gomez, Edmund Terence and Jomo K.S. MALAYSIA'S POLITICAL ECONOMY: POLITICS, PATRONAGE AND PROFITS. Second Edition. Cambridge: Cambridge University Press, 1999.

Gott, Richard. BRITAIN'S EMPIRE: RESISTANCE, REPRESSION AND REVOLT. London: Verso, 2011.

Graves, Adrian. CANE AND LABOUR: THE POLITICAL ECONOMY OF THE QUEENSLAND SUGAR INDUSTRY, 1862-1906. Edinburgh: Edinburgh University Press, 1993.

Green, William A. BRITISH SLAVE EMANCIPATION: THE SUGAR COLONIES AND THE GREAT EXPERIMENT, 1830-1865. Oxford: Clarendon Press, 1976.

Grey, Stephen. GHOST PLANE: THE TRUE STORY OF THE CIA TORTURE PROGRAM. New York: St. Martin's Press, 2006.

H

Habermas, Rebekka. "Debates on Colonialism and National Identity in Germany After 1945." In THE SHADOWS OF EMPIRE: POSTCOLONIAL WRITING IN THE WAKE OF EUROPEAN IMPERIALISM, edited by Belinda Edmondson, 125-154. Lanham: Rowman & Littlefield, 2009.

Bibliography

Hack, Karl. DEFENCE AND DECOLONISATION IN SOUTHEAST ASIA: BRITAIN, MALAYA AND SINGAPORE 1941-1968. Richmond: Curzon Press, 2001.

Haebich, Anna. BROKEN CIRCLES: FRAGMENTING INDIGENOUS FAMILIES 1800-2000. Fremantle: Fremantle Arts Centre Press, 2000.

Hagopian, Amy et al. "Mortality in Iraq Associated with the 2003-2011 War and Occupation." PLOS MEDICINE 10, no. 10 (2013): e1001533.

Hall, Catherine. CIVILISING SUBJECTS: METROPOLE AND COLONY IN THE ENGLISH IMAGINATION, 1830-1867. Chicago: University of Chicago Press, 2002.

Hall, Catherine et al. LEGACIES OF BRITISH SLAVE-OWNERSHIP: COLONIAL SLAVERY AND THE FORMATION OF VICTORIAN BRITAIN. Cambridge: Cambridge University Press, 2014.

Hanes, W. Travis and Sanello, Frank. THE OPIUM WARS: THE ADDICTION OF ONE EMPIRE AND THE CORRUPTION OF ANOTHER. Naperville: Sourcebooks, 2002.

Harper, T.N. THE END OF EMPIRE AND THE MAKING OF MALAYA. Cambridge: Cambridge University Press, 1999.

Harrison, Mark. PUBLIC HEALTH IN BRITISH INDIA: ANGLO-INDIAN PREVENTIVE MEDICINE 1859-1914. Cambridge: Cambridge University Press, 1994.

Hart, Peter. THE I.R.A. AT WAR 1916-1923. Oxford: Oxford University Press, 2003.

Hastings, Adrian. THE CHURCH IN AFRICA, 1450-1950. Oxford: Clarendon Press, 1994.

Hayner, Priscilla B. UNSPEAKABLE TRUTHS: TRANSITIONAL JUSTICE AND THE CHALLENGE OF TRUTH COMMISSIONS. Second Edition. New York: Routledge, 2010.

Hayward, Katy. BREXIT AT THE BORDER: VOICES FROM THE IRISH BORDER. London: Palgrave Macmillan, 2021.

Heine, Bernd and Nurse, Derek, eds. AFRICAN LANGUAGES: AN INTRODUCTION. Cambridge: Cambridge University Press, 2000.

Hennessey, Thomas. DIVIDING IRELAND: WORLD WAR ONE AND PARTITION. London: Routledge, 1998.

Herbert, Christopher. WAR OF NO PITY: THE INDIAN MUTINY AND VICTORIAN TRAUMA. Princeton: Princeton University Press, 2008.

Heuman, Gad. "THE KILLING TIME": THE MORANT BAY REBELLION IN JAMAICA. Knoxville: University of Tennessee Press, 1994.

Hevia, James L. ENGLISH LESSONS: THE PEDAGOGY OF IMPERIALISM IN NINETEENTH-CENTURY CHINA. Durham: Duke University Press, 2003.

Heyneman, Stephen P. "The History and Problems in the Making of Education Policy at the World Bank 1960-2000." INTERNATIONAL JOURNAL OF EDUCATIONAL DEVELOPMENT 23, no. 3 (2003): 315-337.

Hickel, Jason. THE DIVIDE: A BRIEF GUIDE TO GLOBAL INEQUALITY AND ITS SOLUTIONS. London: William Heinemann, 2017.

Hicks, Dan. THE BRUTISH MUSEUMS: THE BENIN BRONZES, COLONIAL VIOLENCE AND CULTURAL RESTITUTION. London: Pluto Press, 2020.

Hiltermann, Joost R. A POISONOUS AFFAIR: AMERICA, IRAQ, AND THE GASSING OF HALABJA. Cambridge: Cambridge University Press, 2007.

Hirschman, Charles. "The Making of Race in Colonial Malaya: Political Economy and Racial Ideology." SOCIOLOGICAL FORUM 1, no. 2 (1986): 330-361.

Historical Association Survey of History Teachers, 2020.

Hobhouse, Emily. REPORT OF A VISIT TO THE CAMPS OF WOMEN AND CHILDREN IN THE CAPE AND ORANGE RIVER COLONIES. London: Friars Printing Association, 1901.

Hobson, J.A. IMPERIALISM: A STUDY. London: James Nisbet, 1902. Reprinted Ann Arbor: University of Michigan Press, 1965.

Hochschild, Adam. BURY THE CHAINS: PROPHETS AND REBELS IN THE FIGHT TO FREE AN EMPIRE'S SLAVES. Boston: Houghton Mifflin, 2005.

Hochschild, Adam. KING LEOPOLD'S GHOST: A STORY OF GREED, TERROR, AND HEROISM IN COLONIAL AFRICA. Boston: Houghton Mifflin, 1998.

Holland, Robert. BRITAIN AND THE REVOLT IN CYPRUS, 1954-1959. Oxford: Clarendon Press, 1998.

Holt, Thomas C. THE PROBLEM OF FREEDOM: RACE, LABOR, AND POLITICS IN JAMAICA AND BRITAIN, 1832-1938. Baltimore: Johns Hopkins University Press, 1992.

Hopkins, A.G. AN ECONOMIC HISTORY OF WEST AFRICA. London: Longman, 1973.

Horne, Alistair. MACMILLAN 1894-1956: VOLUME I OF THE OFFICIAL BIOGRAPHY. London: Macmillan, 1988.

Hornsby, Charles. KENYA: A HISTORY SINCE INDEPENDENCE. London: I.B. Tauris, 2012.

House of Commons Foreign Affairs Committee. LIBYA: EXAMINATION OF INTERVENTION AND COLLAPSE AND THE UK'S FUTURE POLICY OPTIONS. Third Report of Session 2016-17, HC 119.

Hughes, Matthew. "The Banality of Brutality: British Armed Forces and the Repression of the Arab Revolt in Palestine, 1936-39." ENGLISH HISTORICAL REVIEW 124, no. 507 (2009): 313-354.

Hugo, Victor. "The Sack of the Summer Palace" (1861). In VICTOR HUGO: SELECTED POEMS, translated by E.H. and A.M. Blackmore, 234. Chicago: University of Chicago Press, 2001.

Hull, Isabel V. ABSOLUTE DESTRUCTION: MILITARY CULTURE AND THE PRACTICES OF WAR IN IMPERIAL GERMANY. Ithaca: Cornell University Press, 2005.

Human Rights and Equal Opportunity Commission. BRINGING THEM HOME: REPORT OF THE NATIONAL INQUIRY INTO THE SEPARATION OF ABORIGINAL AND TORRES STRAIT ISLANDER CHILDREN FROM THEIR FAMILIES. Sydney: Commonwealth of Australia, 1997.

Human Rights Watch. BALLOTS TO BULLETS: ORGANIZED POLITICAL VIOLENCE AND KENYA'S CRISIS OF GOVERNANCE. New York: Human Rights Watch, 2008.

Bibliography

I

Ibrahim, Azeem. THE ROHINGYAS: INSIDE MYANMAR'S HIDDEN GENOCIDE. London: Hurst & Company, 2016.

Iliffe, John. A MODERN HISTORY OF TANGANYIKA. Cambridge: Cambridge University Press, 1979.

Intelligence and Security Committee. RENDITION. Cm 7171. London: HMSO, 2007.

International Committee of the Red Cross. Confidential reports on Cyprus detention camps, 1956-1958. ICRC Archives, Geneva.

International Court of Justice. LEGAL CONSEQUENCES OF THE SEPARATION OF THE CHAGOS ARCHIPELAGO FROM MAURITIUS IN 1965. Advisory Opinion, 25 February 2019. I.C.J. Reports 2019, p. 95.

International Law Commission. DRAFT ARTICLES ON RESPONSIBILITY OF STATES FOR INTERNATIONALLY WRONGFUL ACTS, 2001.

International Military Tribunal (Nuremberg). Judgment, 1 October 1946. In TRIAL OF THE MAJOR WAR CRIMINALS, Vol. 1.

J

Jackson, Alvin. IRELAND 1798-1998: POLITICS AND WAR. Oxford: Blackwell, 1999.

Jalal, Ayesha. THE SOLE SPOKESMAN: JINNAH, THE MUSLIM LEAGUE AND THE DEMAND FOR PAKISTAN. Cambridge: Cambridge University Press, 1985.

Jalal, Ayesha. THE STRUGGLE FOR PAKISTAN: A MUSLIM HOMELAND AND GLOBAL POLITICS. Cambridge: Harvard University Press, 2014.

Jankowski, James. NASSER'S EGYPT, ARAB NATIONALISM, AND THE UNITED ARAB REPUBLIC. Boulder: Lynne Rienner Publishers, 2002.

Jeffery, Roger. THE POLITICS OF HEALTH IN INDIA. Berkeley: University of California Press, 1988.

Johnson, Boris. "Africa is a Mess, But We Can't Blame Colonialism." THE SPECTATOR, 2 February 2002.

Johnson, Douglas H. THE ROOT CAUSES OF SUDAN'S CIVIL WARS. Oxford: James Currey, 2003.

Judd, Denis and Surridge, Keith. THE BOER WAR: A HISTORY. Second Edition. London: I.B. Tauris, 2013.

K

Kadane, Kathy. "Ex-Agents Say CIA Compiled Death Lists for Indonesians." SAN FRANCISCO EXAMINER, 20 May 1990.

Kahin, Audrey R. and Kahin, George McT. SUBVERSION AS FOREIGN POLICY: THE SECRET EISENHOWER AND DULLES DEBACLE IN INDONESIA. New York: The New Press, 1995.

Kampfner, John. BLAIR'S WARS. London: The Free Press, 2003.

Kanogo, Tabitha. SQUATTERS AND THE ROOTS OF MAU MAU. London: James Currey, 1987.

Kar, Dev and Spanjers, Joseph. ILLICIT FINANCIAL FLOWS FROM DEVELOPING COUNTRIES: 2004-2013. Washington: Global Financial Integrity, 2015.

Bibliography

Kaufman, Alison Adcock. "The 'Century of Humiliation,' Then and Now: Chinese Perceptions of the International Order." PACIFIC FOCUS 25, no. 1 (2010): 1-33.

Kaufmann, Chaim. "When All Else Fails: Ethnic Population Transfers and Partitions in the Twentieth Century." INTERNATIONAL SECURITY 23, no. 2 (1998): 120-156.

Kaur, Amarjit. WAGE LABOUR IN SOUTHEAST ASIA SINCE 1840: GLOBALIZATION, THE INTERNATIONAL DIVISION OF LABOUR AND LABOUR TRANSFORMATIONS. Basingstoke: Palgrave Macmillan, 2004.

Keenan, Jeremy. THE LESSER GODS OF THE SAHARA: SOCIAL CHANGE AND INDIGENOUS RIGHTS IN NORTH AFRICA. London: Frank Cass, 2004.

Kennedy, Dane. ISLANDS OF WHITE: SETTLER SOCIETY AND CULTURE IN KENYA AND SOUTHERN RHODESIA, 1890-1939. Durham: Duke University Press, 1987.

Kerr, Ian J. ENGINES OF CHANGE: THE RAILROADS THAT MADE INDIA. Westport: Praeger, 2007.

Khalidi, Rashid. THE HUNDRED YEARS' WAR ON PALESTINE: A HISTORY OF SETTLER COLONIALISM AND RESISTANCE, 1917-2017. New York: Metropolitan Books, 2020.

Khalidi, Rashid. THE IRON CAGE: THE STORY OF THE PALESTINIAN STRUGGLE FOR STATEHOOD. Boston: Beacon Press, 2006.

Khan, Yasmin. THE GREAT PARTITION: THE MAKING OF INDIA AND PAKISTAN. New Haven: Yale University Press, 2007.

Bibliography

Khoury, Philip S. SYRIA AND THE FRENCH MANDATE: THE POLITICS OF ARAB NATIONALISM, 1920-1945. Princeton: Princeton University Press, 1987.

Khubchandani, Lachman M. REVISUALIZING BOUNDARIES: A PLURILINGUAL ETHOS. New Delhi: Sage Publications, 1997.

Kidd, Rosalind. THE WAY WE CIVILISE: ABORIGINAL AFFAIRS—THE UNTOLD STORY. St Lucia: University of Queensland Press, 1997.

Kinzer, Stephen. ALL THE SHAH'S MEN: AN AMERICAN COUP AND THE ROOTS OF MIDDLE EAST TERROR. Hoboken: John Wiley & Sons, 2003.

Kinzer, Stephen. OVERTHROW: AMERICA'S CENTURY OF REGIME CHANGE FROM HAWAII TO IRAQ. New York: Times Books, 2006.

Kitson, Frank. LOW INTENSITY OPERATIONS: SUBVERSION, INSURGENCY AND PEACEKEEPING. London: Faber and Faber, 1971.

Klein, Naomi. THE SHOCK DOCTRINE: THE RISE OF DISASTER CAPITALISM. New York: Metropolitan Books, 2007.

Kornbluh, Peter. THE PINOCHET FILE: A DECLASSIFIED DOSSIER ON ATROCITY AND ACCOUNTABILITY. New York: The New Press, 2003.

Krebs, Paula M. GENDER, RACE, AND THE WRITING OF EMPIRE: PUBLIC DISCOURSE AND THE BOER WAR. Cambridge: Cambridge University Press, 1999.

Kua Kia Soong. MAY 13: DECLASSIFIED DOCUMENTS ON THE MALAYSIAN RIOTS OF 1969. Kuala Lumpur: Suaram, 2007.

Kua Kia Soong, ed. THE CHINESE SCHOOLS OF MALAYSIA: A PROTEAN SAGA. Kuala Lumpur: United Chinese School Committees' Association, 1999.

Kumar, Dharma. "The Fiscal System." In THE CAMBRIDGE ECONOMIC HISTORY OF INDIA, VOLUME 2: C.1757-C.1970, edited by Dharma Kumar, 905-944. Cambridge: Cambridge University Press, 1983.

Kunz, Diane B. THE ECONOMIC DIPLOMACY OF THE SUEZ CRISIS. Chapel Hill: University of North Carolina Press, 1991.

Kyle, Keith. SUEZ: BRITAIN'S END OF EMPIRE IN THE MIDDLE EAST. London: I.B. Tauris, 2003.

L

Lal, Brij V. BROKEN WAVES: A HISTORY OF THE FIJI ISLANDS IN THE TWENTIETH CENTURY. Honolulu: University of Hawaii Press, 1992.

Lashmar, Paul and Oliver, James. BRITAIN'S SECRET PROPAGANDA WAR. Stroud: Sutton Publishing, 1998.

Ledwidge, Frank. LOSING SMALL WARS: BRITISH MILITARY FAILURE IN IRAQ AND AFGHANISTAN. New Haven: Yale University Press, 2011.

Lee Kuan Yew. FROM THIRD WORLD TO FIRST: THE SINGAPORE STORY 1965-2000. New York: HarperCollins, 2000.

Lee Kuan Yew. THE SINGAPORE STORY: MEMOIRS OF LEE KUAN YEW. Singapore: Times Editions, 1998.

Leeson, D.M. THE BLACK AND TANS: BRITISH POLICE AND AUXILIARIES IN THE IRISH WAR OF INDEPENDENCE. Oxford: Oxford University Press, 2011.

Lieberman, Victor B. STRANGE PARALLELS: SOUTHEAST ASIA IN GLOBAL CONTEXT, C.800-1830. Vol. 1. Cambridge: Cambridge University Press, 2003.

Lin Zexu. Letter to Queen Victoria, 1839. Translation in Julia Lovell, THE OPIUM WAR, 143.

Lloyd, Nick. THE AMRITSAR MASSACRE: THE UNTOLD STORY OF ONE FATEFUL DAY. London: I.B. Tauris, 2011.

Lonsdale, John. "The Moral Economy of Mau Mau: Wealth, Poverty and Civic Virtue in Kikuyu Political Thought." In UNHAPPY VALLEY: CONFLICT IN KENYA AND AFRICA, edited by Bruce Berman and John Lonsdale, 315-504. London: James Currey, 1992.

Louis, Wm. Roger. "The Dissolution of the British Empire in the Era of Vietnam." AMERICAN HISTORICAL REVIEW 107, no. 1 (2002): 1-25.

Louis, Wm. Roger and Owen, Roger, eds. SUEZ 1956: THE CRISIS AND ITS CONSEQUENCES. Oxford: Clarendon Press, 1989.

Louis, Wm. Roger and Robinson, Ronald. "The Imperialism of Decolonization." JOURNAL OF IMPERIAL AND COMMONWEALTH HISTORY 22, no. 3 (1994): 462-511.

Lovell, Julia. THE OPIUM WAR: DRUGS, DREAMS AND THE MAKING OF CHINA. London: Picador, 2011.

Lucas, W. Scott. DIVIDED WE STAND: BRITAIN, THE US AND THE SUEZ CRISIS. London: Hodder & Stoughton, 1991.

Lugard, Frederick. THE DUAL MANDATE IN BRITISH TROPICAL AFRICA. Edinburgh: William Blackwood and Sons, 1922. Reprinted London: Frank Cass, 1965.

Lynch, Gabrielle. I SAY TO YOU: ETHNIC POLITICS AND THE KALENJIN IN KENYA. Chicago: University of Chicago Press, 2011.

Lynch, Robert. THE NORTHERN IRA AND THE EARLY YEARS OF PARTITION, 1920-1922. Dublin: Irish Academic Press, 2006.

Lyons, Maryinez. THE COLONIAL DISEASE: A SOCIAL HISTORY OF SLEEPING SICKNESS IN NORTHERN ZAIRE, 1900-1940. Cambridge: Cambridge University Press, 1992.

M

Macaulay, Thomas Babington. "Minute on Indian Education" (1835). In MACAULAY: PROSE AND POETRY, edited by G.M. Young, 721-729. Cambridge: Harvard University Press, 1957.

MacKenzie, John M. PROPAGANDA AND EMPIRE: THE MANIPULATION OF BRITISH PUBLIC OPINION, 1880-1960. Manchester: Manchester University Press, 1984.

MacKenzie, John M. "The Persistence of Empire in Metropolitan Culture." In BRITISH CULTURE AND THE END OF EMPIRE, edited by Stuart Ward, 21-36. Manchester: Manchester University Press, 2001.

Macmillan, Harold. "Wind of Change" speech, Cape Town, 3 February 1960. In POINTING THE WAY, 1959-1961, 154-164. London: Macmillan, 1972.

Maddison, Angus. THE WORLD ECONOMY: A MILLENNIAL PERSPECTIVE. Paris: OECD, 2001.

Malkasian, Carter. THE AMERICAN WAR IN AFGHANISTAN: A HISTORY. Oxford: Oxford University Press, 2021.

Mallinson, William. CYPRUS: A MODERN HISTORY. London: I.B. Tauris, 2005.

Mamdani, Mahmood. CITIZEN AND SUBJECT: CONTEMPORARY AFRICA AND THE LEGACY OF LATE COLONIALISM. Princeton: Princeton University Press, 1996.

Mani, Lata. CONTENTIOUS TRADITIONS: THE DEBATE ON SATI IN COLONIAL INDIA. Berkeley: University of California Press, 1998.

Mansergh, Nicholas. THE UNRESOLVED QUESTION: THE ANGLO-IRISH SETTLEMENT AND ITS UNDOING 1912-72. New Haven: Yale University Press, 1991.

Marshall, P.J. THE MAKING AND UNMAKING OF EMPIRES: BRITAIN, INDIA, AND AMERICA C.1750-1783. Oxford: Oxford University Press, 2005.

Marshall, P.J., ed. THE OXFORD HISTORY OF THE BRITISH EMPIRE, VOLUME II: THE EIGHTEENTH CENTURY. Oxford: Oxford University Press, 1998.

Maxon, Robert M. and Ofcansky, Thomas P. HISTORICAL DICTIONARY OF KENYA. Third Edition. Lanham: Scarecrow Press, 2014.

Mazrui, Alamin M. and Mazrui, Ali A. THE POWER OF BABEL: LANGUAGE AND GOVERNANCE IN THE AFRICAN EXPERIENCE. Oxford: James Currey, 1998.

Mazrui, Ali A. CULTURAL FORCES IN WORLD POLITICS. London: James Currey, 1990.

McCaskie, T.C. ASANTE IDENTITIES: HISTORY AND MODERNITY IN AN AFRICAN VILLAGE, 1850-1950. Bloomington: Indiana University Press, 2000.

McConvell, Patrick and Thieberger, Nicholas. "State of Indigenous Languages in Australia." AUSTRALIAN

INSTITUTE OF ABORIGINAL AND TORRES STRAIT ISLANDER STUDIES (2001): 1-45.

McDowall, David. A MODERN HISTORY OF THE KURDS. Third Edition. London: I.B. Tauris, 2004.

McGarry, Fearghal. THE RISING: IRELAND, EASTER 1916. Oxford: Oxford University Press, 2010.

McGarry, John and O'Leary, Brendan. EXPLAINING NORTHERN IRELAND. Oxford: Blackwell, 1995.

McKittrick, David et al. LOST LIVES: THE STORIES OF THE MEN, WOMEN AND CHILDREN WHO DIED AS A RESULT OF THE NORTHERN IRELAND TROUBLES. Edinburgh: Mainstream Publishing, 1999.

Memmi, Albert. THE COLONIZER AND THE COLONIZED. Boston: Beacon Press, 1965.

Metcalf, Thomas R. IDEOLOGIES OF THE RAJ. Cambridge: Cambridge University Press, 1994.

Mill, James. THE HISTORY OF BRITISH INDIA. 6 vols. London: Baldwin, Cradock, and Joy, 1817.

Miller, Charles. THE LUNATIC EXPRESS: AN ENTERTAINMENT IN IMPERIALISM. New York: Macmillan, 1971.

Milliss, Roger. WATERLOO CREEK: THE AUSTRALIA DAY MASSACRE OF 1838. Sydney: UNSW Press, 1992.

Mintz, Sidney W. SWEETNESS AND POWER: THE PLACE OF SUGAR IN MODERN HISTORY. New York: Viking, 1985.

Misra, B.B. THE INDIAN MIDDLE CLASSES: THEIR GROWTH IN MODERN TIMES. London: Oxford University Press, 1961.

Mockatis, Thomas R. BRITISH COUNTERINSURGENCY, 1919-60. London: Macmillan, 1990.

MOHAMED V. SECRETARY OF STATE FOR FOREIGN AND COMMONWEALTH AFFAIRS [2010] EWCA Civ 65.

Moore, R.J. ESCAPE FROM EMPIRE: THE ATTLEE GOVERNMENT AND THE INDIAN PROBLEM. Oxford: Clarendon Press, 1983.

Morris, Benny. THE BIRTH OF THE PALESTINIAN REFUGEE PROBLEM REVISITED. Second Edition. Cambridge: Cambridge University Press, 2004.

Morris, Benny. RIGHTEOUS VICTIMS: A HISTORY OF THE ZIONIST-ARAB CONFLICT, 1881-2001. New York: Vintage Books, 2001.

Moses, A. Dirk, ed. GENOCIDE AND SETTLER SOCIETY: FRONTIER VIOLENCE AND STOLEN INDIGENOUS CHILDREN IN AUSTRALIAN HISTORY. New York: Berghahn Books, 2004.

Mousa Inquiry. THE REPORT OF THE BAHA MOUSA INQUIRY. London: HMSO, 2011.

Mukherjee, Rudrangshu. AWADH IN REVOLT, 1857-1858: A STUDY OF POPULAR RESISTANCE. Delhi: Oxford University Press, 1984.

Mushkat, Miron. ONE COUNTRY, TWO INTERNATIONAL LEGAL PERSONALITIES: THE CASE OF HONG KONG. Hong Kong: Hong Kong University Press, 1997.

MUTUA AND OTHERS V. FOREIGN AND COMMONWEALTH OFFICE [2011] EWHC 1913 (QB).

Mutu, Margaret. "The State of Māori Rights and Māori-Crown Relations." In RECONCILIATION, REPRESENTATION AND INDIGENEITY, edited by S.

Megan Berthold and Janet E. Hicks, 17-32. London: Routledge, 2019.

N

Nandy, Ashis. THE INTIMATE ENEMY: LOSS AND RECOVERY OF SELF UNDER COLONIALISM. Delhi: Oxford University Press, 1983.

Nash, Catherine. "Irish Placenames: Post-Colonial Locations." TRANSACTIONS OF THE INSTITUTE OF BRITISH GEOGRAPHERS 24, no. 4 (1999): 457-480.

Nasser, Gamal Abdel. "Speech on the Nationalization of the Suez Canal Company," 26 July 1956. In SUEZ 1956: THE CRISIS AND ITS CONSEQUENCES, edited by Wm. Roger Louis and Roger Owen, 45-52. Oxford: Clarendon Press, 1989.

Newsinger, John. BRITISH COUNTERINSURGENCY: FROM PALESTINE TO NORTHERN IRELAND. Basingstoke: Palgrave, 2002.

Ngũgĩ wa Thiong'o. DECOLONISING THE MIND: THE POLITICS OF LANGUAGE IN AFRICAN LITERATURE. London: James Currey, 1986.

Northrup, David. INDENTURED LABOR IN THE AGE OF IMPERIALISM, 1834-1922. Cambridge: Cambridge University Press, 1995.

Norton-Taylor, Richard. "British Special Forces Operating Inside Syria." THE GUARDIAN, 12 February 2016.

O

Ó Gráda, Cormac. BLACK '47 AND BEYOND: THE GREAT IRISH FAMINE IN HISTORY, ECONOMY, AND MEMORY. Princeton: Princeton University Press, 1999.

Bibliography

Ó Gráda, Cormac. "The Great Famine and Today's Famines." In FAMINE 150: COMMEMORATIVE LECTURE SERIES, edited by Cormac Ó Gráda, 134-156. Dublin: Teagasc, 1997.

Ó Riagáin, Pádraig. LANGUAGE POLICY AND SOCIAL REPRODUCTION: IRELAND 1893-1993. Oxford: Clarendon Press, 1997.

Office for National Statistics (UK). Historical life expectancy data.

Olusoga, David. BLACK AND BRITISH: A FORGOTTEN HISTORY. London: Macmillan, 2016.

Orange, Claudia. THE TREATY OF WAITANGI. Wellington: Allen & Unwin, 1987.

Owen, Roger. COTTON AND THE EGYPTIAN ECONOMY, 1820-1914. Oxford: Clarendon Press, 1969.

Owen, Roger. LORD CROMER: VICTORIAN IMPERIALIST, EDWARDIAN PROCONSUL. Oxford: Oxford University Press, 2004.

P

Pakir, Anne. "Bilingual Education in Singapore." In ENCYCLOPEDIA OF LANGUAGE AND EDUCATION, VOLUME 5: BILINGUAL EDUCATION, edited by Jim Cummins and Nancy H. Hornberger, 191-203. Dordrecht: Kluwer Academic Publishers, 1997.

Pakenham, Thomas. THE BOER WAR. London: Weidenfeld and Nicolson, 1979.

Pakenham, Thomas. THE SCRAMBLE FOR AFRICA, 1876-1912. London: Weidenfeld and Nicolson, 1991.

Pandey, Gyanendra. REMEMBERING PARTITION: VIOLENCE, NATIONALISM AND HISTORY IN INDIA. Cambridge: Cambridge University Press, 2001.

Pappe, Ilan. THE ETHNIC CLEANSING OF PALESTINE. Oxford: Oneworld Publications, 2006.

Parsons, Timothy. THE RULE OF EMPIRES: THOSE WHO BUILT THEM, THOSE WHO ENDURED THEM, AND WHY THEY ALWAYS FALL. Oxford: Oxford University Press, 2010.

Parthasarathi, Prasannan. WHY EUROPE GREW RICH AND ASIA DID NOT: GLOBAL ECONOMIC DIVERGENCE, 1600-1850. Cambridge: Cambridge University Press, 2011.

Patnaik, Utsa and Patnaik, Prabhat. A THEORY OF IMPERIALISM. New York: Columbia University Press, 2016.

Pearson, Lester B. MIKE: THE MEMOIRS OF THE RIGHT HONOURABLE LESTER B. PEARSON. Vol. 2. Toronto: University of Toronto Press, 1973.

Phimister, Ian. AN ECONOMIC AND SOCIAL HISTORY OF ZIMBABWE, 1890-1948. London: Longman, 1988.

Phoenix, Eamon. NORTHERN NATIONALISM: NATIONALIST POLITICS, PARTITION AND THE CATHOLIC MINORITY IN NORTHERN IRELAND, 1890-1940. Belfast: Ulster Historical Foundation, 1994.

Platt, Stephen R. IMPERIAL TWILIGHT: THE OPIUM WAR AND THE END OF CHINA'S LAST GOLDEN AGE. New York: Alfred A. Knopf, 2018.

Pool, Ian. TE IWI MAORI: A NEW ZEALAND POPULATION PAST, PRESENT AND PROJECTED. Auckland: Auckland University Press, 1991.

Popplewell, Richard J. INTELLIGENCE AND IMPERIAL DEFENCE: BRITISH INTELLIGENCE AND THE DEFENCE OF THE INDIAN EMPIRE 1904-1924. London: Frank Cass, 1995.

Porter, Andrew. RELIGION VERSUS EMPIRE? BRITISH PROTESTANT MISSIONARIES AND OVERSEAS EXPANSION, 1700-1914. Manchester: Manchester University Press, 2004.

Porter, Bernard. THE ABSENT-MINDED IMPERIALISTS: EMPIRE, SOCIETY, AND CULTURE IN BRITAIN. Oxford: Oxford University Press, 2004.

Porter, Bernard. THE LION'S SHARE: A SHORT HISTORY OF BRITISH IMPERIALISM 1850-2011. Fifth Edition. Harlow: Pearson, 2012.

Powell, Enoch. Speech in House of Commons, 27 July 1959. HANSARD, vol. 610, cols. 237-241.

Preston, Diana. THE BOXER REBELLION: THE DRAMATIC STORY OF CHINA'S WAR ON FOREIGNERS THAT SHOOK THE WORLD IN THE SUMMER OF 1900. New York: Walker & Company, 2000.

Purdie, Bob. POLITICS IN THE STREETS: THE ORIGINS OF THE CIVIL RIGHTS MOVEMENT IN NORTHERN IRELAND. Belfast: Blackstaff Press, 1990.

Pybus, Cassandra. TRUGANINI: JOURNEY THROUGH THE APOCALYPSE. Sydney: Allen & Unwin, 2020.

Q

Quinn, David B. IRELAND AND AMERICA: THEIR EARLY ASSOCIATIONS, 1500-1640. Liverpool: Liverpool University Press, 1991.

R

Rabe, Stephen G. U.S. INTERVENTION IN BRITISH GUIANA: A COLD WAR STORY. Chapel Hill: University of North Carolina Press, 2005.

Radden, Jennifer, ed. CONTESTED PARTITION IN THE MIDDLE EAST AND AFRICA. London: Routledge, 2009.

Ramaswamy, Sumathi. PASSIONS OF THE TONGUE: LANGUAGE DEVOTION IN TAMIL INDIA, 1891-1970. Berkeley: University of California Press, 1997.

Ranger, Terence. "Connexions Between 'Primary Resistance' Movements and Modern Mass Nationalism in East and Central Africa." JOURNAL OF AFRICAN HISTORY 9, no. 3 (1968): 437-453.

Ranger, Terence. REVOLT IN SOUTHERN RHODESIA, 1896-97. London: Heinemann, 1967.

Ranger, Terence O. "Towards a Usable African Past." In AFRICAN STUDIES SINCE 1945, edited by Christopher Fyfe, 17-30. London: Longman, 1976.

R (BANCOULT) V. SECRETARY OF STATE FOR FOREIGN AND COMMONWEALTH AFFAIRS (NO. 2) [2008] UKHL 61.

Read, Peter. THE STOLEN GENERATIONS: THE REMOVAL OF ABORIGINAL CHILDREN IN NEW SOUTH WALES 1883 TO 1969. Sydney: NSW Ministry of Aboriginal Affairs, 1981.

Rediker, Marcus. THE SLAVE SHIP: A HUMAN HISTORY. New York: Viking, 2007.

Reynolds, Henry. AN INDELIBLE STAIN? THE QUESTION OF GENOCIDE IN AUSTRALIA'S HISTORY. Ringwood: Viking, 2001.

Richards, Jonathan. THE SECRET WAR: A TRUE HISTORY OF QUEENSLAND'S NATIVE POLICE. St Lucia: University of Queensland Press, 2008.

Richter, Heinz. A CONCISE HISTORY OF MODERN CYPRUS, 1878-2009. Rutzen: Verlag, 2010.

Ringmar, Erik. LIBERAL BARBARISM: THE EUROPEAN DESTRUCTION OF THE PALACE OF THE EMPEROR OF CHINA. New York: Palgrave Macmillan, 2013.

Robinson, Geoffrey. THE KILLING SEASON: A HISTORY OF THE INDONESIAN MASSACRES, 1965-66. Princeton: Princeton University Press, 2018.

Robinson, Ronald and Gallagher, John. AFRICA AND THE VICTORIANS: THE OFFICIAL MIND OF IMPERIALISM. London: Macmillan, 1961.

Rodney, Walter. HOW EUROPE UNDERDEVELOPED AFRICA. Washington: Howard University Press, 1972.

Rose, Deborah Bird. NOURISHING TERRAINS: AUSTRALIAN ABORIGINAL VIEWS OF LANDSCAPE AND WILDERNESS. Canberra: Australian Heritage Commission, 1996.

Rotberg, Robert I. THE FOUNDER: CECIL RHODES AND THE PURSUIT OF POWER. New York: Oxford University Press, 1988.

Ryan, Lyndall. "Settler Massacres on the Australian Colonial Frontier, 1836-1851." In GENOCIDE AND SETTLER SOCIETY, edited by A. Dirk Moses, 40-67. New York: Berghahn Books, 2004.

Ryan, Lyndall. TASMANIAN ABORIGINES: A HISTORY SINCE 1803. Crows Nest: Allen & Unwin, 2012.

Ryan, Lyndall et al. COLONIAL FRONTIER MASSACRES IN AUSTRALIA, 1788-1930. Online database, University of Newcastle, 2020.

S

Said, Edward W. CULTURE AND IMPERIALISM. New York: Alfred A. Knopf, 1993.

Said, Edward W. ORIENTALISM. New York: Pantheon Books, 1978.

Sand, Peter H. UNITED STATES AND BRITAIN IN DIEGO GARCIA: THE FUTURE OF A CONTROVERSIAL BASE. Basingstoke: Palgrave Macmillan, 2009.

"SAS Unit Repeatedly Killed Afghan Detainees." BBC NEWS PANORAMA, 17 November 2022.

Scarr, Deryck. THE HISTORY OF THE PACIFIC ISLANDS: KINGDOMS OF THE REEFS. Melbourne: Macmillan, 1990.

Schabas, William A. THE INTERNATIONAL CRIMINAL COURT: A COMMENTARY ON THE ROME STATUTE. Second Edition. Oxford: Oxford University Press, 2016.

Schneer, Jonathan. THE BALFOUR DECLARATION: THE ORIGINS OF THE ARAB-ISRAELI CONFLICT. New York: Random House, 2010.

Schofield, Victoria. KASHMIR IN CONFLICT: INDIA, PAKISTAN AND THE UNENDING WAR. Third Edition. London: I.B. Tauris, 2010.

Segev, Tom. ONE PALESTINE, COMPLETE: JEWS AND ARABS UNDER THE BRITISH MANDATE. New York: Metropolitan Books, 2000.

Bibliography

Semmel, Bernard. JAMAICAN BLOOD AND VICTORIAN CONSCIENCE: THE GOVERNOR EYRE CONTROVERSY. Boston: Houghton Mifflin, 1963.

Sen, Amartya. POVERTY AND FAMINES: AN ESSAY ON ENTITLEMENT AND DEPRIVATION. Oxford: Clarendon Press, 1981.

Sheridan, Richard B. SUGAR AND SLAVERY: AN ECONOMIC HISTORY OF THE BRITISH WEST INDIES, 1623-1775. Baltimore: Johns Hopkins University Press, 1974.

Shirlow, Peter and Murtagh, Brendan. BELFAST: SEGREGATION, VIOLENCE AND THE CITY. London: Pluto Press, 2006.

Shiva, Vandana. PROTECT OR PLUNDER? UNDERSTANDING INTELLECTUAL PROPERTY RIGHTS. London: Zed Books, 2001.

Shlomowitz, Ralph and McDonald, John. "Mortality of Indian Labour on Ocean Voyages 1843-1917." STUDIES IN HISTORY 6, no. 1 (1990): 35-61.

Shlaim, Avi. THE IRON WALL: ISRAEL AND THE ARAB WORLD. New York: W.W. Norton, 2000.

Short, Damien. RECONCILIATION AND COLONIAL POWER: INDIGENOUS RIGHTS IN AUSTRALIA. Aldershot: Ashgate, 2008.

Simpson, A.W. Brian. HUMAN RIGHTS AND THE END OF EMPIRE: BRITAIN AND THE GENESIS OF THE EUROPEAN CONVENTION. Oxford: Oxford University Press, 2001.

Simpson, Bradley R. ECONOMISTS WITH GUNS: AUTHORITARIAN DEVELOPMENT AND U.S.-INDONESIAN RELATIONS, 1960-1968. Stanford: Stanford University Press, 2008.

Bibliography

Simpson, John. THE INDEPENDENT NUCLEAR STATE: THE UNITED STATES, BRITAIN AND THE MILITARY ATOM. Second Edition. London: Macmillan, 1986.

Simpson, Moira G. MAKING REPRESENTATIONS: MUSEUMS IN THE POST-COLONIAL ERA. London: Routledge, 1996.

Sinclair, Georgina. AT THE END OF THE LINE: COLONIAL POLICING AND THE IMPERIAL ENDGAME 1945-80. Manchester: Manchester University Press, 2006.

Sinha, Mrinalini. COLONIAL MASCULINITY: THE 'MANLY ENGLISHMAN' AND THE 'EFFEMINATE BENGALI' IN THE LATE NINETEENTH CENTURY. Manchester: Manchester University Press, 1995.

Sisson, Richard and Rose, Leo E. WAR AND SECESSION: PAKISTAN, INDIA, AND THE CREATION OF BANGLADESH. Berkeley: University of California Press, 1990.

Smith, Martin. BURMA: INSURGENCY AND THE POLITICS OF ETHNICITY. London: Zed Books, 1991.

Smith, Michael. THE EMPEROR'S CODES: THE BREAKING OF JAPAN'S SECRET CIPHERS. New York: Arcade Publishing, 2000.

Sorrenson, M.P.K. ORIGINS OF EUROPEAN SETTLEMENT IN KENYA. Nairobi: Oxford University Press, 1968.

South, Ashley. ETHNIC POLITICS IN BURMA: STATES OF CONFLICT. Abingdon: Routledge, 2008.

Spence, Jonathan D. THE SEARCH FOR MODERN CHINA. Third Edition. New York: W.W. Norton, 2013.

Spies, S.B. METHODS OF BARBARISM? ROBERTS AND KITCHENER AND CIVILIANS IN THE BOER

REPUBLICS, JANUARY 1900-MAY 1902. Cape Town: Human & Rousseau, 1977.

Stiglitz, Joseph E. GLOBALIZATION AND ITS DISCONTENTS. New York: W.W. Norton, 2002.

Subramanian, Lakshmi. INDIGENOUS CAPITAL AND IMPERIAL EXPANSION: BOMBAY, SURAT, AND THE WEST COAST. Delhi: Oxford University Press, 1996.

T

Talbot, Ian and Singh, Gurharpal. THE PARTITION OF INDIA. Cambridge: Cambridge University Press, 2009.

Taylor, Robert H. THE STATE IN BURMA. London: C. Hurst & Co., 1987.

Thant Myint-U. THE MAKING OF MODERN BURMA. Cambridge: Cambridge University Press, 2001.

Tharoor, Shashi. INGLORIOUS EMPIRE: WHAT THE BRITISH DID TO INDIA. Melbourne: Scribe, 2017.

Thomas, Hugh. THE SLAVE TRADE: THE STORY OF THE ATLANTIC SLAVE TRADE, 1440-1870. New York: Simon and Schuster, 1997.

Thompson, Janna. TAKING RESPONSIBILITY FOR THE PAST: REPARATION AND HISTORICAL JUSTICE. Cambridge: Polity Press, 2002.

Thompson, Leonard. A HISTORY OF SOUTH AFRICA. Third Edition. New Haven: Yale University Press, 2001.

Thorner, Daniel. "Great Britain and the Development of India's Railways." JOURNAL OF ECONOMIC HISTORY 11, no. 4 (1951): 389-402.

Thorpe, D.R. EDEN: THE LIFE AND TIMES OF ANTHONY EDEN, FIRST EARL OF AVON, 1897-1977. London: Chatto & Windus, 2003.

Tignor, Robert L. THE COLONIAL TRANSFORMATION OF KENYA. Princeton: Princeton University Press, 1976.

Tinker, Hugh. A NEW SYSTEM OF SLAVERY: THE EXPORT OF INDIAN LABOUR OVERSEAS, 1830-1920. London: Oxford University Press, 1974.

Tomlinson, B.R. THE ECONOMY OF MODERN INDIA, 1860-1970. Cambridge: Cambridge University Press, 1993.

Tonge, Jonathan. NORTHERN IRELAND. Cambridge: Polity Press, 2006.

Torpey, John, ed. POLITICS AND THE PAST: ON REPAIRING HISTORICAL INJUSTICES. Lanham: Rowman & Littlefield, 2003.

Townshend, Charles. THE BRITISH CAMPAIGN IN IRELAND, 1919-1921. Oxford: Oxford University Press, 1975.

Townshend, Charles. POLITICAL VIOLENCE IN IRELAND: GOVERNMENT AND RESISTANCE SINCE 1848. Oxford: Clarendon Press, 1983.

Trevor-Roper, Hugh. "The Rise of Christian Europe." THE LISTENER 70 (28 November 1963): 871.

Tripp, Charles. A HISTORY OF IRAQ. Third Edition. Cambridge: Cambridge University Press, 2007.

Tsang, Steve. A MODERN HISTORY OF HONG KONG. London: I.B. Tauris, 2004.

U

UN General Assembly Resolution 73/295. "Advisory opinion of the International Court of Justice on the legal consequences of the separation of the Chagos Archipelago from Mauritius in 1965." A/RES/73/295, 22 May 2019.

UN General Assembly Resolution 1514 (XV). "Declaration on the Granting of Independence to Colonial Countries and Peoples." 14 December 1960.

UNESCO. WORLD ILLITERACY AT MID-CENTURY. Paris: UNESCO, 1957.

UNRWA. "Palestine Refugees." Accessed 2024.

Urban, Mark. TASK FORCE BLACK: THE EXPLOSIVE TRUE STORY OF THE SAS AND THE SECRET WAR IN IRAQ. London: Little, Brown, 2010.

V

Van der Veer, Peter. IMPERIAL ENCOUNTERS: RELIGION AND MODERNITY IN INDIA AND BRITAIN. Princeton: Princeton University Press, 2001

Van Onselen, Charles. CHIBARO: AFRICAN MINE LABOUR IN SOUTHERN RHODESIA, 1900-1933. London: Pluto Press, 1976.

Van Reenen, Rykie, ed. EMILY HOBHOUSE: BOER WAR LETTERS. Cape Town: Human & Rousseau, 1984.

Vandervort, Bruce. WARS OF IMPERIAL CONQUEST IN AFRICA, 1830-1914. Bloomington: Indiana University Press, 1998.

Varble, Derek. THE SUEZ CRISIS 1956. Oxford: Osprey Publishing, 2003.

Varnava, Andrekos. BRITISH IMPERIALISM IN CYPRUS, 1878-1915. Manchester: Manchester University Press, 2009.

Vatikiotis, P.J. NASSER AND HIS GENERATION. London: Croom Helm, 1978.

Veg, Sebastian. "The Rise of 'Localism' and Civic Identity in Post-handover Hong Kong." THE CHINA QUARTERLY 230 (2017): 323-347.

Vernon, Patrick and Osborne, Angelina. 100 GREAT BLACK BRITONS. London: Robinson, 2020.

Vertovec, Steven. HINDU TRINIDAD: RELIGION, ETHNICITY AND SOCIO-ECONOMIC CHANGE. London: Macmillan, 1992.

Vine, David. ISLAND OF SHAME: THE SECRET HISTORY OF THE U.S. MILITARY BASE ON DIEGO GARCIA. Princeton: Princeton University Press, 2009.

Visaria, Leela and Visaria, Pravin. "Population (1757-1947)." In THE CAMBRIDGE ECONOMIC HISTORY OF INDIA, VOLUME 2: C.1757-C.1970, edited by Dharma Kumar, 463-532. Cambridge: Cambridge University Press, 1983.

Viswanathan, Gauri. MASKS OF CONQUEST: LITERARY STUDY AND BRITISH RULE IN INDIA. New York: Columbia University Press, 1989.

Vohra, Ranbir. THE MAKING OF INDIA: A HISTORICAL SURVEY. Second Edition. Armonk: M.E. Sharpe, 2001.

W

Walker, Ranginui. KA WHAWHAI TONU MATOU: STRUGGLE WITHOUT END. Auckland: Penguin Books, 1990.

Walvin, James. ATLAS OF SLAVERY. Harlow: Pearson, 2006.

Walvin, James. BLACK IVORY: SLAVERY IN THE BRITISH EMPIRE. Second Edition. Oxford: Blackwell, 2001.

Ward, Stuart, ed. BRITISH CULTURE AND THE END OF EMPIRE. Manchester: Manchester University Press, 2001.

Watts, Michael. SILENT VIOLENCE: FOOD, FAMINE, AND PEASANTRY IN NORTHERN NIGERIA. Berkeley: University of California Press, 1983.

Weiner, Tim. LEGACY OF ASHES: THE HISTORY OF THE CIA. New York: Doubleday, 2007.

Weiss, Meredith L. PROTEST AND POSSIBILITIES: CIVIL SOCIETY AND COALITIONS FOR POLITICAL CHANGE IN MALAYSIA. Stanford: Stanford University Press, 2006.

Wesseling, H.L. DIVIDE AND RULE: THE PARTITION OF AFRICA, 1880-1914. Westport: Praeger, 1996.

White, Nicholas J. BRITISH BUSINESS IN POST-COLONIAL MALAYSIA, 1957-70: 'NEO-COLONIALISM' OR 'DISENGAGEMENT'? London: RoutledgeCurzon, 2004.

Whitcombe, Elizabeth. AGRARIAN CONDITIONS IN NORTHERN INDIA: THE UNITED PROVINCES UNDER BRITISH RULE, 1860-1900. Berkeley: University of California Press, 1972.

Whitehead, Clive. COLONIAL EDUCATORS: THE BRITISH INDIAN AND COLONIAL EDUCATION SERVICE 1858-1983. London: I.B. Tauris, 2003.

WikiLeaks Cable 09LONDON1156. "HMG Floats Proposal for Marine Reserve Covering the Chagos Archipelago." 15 May 2009.

Williams, Eric. CAPITALISM AND SLAVERY. Chapel Hill: University of North Carolina Press, 1944.

Williams, Eric. INWARD HUNGER: THE EDUCATION OF A PRIME MINISTER. London: Andre Deutsch, 1969.

Wilson, Mary C. KING ABDULLAH, BRITAIN, AND THE MAKING OF JORDAN. Cambridge: Cambridge University Press, 1987.

Wong, J.Y. DEADLY DREAMS: OPIUM AND THE ARROW WAR (1856-1860) IN CHINA. Cambridge: Cambridge University Press, 1998.

Worthington, Andy. THE GUANTANAMO FILES: THE STORIES OF THE 774 DETAINEES IN AMERICA'S ILLEGAL PRISON. London: Pluto Press, 2007.

Y

YouGov Survey. "How (Un)Proud Are Britons of the Empire?" 26 July 2020.

Z

Zheng Yangwen. THE SOCIAL LIFE OF OPIUM IN CHINA. Cambridge: Cambridge University Press, 2005.

NEWS ARTICLES AND ONLINE SOURCES

"Barbados Becomes a Republic and Parts Ways with the Queen." BBC NEWS, 30 November 2021.

Bibliography

"Chagos Islands Deal: What It Means." THE GUARDIAN, 3 October 2024.

"Chagossians Excluded from Sovereignty Deal." AL JAZEERA, 4 October 2024.

"David Cameron Criticized for Offering Jamaica Prison Instead of Slavery Reparations." THE GUARDIAN, 30 September 2015.

"Kenya Mau Mau Victims Receive UK Compensation." BBC NEWS, 6 June 2013.

"UK Compensates Kenya's Mau Mau Torture Victims." BBC NEWS, 6 June 2013.

"UK to Return Chagos Islands to Mauritius." BBC NEWS, 3 October 2024.

OFFICIAL DOCUMENTS & GOVERNMENT REPORTS

CARICOM Reparations Commission. "The Case for Reparations." March 2014.

CARICOM Reparations Commission. "Ten Point Plan." March 2014.

Foreign and Commonwealth Office. STATEMENT ON THE SETTLEMENT OF MAU MAU CLAIMS. Cm 8661, June 2013.

Foreign Secretary William Hague. Statement on Kenya settlement, 6 June 2013. HANSARD, HC Deb, vol. 564, col. 31WS.

Treaty of Nanjing, 1842. Full text in John King Fairbank, TRADE AND DIPLOMACY ON THE CHINA COAST, 463-469.

Treaties of Tianjin (1858) and Convention of Beijing (1860). Full texts in John King Fairbank, TRADE AND DIPLOMACY ON THE CHINA COAST, 470-485.

END Bibliography.